JavaScript Objects

Alexander Nakhimovsky and Tom Myers

Wrox Press Ltd. ®

JavaScript Objects

© 1998 Wrox Press

Published by Wrox Press Ltd. 30 Lincoln Road, Olton, Birmingham, B27 6PA
Printed in USA
ISBN 1-861001-8-49

Trademark Acknowledgements

Wrox has endeavored to provide trademark information about all the companies and products mentioned in this book by the appropriate use of capitals. However, Wrox cannot guarantee the accuracy of this information.

Credits

Author
Alexander Nakhimovsky
Tom Myers

Development Editor
Anthea Elston

Editors
Jeremy Beacock
Soheb Siddiqi

Technical Reviewers
Michael Corning
Alex Fedorov
Nigel McFarlane
Mary McKenzie
Josh Pava
Simon Oliver
Jesse Reisman
David Whitney

Cover
Andrew Guillaume
Concept by Third Wave
Photo by Warren Wheeler

Design/Layout
Frances Olesch
Noel Donnelly

Index
Julian Skinner

About the Authors

Alexander Nakhimovsky has been a member of Colgate's Computer Science department since 1985. He is the author of several Russian language textbooks, a book and numerous articles on linguistics, and several articles on computational linguistics, in addition to ventures into other fields in frequent collaboration with Alice Nakhimovsky.

Tom Myers taught computer science at the University of Delaware and at Colgate before becoming a full-time programmer (while occasionally teaching a course or two at Colgate). He is the author of Equations, Models and Programs: A Mathematical Introduction to Computer Science (Prentice Hall 1988) and several theoretical articles.

Acknowlegements

We would like to thank the many people who made this book possible.

At WROX, our editors showed both good cheer and professionalism of the highest caliber; it was a real pleasure working with Anthea Elston, Jeremy Beacock and Soheb Siddiqi. Our reviewers were tough but supportive, and their comments have significantly improved the final product. On several occasions, their positive attitude gave a badly needed boost to our flagging spirits.

At Colgate, we've been able to use excellent equipment and good advice from colleagues and administration. Our special thanks go to the Information Technology Services whose enlightened support was crucial at several junctures. Some of the book's material, especially in chapter 9, overlaps with a project that was supported by the Mellon grant to Colgate University and Hamilton College. Our collaborators on that project -- John Gallucci, Carol Kinne and Naeem Sheikh -- are wonderful imaginative people who contributed beautiful ideas to it.

Some of the book's ideas started life as lecture notes for CS303, Design of Large Systems, in the Spring of 1998. The students in the course deserve a special mention: they did a terrific job on the course projects during that semester.

We separately thank our families:

Alice, without you there would be no book, no nothing. Isaac and Sharon, thanks for being around; this whole thing would be pretty meaningless otherwise.

and

Tamsin, if you'd been a less demanding baby, I'd have slept more and this book would have many more bad ideas in it. tjm

Table of Contents

JavaScript is Great

Introduction

The World Wide Web has developed rapidly since its inception back in 1983 and especially since the release of the first graphical browser, Mosaic, in 1991. Another major advance was the release of the Netscape browser with an embedded scripting language, JavaScript. In 1997, extremely powerful (but incompatible) upgrades to the language were released, both by Netscape and Microsoft, as part of their 4th generation browsers. At about the same time, HTML 4.0, the style sheet language, and many aspects of JavaScript were standardized by the World Wide Web Consortium (W3C) and the European Computer Manufacturers Association (ECMA). Together, these developments made totally new styles of programming in JavaScript possible. This book explores the new possibilities. It's probably the first book that takes JavaScript completely seriously, the way it deserves to be treated.

In this introductory chapter we'll talk about scripting languages in general and JavaScript in particular. We'll try to show why JavaScript is a truly outstanding tool for many interesting and useful projects, and why it is likely to become even more useful in the future. In order to do that, we have put it in a larger context, to show how it fits in with large-scale trends in software development.

About JavaScript

JavaScript, as the name suggests, is a scripting language. What's a scripting language? There are no hard-and-fast definitions, but usually scripting languages are interpreted, weakly-typed, over-permissive, embedded into an application, and serve as glue to hold together components written in other languages. We'll take up these features one at a time. The examples we use to illustrate the features will be fully explained in the chapters that follow.

JavaScript is an Interpreted Language

Before the text of a program can be used by a computer, it needs to be translated from the language it was written in, to something the computer understands. The translation can be done in one of two ways, called **compile** and **interpret**. If a program is compiled, its entire text is translated into machine code before any of it is used. The translation is performed by a special program called **compiler**. The output of the compiler is a file of machine codes that constitutes an executable program.

If a program is interpreted, there's no intermediate compilation step between writing your code and using it. The text of the program is translated line-by-line (more or less) and used immediately, without any machine code files created. This makes the programming experience more immediate and gratifying: you type in your code, click on a button, and if (this is a big if) it has no bugs you see it perform right away. The flip side is that a good compiler catches a lot of errors, and without it you have to catch them yourself (although a script debugger may help). Also, because the interpreter has to translate the computer language 'on the fly' it is much slower than the compiled equivalent.

JavaScript is Weakly-Typed

The weakly-typed feature of scripting languages has to do with data types. In a strongly-typed language, you commit each variable to a specific data type: e.g., once an integer, always an integer. When you declare a new variable in C, you specify its data type: e.g., `int i`. In JavaScript, a variable can take on values of different data types during its lifetime. So, in declaring a variable, you don't specify a type, you simply say:

```
var a = 17;          // variable a is given an integer (whole number) value
a = 15.3;            // type has changed from an integer to a floating point number
a = "I've decided to change my type again";      // now a string literal
a = new Array(25);   // variable a is now an array of 25 items
```

An array is just a collection of variables indexed by integers, where the first item/element of the array is given the index 0. Since variables are untyped, an array can contain elements of different data types:

```
a[0] = 32;           // the first item of array a is an integer
a[1] = "I'm the second item of this array";
a[2] = true;         // true is a boolean value
```

A function, as you know, is like a little piece of machinery that takes inputs (called arguments) and returns a value. In JavaScript, a function doesn't have to declare the type of value it returns, or the data types of its arguments, so we define functions simply as:

```
function square(x) {return x * x;}
```

A fuller explanation of all these concepts in programming follows in Chapter 1.

JavaScript is a bit too Permissive

Scripting languages tend to be over-permissive when it comes to syntax rules. For instance, you don't really have to declare your variables before using them, and you don't have to put a semicolon after every statement. Such laxity comes at a price: debugging becomes more difficult. In this book we preach the virtue of self-imposed discipline: always declare your variables and terminate your statements with a semicolon. If you catch us breaking our own rules and lapsing into laxity, condemn us immediately and severely.

JavaScript is Embedded in the Browser

The most important feature of a scripting language is that it comes equipped with an intimate knowledge of a very common and powerful application, such as a word processor, a spreadsheet, or, in the case of JavaScript, a web browser. The reason we like JavaScript so much is not only that it is a very nice, well-designed language but also because we can use it, out of the box, to manipulate the browser window and the document it contains. It is possible to use JavaScript as a self-standing language, or use it with applications other than the browser (see *Instant JavaScript* from Wrox Press, ISBN 1-861001-27-4 for a complete discussion) but in this book, we do only web browser JavaScript. We refer to it as client-side JavaScript or browser JavaScript, and we refer to the browser as its host application.

JavaScript can Call on Java Easily

Finally, scripting languages are usually set up so that it's easy to make "outside calls" from them. An outside call uses components—small programs—written in another language, usually a compiled one. This greatly increases the usefulness of scripting languages. You can write CPU-intensive functions in C, C++ or Java, compile them into a component, and call on it from the web page using a JavaScript function. In Chapters 6-8, we'll use Java components, called "applets" (which are designed specifically for use in web pages), as one way to save and load our database files. You'll learn to develop Java applets and use them from JavaScript functions in Chapter 9. If the applet is "trusted", then it can itself use components written in C, Java or whatever, and the range of functions callable from JavaScript gets greatly expanded.

Even without such extensions, JavaScript can do a great deal for you because it knows HTML very well: it can read and write it, after the page is already loaded, in response to actions by the user.

Why is JavaScript Great?

Serious programmers sometimes stay away from scripting languages. This may change, and we hope that this book will help to bring this change about. As new and better scripting languages are developed, they become a good medium for large scale applications. In the case of JavaScript, we can draw attention to at least six features.

Familiar Syntax makes the Learning Curve Pleasant

Much of JavaScript syntax and some of its semantics are adopted from C and C++. If you're a C or C++ programmer, it should be easy for you to learn how to *read* JavaScript and to start writing simple applications.

Regular Expressions help in Working with Text

Although a recent addition to the language, regular expressions are well integrated into JavaScript, becoming one of its prominent features. In combination with the `TextRange` class (available in IE4 on Win95), they make JavaScript a powerful tool for manipulating the textual content of web pages. There's more on regular expressions in Chapter 1. We also use them for form validation in Chapter 3 and as a way for non-programmers to define editing tools in Chapter 8.

4

Functional Programming Constructs make Code Concise

Although it looks like C, much of JavaScript is influenced by other programming languages, including totally unexpected ones, like Scheme. The details and examples are found throughout the book. For now, we simply note that functions are treated as first class objects, which frequently makes code concise and elegant. (We're praising the language, of course, not our own code.)

JavaScript is Well Designed for Object-Oriented Programming

If we didn't believe it, we would not have written this book. JavaScript can be used very effectively, not only to manipulate web pages, but also to create large-scale applications and reusable components. These applications still work with web pages, but in the context of a world of objects that they themselves create. Thanks to JavaScript's intimate relationship with the browser, programmer-created objects mesh well with the objects on the web page. To recreate and reuse the objects, all you have to do is include a file of code in your HTML document.

JavaScript Objects are Associative Arrays

JavaScript objects, including web page objects, are associative arrays. You can refer to `obj.propName` as `obj["propName"]`, and call `obj.methodName()` as `obj["methodName"]`. Since functions are treated as first-class objects, you can add methods by simple assignment. The strings that index the properties and methods of an object can be constructed at run time. We describe this in Chapter 2.

Why Do OOP in JavaScript?

As we've just said, one *can* do object-oriented programming in JavaScript, but why would one *want to*? In this section, we address the notion that object-oriented techniques are not needed for JavaScript programming because JavaScript is mostly used for small enhancements to web pages. Now, it is true that there are many more JavaScript programmers than there are, say, C++ programmers, and most of them write small pieces of fairly trivial code most of the time. (To quote a Wrox author, "Most client-side JavaScript code is small and uninspired." McFarlane, *Instant JavaScript* from Wrox Press, ISBN 1-861001-27-4, p.167.) However, this picture is changing rapidly, because of the enormous changes that have taken place since 1997 in the status and potential of JavaScript and HTML. IE4, and to a lesser extent NC4, already provide a powerful programming platform; once browser-embedded JavaScript is standardized and the two browsers narrow, if not completely eliminate, their differences, JavaScript will take off.

Object-oriented programming has been of little importance to web scripts because they have been small in code-size, small in team-size, and small in time-scale. All three of these factors are changing. Firstly, increasing power of the language (both JavaScript and the underlying HTML, not to mention the Java and database connections) makes larger projects more attractive, while increasing machine speed reduces the penalty for extensive interpretive scripting. As a result, larger groups, with disparate skills, are tackling projects which will last for a long time: code will last after its author is no longer involved, or has simply forgotten how a given piece of script was to work. Each of these changes generates problems; object-oriented programming won't magically solve them, but it will help. See the rest of the book, especially Chapters 4-8, for examples.

Our Approach to JavaScript Applications

To give a slightly more detailed preview, we'll spell out (very briefly!) our approach to large-scale applications in JavaScript. All such applications will involve large computational objects that need visual counterparts (think of Model-View-Control architecture of Smalltalk, or Document-View architecture of the Microsoft Foundation Classes, or MFC). In the case of JavaScript, the view and control elements come from the web page. We treat HTML elements as data structures, and associate an "HTML structure", such as a table of a form, with a JavaScript class. In addition to modular design, this approach makes JavaScript classes controllable and customizable from HTML. As a result, our classes can be used and customized by people with only HTML skills, or even people who only know how to fill out a form. For more detail on this last point, see the section "*Who Should Read This Book?*"

A Word to Non-Serious Programmers

Predicting the Web's future in any concrete detail is, of course, foolish, but we believe in a couple of large trends. One of them is that more and more people will program, without becoming programmers. If you're one of such programming people, please heed our advice: learn several important principles early and apply them in their programming practice. They will make your programming both more effective and more pleasurable, because most people derive pleasure from producing well-designed, well-crafted things. JavaScript is a great language to start programming, and to start it well.

The Big Picture

Ultimately, we're interested in documents (web pages). A document has appearance, structure and behavior. Each aspect of a document can and should be controlled by a separate software module. The structure of the document is determined by HTML tags, its appearance is controlled by a style sheet, and its dynamic behavior is produced by JavaScript code.

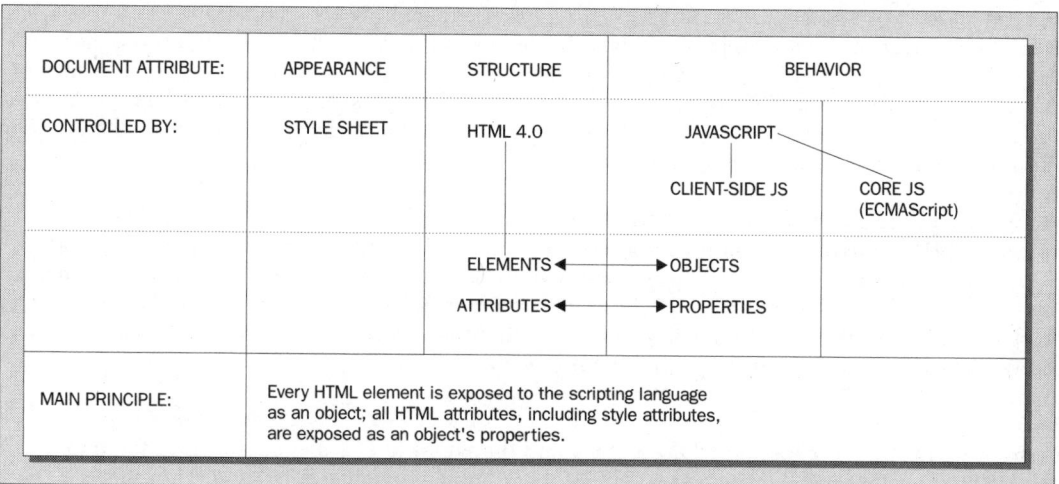

DOCUMENT ATTRIBUTE:	APPEARANCE	STRUCTURE	BEHAVIOR	
CONTROLLED BY:	STYLE SHEET	HTML 4.0	JAVASCRIPT	
			CLIENT-SIDE JS	CORE JS (ECMAScript)
		ELEMENTS ◄──────► OBJECTS		
		ATTRIBUTES ◄──────► PROPERTIES		
MAIN PRINCIPLE:	Every HTML element is exposed to the scripting language as an object; all HTML attributes, including style attributes, are exposed as an object's properties.			

In order to make a web page "behave", JavaScript needs access to the page. The building blocks of the document's structure and appearance—tags and their attributes, style properties and their values—should be exposed to JavaScript code so it can retrieve and change every detail of both the HTML markup and the Style Sheet specifications. This is the goal. IE4 comes close to it, and the next set of recommendations from W3C will probably spell it out in detail. In the meantime, the following is largely true about the IE4 DOM, and not true about NC4 DOM:

- ❏ Every HTML element in the page is a JavaScript object.
- ❏ Every HTML attribute of an HTML element is a property or method of the corresponding JavaScript object.
- ❏ Every HTML element in the page can be individuated, for ease of reference, by a unique ID attribute.
- ❏ Every HTML element in the page can be replaced by an assignment statement in JavaScript

We will elaborate on these principles in Chapter 2 and throughout the book.

Which JavaScript do We Use?

As the diagram above illustrates, JavaScript falls into two parts: the core language and the host application (browser) part. The core language has literals and variables, expressions and statements, conditional and iterative constructs, and all the other things we've come to expect from a programming language. We cover the core language in Chapters 1 and 2. The core language is relatively easy to codify, and in fact it has been codified by ECMA (the European Computer Manufacturers Association). Both Netscape and Microsoft support the ECMA standard, and their fifth-generation browsers are expected to be in full compliance with it.

When it comes to the host application, a very important notion is the Document Object Model, or DOM for short. It specifies how JavaScript makes references to HTML elements and navigates around a web page. The WWW Consortium (W3C) is working on a DOM standard, which has just reached the status of a recommendation. You can read the full standard at `http://w3.org/TR/REC-DOM-Level-1.htm`, and expect browser compatibility to improve dramatically over the next couple of releases. In the meantime, the DOMs of Microsoft and Netscape are completely at odds with each other, much like the Houses of Montague and Capulet. It may or may not be possible for a Microsoft programmer to marry somebody from the house of Netscape and live happily ever after, but writing a cross-browser program of any complexity is out of the question: you pretty much have to write two different versions.

We wouldn't even mind writing two different versions, but it so happens that the approach to programming we advocate is simply impossible in NC4. As the list of features in the preceding section shows, NC4 DOM does not provide any uniform way to individuate an object or to change it. For this reason, all the programs in this book are IE4 specific. Some of them (in Chapter 8) are even more narrowly specific to IE4 on Win32 machines, because IE4 on the Mac is not a complete port of the Windows version. It is our hope that the fifth-generation browsers will be more uniform across manufacturers and platforms.

In order to illustrate the limited DOM of NC4 and the DOM of IE4 that conforms to the four principles above, we have provided two HTML pages of very similar functionality, in the `http://webdev/wrox.co.uk/books/1894/introduction` directory. The first of them is `docWrite.htm`, the only cross-browser program in this book. If you compare it with the IE4-specific `innerOb.htm`, you will understand why. The new, "object-oriented" DOM is essential for what we do.

Where does JavaScript code Live?

JavaScript code is mostly found in four places:

- ❏ as a SCRIPT element on the page, either within the HEAD or within the BODY;
- ❏ in a source file whose name is given as the SRC attribute of a SCRIPT element;
- ❏ as a value of an event handler attribute.

It can also be placed in a URL, as in:

```
javascript: alert("JavaScript is running");
```

but we use this option rarely. There are several other browser-specific options, but the main three really give you enough flexibility. You will see a lot of examples throughout the rest of the book, beginning with the next chapter.

The Rest of the Book

- ❏ Chapter 1 is a condensed look at core JavaScript which will not try to replace many existing introductory and reference texts. The point is rather to concentrate on some essential features of the language that will be extensively used in the main chapters.
- ❏ Chapter 2 is about programming with objects, as distinct from object-oriented programming. We're still in core JavaScript, but we talk more about arrays, strings, functions, and regular expressions. We also pay more attention to advanced control structures. Without going into a lot of theory about it, we introduce iteration and recursion (including tail-recursion); functions as first-class objects that can be passed as parameters, stored in data structures and returned as values; and the functions eval and quote.
- ❏ Chapter 3 is about browser JavaScript. We introduce the document tree early and provide tools for exploring and modifying it.
- ❏ Chapter 4 is an overview of object-oriented programming, both in general and with particular reference to JavaScript. Keeping jargon to a minimum, we show why object-oriented programming is good for JavaScript code and for collaboration between the programmer, the content provider and the graphical artist.
- ❏ Chapters 5 through 8 implement several classes of objects and use them in fairly large applications. In particular, we implement a Tree and a TreeTraverser classes in Chapter 5, a Database class in Chapter 6 (enhanced in Chapter 7), and a variety of classes to support a Web-page annotator in Chapter 8.
- ❏ Chapter 9 shows how to control Java applets from JavaScript to give the language such additional capabilities as file input and output and graphics.

Who Should Read This Book?

You should read this book if you want to be able to take your scripting–and your web-pages– to a new level of sophistication. Object-Oriented Programming is the programming trend of the future, and JavaScript is well adapted to be a part of that trend.

This book assumes you have good working knowledge of HyperText Markup Language (HTML), including elements of style sheets. Everything else is built from scratch. In particular, no prior knowledge of JavaScript or any other programming language is presupposed. On the other hand, some of the material assumes that you're comfortable with formal notations, and have been around computers long enough to know what the CPU is. So, the audiences that will benefit most from *all* of the book's material are professional programmers and students in computer science departments. These audiences can use the book for self-study or in the context of an instructor-led course. (In the US, the book would be appropriate for a senior undergraduate or introductory graduate course on software engineering or internet programming.)

The book is also addressed to those people who are not programmers but may be interested in our example applications. They are large, industrial strength programs for advanced document processing and for developing computer-aided instructional materials. Many sections in the book are specifically addressed to competent users of large applications who can install an application and customize it by changing elements of an HTML page. Such sections are marked as HTML-only in the book's table of contents. Some of them are written in the tutorial fashion, taking the reader step-by-step through the process of using and customizing our applications.

Some of the applications in the book have been developed in collaboration with humanities faculty at Colgate University. We hope that their colleagues elsewhere will recognize the educational potential of our applications and buy the book, or tell their technical support people to buy it. The applications, especially in Chapters 5 through 8 are, in effect, authoring systems for creating computer-aided educational materials. Although created in collaboration with humanities faculty (which shows in the examples in the book), they can be equally well used in other academic fields, or outside academia altogether, wherever computer-aided instruction and advanced document processing are practiced.

As long as you've created a few pages before, and have done a little scripting before, you'll have no problems keeping up with what's going on. Programmers from other languages, such as C++ or Java, who are looking to mimic some of the power and approach of these languages in their JavaScript code will also find this book invaluable.

What Do I Need to Use This Book?

All you'll need to write your own JavaScript applications is a text editor capable of saving files in ASCII format, and an IE4.x web browser. The browser can be downloaded from:

```
http://www.microsoft.com/windows/ie/
```

Apart from that, everything you need is here in this book. The examples and screenshots were all taken from a PC running Windows 95. All JavaScript and Java code has been written using Pfe, a wonderful freeware program available from:

```
http://www.lancs.ac.uk/people/cpaap/pfe/
```

Others have successfully used Windows Notepad for that purpose.

For programs in Chapter 9, you will need the Java Development Kit (jdk1.1.x) and the Java Plugin available from:

```
http://java.sun.com
```

Some programs from Chapter 9 are used in Chapters 6-8 for loading and saving the database files without using a web server and CGI. See the **jclasses/dbreadme.htm** file in the directory of samples and tools.

Where You'll Find the Samples and Tools

If you want to try out the examples in this book, you can run them straight from our web site or you can download them as compressed files from the same site. The index page can be found at:

```
http://www.wrox.com/Store/Details.asp?Code=1894
```

Throughout the book, we've also suggested further examples and exercises. Although these aren't crucial to understanding, they're intended to reinforce your knowledge as well as provide a demonstration of how our programs can be easily expanded. Like the samples, a full list of suggested solutions is available from our website.

If you're located in Europe or the United Kingdom, or you find that the site in the United States is down for maintenance, then you may want to try our mirror site which can be found at:

```
http://webdev.wrox.co.uk/books/1894/
```

Conventions

We have used a number of different styles of text and layout in the book to help differentiate between the different kinds of information. Here are examples of the styles we use and an explanation of what they mean:

> **Important pieces of information come in boxes like this**

- ❑ *Advice, hints, or background information comes in this type of font.*
- ❑ **Important Words** are in a bold type font
- ❑ Words that appear on the screen in menus like the File or Window are in a similar font to the one that you see on screen
- ❑ Keys that you press on the keyboard, like *Ctrl* and *Enter*, are in italics
- ❑ Code has several fonts. If it's a word that we're talking about in the text, for example, when discussing the **For...Next** loop, it's in a bold font. If it's a block of code that you can type in as a program and run, then it's also in a gray box:

```
<STYLE TYPE = "text/javascript">
… Some Javascript …
</STYLE>
```

❑   Sometimes you'll see code in a mixture of styles, like this:

```
<HTML>
<HEAD>
<TITLE>Javascript Style Sheet Example</TITLE>
<STYLE  TYPE = "text/javascript">
tags.BODY.color = "black"
classes.base.DIV.color = "red"
</STYLE>
</HEAD>
```

❑   The code with a white background is code we've already looked at and that we don't wish to examine further.

These formats are designed to make sure that you know what it is you're looking at. I hope they make life easier.

We'll frequently use these abbreviations:

NC4	Netscape Communicator 4.x
IE4	Internet Explorer 4.x
ECMA	European Computer Manufacturers Association
W3C	World Wide Web Consortium
DOM	Document Object Model
OOP	Object-oriented programming

Tell Us What You Think

We've worked hard on this book to make it useful. We've tried to understand what you're willing to exchange your hard-earned money for, and we've tried to make the book live up to your expectations.

Please let us know what you think about this book. Tell us what we did wrong, and what we did right. This isn't just marketing flannel: we really do huddle around the email to find out what you think. If you don't believe it, then send us a note. We'll answer, and we'll take whatever you say on board for future editions. The easiest way is to use email:
feedback@wrox.com

You can also find more details about Wrox Press on our web site. There, you'll find the code from our latest books, sneak previews of forthcoming titles, and information about the authors and editors. You can order Wrox titles directly from the site, or find out where your nearest local bookstore with Wrox titles is located. The address of our site is:
http://www.wrox.com

Customer Support

If you find a mistake, please have a look at the errata page for this book on our web site first. Appendix G outlines how you can submit an errata in much greater detail, if you are unsure. The full URL for the errata page is:

```
http://www.wrox.com/Scripts/Errata.idc?Code=1894
```

If you can't find an answer there, tell us about the problem and we'll do everything we can to answer promptly!

Just send us an email to: support@wrox.com.

Overview of the Core Language

Introduction

In this chapter, you will start learning and using core JavaScript. Much of JavaScript, as you will discover, is about objects and classes of objects and the next chapter will cover programming with objects. Here, we cover the basic building blocks of a computer language: **literals** and **variables**; **tokens** and **data types**; **operators**, **expressions** and **statements**. Many of the concepts will probably be familiar to you but the details may not be. We've tried to make this overview comprehensive but brief. We've left out some of the more obscure details, which you can find either in the appendices or in another book on JavaScript, such as Nigel McFarlane's *Instant JavaScript* from Wrox Press (ISBN 1-861001-27-4). Our goal in this chapter is to cover the basic concepts, to show how they are fleshed out in our language, and to build a foundation for the chapters to follow. Here's an outline of the chapter:

- ❏ terminology and basic concepts, with examples
- ❏ JavaScript statements, subdivided into variable declarations, function definitions, conditional statements, loops, and more
- ❏ expressions and operators, including a handy operator table
- ❏ data types and automatic type conversion
- ❏ identifiers and literals in JavaScript
- ❏ regular expression literals

As you probably know, overview chapters can be boring to read. We've done our best to avoid this! One device that helped was to start with the larger building blocks, the statements, so that from the beginning we could write something meaningful for you to read. Another helpful prop is a little application, called `EvalExp.htm`, which you can use to instantly try out any new construct or statement or operator that comes up in the discussion. It's a web page with two text boxes; you can type JavaScript in one box, click the Eval button, and see the result in the other box.

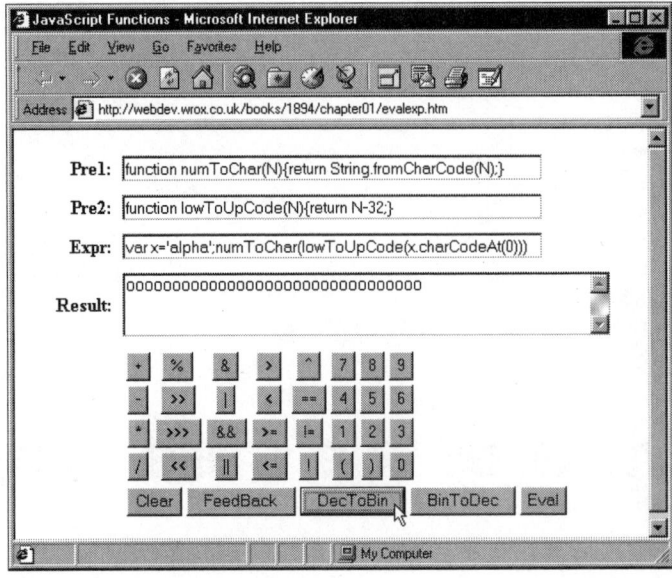

Instead of typing in digits, parentheses and JavaScript operators, you can click on the labeled buttons that show them. You can then feed the results of one computation into the next computation by clicking the **Feedback** button. The **Clear** button clears the display. Furthermore, if you want to test some of the longer programs we give later then you can use `EvalExp.htm` to generate instant feedback. Simply type the program as a single line into the expression box, remembering to use the semi colons to mark the end of each statement, and press **Eval**. Ignore the `undefined` comment in the results box and use a dialog box to display the result.

We've also provided another application, `tstTable.htm`, to help you understand how binary operators work.

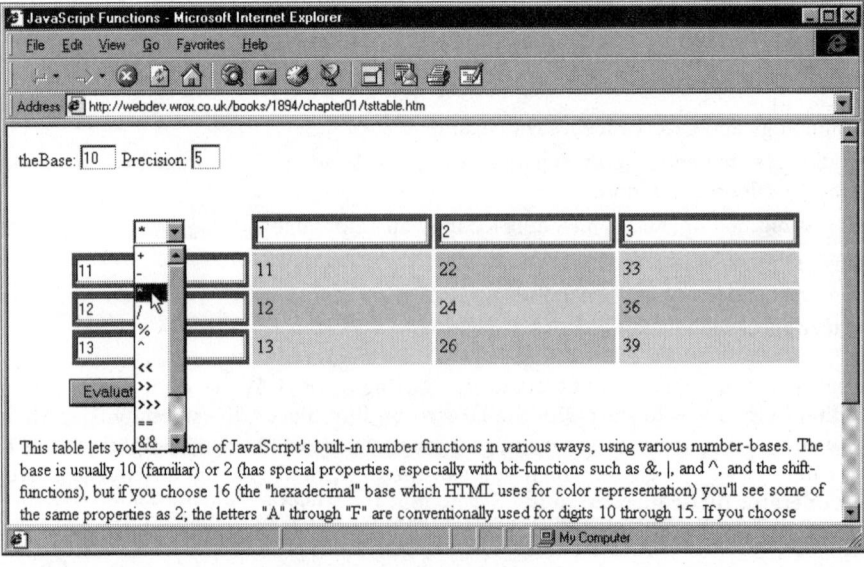

You can specify sets of values in the top column and the left-hand row, and get a table of the results you would get with various expressions. This may be particularly useful for learning bitwise operations where the goal is to understand the bit patterns of arguments and results.

Try It Out

Point your browser at `http://webdev.wrox.co.uk/books/1894/chapter01/EvalExp.htm` or `tstTable.htm` and click away.

Terminology and a Couple of Ideas

This preliminary section introduces the necessary terminology and essential concepts. They're the building blocks for the later sections.

Text, Comments, Separators, Tokens

A JavaScript program is a human-readable text. The main "story line" of that text is the **code** of the program. The code is translated into internal instructions for the browser by a specialized program called 'the JavaScript interpreter', which comes with the browser. In addition to code, the program contains **comments** that are addressed to human readers of the program and ignored by the interpreter. Comments are interspersed through the code part of the program, separated from it by **comment delimiters**. There are two kinds of delimiters. The `//` delimiter says: "everything from here to the rest of the line is a comment". The `/*` delimiter says: "everything from here to the matching `*/` companion is a comment". The second kind of comment can be many lines long and is called a **block comment**. For example, if you look at this code from the Introduction, when we were discussing data-types, you can see the first type of comment, and we've added another comment to show the second type.

```
var a = 17;          // variable a is given an integer (whole number) value
a = 15.3;            // type has changed from an integer to a floating point number
a = "I've decided to change my type again";     // now a string literal
a = new Array(25);   // variable a is now an array of 25 items

/*Don't worry if this code is unclear; later on in this chapter we'll look at
datatypes in more depth*/
```

That's all there is to say about comments; from now on, when we talk about the text of a program, we mean the code part of it. This doesn't mean that comments are unimportant: indeed, a program without comments is hard to share with others and even harder to maintain. Writing comments is an essential skill for the programmer, and we try to practice it when writing our code.

A text is a sequence of characters that express some meaning. Characters form meaningful units (like words), or serve as separators between meaningful units, or both. Consider a simple piece of code which declares a variable and assigns a value to it:

```
var x = 17 + 5;
```

What are the meaningful units here? Let's list them one per line:

Unit	Description
`var`	Declaration: there shall be a variable
`x`	the name of the variable, also known as an **identifier**
`=`	Assignment operator; also indicates the end of the name (cannot be part of it)
`17`	a special kind of meaningful unit called a **literal**; a number literal, to be precise
`+`	an arithmetic operator; also indicates the end of the number literal
`5`	another number literal
`17+5`	an **expression**, which is a unit that may consist of several units, like a phrase in English
`;`	terminates assignment statement; also indicates the end of the number literal

A general term for the most elementary meaningful items in a programming language is **token**. What kinds of tokens are there? The first division is into punctuation, operators and "the rest". (The rest includes **reserved words**, **identifiers**, number literals, and quoted strings.) There isn't much punctuation in JavaScript: commas to separate items in a list, semicolons to terminate statements, and braces to group statements together into one compound statement.

Operators also serve as a kind of punctuation, indicating the end of a token. Some traditional punctuation marks in English grammar, such as period and colon, are actually operators in JavaScript. An operator, in case you need a definition, is something that combines expressions into larger expressions. They're much easier to understand than to define. Once you see them used, you'll have no problem with them. (A complete table of operators, with comments, is given later in the chapter.)

Literals and Names (Identifiers)

Within words, the big distinction is between literals and names. **Literals** are raw data, what you see is what they are. There are number literals (e.g., 1725), string literals (e.g., "a quoted string"), and **boolean** literals (true or false; yes or no; 0 or 1), which are named after a 19th century British logician, George Boole. You cannot make a literal mean something other than what it literally means. Names, by contrast, acquire their meanings by convention or by decree. The connection between a name and its meaning is arbitrary: a rose, as you know, "by any other name would smell as sweet". Names used in computer programs are called **identifiers**.

Some identifiers mean what the language designers decided they would mean. These are called **reserved words**. They include, for instance, `if`, `break` and `function`. (We give a complete list in Appendix E). All other legal identifiers are free for programmers to use. What's legal? The restrictions in JavaScript are that identifiers may only consist of letters, digits, the dollar sign, and the underscore character, but they may not begin with a digit. This still gives you a lot of options.

Good programmers try to make their identifiers descriptive of what they mean in the program. Let's say you have an entity in your program that represents a list of words. You might want to call it `word_list` or `WordList` or `wdLst` (if you always abbreviate "word" to "wd" in your program). There are many good styles, but to be good a style has to be consistent. We use the `wdLst` style, but we do use underscores in one very specific kind of identifier. We also start our names with a lower-case letter, except for another very specific kind of identifier. Both of those specific kinds are introduced in Chapter 4.

Speaking of lower and upper case names, JavaScript is case-sensitive, so `x` and `X` are two different names, as are `wdLst` and `WdLst`. If you come from Visual Basic, this may take some getting used to.

Values and Data Types

In addition to its meaning in the program, an identifier has a **value**. A value is a data item of a specific data type. If you say `x = 17;` the value of `x` is 17, an integer. Can `x` change its value? Some languages make a distinction between identifiers that can change their value in the course of the program, and those that cannot. The former are called **variables**, and the latter are called **constants**. In C++ you can say:

```
const int x = 17;
```

This means that `x` is an *integer const*ant and you cannot change its value. Notice that the data type is also specified. This is yet another rule that some languages make: an identifier can only have values of the same data type. You can think of it as a caste system (if you're born an integer, you remain an integer forever), and you won't find any of that in JavaScript. There are no constants, only variables, and they can have values of any data type in the same program. It's perfectly legal to say:

```
var x = 17;              // x is an integer
x = "I've changed my mind"   // x is a string now
x = 12.45;              // changed my mind again
```

Even though JavaScript variables are not typed, their values are. Each value belongs to a specific data type to which specific functions and operators apply. If you apply a wrong function to a data type, you will get an error message or, worse, you may get no error message and wrong but plausible results. You need to know your data types.

There are two kinds of data types, **primitive** and **compound**. The primitive data types are numbers, booleans, strings, null and the `undefined` value. There are many little details about primitive data types that are worth knowing, but they're best learnt by using the data types than by reading about them. We'll save those details for the end of the chapter. If by the time you reach that section you feel that you'd like to know more about primitive data types please, help yourself. Otherwise, skip it and return as the need arises.

Compound data types, as the name implies, consist of components. These components can be of primitive data types or they can be compound data types that in turn consist of components, and so on, until you bottom out. Compound data types include arrays and objects. There are also associative arrays, but it turns out that they're the same as objects, so we'll leave them for a separate chapter, right after this one. However, so much of JavaScript is put into objects that we'll probably bump into them a couple of times in the course of this chapter. Just in case, let's define what an object is right here:

JavaScript Objects

An object is a collection of properties. Each property has a name and a value. The value of a property can be of any data type, including a function and an object.

You create new objects using the new operator:

```
var joe = new Object();
var jane = new Object();
```

As an example, lets look at arrays, which are both a compound data type and an object.

Arrays

Here's an example, using the array data type. An array is a collection of numbered items, such that you can refer to each item in the collection by number. The numbering (in JavaScript, C, C++ and Java) starts at 0. For instance, you can have an array of words called wdArray that has three items in it: "I", "love" and "Lucy." The expression wdArray[0] refers to the word "I", wdArray[1] refers to "love", and wdArray[2] refers to "Lucy". We'll talk about arrays at great length in the next chapter, so you can just skim or skip this section.

Suppose you want to make yourself a new, freshly minted array and initialize it to have three elements, the letters "x", "y" and "z". One way to do it is by saying:

```
var myArr = new Array("x","y","z");
```

This immediately gives away the secret: arrays are objects, because new is an operator that creates an object. However, once you have an array and have given it a name, you handle it the same way as in C or C++. You refer to myArr's elements as myArr[0], myArr[1], and myArr[2]. The length of newArr is 3. The index of the last element is always one less than the length because all arrays start at 0.

JavaScript arrays are very flexible. You can put values of different data types in the same array: myArr[0] can be a number, and the rest of them can be boolean values, or strings, or other arrays, for that matter. The arrays are also easily expandable. If you have an array of length 3 and you want to put more data into it, you can simply say:

```
myArr[3] = "new data";          // myArr's length becomes 4
```

Moreover, the arrays can be sparse, with holes in them. After filling myArr[0]...myArr[3], you can say:

```
myArr[51] = "totally new data";
```

The length of the array becomes 52. Elements 4 through 50 have the value undefined. This can easily become confusing; we recommend that you keep your arrays dense.

Expressions and Statements

An expression is anything that has a value. Since identifiers and literals have values, they're expressions of the simplest kind. Usually, by expression we mean a compound expression, something like "(myArr[0] + x) * 7 - 15 * y". Compound expressions are put together with identifiers, literals, operators, parentheses and function calls. Here's an example of a function call:

```
var z = Math.sqrt(16);        // z equals 4
```

This is quite straightforward, but what's `Math.` doing there? This is another example of how a lot of JavaScript is parceled out into separate "name spaces" called objects. Think of a name space as a place where a name is associated with a meaning, so that the same name can have different meanings in different name spaces. So, all mathematical functions are prefixed by `Math.` because, to use the proper terminology, they're all methods of the built-in `Math` object. If this terminology is new to you, wait till the next chapter where it is explained at length. For the time being, just accept the inconvenience of adding a few keystrokes to every call on a mathematical function.

An expression has a value, but it doesn't tell the program what to do with it. This is done by statements. In ordinary English a statement is something that can be true or false, but programming statements are really commands that instruct the computer to do something. The usage has by now been firmly established, and we're not going to waste any more time quibbling about it.

One thing to note about expressions and statements is that many of them are both. For instance, an assignment statement which assigns a value to a variable is also an expression that produces a value, the value being assigned. So, you can end your function, for example, by saying:

```
return x = 17;
```

This sets x to be 17, and the value 17 is returned by the function.

What's Next?

This concludes our quick run through the terminology and concepts. We're now faced with the task of going through all the possible kinds of statements, expressions, operators and data types. To make the task more enjoyable, we'll proceed in the top-down fashion, from statements to expressions to operators to identifiers. This way, you will have something meaningful to read (and test in `EvalExp.htm`) from the start.

This strategy is not without risks because early examples may contain elements of the language that have not yet been discussed, and may be unfamiliar to some readers. If this happens, we request that you suspend your curiosity (or anxiety) and concentrate on the point of the example rather than the unfamiliar elements of its context. By the time you reach the end of the chapter, everything should have been explained.

Statements

JavaScript statements fall into the following categories:

- variable declaration (`var`) and function definition (`function`) statements
- function call statements
- assignment statements, frequently combined with an operation
- increment and decrement statements (`++`, `--`)
- conditional statements (`if...`; `if...else...`; `switch...`)
- iterative statements (`for`, `while`)
- other flow of control statements (`break`, `continue`, `return`)
- object support statements (`for...in...`, `with`)

Let's take them up in order and cover them all, except for a couple of rather esoteric possibilities that we never use, but that you can find in the appendix or in a definitive guide like *Instant JavaScript* from Wrox Press (ISBN 1-861001-27-4).

Variable Declarations and Function Definitions

Theoretically, variable declarations are optional. In practice, **always declare your variables before using them**. Not only will your readability improve, but you will also be spared some nasty name conflicts in unexpected places. In particular, when you have a for loop, always get yourself a fresh counter variable to keep track of the number of times you've been round the loop:

```
for (var i=0; i<len; ++i) ...        // don't leave out var
```

Function definitions are not optional. There's a lot to say about them but we'll delay most of it till the next chapter, Programming with Objects, because, guess what: functions are objects. Only the basics of notation and terminology are covered here: **function name**, **argument list**, the body of the function (a compound expression within braces), **local variables**, and the **return value**. An example illustrates:

```
function square(x)
{                         // function name and argument list, in parentheses
   var res = x * x;       // local variable is declared and given a value
   return res;            // the value of the variable is returned by the function
}     //the brace closes compound expression which is the body of the function
```

We didn't really need a local variable in this particular function:

```
function square(x)
{                         // function name and argument list, in parentheses
   return x * x;          // return statement
}
```

Function Call Statements and Dialog Boxes

Strictly speaking, function calls are expressions: if you say square(4), you'll get yourself a value, the number 16, but nothing will happen to it. However, some functions are used for their side effects rather than the value (if any) that they return. Calling on such a function constitutes a statement. An example you'll see a lot is the **alert**() function that puts a modal dialog box on the screen. (A dialog is called modal if it doesn't let you do anything else until you dismiss it by clicking on a button.)

```
alert ("Click on my OK button to dismiss me");
```

Alert dialogs are great for program development and debugging. There are "integrated debuggers" out there that allow you to insert breakpoints and inspect values of variables, but an alert dialog does it very well, too.

JavaScript has two more kinds of dialog functions: confirm() and prompt(). While alert() doesn't return any value, confirm() asks you to click on either OK or Cancel button, and returns true or false, respectively. A call on prompt() returns a string value, the string that the user has typed in:

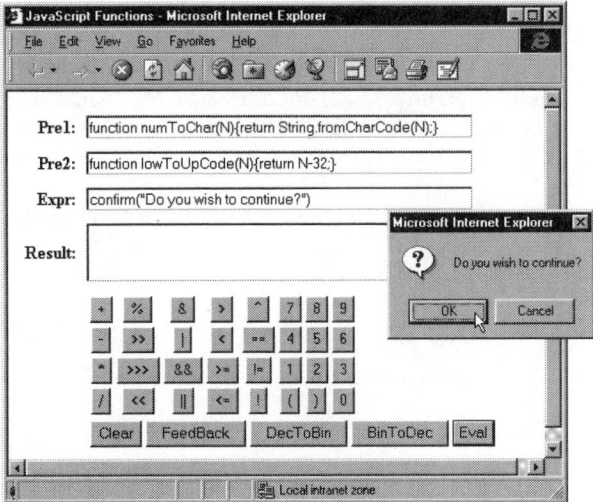

It will turn out (in Chapter 3) that these dialog-producing functions, as well as the functions that you define yourself, are, in fact, methods of a window object. Truly, objects are everywhere in JavaScript.

Strictly speaking, with our last example we've stepped outside ECMA-codified JavaScript into the client-side JavaScript, which is a specific implementation of the core language. There may be other versions of JavaScript that don't have window objects (or dialog boxes, for that matter) but none of them are considered in this book.

Assignment Statements

You've seen assignment statements already, both separately and combined with a variable declaration. Another common combination is with an operator that applies to the variable on the left side, as in:

```
a += 7;                      // equivalent to: a = a + 7;
var str = "ab"; str += "cde"; // str is now "abcde"
```

Almost every binary operator can be combined with assignments in this way. It may take a little practice before you can read and write them fluently. Some mnemonic device can help; think of a little dance or animation that the characters in "a = a + 7" have to perform to become "a += 7".

All existing combinations of assignment with binary operators are listed in the *Expressions and Objects* section later in this chapter.

Conditional Statements

Conditional statements test some condition and proceed in different ways depending on the outcome. The most common and important conditional is the if statement. Its meaning is pretty much what you would expect—it tests a condition, and **if** the condition is met, then the function performs an operation of some sort.

The if... and if...else... Statements

We can start with an example:

```
var a = 23;
if (a == 23) alert ("Success");
```

While the meaning of if is quite straightforward, the difference between = and == is quite subtle. The first means assignment ("Make a equal to 23"!), the second forms an expression that describes a state of affairs ("a is equal to 23"), and can be true or false.

There can be an else part following the if part, as in the following function:

```
function max(a,b)
{
  if (a > b) return a;        // return the larger of the two arguments
  else return b;
}
```

The Ternary Conditional

This is a very common pattern: test a condition and choose one of two alternatives depending on the outcome. There is a special ternary (three-place) expression that achieves the same effect: write down the test followed by a question mark followed by the two alternatives separated by a colon. Since ? : is an operator and creates an expression, you can put that expression inside the return statement. The preceding example becomes:

```
return a>b ? a : b;          // concise and elegant
```

This pattern is appropriate when both alternatives are short one-liners. If they are long, use if...else....

The Compound Statement in Curly Brackets

If you want to perform more than one statement in each of the if...else... branches of the conditional, you have to group several statements into one compound statement using the curly brackets {}. We recommend putting curly brackets around a single statement as well because it helps readability, and it helps in debugging:

```
if (someCondition() == true)
{
  doThis();
  doThat();
  doAnotherThing();
}
else
{
  doSomethingCompletelyDifferent();
}
```

There are many other situations when you have to group several statements together into one compound statement. You'll see more examples in the section on iterative statements.

The Switch Statement

The `switch` statement properly belongs with conditional statements, but it requires a bit more explanation, so we put it in a section by itself. It's also a recent addition that is not even part of the ECMA specification, but since both Netscape Communicator 4 and IE4 support it, it's a de-facto standard.

You don't really have to use the `switch` statement ever, if you're content to write multiple `if...then...else...` branches, as in:

```
if (myAge == 1) str = "I had just begun";
else if (myAge==2) str = "I was nearly new";
else if (myAge==3) str = "I was hardly Me";
else if (myAge==4) str = "I was not much more";
else if (myAge==5) str = "I was just alive";
else str = "but now I am six, I'm as clever as clever, "+
            "so I think I'll be six now for ever and ever";
```

The switch statement is exactly for situations like that, when you have multiple choices, each determined by a specific value. Recast as a switch, the little poem looks like this:

```
switch (myAge)
{          // a compound statement follows
  case 1: str = "I had just begun"; break;
  case 2: str = "I was very new"; break;
  case 3: str = "it was barely me"; break;
  case 4: str = "I was not much more"; break;
  case 5: str = "I was just alive"; break;
  default: str = "but now I am six, ...";
}
```

Why do we need `break` statements in the end of each branch? Because without them, switch assumes that the same action applies to more than one case. This is easier to show than explain. Suppose the correct dosage for a certain medicine is as follows: half a pill for ages 2 and younger, one pill for ages 3 to 6; a pill and a half for ages 7 to 9, and 2 pills for the rest of us. This would be expressed as follows:

```
switch(age)
{
  case 0: ;
  case 1: ;
  case 2: dosage = 0.5; break;
  case 3: ;
  case 4: ;
  case 5: ;
  case 6: dosage = 1; break;
  case 7: ;
  case 8: ;
  case 9:
  dosage = 1.5; break;
  default: dosage = 2;
}
```

In other words, the action applies to all the cases before the `break`.

Increment, Decrement

The increment and decrement operators can be used in a statement by themselves:

```
b++;       // equivalent to b += 1 or b = b + 1;
--b;       // equivalent to b -= 1 or b = b - 1
```

Increment and decrement operators appear in two forms, postfix (b++, b--) and prefix (++b, --b). When used in a statement by themselves, there is no difference between the two forms. When they are used in a statement that has other things going on, the difference is in timing. Consider these examples:

```
var i = 0, j = 0; // comma separates two actions within the same statement
if (++i == 1)
  alert("i has been incremented"); else alert("not yet");
if (j++ == 1)
  alert("j has been incremented"); else alert("not yet");
```

The first alert will show "i has been incremented" because the condition uses the prefix form of the increment operator. The prefix form is executed before the check for equality, so the check returns true. The second alert will show "not yet" because the postfix form is executed after the check for equality, so at the time of checking j is still equal to 0. In general, the *prefix* operator increments or decrements *before* its value is used, while the *postfix* operator increments or decrements *after* its value is used.

Iterative Statements

JavaScript has two kinds of loops, or iterative statements. One repeats its actions a specified number of times. The other repeats its actions as long as some condition holds. Both are copied from C/C++/Java unchanged.

For Loop

The syntax of the for loop is best explained by an example:

```
var sum = 0;
for(var i=0; i<5; ++i)
{
  sum += i;
}
alert(sum);      // shows 10
```

The first line of the loop says: "get yourself a counter variable and set it to 0; repeat the actions of the body of the loop as long as the condition i<5 holds; increment the counter by 1 every time after going through the loop". The body of the loop is in curly brackets even if it's a single statement. Here's something a trifle more complicated:

```
var sum = 0, str = "0";              // str has one character, '0'
for(var i=1; i<5; ++i)
{
  sum += i; str += "+" + i;
}
alert(str + "==" + sum);             // shows 0+1+2+3+4==10
```

The statement `str += "+" + i;` is admittedly tricky. The order of events in it is as follows. First we carry out the right-hand side of it, `"+" + i`. This starts with a character string, `"+"`, and asks to concatenate `i` to it. Now, `i` is an integer, not a string, so JavaScript automatically converts it to a string and does the concatenation. The result is appended to the end of the current value of `str`. In JavaScript, you do a great deal of this kind of programming, constructing strings out of disparate pieces to get the expression that you want.

While Loop

The same example using the `while` loop is as follows:

```
var i = 0, sum = 0, str = "0";
while(i < 5)
{
  sum += i;
  str += "+" + i; i++;
}
```

Instead of putting the increment operator in a separate statement, we could have inserted it in the preceding one, which would become:

```
str += "+" + i++;  // postfix increment is performed after everything else
```

This can probably qualify as a JavaScript tongue twister. Avoid them in your programs because they are extremely confusing and politically incorrect.

Do...While Loop

This version of the while loop puts the condition in the end, rather than in the beginning of the statement. The main difference is that the body of the loop gets done at least once even if the condition is false from the beginning. This makes `do...while` more appropriate in some contexts, less so in many more contexts. The `while` loop is more commonly used.

Flow of Control: Return, Break, Continue

You've already seen the `return` statement: it terminates a function call and returns control to wherever that call came from. If it occurs inside a loop, it terminates both the loop and the function call. The `break` and `continue` statements are used only in loops: `break` breaks the loop completely, `continue` interrupts the current iteration:

```
var str = "";
for(var i=0; i<5; ++i)
{
  if (i == 3) break;
  str += "+" + i;
}
alert(str);             // shows "+0+1+2"
```

```
var str= "";
for(var i=0; i<5; ++i)
{
  if (i == 3) continue;
  str += "+" + i;
}
alert(str);             // shows "+0+1+2+4"
```

The two statements work exactly the same way with while loops. It's a fairly common idiom to let your loop condition be true forever, and terminate the loop by a `break` or `return`:

```
while (1 > 0)
{
  ...                        // loop forever
  if (some condition) break;
  ...
}
```

Object Support

A lot of JavaScript programming, even when not object-oriented, involves objects, and we will talk about them at great length in Chapter 2 and forever after. For now, let's just repeat and expand upon the definition given earlier in this chapter:

An object is a collection of properties. Each property has a name and a value. The value of a property can be of any data type, including a function and an object. A property whose value is a function is called "a method" of the object.

Think of properties as variables and methods as functions, except that their full names are a combination of the object's name and their own. (In fact, an even stronger statement is true: all variables are properties of a global object that we simply don't have to mention, and all functions are methods of that global object. There's nothing mysterious or mystical about that Global Object, either: in client-side JavaScript, it's just the browser's main window.)

To introduce the object-support statements, let's consider the built-in JavaScript Date class of objects. You create a variable whose value is an object of the Date class by saying:

```
var aDate = new Date(1998,7,11);    // aDate corresponds to July 11, 1998
```

The Date class of objects has the methods `getDate()`, `getMonth()` and `getYear()` for extracting the components of a date. In order to use them, you have to combine their names with the name of the object whose components you want to extract, like so: `aDate.getDate()`, `aDate.getMonth()` and `aDate.getYear()`. The dot operator is used for that purpose, as it is in virtually every language that has objects as a data type. A typical usage would be:

```
var d = aDate.getDate();     // d==11
var m = aDate.getMonth();    // m==7
var y = aDate.getYear();     // y==1998
```

Terminologically speaking, an object creates its own **namespace** within which the names of its properties and methods are unique. Since we often want to do several things with the same object, there is a language construct that reduces the amount of repetitive typing in such situations: we can rewrite the code above as:

```
var d,m,y;
with (aDate)
{                          // enter the object's name space
  d = getDate();
  m = getMonth();
  y = getYear();
}                          // leave the object's name space
```

Another common thing to do is to iterate through all the properties of an object. JavaScript provides a special iterative statement for that purpose:

```
for prop in obj { /* do something to each prop */ }
```

We will discuss this statement in detail in the next chapter.

This concludes our whirlwind introduction to statements. You may want to go back to our `EvalExp.htm` application and practice a few of them, especially if you've come to this book without prior knowledge of any of the Big Three languages (Java, C and C++), and the syntactic detail is new to you.

Expressions and Operators

As we said in the beginning of the chapter, there are primitive expressions (names and literals) and compound expressions (function calls and operator expressions). In this section, we go over operator expressions, such as

```
3+40/4/2
```

The value of this expression is 8 because addition has **lower precedence** than division, and division is **left-associative**. Our first task is to understand what those words mean.

Precedence, Associativity, and the Number of Operands

The term **precedence** is to do with the order in which operations are carried out. Our example expression begins with 3+40, and if we always performed operations from left to right, we'd start by adding the two numbers. We don't: the operators are arranged in a pecking order, from the highest precedence to the lowest, and, in the absence of parentheses, we perform higher precedence operations first. In our example, this is division.

Associativity has to do with the order in which we perform a sequence of the same operations. Looking at our example again, we could think of the second part of it as meaning (40/(4/2)), where the inner parentheses are evaluated first, giving a value of 20. We don't: if we have a series of divisions, we perform them from left to right, giving an answer of 5, and that's what **left-associative** means. For many operators, such as addition, it doesn't matter whether we think of them as left- or right-associative but for some it does.

What would be right-associative operators? It's good you've asked, because we're going to present all operators in one big table, in the order of precedence from top to bottom, and for each group of operators, we'll put L or R, to indicate their associativity.

Finally, operators are described as unary, binary or ternary, depending on whether they require 1, 2 or 3 values to work on. Most operators are binary, like + or /. There are several unary operators, like unary minus as in -17 (negative seventeen), or the increment and decrement operators you've seen recently. You've also seen the one ternary operator of JavaScript, the conditional ?: operator.

The Operator Table

The table lists operators in order of precedence, from the highest—those which will be evaluated first—to the lowest. The letters L and R indicate associativity. We give a brief comment in the table and more detailed comments below.

P	A	Description	Syntax
1	L	Access operators: components of object or array; arguments of function	`. [] ()`
2	R	Unary operators: unary minus, increment, decrement; bitwise, complement and logical negation; object and data type operators	`- -- ++ ~ !` `type of new` `void`
3	L	Arithmetic operators: multiply, divide, remainder	`* / %`
4	L	Arithmetic operators: add, subtract; string concatenation	`+ - +`
5	L	Binary shift operators	`<< >> >>>`
6	L	Less-than, greater-than on numbers; strings	`<= < > >=`
7	L	Equality and identity of any object or type	`== != === !==`
8	L	Bitwise AND	`&`
9	L	Bitwise XOR	`^`
10	L	Bitwise OR	`/`
11	L	Logical AND	`&&`
12	L	Logical OR	`//`
13	R	The conditional ternary operator	`?:`
14	R	Assignment, assignment with operators	`= *= /= %= +=` `-= <<= >>=` `>>>= &= ^= /=`
15	L	Sequence of statements to evaluate	`,`

P = Precedence; A = Associativity

Comments

We're going to comment selectively on those operators that are less well known. To help locate the operators in the table, we give their precedence number in parentheses.

Bitwise and Binary Operators

All operators in this section operate on binary representation of numbers, so we have to assume that the reader has some familiarity with those. (If you don't, get yourself a book with a chapter on binary numbers—or skip this section and never use the operators. It's possible to be a very productive and successful programmer without ever going binary.) The operators include: bitwise complement (2), binary shifts (5) and bitwise AND, XOR and OR (8-10).

The binary complement changes each 1 to 0 and 0 to 1, so that `001010` becomes `110101`. The AND, XOR and OR combine bits according to these rules:

Bit 1	Bit 2	AND	XOR	OR
1	1	1	0	1
1	0	0	1	1
0	1	0	1	1
0	0	0	0	0

To see how it works with actual numbers, try these operators with the `EvalExp.htm` application.

For ultimate clarity, `EvalExp.htm` is outfitted with a pair of friendly functions, `intToBin()` and `binToInt()`, which convert from decimal integers to binary strings and back. Enter something like

```
intToBin(5) + "\n" + intToBin(3) + "\n" + intToBin(5^3);
```

and you will really see what's
going on.

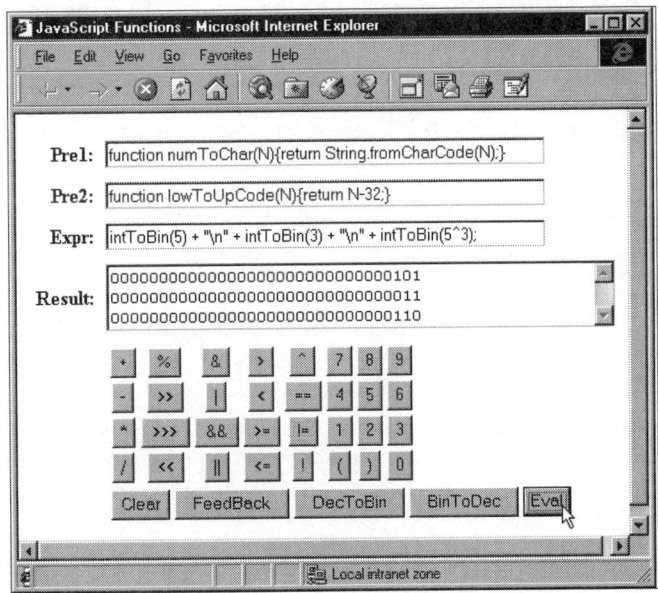

The shifts do what they say they do: shift all the 0s and 1s to the left or to the right. When you shift to the left, the vacated positions on the right are filled with 0s; it is equivalent to multiplying by a power of 2 (just as adding 0s to a decimal number is equivalent to multiplying by the powers of 10). So, `3<<2` is `12`, or, using binary strings on the left side of the operator, `11<<2` is `1100`.

Right shift is equivalent to dividing, without remainder, by the powers of 2. When you shift right, you have the choice of preserving the sign (`>>`) or discarding it (`>>>`). To preserve the negative sign, the vacated positions on the left are filled with 1s, otherwise they're filled with 0s. All operations are 32 bit. As we said in the beginning of the section, if this sounds mysterious to you, consult a book with a chapter on binary numbers.

JavaScript Objects

Arithmetic Operators

The only arithmetic operator that may require a comment is the remainder "%" (3), also known as **modulo**. It produces the remainder of integer division: if you try to divide ten apples equally among three kids, you're left with exactly one apple for yourself. The examples below illustrate; try a few more if you have any lingering doubts.

```
16 % 3 == 1;   // the value of this JavaScript expression is true
-27 % 4 == -3; // same comment
```

Equality vs. Identity

This is a difficult subject that has to do with type conversions. The equality operator (==) converts the two operands to the same type before doing the comparison. So, for instance, the following are true:

```
4 == "4"; true == 1; true == "1"; false == ""; false == 0;
```

None of them would be true if we replaced equality with identity (===).

The identity operator is supported by IE4 and Netscape Communicator 4.5, but not earlier versions. It is expected to be canonized by the next ECMA standard.

The Typeof Operator

As its name suggests, it returns the type of the operand. More precisely, it returns a string that is the name of the type of the operand. The following expressions are true:

```
typeof "abc" == "string";
typeof 13 == "number";
typeof (3>2) == "boolean";
typeof typeof 13 == "string";
```

No parentheses are needed in the last example because `typeof` is right-associative.

The Void Operator

This peculiar operator takes an operand of any type, ignores it, and returns an undefined value. Why would you want such an operator? We're not sure. One reason given is to test whether an object's property is defined or not. Suppose we have an object `obj`, and we want to know whether `obj.prop` is defined or not; a possible way to do this is to say:

```
if (obj.prop === void 0)                 // it could be void anything
{
  /* assume that prop is undefined */
}
else
{
  /* assume it is defined */
}
```

However, you can achieve the same effect by saying, as we often do:

```
if (typeof obj.prop == "undefined") ...
```

If you know for a fact that the value of obj.prop is not 0, the empty string or null then you can achieve the same effect by simply saying:

```
if (!obj.prop)
{
  /* assume that prop is undefined */
}
```

The undefined value means the same as false in the if statement. So do 0, the empty string, and the null value. This brings us to the subject of automatic type conversion.

Operators and Type Conversion

Quite often, operators are applied to values of different data types. Suppose we have a numeric variable x in our program and we want to see what its value is. A natural thing to say is:

```
alert("x==" + x);        // if x is 12, we'll see "x==12"
```

In order for this to work, JavaScript should be clever enough to figure out that we want the value of x, which is the number 12, to be converted to the two-character string "12" and use + as the string concatenation operator. That's precisely what it does, and conversion of numbers to strings is probably the most common example of automatic type conversion.

Conversion to String

Almost anything else can also be converted to a string. If arr is an array of three elements, 1,2,3, then alert(arr) will produce 1,2,3. Or is it [1,2,3]? As usual, the best thing to do is experiment to see what happens; our friendly EvalExp.htm is there to help.

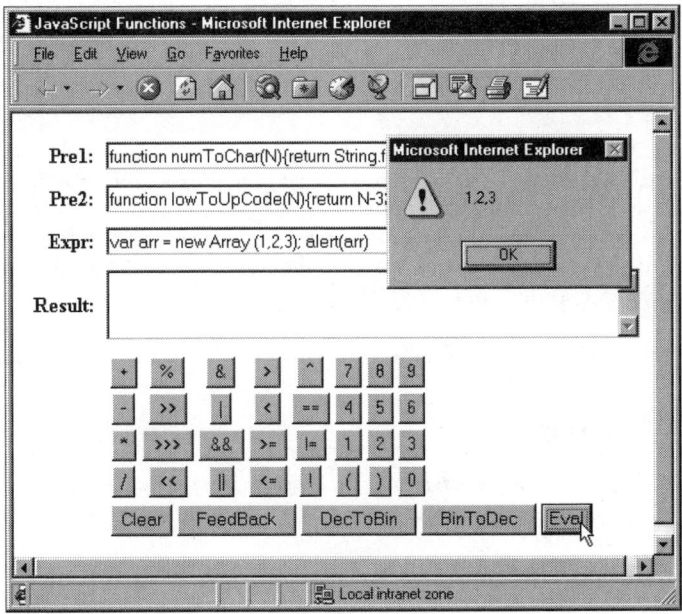

Strings to Numbers

The opposite conversion is also fairly common, as in:

```
var x = "372.25" - 2;            // x == 370.25
```

This type of conversion has limitations: the string must contain only the number, with no trailing characters, and it is always converted to a decimal number. For more sophisticated conversions, use the functions parseInt() and parseFloat(). These take two arguments, a string to convert and the base of conversion. To get a decimal number corresponding to the binary 1011, you say parseInt("1011",2). If no second argument is given, then the base is taken to be 10, 8 or 16, depending on how the string starts:

```
parseInt("2.718");
        // starts with a non-zero digit, base==10, result is 2.718
parseInt("027");      // starts with 0, base==8, result is 23
parseInt("0xf0");     // starts with 0x, where x is a-f, base==16, result is 240
```

Beware of a difficult bug: if you run parseInt() on constructed strings that may accidentally begin with 0, and you don't provide a second argument, your string will be interpreted as octal, not decimal, and you'll get plausible-looking but wrong results. It may be a good habit always to provide that argument, even when it's the default.

With parseInt(), the string you're converting can have any number of trailing characters, as in:

```
parseInt("15 men on the dead man's chest")    // result==15
```

Conversion to Booleans

Another very common example is the one we mentioned in the section discussing void: conversion of the number 0, the empty string, the null value and the undefined value, to the boolean value false, in if statements. Pretty much everything else is converted to true in that context. Netscape Communicator 4 converts an array of 0 length to false, in deviation from the ECMA standard, but this will change in version 5.

There are less obvious cases of type conversion: how do you convert an array to a number? The rule in IE4, in agreement with ECMA's implicit guidelines, is that if an array has only one element then you take the value of that element and convert according to the rules of its data type; otherwise, you convert it to NaN. What's a NaN? That's explained in the next section. The subject of type conversion has many small nooks and crannies, but we've already listed all the cases we ever use, and it's time to move on.

Literals and Names

For almost every data type there are corresponding literals. Data types, as you remember, can be primitive or compound. Primitive data types are numbers, booleans, strings, null and the undefined value. What are their literals like?

Primitive Data Type Literals

Number Literals

We'll start with numbers. Number literals may seem like the most obvious of subjects, but there are interesting twists. For instance, what happens when you try to convert an array to a number. Instead of saying that it's an error, it's more useful to say that it's a very special number called "Not a Number," or NaN for short. Why is this good? Because then you can test whether the result of what you're trying to do is equal to NaN, you can see that result in the result text box of our EvalExp.htm application, and you can even display that result in an alert box. (Try alert(parseInt("abc")))

What other interesting number literals are there? Well, you want to return something useful even if the user tries to divide by 0. The useful thing to return is Infinity, of course. What can you do with Infinity? You can add a number to it, or subtract one; the answer should be Infinity. (Try 1/0 -17.) You can put it in an if statement (it converts to true). You can try to subtract another Infinity from it, as in 1/0-1/0 but the result is not 0, it's NaN. Finally, you can subtract it from a number, and you'll get -Infinity, "negative infinity".

Otherwise, number literals are rather uneventful. You do need to remember that literals beginning with 0x are hexadecimal numbers (numbers in base 16), and literals beginning with 0 are octals (numbers in base 8).

String Literals

Anything inside a matching pair of quotes is a string literal. Single quotes may appear inside double quotes and vice versa:

```
<input type = button onclick = "alert('you clicked me!');" ...
```

What if you want to say something like: "You know what she said?" he said. "She said: 'No way. It ain't gonna work.'" We're in trouble here because we have an apostrophe inside single quotes and we don't want to change it to a double quote. If we want JavaScript to process this correctly, we have to help the apostrophe to "escape" the normal rules of evaluation, so it's interpreted literally. This is called "to escape an apostrophe". In order to escape a character, you put a special escape character in front of it. The escape character is \ and so to include a single quote inside single quotes you type \ ', and to include a double quote inside double quotes you type \ ". To include the escape character itself you type \ \. (A reminder: even though we keep talking about characters, there's no such data type in JavaScript. As we will see in Chapter 2, it uses single-character strings instead.)

The escape character is also used in **escape sequences** that represent several frequently used control characters. Here's a listing:

Escape sequence	Character
\f	Formfeed
\n	Newline
\r	Return
\t	Tab
\v	Vertical Tab

The backspace character can be represented by \b, but only when used within [], as explained below. The sequence \b by itself represents a word boundary.

The escape character is also needed to enter characters by their ASCII numerical codes (or Latin-1 encodings, as they're properly called). You can say \015 (octal) or \x0F (hexadecimal) instead of \n. Finally, ECMA stipulates and IE4 provides support for Unicode characters. Each one of those requires two bytes, and can be entered as \uXXXX, where each X is a hexadecimal digit. Be aware that alert boxes are not yet fully conversant with Unicode and mangle some characters beyond recognition.

Booleans and Others

The boolean literals are true and false. The only literal of type null is null. There are no literals of type undefined (the only way to create an undefined value is by using the void operator), but if you apply the typeof operator to an undefined variable or object property, you'll get back the string "undefined".

Array, Object and Regular Expression Literals

Array and Object Literals

Array and object literals are recent additions to JavaScript. Array literals look like this:

```
var arr = [1,2,"the third element",true,["an","embedded","array"]];
```

There's nothing conceptually difficult about them. We'll discuss arrays in greater detail in Chapter 2, Programming with Objects, because, as you already know, JavaScript arrays are objects.

Objects that are not arrays can also be initialized by a literal. Object literals look like this:

```
var car17 = {make:"Ford", model:"SymphonyGL", year:2000, door:4, color:"green"}
```

This is a comma-separated list of colon-separated attribute-value pairs. After you see a few such examples, it shouldn't come as a surprise that objects are implemented as associative arrays in JavaScript. An associative array is an array that is not indexed by numbers, but by something else; very often, by strings. That's what JavaScript objects are: you can refer to car17's make either as car17.make (it's an object) or as car17["make"] (it's an associative array). The answer in both cases is "Ford." The next chapter goes on and on about these subjects.

Regular Expression Literals

Like almost everything else in JavaScript, regular expressions (RE) can be wrapped into and manipulated as objects but much of the time we deal with RE literals. The same is true about strings. The difference is that string literals are very familiar, while RE literals can look forbidding. Learning REs is like learning another language. (In fact, if you learn all there is to know about REs in JavaScript, you will have learned a good deal of Perl.) We will only cover the basics here, but you will see REs again and again throughout the book.

The Language of Regular Expressions

Regular expressions are written in a special language. The purpose of the language is to describe patterns of characters. The main operation is matching; the main activity is to find a pattern (a regular expression) that matches exactly the set of strings that we want to do something with, or to, or about. The pattern-matching activity always takes place in the context of some operation, such as find-and-replace. Once the pattern is found, the operation is carried out.

Just as string literals are delimited by a pair of quotes, RE literals are delimited by a pair of slash characters. The second slash can be followed by the letters "i" or "g" or both. The letter "g" (as in "global") means "find all the strings that match the pattern, not just the first one, which is the default." The letter "i" means "make your match case-insensitive". These are the only two post-second-slash modifiers that are implemented in JavaScript 1.2. There are more of them in Perl, and we can expect them to gradually migrate to JavaScript.

Experimenting with Regular Expressions

You can use our `EvalExp.htm` to experiment with regular expressions. Borrowing from the next chapter, you can use regular expressions to find and replace substrings of a string. For instance, you can type this into the expression window:

```
var s = "Mississippi is history"; var t = s.replace(/is/gi,"are "); t;
```

This says: "Replace all occurrences of "is", globally and case-insensitively, with "are". The result window will show "Mare sare sippi are hare tory". As RE patterns become more complex, you may want to try them out as you read about them.

Alphanumeric Characters, Sequences and Grouping

A very simple RE pattern is `/ab/`. It matches the string "ab". This is rule 1 of RE matching: alphanumeric characters match themselves. The rule is simple but not very helpful because for every pattern there's only one sequence of characters that matches it. We want our patterns to be both precise and concise, so that every pattern can match a lot of different strings, very precisely described. That's what RE language is for.

We can group characters into classes such that the class matches any one character in it. Square brackets `[]` are used for that purpose. Suppose you always use the letters i, j and k to name your integer variables. You can match them all by the pattern `/[ijk]/`. Then you may notice that these letters form a sequence (come together in the alphabet and the Latin-1 encoding), and abbreviate your pattern to `/[i-k]/`. This is not much of an abbreviation, but consider `/[a-z]/` (matches any lowercase letter) and `/[0-9]/` (matches any digit). The pattern `/[a-z][0-9]/` then matches any identifier that consists of a lower-case letter followed by a digit. That's getting better; one little pattern matches 260 precisely specified strings.

Negated Classes

Actually, we cheated a little in the last paragraph: the pattern `/[ijk]` will match not only single-letter identifiers but **any** occurrence of those three letters anywhere. To catch only the identifiers, you want to say: "find any one of those letters preceded and followed by a non-identifier character". What's a non-identifier character? Recall the beginning of the chapter: identifiers have to start with a letter, underscore or dollar sign, and may also contain digits. The $ character presents some difficulties which we will address in a page or two; for the time being let's pretend that we're in JavaScript 1.0 and no dollar signs are allowed. The pattern `/[_A-Za-z0-9]/` matches any legitimate identifier character. To match anything that is not in this class, put the ^ character right after the opening square bracket. The entire pattern for our identifiers becomes:

```
/[^_A-Z a-z 0-9][ijk][^_A-Z a-z 0-9]/
```

This is rather a mouthful; can't we write it more concisely? The sequence A-Za-z0-9 seems to repeat often. The answer is yes; we'll get to abbreviations for popular classes soon.

Repetition

We can now pose ourselves a real-life problem: write a regular expression that matches all and only the legitimate identifiers of JavaScript. Something like this regular expression is sitting inside the JavaScript interpreter in the bowels of your browser and finds identifier tokens in your program.

As we were just reminded, an identifier has to start with a letter or an underscore. So the beginning is easy: /[_A-Za-z]. This can be followed by the same set, plus digits, repeated any number of times, including 0 times. How do we express that? Remarkably easily. We just put together the expression we want repeated and put an * after it. The entire pattern is:

```
/[_A-Za-z][_A-Za-z0-9]*/
```

Note that we don't have to add anything after the * character because of the "maximal match" principle. The pattern will try to find the maximal possible expression it matches, and will stop only when it comes across a non-identifier character.

There are other frequent repetition patterns. Suppose you need more than three integer variables and you've started using names like i2 or k7. In other words, you want to match i, j, k followed by none or one digit. Easy: use the ? instead of the *:

```
/[ijk][0-9]?/
```

Finally, the + sign means "repeat one or more times." The pattern /[ijk][0-9]+/ will match j23 or k29856, but not just j or k.

That's good, but what if we want something repeated exactly 2 or 3 or 4 times, and not any other number of times? The most precise way to indicate repetition is by using braces, as follows:

```
/a{3}/          // matches aaa and nothing else
/a{2,4}/        // matches 2 or 3 or 4 a's
/a{2,}/         // matches 2 or more a's
```

Now you can see that +,* and ? are just abbreviations for the most common braced intervals: + means {1,}, * means {0,}, and ? means {0,1}.

Alternation and Grouping

We know how to express the idea "match this OR that" with respect to individual characters: /[ijk]/ matches i or j or k. What if we want to match this string OR that string? In that case, we have to use an explicit OR character, which is the vertical bar. To match either "ab" or "bc" you say: /ab|bc/. Now the next question is: how do you match "ab" or "bc" followed by "ef"? This is ambiguous; the two interpretations are:

```
"ab" or ("bc" followed by "ef")
("ab" or "bc") followed by "ef"
```

To disambiguate we need parentheses, used exactly the same way in English and in RE.

```
/(ab|bc)ef/              // the second interpretation
```

Special Characters

By now we have accumulated quite a few characters that have specialized meaning in RE. Let's review them all before we proceed:

Character(s)	Meaning
/	mark beginning and end of pattern
[...]	match any character in the class
[^...]	match any character not in the class
.	match any character other than new line
-	match any character in a range
* + ? {..}	repetitions of various kinds
( )	parentheses for grouping
/	alternation: match this or that

What if we wanted to match one of those special characters literally, letting them escape their specialized meaning? You can probably guess the answer: use the same "\" escape character that goes back at least to those glorious times in the early 1970s when Ken Thompson was inventing Unix and Dennis Ritchie was inventing the C programming language (and they both worked in the same Bell Labs where Al Aho was inventing regular expressions). At this point, you may start to feel that you're part of a long and illustrious history.

Alphabetical Characters with Special Meaning

For non-alphabetical characters, you use the escape character to have them interpreted literally. With alphabetical characters it's the other way around: you use the escape character to give them a special meaning. Some of them are the familiar escapees from string literals: \f \n \r \t \v, meaning Formfeed, Newline, Return, Tab and Vertical Tab, respectively. These are collectively known as whitespace. A very special case is the backspace character: to match it, you have to make it into a single-character class [\b]. You'll see why in a moment.

Another big set of escaped letter characters contains abbreviations for popular character classes:

Character(s)	Meaning
\w	Any word character. Same as [A-Za-z0-9]
\W	Any non-word character. Same as [^A-Za-z0-9]
\s	Any whitespace character. Same as [\f\n\r\t\v]

Table Continued on Following Page

Character(s)	Meaning
\S	Any non-whitespace character. Same as [^\f\n\r\t\v]
\d	Any digit. Same as [0-9]
\D	Any non-digit. Same as [^0-9]

We'd like to remind you here that there is also a non-alphabetic abbreviation for a character class. It is the . (dot) character which stands for "any character except Newline", or [^\n]. It is used unescaped in its special meaning, and has to be escaped to be used literally.

Now we can go back and rewrite our pattern for JavaScript identifiers using the new abbreviations. Or rather you can: we're going to give it to you as an exercise, but not before we introduce yet another small set of three special characters, including the dollar sign.

Anchoring the Match at a Specific Position

The dollar sign character has to be escaped if you want to match it literally, because unescaped it has a special meaning. The meaning is unusual. The dollar sign doesn't match any particular character or group of characters. Rather, it stipulates that the preceding pattern has to be found at the end of the string, or, in a multi-line string, at the end of a line. For instance, the pattern /!$/ matches all and only lines that end with the exclamation point. We can say that the dollar sign **anchors** the match to a specific position in the text, or we can say that it matches a position in the text.

To anchor the match at the beginning of a line, the ^ character is called into duty again. To find the next occurrence of a digit at the beginning of a line you'd use the pattern /^[0-9]/.

You can also anchor the match at the word boundary, i.e., at a position between \w, a word character, and \W, a non-word character. That anchor is performed by the b character, escaped. This explains why the backspace character can only be matched by [\b]: the reason is that \b by itself is used as an anchor. The \B pattern matches any position that is not a word boundary.

And Much More...

Regular expressions form a large topic; there are books written about them. In JavaScript, they also form a moving target. It seems that the final goal is to transport the entire Perl syntax of regular expressions into JavaScript. This guarantees that with every new release there will be more of it. What we've described in this section is sufficient for very vigorous pattern matching. In the next chapter (which is drawing close) we'll show you how to set those patterns in action, by giving them as arguments to the methods of the String and RegExp objects.

Conclusions

This chapter has laid the foundation of JavaScript. We have covered the main rules of grammar, including rules for forming words (literals and identifiers), phrases (expressions), and sentences (statements). Let's check off the main points:

- ❑ terminology: what are literals, identifiers, expressions and statements?
- ❑ variables, values and data types: what does it mean that variables are untyped?
- ❑ statements: what kind of statements are there?
- ❑ expressions and operators: what kind of operators are there?
- ❑ precedence and associativity
- ❑ literals, especially regular expression literals.

Several times in the course of the chapter, we have emphasized the central role of objects in JavaScript, and we have given examples of what they look like. It is now time to move on to the real center of JavaScript, the objects.

2

Programming with Objects

Introduction

In this chapter we will begin to come to grips with objects. This is not yet object-oriented programming, but a necessary first step toward it. We'll start with a brief general introduction to objects and classes of objects, and proceed to a systematic treatment of the specific objects that are native to JavaScript. In the next chapter, we'll give an equally systematic treatment of the objects that populate the browser window and the web page.

With one introductory chapter already behind us, we can try to make our examples more realistic and useful. For instance, they will include a library of utility functions for working with arrays and strings. We'll use those utility functions in applications that make sense in the world outside computing. To make it all hang together, our examples will be cumulative; they will develop a theme. For this chapter, the theme is text-processing; later chapters will also each have a theme.

Our first text-processing utility produces an alphabetical word list that contains all the words in a web document. The next step is a frequency count that associates each word with its frequency in the text. Our most ambitious effort will be a dictionary that is embedded in the same page as your text, so that if you click on a word, the dictionary will bring up its definition. The *Try It Out* section below shows all three applications together. Although relatively simple (hey, this *is* an introductory chapter!), our examples should make sense, and make your pages more informative.

In summary, our chapter will move along three parallel lines: a descriptive coverage of native JavaScript objects; a library of utilities for working with strings and arrays, and a suite of text-processing applications. The subjects covered are:

- ❑ objects, classes, prototypes, properties and methods
- ❑ how to define your own properties (for existing objects)
- ❑ native JavaScript classes, especially strings, arrays, RegExp, functions, and objects
- ❑ how to add new methods to them, using their prototypes
- ❑ functions as data, functions as objects and functions as properties of objects
- ❑ reference and value semantics (don't worry, it's not too bad)
- ❑ objects and associative arrays

Try It Out

To try out our applications, point your browser at `http://webdev.wrox.co.uk/books/1894/Chapter02/txtUtils.htm`. Click on the ListWords button to see the alphabetized list of words in the page. Click Refresh to get the document back. Do the same with Frequency Count. Finally, click on Apply Dictionary. To extend and format the dictionary, use the instructions in the page.

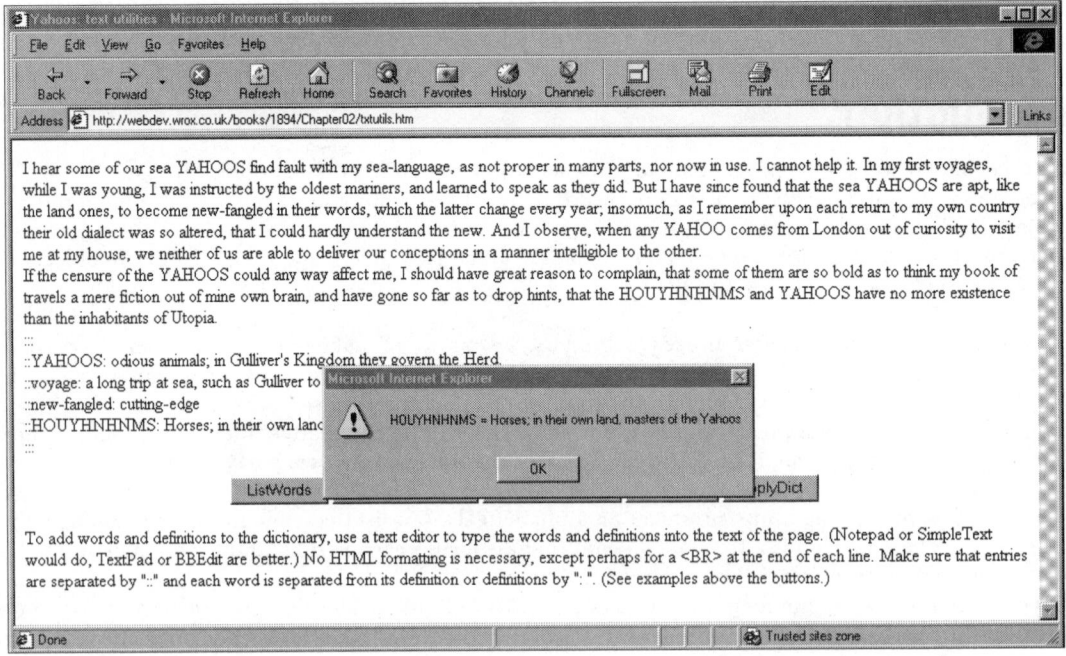

How It Works

Sorry. You can try out our applications and extend them in some ways (e.g., make the dictionary better or put it in a separate frame), but in order to understand how they work you'll have to read the chapter. By the end of it, you will be able to understand every line of our code, and develop it even further.

Objects, Classes, Prototypes, Properties, Methods

We think of the world as consisting of objects. An object has a unique identity and usually belongs to a class of objects that have the same properties. Consider the book you're reading right now: it has the same properties (title, price, number of pages) as other books. We can express this by saying that the book is an object of the class `Book`. There are two ways, at least, to think about classes: as **sets** or as **prototypes**. In the first view, the name of the class ("`Book`") refers to the set of all books, and each individual book is a member (or *instance*) of that class. In the second view, the name of the class refers to the "typical book" or "the concept of book" that has all the properties that all books have in common.

From either perspective, a Book object is like a collection of various properties, for instance:

- ❑ a Book has an author, which is a list of Persons (with perhaps a single Person in it);
- ❑ and a page-count, which is an Integer > 0;
- ❑ and a list-price, which is a Number > 0;
- ❑ and a title, which is a list of Words;
- ❑ and a copyright-date, which is a Date;
- ❑ ... and so on, until you have enough for the task at hand

Where would these properties be stored and found? If you think of a class as a set that contains all its objects, including those that do not yet exist, then you could put all the properties into the class itself and have it manufacture new objects. If you think of a class as a prototype, you would put all the properties in the prototype object and make sure that when a new object is created, it copies all the properties from the prototype. In either case, you need some mechanism for constructing new objects of a given class; let's call it a constructor, because that's what it's usually called in programming languages.

In programming languages, it proves very useful to build programs out of interacting objects. Just as in the real world, objects are instances of classes, but the classes in this case are either built into the language, or have been defined by the programmer. A class is a collection of named properties. These properties can be of any data type, including functions; function-properties are called **methods**. (If this is the first time you're encountering the idea of function as a property and it makes you feel uneasy, suspend your sense of unease until the section on functions as objects.)

Each class also includes one or several functions, called **constructors**, that create individual objects. The name of the constructor function is usually the same as the name of the class itself.

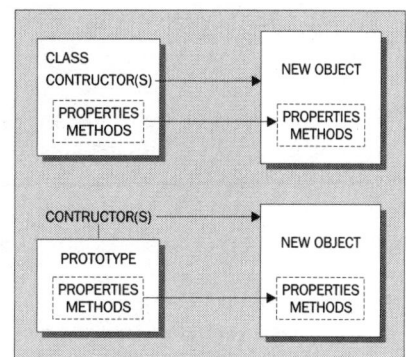

In order to program with objects of a given class, you need to know the class constructors, properties, methods, and the operators that apply to it.

JavaScript, unlike C++ or Java, does not have a reserved word Class. It does, however, provide a prototype for each class, in which all the common properties of the class are stored. The prototype itself is a property of the constructor function.

An Example: the String Class

Time for an example. JavaScript has a built-in class `String` which is, in effect, a collection of facilities to manipulate character strings. `String` has three constructors, or three ways of using one constructor function. To see them in action, let's look at the three statements below:

```
var theWord = new String("Lettuce");
                        // make a String object out of a string literal
var theWord2 = new String(theWord); // make a copy of theWord
var theDef = new String();      // create an empty string; we will add to it
                                later
```

The variable `theWord` is created by the `String` constructor from a string literal. This is a very common use of a constructor: take pure data and wrap it into an object that has many predefined properties and methods. Since it was created by a constructor, `theWord` has various properties, such as length: `theWord.length` evaluates to 7 because "Lettuce" is indeed a word of seven letters. What letters? Well, every String object has a method, `charAt()`, that lets you inspect its individual characters: `theWord.charAt(0)=="L"`, `theWord.charAt(1)=="e"`, and so on. (In spite of its name, the `charAt()` method really returns a string that is one character long. JavaScript doesn't have a separate data type for characters, but it manages quite nicely with single-character strings.)

In the second line, the constructor takes an already existing object as an argument and creates a copy of it. This is called "the copy constructor"- in this case, we're creating a copy of `theWord` string object.

In the third line, the constructor is a function of no arguments. A constructor that takes no arguments is called "the default constructor." It is used to create an object that is either minimal in some way or serves as a default for the class. In the case of `String`, it creates an empty string whose length is 0. (You may think that `theDef.charAt(0)` would be undefined, but in fact it is also an empty string.) You can add to the empty string, or any string, using the + or += operator:

```
theDef = theDef + " basic stuff for salad";  // add to theDef
theDef += "; also good in sandwiches";      // add some more
```

The three constructors we've just shown are very common, you'll see them in many classes. However, in the case of `String`, the first constructor is not used very often. It's more common to assign a string literal, as in:

```
var allCaps = "LETTUCE"; // assign string literal "LETTUCE"; no constructor here
```

This variable looks like pure data, not an object at all. Indeed it is pure data, but you can still use all the properties and methods of the class `String`. If you try `allCaps.length`, you'll still get 7, and `allCaps.charAt(0)` will return `"L"`. JavaScript is happy to add the obvious object properties to our string literal. It does so by creating a temporary "wrapper" string object, which it will use and then discard. You can also use operators with a string literal:

```
var theWord = new String("Lettuce");
var sandwich1 = allCaps + "TOMATO";
theWord == allCaps;
   // returns false because the == operator is case-sensitive
theWord.toLowerCase() == allCaps.toLowerCase();  // evaluates to true;
```

In the last example, note that the method `toLowerCase()` applies equally well to a regular object on the left and to the literal on the right. The only situation in which there is a difference between them is when you start adding your own properties and methods to the `String` class, or any other built-in class.

Adding Your Own Properties

You can add your own properties to any object. No special declarations are necessary: you just choose a name for your property and start using it. Let's go back to `theWord`, but now give it a definition as a property:

```
theWord.theDef = "basic stuff for salad";
alert(theWord+ "=" + theWord.theDef);          // show word and definition
```

This will produce `"Lettuce=basic stuff for salad"`. Can we do the same thing with a string literal? Let's try it with `allCaps`, which we defined earlier:

```
allCaps.theDef = "good in sandwiches; mayonnaise, lettuce and tomato make a good
                  one"
alert(allCaps + "=" + allCaps.theDef);          // show word and definition
```

This time, we'll get `"LETTUCE=undefined"` What happened? Remember that `allCaps` is pure data. When we assigned it a `"theDef"` property, a `String` object was created and given that property, so there's no error message. However, it was a temporary wrapper object that was thrown away after use. When we say `allCaps.theDef` in the next line, a new wrapper object is created, for which the property is undefined.

The moral is that if you're going to set properties, you've got to use objects. In particular, if you want to associate names with definitions through the property mechanism, the definitions have to be properties of a real persistent object rather than transient wrappers of literal strings. To make our dictionary, we'll create a dictionary object such that words are its properties and definitions are the values of those properties:

```
var theDict = new Something();        // Something that will have properties.
theDict.lettuce = "basic stuff for salad ";
```

This will work quite well, as we'll see later in the chapter.

Adding Methods

In addition to adding value properties to the `String` class, we can also add **methods** (i.e., function properties). This time, let's take up a slightly more involved example that qualifies as a useful utility: a method that replaces all occurrences of a target sequence of characters with the specified replacement:

```
var str1 = new String("best test");
str1.replaceLiteral("e","oa");          // str1 == "boast toast"
```

In Chapter 1, you saw the `String.replace()` method that uses regular expressions. Here, we're defining a simpler and more limited method that is also easier to use (especially if regular expressions give you headache or indigestion). Our method is, of course, redundant: the second line in the example above can be rewritten using `replace()`:

```
str1.replace(/e/g,"oa");
```

However, `replaceLiteral()` is adequate for many tasks, and very good for illustrating the process of defining your own method. That process consists of three steps. You may find them puzzling at first reading, but as you work through the example, things will become clearer. To achieve complete clarity, roll up your sleeves and define some methods of your own.

These are the steps:

❑ define a global function that does the same thing to one of its arguments as the method will do to its "owner" object

❑ rewrite the function using the word "this" to refer to the argument that will be the object.

❑ make the revised function a property of the prototype

Since this is our first try, we'll go through the steps very carefully. In Chapter 4 and later, where we'll be defining methods all the time, we'll usually skip the first one.

Defining a Global Function

In our example, the global function `replaceLiteral()` would behave as follows:

```
var str2 = replaceLiteral("best test", "e","oa");  // str2 == "boast toast"
```

As you can see, the global function does the same thing to its first argument, in this case `"best test"` as the future method will do to its owner object. We'll consider two different implementations of this function. The first follows the algorithm below:

❑ create a new String;

❑ go to the first occurrence of target in initial string;

❑ copy the material up to that occurrence from the initial string to the new string;

❑ add the replacement where the original string has the target sequence;

❑ repeat until there are no more occurrences of the target in the initial string.

In writing it up, we'll make use of two helpful methods that are defined for the `String` class: `indexOf()` and `substring()`. The `indexOf()` method takes a target substring as an argument and returns the position of the target or -1 if the target is not found. The `substring()` method can take one or two arguments. The first argument is the starting position of the substring, and the second argument, if present, is the end position. If no second argument is given the substring stretches to the end of the string.

```
function replaceLiteral(str, target, repl){
        // in str, replace all occurrences of target with repl
  var res = new String();          // 'res' is the resulting string
  var len = target.length;
  var pos = 0;                      // 'pos' is the position in the source string
  var newpos = str.indexOf(target); // find first occurrence of target
  while (newpos != -1)
  {
   res += str.substring(pos,newpos) + repl;
   pos = newpos + len;
   newpos = str.indexOf(target, pos);
  }
  res += str.substring(pos);
  return res;
}
```

This is a solid and established, if somewhat pedestrian, way of doing this sort of thing. Looking further into available objects and methods, we can come up with a much snappier version. The String class has a split() method that splits a string at every occurrence of the specified separator and puts the resulting pieces into an array of strings. For instance:

```
var theDef = new String("basic stuff for salad"); // a definition for"lettuce"
theDef += ";also good in sandwiches";             // another definition
var defList = theDef.split(";");
  // defList == ["basic stuff for salad","also good in sandwiches"]
```

Array is another JavaScript class equipped with its own collection of properties and methods. One of them is the join() method designed specifically for arrays whose elements are strings. (If they are not, they are converted to strings.) The join() method concatenates all the elements of the array together, adding a specified separator. We can therefore use split() to remove all occurrences of target, and use join() to insert the replacement. Our function becomes:

```
replaceLiteral(str,target,replacement){
  return str.split(target).join(replacement);
}
```

This is cool, but it's a global function, not a method of the String class. So what, you might say, why not use it as a global function? Let's rewrite it as a method first, then address the question why it is a Good Thing to do.

Rewrite as a Method; Make a Prototype Property

Rewriting a global function as a method is a fairly mechanical task. Our function no longer needs its first argument because the method will operate on the object that calls it:

```
var str = new String("Mary was wary");
str.replaceLiteral("ary","oosy");        // str == "Moosy was woosy"
```

In order for this to work, the method needs some way to refer to the object that owns it. The word this is reserved precisely for that purpose: when the keyword this is mentioned in the text of a method, the reference is to the method's owner object. So the only change in the code is that we use this instead of str.

```
function str_replaceLiteral(target, replacement) {
  return this.split(target).join(replacement);
}
```

The final step is to install the code as a method of the `String` class:

```
String.prototype.replaceLiteral = str_replaceLiteral;
```

With this code evaluated, every object of class `String` will have our `replaceLiteral()` method. Why this is better than a global function with the same name and an extra argument?

Why Methods are Better than Global Functions

There are, as far as we know, two reasons why methods are better than global functions: a simple one and a profound one. The simple reason is that you have one less argument to get wrong, or to place in the wrong order. It's quite a burden, we feel, to have to remember whether you should say `replaceLiteral(str,targ,rep)` as in "within str, replace every target by replacement," or `replaceLiteral(targ,rep,str)`, as in "I want to replace every target by replacement in str". It's much easier to remember the order of two arguments (with two possibilities) than three (with six possibilities). And you never have to worry that your String argument is of a wrong type, if what you're calling is a method of a String object.

The second, more profound, reason is that a method is packaged together with the data it operates on, in a single object that is also an enclosed name space. The name of your method does not preclude another class from having a method of the same name. For instance, we might want to give a `replaceLiteral()` method to the Array class, that would be applicable to arrays of strings. The method would tell each string in the array to apply its own `replaceLiteral()` method to itself:

```
function arr_replaceLiteral(target,repl){
  var len = this.length;      // length of the Array owner of the method
  res = new Array(len);       // create a new array of that length
  for(var i=0; i<len; i++)
    res[i] = this[i].replaceLiteral(target,repl);
  return res;
  }
Array.prototype.replaceLiteral = arr_replaceLiteral;  // install in prototype
```

Suppose, we want to be able to apply that method to arrays that contain numbers as well as strings. Easy: let's define a `replaceLiteral()` method for the Number class. In the code below, we convert the number object to a string by saying `this.toString()`; we apply `replaceLiteral()` to the resulting string to make the replacement; and we convert the result back to number by putting a + in front of it:

```
function num_replaceLiteral(a,b){
  return + this.toString().replaceLiteral(a,b);
  }
Number.prototype.replaceLiteral = num_replaceLiteral;
```

Now, suppose we have a mixed array called `mixedArray`, that contains strings, numbers and sub-arrays. Scattered throughout the array is a magical sequence of digits that we want to replace with an encoding that only our trusted friends can decode. We can do it by simply saying:

```
mixedArray.replaceLiteral(magicDigits,encoding);
```

To work through a specific example, let's define the variables:

```
var mixedArray = new Array("17B","or",new Array("not",17,"bee"));
var magicDigits = 17, encoding = 2;
mixedArray.replaceLiteral(magicDigits,encoding);
        // mixedArray becomes ["2B","or",["not",2,"bee"]]
```

This style of programming is frequently described as follows: we send each element of `mixedArray` a message saying: "apply your `replaceLiteral()` method to yourself." Each element is smart enough to know how to do it. Replacing global functions with methods adds intelligence to data, and this is a Good Thing to do. If our `replaceLiteral()` were a global function, it would have to contain a long 'switch' or 'if...else if...' statement whose different branches would contain the versions of the code for different data types. Separating those versions into methods that are kept **within** the matching data type is a much better, more modular solution. Consider how we added Numbers to those data types that can be placed in a "mixed array" to which `replaceLiteral()` applies. If it were a global function, we would have to go into its code and add a branch to its conditional. Since it's a method, all we had to do was define a new `replaceLiteral()` method for the Number class.

Another Example: the Array Class and Sorting

To give the Array class another workout, suppose we have a list of definitions somewhere on a web page, represented in this form:

```
:::
::lettuce: basic stuff for salad
::tomatoes: add color and juice
::mushrooms: add body and taste
::peppers: only if you have some lying around the house
::croutons: we're going Caesar
::hunger: the authors' strongest feeling right now
:::
```

Assume that the sequence of three colons is used only twice in the page. Assume also that we can somehow extract the full text of the page and assign it to a JavaScript variable `pageText`. we could easily extract these definitions, ignoring everything before and after, by saying:

```
var pageParts = pageText.split(":::"); // an array of three items
var theDefListText = pageParts[1];  // the middle item; pageParts[0] precedes,
                                    // pageParts[2] follows
```

We can further split into individual entries, and entries into words and definitions:

```
var theDefList = theDefListText.split("::");
var entry1 = theDefList[0];          // entry1 == "lettuce: basic stuff for salad"
var wrd1 = theDefList[0].split(": ")[0];    // wrd1 == "lettuce"
var def1 = theDefList[0].split(": ")[1];    // definition of wrd1
```

So far, we seem to be in good shape, but how do we get the text of the page into a JavaScript variable? This is what you have to say:

```
var pageText = document.body.innerText;
```

All we needed from the page, it turns out, was its body's "innerText" property. This property is a string which can be used like any other string. It contains the whole text of your page, with the HTML codes removed. If we wanted to keep those codes, we'd ask for the "innerHTML" property, and soon we'll be doing that. Those are the only two document properties used in this chapter.

Suppose you have an array of strings which contains your definitions, and you want to sort it alphabetically. Before you roll out your high-powered sorting algorithm, check to see whether the Array class has a sort method. It turns out that it does, so you simply say theDefList.sort(), and it is sorted. However, there is a problem: it is sorted in the ASCII order, with all the capital letter words preceding all the lower-case words. To sort some other way, you need to supply a comparison function as an argument to sort(). A comparison function takes two items as arguments and returns -1, 0 or 1, if the first item is less than, equal to, or greater than the second. It's like subtraction, but with the result simplified to one of three possibilities: compare(3,5) should be negative (-1), compare(3,3) is 0, but compare(5,3) should be positive (1). If you want to sort alphabetically, your function should compare strings alphabetically, with case as a secondary issue.

Again the first thing to do is to check whether the String class has an appropriate method. The answer is no (in Java it does...), but it does have a very handy pair of case-conversion methods, toUpperCase() and toLowerCase(). To compare two strings alphabetically we'll just convert both to uppercase, then do the comparison. If the uppercase strings are equal, we'll do an additional comparison of the initial strings to check for the possibility that they differ in case; we'll put uppercase words first.

```
function strLessThan(a,b)
{                            // examples: "That" < "that" < "This" < "this"
  var aU = a.toUpperCase(); var bU = b.toUpperCase();
  return aU<bU?-1: aU>bU?1: a==b?0: a<b?-1: 1;}
```

This use of the "?:" operator is equivalent to: "if (aU<bU) return -1; else if ... ", which was explained in the *Statements* section of Chapter 1. The long line simply of operations simply checks every possibility, first checking to see if the uppercased strings are different words, then, if they are the same, comparing their original forms to see if they are identical (a==b?0), such as when both a & b are "this", or going on to establish a precedent based on their original forms.

Now that the comparison function is defined, we sort alphabetically by saying:

```
theDefList.sort(strLessThan)
```

If this kind of programming—passing functions as arguments to other functions—is new to you, wait till the *Functions* section below for explanations and examples.

What Kinds of Objects are There?

JavaScript classes of objects come from three sources:

- ❑ built-in classes of the core language (covered in the rest of this chapter)
- ❑ the classes of the host application (covered in Chapter 3)
- ❑ user-defined classes (covered in Chapter 4)

Built-in classes fall into two categories: wrapper classes for primitive data types and "the rest of them". Wrapper classes, as we already explained, are used for wrapping temporary objects around pure data so you can apply the methods and properties of the wrapper class. In the case of the Number and Boolean classes, that's the only reason for having them. The String class, in addition to being a wrapper, is a terrific programming tool.

What about "the rest of them", specifically Math, Date, RegExp, Function, Array, and Object? We're going to present Date and Math in the remainder of this section, while RegExp, Function, Array, and Object will get a separate section each.

The Date class is pretty much what you would expect. It has constructors that create Date objects and a bunch of methods to extract or modify a Date object's year, month, day, and other components. Math is an unusual class in that it has no objects and therefore no constructors: it's just a name space for holding references to mathematical constants and functions. So, if you need the value of *pi* (π) in your JavaScript code you obtain it by saying Math.PI, and if you want the logarithm in base 2 of arctan of 17, you say: Math.LOG2E(Math.atan(17)). Read about it in Appendix A; we're going to move on to more interesting things: regular expressions, functions as data, functions as objects, arrays as objects, and objects as arrays.

The RegExp Object

We have seen regular expression literals that are typed in by the programmer before the program starts to run, and cannot be changed when the program is running. What if we want to create a regular expression in response to a user action or a changing situation in the program? This is what the RegExp object is for. It constructs regular expressions out of strings, which themselves can be constructed on the fly, in the course of the program.

The Constructor and the compile() Method

The RegExp constructor takes one or two string arguments. The first argument is the body of the regular expression. The second argument, if present, is the modifier. For instance, to construct a RegExp object that would match a consonant letter, whether capital or lower-case, you'd call the constructor as follows:

```
var cons1RE = new RegExp("[^aeiou]","i");   // the reg exp is /[^aeiou]/i
```

If your regular expression is to contain the escape character \, it has to be itself escaped in the string that is given to the constructor, because the backslash is an escape character for strings also. To create an object that would match a consonant right after a non-word character, you'd say:

```
var cons2RE = new RegExp("\\W[^aeiou]","i"); // the reg exp is /\W[^aeiou]/i
```

The following pattern matches five-digit zipcodes:

```
var zip5 = new RegExp("\\d{5}");
```

We leave it as an exercise for the reader to create a regular expression that matches both five-digit and nine-digit zip codes. Such a regular expression would be useful in validating input from an HTML form. (We present a form validator based on regular expressions in Chapter 3.)

In addition to a constructor, RegExp has a `compile()` method that takes the same arguments as the constructor. It makes it possible to "reuse" an existing RegExp object by giving it a new value:

```
var aPat = new RegExp("^silly$")    // matches only the "silly" string
aPat.compile("^clever$","i")        // matches "clever" case-insensitively
```

Using RegExp objects

Once you've constructed a RegExp object, how do you use it for matching? The most general answer is that you invoke one of its methods, and give it a string to work on as an argument. There are two such methods, `test()` and `exec()`.

The test() Method and the lastIndex Property

The `test()` method is the simpler of the two; it returns true or false, reporting success or failure of the match:

```
zip5.test("12z45"); /* returns false */  zip5.test("12345"); // returns true
```

If the pattern of the RegExp object has the g (global) attribute, then the `test()` method works together with the `lastIndex` property of the object. Upon a successful match, the method not only returns `true`, but also sets the value of `lastIndex` to the position immediately following the match:

```
var zip5g = new RegExp("\\d{5}","g");    // the pattern is /\d{5}/g
zip5g.test("try 12345 or 54321, see what happens");
```

The last line returns `true` and also sets `zip5g.lastIndex` to 9, which is the index of the blank character immediately following the last digit of the first match. Next time `test()` is called, it starts the search for a match from the `lastIndex` position in the string. If no more matches are found, `lastIndex` is set to 0. Everything is set up very nicely so we can loop through the string visiting each match. The code below stores the starting index of each zip code in an array:

```
var zipStr="zips: 12345, 34567, 99543, and many others";
var zipStartPos=new Array(); var zipCount=0;
while(zip5g.test(zipStr)) zipStartPos[zipCount++]=zip5g.lastIndex-5;
```

In the last line, the loop condition sets `lastIndex` to the position right after a five-digit match; subtracting 5 gives us its starting position. Upon the last match, the loop condition returns 0, which is converted to `false`, and the loop terminates.

The exec() method

On most occasions, we want to know more than the position of the match: we want to know what the match is. For this, we use the `exec()` method. It manipulates the `lastIndex` property in the same way as the `test()` method. However, instead of a Boolean value, `exec()` returns the matching substring. We can use a very similar loop to get an array of all matches:

```
var zips = new Array(); var matchResult;
zipCount = 0;
while(matchResult = zip5g.exec(zipStr))     // assignment returns a value
   zips[zipCount++] = matchResult;
```

The loop condition is an assignment statement that also returns a value. If the match is successful, the returned value is the matching substring, which is converted to `true`. If the match fails, the returned value is `null`, which is converted to `false`, and the loop terminates.

Properties of the RegExp Object and Class

Each RegExp object has the following properties:

Property	Data type	Access type	Description
source	String	read-only	the text of the regular expression
global	Boolean	read-only	is the global attribute set?
ignoreCase	Boolean	read-only	is the ignoreCase attribute set?
lastIndex	Integer	read-write	position after the last match

Note that `lastIndex` is a read-write property, so you can set it to 0 yourself if you want to terminate the loop before the last match is found (for instance, if you're looking for a specific match, or the first match satisfying some conditions).

In addition to **instance properties** of individual objects, RegExp also has **class** or **static** properties. We discuss static properties of JavaScript classes in the section on function objects later in this chapter. For now, we'll just give a quick definition. A class property, as you can guess, is a property of the entire class. While the same `lastIndex` property can have different values for different objects, a class property can only have one value at any given time. It can have a value before any objects of the class are created. An example of a RegExp's static property would be `lastMatch`, the most recently matched text by whatever RegExp object did the last matching. Since we don't use the static properties of RegExp in this book, we only list them in Appendix B, with explanations.

String Methods That Use Regular Expressions

Although slightly off-topic, string methods that take regular expressions as arguments are most conveniently discussed here, because they often have the same functionality as RegExp methods that take strings as arguments. There are four string methods that use regular expressions. One of them is `replace()`: you've already seen a lot of it, and will see much more, especially in Chapter 8. Another one is `split()`: although we have used it only with string literals, it would be happy to work with regular expressions as well. The remaining two methods are `search()` and `match()`.

The `search()` method takes a regular expression (or a RegExp object) as argument, and returns the position of the first match, or -1 if no match is found. If the expression contains the g attribute, it is ignored by the method:

```
var pos = "alma mater".search(/ma/g);      // pos == 2
```

(Recall that although "alma mater" is a string literal, a wrapper object is created behind the scenes in order to call the String object's method.)

The `match()` method takes a regular expression and returns an array. If the expression has the g attribute, the array contains all the matches. Returning to our zip code example, we could extract all zip codes from a string using the `match()` method as follows:

```
var zipStr = "zips: 12345, 34567, 99543, and many others";
var zips = zipStr.match(/\d{5}/g);      // zips is an array of three elements
```

If the regular expression does not have a g attribute, it still returns an array. The first element of the array, at index 0, contains the entire match. If the matched expression has subexpressions enclosed in parentheses, those substrings of the input string that match the parenthesized subexpressions are stored as the remaining elements of the array. Here's an example:

```
var str = "My zip code is 12345-3333, in full detail";
var zipPat = /(\d{5})-(\d{4})/;              // five digits, then -, then four digits
var res = str.match(zipPat);
var fullZip = res[0]   // contains 12345-3333
var zip5 = res[1];     // contains 12345
var zip4 = res[2];     // contains 3333
```

In addition, the resulting array object has two special properties. One is index, which contains the position of the match in the input string. (In our example, res.index == 15, the index of digit 1.) The other property is input, and contains, unsurprisingly, the entire input string. (In our example, res.input == str.)

Referring to substrings matched by subexpressions

Subexpressions enclosed in parentheses play another special role in the regular expressions language. We'll illustrate it with a `replace()` example. Suppose you want to take a string that contains an address and a zip code and replace the address with the string "xxx" but leave the zip code intact. First, let's construct a match:

```
var addrPat = /(.*)(\d{5}-\d{4})/; // two subexpressions in parentheses
```

The special role of parenthesized subexpressions is that you can refer to them by using names of the form $d, where d is a digit 0..9. For instance, our addrPat matches an address such as the following:

```
var addr = 73 Park Ave Nowhere NS 12345-3333;
```

Once we perform the match, we can refer to the entire input string and its substrings matched by subexpressions as follows:

❑ $0 refers to the entire input string
❑ $1 refers to the substring matched by first subexpression ("73 Park Ave Nowhere NS ")
❑ $2 refers to the substring matched by second subexpression ("12345-3333")

In general, if `str.match(pat)` returns an array `res`, then we can refer to `res[i]` as `$1`. We can now complete our example. To produce a desired transformation of the input string, we call the `replace()` method as follows:

```
addr.replace(addrPat,"xxx$2"); // output "xxx" followed by $2 substring
```

We'll use this feature extensively in Chapter 8, "Working with Text."

Functions as Data

Treating functions as data is not new to JavaScript. You find the same idea in older languages such as Perl, Scheme (a dialect of Lisp) or ML. (In this section we are, in effect, translating some very common Scheme/Lisp idioms into JavaScript.) Briefly, the idea is to give functions the same "rights" that are afforded numbers or strings: to be assigned to a variable, stored in a data structure, passed as an argument to another function, and returned as the result of a function call. Consider these statements:

```
var foo = 34;
var h = foo;
ar[7] = foo;
var z = g(foo);
return foo;
```

These are totally unremarkable. Now imagine that `foo` is defined as a function but the rest of the expressions are still legitimate:

```
function foo(x) {
  // do something with x
}
```

It turns out that very interesting computational possibilities open up if you start thinking of functions as data—basically, as a list of arguments and a body of code, ready to be run but also packaged to be passed around.

You will see examples of functions as data throughout the rest of the book. For now, we'll follow our practice of illustrating with short general-purpose utilities. One such illustration was given in our discussion of the `sort()` method, which takes a comparison function as an argument to accommodate different data types. (If you're familiar with C, the `qsort` function in the standard C library similarly takes a function pointer as an argument, for the same purpose.) We're going to illustrate another general use of functions as data by defining the functions `map`, `accumulate` and `filter`. All three take a function and an array as arguments to express common patterns of operations on an array of items. (Functions like `map`, `filter`, `accumulate` are sometimes called **higher-order functions**, because they are functions that receive other functions as arguments.) We're going to present them in the next three sections. The order of presentation will be as follows: we'll show how the functions are used in numerical and text processing examples, before defining them all in a concluding section. Our examples will form a reasonably complete `wordList` application.

Map

The function `map()` expresses the following pattern: apply the same function to each element of an array and collect the result in another array. Mathematicians describe this pattern by saying "map a function over an array." To take a simple numerical example, suppose you have an array of numbers and you want to double them all. Assuming that the array's name is `numArr`, and `double()` is a function that multiplies its argument by 2, we want to be able to say simply:

```
var doublesArr = map(double,numArr);
```

To show an example with specific numbers, let's get ourselves a little utility to produce arrays of numbers beginning with 0, and map `double()` over such an array:

```
function upto(N){                // returns [0,1,2,...N-1] as an array
  var R = new Array();
  for(var i=0; i<N; i++) R[i] = i; return R;
}
var d = map (double,upto(50));   // d == [0,2,4,...98]
```

Our next example will take us to our "theme" of text-processing utilities. What's involved in compiling a list of all the words in a page? At first glance, it may seem that the task is completely trivial: take the text of the body of the page (using `document.body.innerText`, as in the dictionary example above), and split it into an array using space as the separating character:

```
var wordList = document.body.innerText.split(" ");
```

Well, the problem is not very hard, but it's not quite so trivial either. Suppose your page contains a sentence like "What's gone's gone, and nobody can bring it back." A moment's reflection will show that our list of "words" will include such items as "What's", "gone's" and "gone,". To get rid of those, we have to inspect each item on the list and trim trailing punctuation marks or apostrophes, and whatever else may follow them. It looks as if we might want to map a function over our `wordList`.

What would that function do? It will copy each word, character by character, to another word until it finds something that is not a "word character". Then it will stop and return the trimmed copy. In order to do its job, this function will need a helper, a function which can decide whether a given character is a "word character" or not. Let's call that helper `isWordCharacter()`; it will return a Boolean value, true or false. It is traditional to refer to functions that return a Boolean value as predicates, so `isWordCharacter()` is an example of a predicate. (Many more are coming soon.)

Now we have to decide for ourselves what a word character is. Let's be fairly restrictive and accept as words any combination of letters but not letters and digits. We'll also allow hyphenated words, so that "mumbo-jumbo" is a word but "AK-47" is not. (The reason we exclude digits is not linguistic purism but an obscure feature in IE4-Win which prepends two digits to those words in `innerText` that immediately follow a tag.) Using our knowledge of the ASCII table, we write:

```
function isLetter(c)             // tests if character c is a letter
{
 return ('a' <= c && c <= 'z' || 'A' <= c && c <= 'Z');
}
function isWordCharacter(c)      // return true if c is a letter or a hyphen
```

```
  {
  return(isLetter(c) || c == '-');
  }
```

That was the hard part. Now we can write a function that trims a single word and map it over the `wordList`:

```
function trimWord(S)
{
  var R = "";
  for(var i=0; i<S.length && isWordCharacter(S.charAt(i)); i++)
  R += S.charAt(i);
  return R;
}
wordList = map(trimWord,wordList);
```

This is pretty good, even if not ideal: the string "don't" will be abbreviated to "don." Strings ending in "n't" should probably receive a special treatment. We leave it as an exercise to write a function that would identify such strings and remove the "n't" from their tail end; then you would map that function over the list. Hmmm... what about "can't" or "won't"? What we see here is a general problem: given a word in text, find its dictionary form. The problem is hard; to give it justice we would have to write a separate book. In the meantime, we have to move on. Our next step in creating a useful wordList application is to remove from our word list all the trivial words, such as "a" or "in." This is an example of another common pattern: filtering an array's values using some test applied to them.

Filter

We start again with a trivial numerical example: take a list of integers and filter all the even ones, leaving the odd ones out. We want to express it as follows:

```
var evens = filter(upto(101),even);          // evens==[0,2,4,...100]
```

Here, `even()` is a function that takes a numeric argument and returns a Boolean value, `true` if the number is even, `false` otherwise. We define it using the remainder operator `%`: a number is even if the remainder of dividing it by 2 is 0:

```
function even(n) {return n%2 == 0;} // even is a predicate
```

`Filter()` takes two arguments, an array and a function. The function is frequently a predicate, i.e., it returns a Boolean value. (If it is not a predicate then the value it returns is converted to a Boolean value, as discussed in Chapter 1.) `Filter()` returns a new array that contains all those elements of the input array for which the filtering function returns the value true.

Resuming the development of `wordList`, we want to filter out trivial words. What's a trivial word? We adopt a flexible definition that shifts the burden of this decision where it belongs, to dictionary makers. We'll say that trivial words are all words that are very short (one or two letters), and also those longer words that are found in a special list of trivial words (and we'll let word professionals work on that list). So, non-trivial words are those whose length is greater than 2 *and* that are not found in the list of trivial words:

```
function nonTrivialWord(w)
{
  return w.length>2 && !isIn(w,trivialWords);
}
var trivialWords = new
Array("all","and","any","but","for","him","this","that","the","them");
```

Assuming that we write `isIn()`, the next step in developing the `wordList` application is a one-liner:

```
wordList = filter(nonTrivialWord,wordList);
```

Our first attempt at `isIn()` is:

```
function isIn(x,A){      // is there some i for which A[i] == x?
  for(var i=0; i<A.length; i++)if (A[i] == x) return true;
  return false;
}
```

However, for our purposes we probably don't want our comparison function to be case-sensitive, so we define a `strEqual()` predicate that is not:

```
function strEqual(a,b){
  var aU = a.toUpperCase(); var bU = b.toUpperCase();
  return aU == bU;
}
function isIn(x,A){     // is there some i for which strEqual(A[i],x) == true?
  for(var i=0; i<A.length; i++)
   if(strEqual(A[i],x)) // replace with (A[i] == x) to make case-sensitive
     return true;
  return false;
}
```

A useful exercise here would be to rewrite `isIn()` so that it takes an extra argument, a function to use as the equality predicate. Then think what you would have to do to pass an operator like `"=="` to it. We'll address this problem in the section on functions as objects, where we will write a peculiar function called `binop()`. It will take one argument, an operator, and return a function that does what the operator does, but in a function-like way.

Well, we're almost done. It only remains to remove duplicates from the list and sort it. Sorting is easy, we'll just call the Array object's `sort()` method. Removing duplicates is more interesting, especially since it's an example of yet another common pattern: `accumulate`.

Accumulate

The `filter` and `map` patterns take us from one sequence to another sequence. The `accumulate` pattern combines the values of an array into a single summary value, as when you want to add or multiply them all together. We want to express this by saying:

```
function plus(x,y) {return x + y;}
var sum = accumulate(plus, ar, 0);
var product = accumulate(mul, ar, 1);
```

Accumulate takes three arguments: a combining function, the array whose values are to be combined, and the initial value. In our examples, 0 is the initial value for summation just as 1 is an initial value for finding a product, `plus()` and `mul()` are combining functions that add or multiply two numbers together, and `ar` is the array to work on.

OK, let's do what we said we were going to do and remove duplicates from the `wordList`. It may seem that accumulate is not really applicable here because it returns a single value, but this single value can be an array! We'll just use the empty array as the initial value, and our combining function will add another word to it unless the word is already there. (Aha! we can reuse our `isIn()` function):

```
function addIfNew(A,x)          // add x to end of A unless it's already in
{
 if (isIn(x,A)) return A;       // x is a duplicate, don't do anything
 A[A.length] = x;               // insert x into A; A.length is incremented automatically
 return A;
}
function remDuplicates(A)
{
 return accumulate(addIfNew,A,new Array());
}
```

One final thing to do to our `wordList` is sort it, a trivial step. We can try the whole application.

Try It Out

The file `wdlist1.htm` is simplicity itself. It includes three source files: `arrUtils.js`, `strUtils.js` and `wdlist1.js` (the main function). The body of the page is a text and a button (see picture). If you click on the button, the text is replaced with its word list. In the next chapter, we'll rewrite this so the text and the wordlist appear next to each other in two frames.

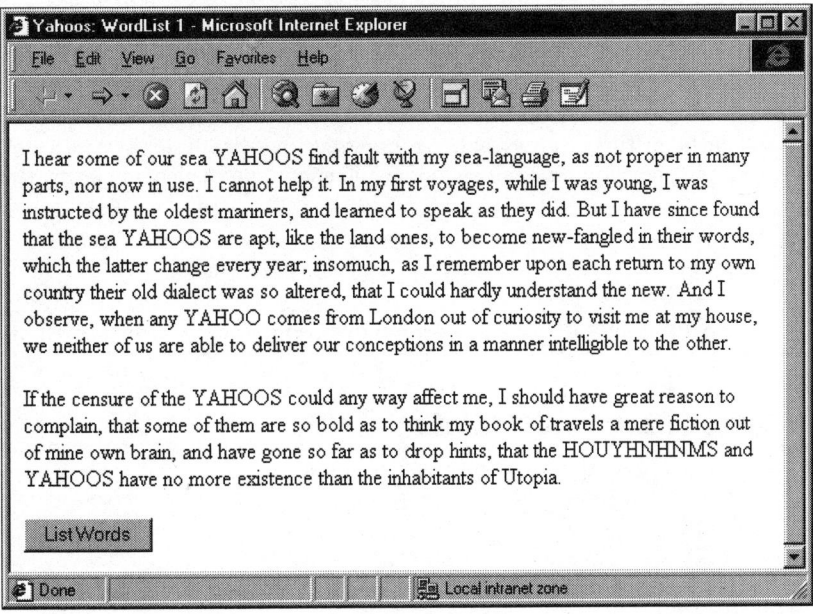

How It Works

Let's look at the main function first. You've seen most of its lines but not the entire thing:

```
function wordList(txt)
{
  var W = txt.split(" ");           // separate the words
  W = map(initLetters,W);           // trim punctuation marks and the rest
  W = filter(nonTrivialWord,W);     // ignore trivial words
  W = remDuplicates(W);             // remove duplicates
  W.sort(strLessThan);              // sort alphabetically, but accounting for case
  document.body.innerHTML = W.join("<BR>");
}
```

The first line of the function splits the text it receives and puts the pieces into an array W. The last line takes the contents of W, converts them to a string using "<BR>" as a separator and makes that string the innerHTML of the document. The lines in the middle of the code massage the initial array into an alphabetized word list without duplicates. Each step of the process has been discussed, so we can sit back and admire the elegant simplicity of the overall structure. Perhaps the main reason why higher-order functions are useful is that they lead you to a step-by-step process of "data massaging", in which the logic is typically less intricate and therefore less bug-prone than the equivalent logic of making a single loop do all the work. The wordList function shown here was developed this way; it worked on the first try. It would be easy to rewrite it to run faster, if we wanted to, but that's an optimization, which is not important now. It would also be easy to rewrite it for any data structure that represents a linear sequence, not necessarily an array. In fact, our code has been clearly influenced by standard Unix utilities that operate on text files rather than arrays.

In addition to general conceptual usefulness, map, filter and accumulate help in avoiding common programming errors:

❑   They are never off-by-one, as when you forget to process the last item in the sequence, or try to process an item that's beyond the last one. Our higher-order functions always work on each item of the sequence, and nothing else.

❑   They never fail to declare the loop variable. (One of the most infuriating JavaScript errors we have committed is "for(i=0; i<N; i++)..." where we haven't declared "i" in the lines preceding the loop. There's no sensible error message: JavaScript simply uses a global value "i", and with looping functions that call on looping functions, the results can be very strange indeed.)

❑   They never fail to return a value; "var x = map(f,seq,val);" will produce a value to assign, whereas a special-purpose function is subject to another infuriating error: you may just happen to forget the "return" statement, leaving "x" undefined.

All in all, map, filter and accumulate are a good deal, so perhaps it's time to see how they're defined.

Definition of Map, Filter, Accumulate

A simple version of map(), adequate for many purposes, is:

```
function map1(f,A){            // a general utility, applies f to each item in A
  var res = new Array(A.length);
  for(var i=0; i<A.length; i++) res[i] = f(A[i]); return res;
}
```

From a mathematical point of view, map() only needs two arguments. However, we can use JavaScript's lax attitude regarding the number of arguments to a function, and throw in another argument to map(), just in case we need another piece of information for our task. For instance, you may want to multiply every item in your array by some fixed scale-factor, or prefix each string on your list of strings with the same label. The function being mapped may also want to know where it is in the array; for instance, you may want to label each word in a list with its position in that list. A more useful, if also a bit more confusing, version of map() can have up to three arguments, and the function we map over the array can also have up to three arguments:

```
function map(f,A,X)    // give "f" each item A[i], along with const X and index i
{
var res = new Array();
for(var i=0; i<A.length; i++) res[i] = f(A[i],X,i);
return res;
}
```

Our previous doubling-map will still work, even though it only uses two arguments. The unused argument X, whose value is undefined, will be passed, together with the index i, to the double() function. Both map() and double() will ignore their extra arguments, and that's perfectly all right within JavaScript. However, we don't need our previous doubling-map any more, because we can express it through a more general multiply-map:

```
function mul(x,y){return x * y;}
var ar = new Array(10, 20, 30);
var doubled = map(mul, ar, 2);      // doubled == [20,40,60]
var tripled = map(mul, ar, 3);      // tripled == [30,60,90]
```

To produce doubled, we call mul(10, 2, 0), mul(20, 2, 1), mul(30, 2, 2). The third argument, which is the array index, is ignored by mul() because it looks only for two arguments. In the next example, the mapping function uses the index to provide numbering for the array items, so that the array ["a","b"] becomes ["1: a","2: b"]. All we need to do is concatenate each index with a constant delimiter and the corresponding word:

```
function addLabel(w,delim,i){return "" + (i+1) + delim + w;}
var labelledWordList = map(addLabel,wordList,": ");
```

Enough about map(); except to note that installing it as a prototype property of the Array class, so that Array has a map() method, is relatively easy. First, we replace each reference to our array, A, with this:

```
function arr_map(f,this,X) /* give "f" each item the array object along with const
  and index I*/
{
var res = new Array();
for(var i=0; i<this.length; i++) res[i] = f(this[i],X,i);
return res;
}
```

Then, we simply install it in the prototype:

```
Array.prototype.arrmap = arr_map;
```

We're also going to spend much less time on the definitions of `filter()` and `accumulate()` because the same design considerations apply. The function `filter()` is defined below. (If needed, refer back to Chapter 1 for the workings of the `++` operator.) Notice how we build the resulting array: when it is of length 0, we want to put something in `res[0]`; when it is of length 1, we assign to `res[1]`, and so on. The value of the length property gets automatically updated.

```
function filter(pred,A,X) {
  var res = new Array();
  for(var i=0; i<A.length; i++) if(pred(A[i],X)) res[res.length] = A[i];
  return res;
}
```

By now we could probably leave it to you to define `accumulate()`, but here it is, (we do leave it as an exercise to define the `filter()` and `accumulate()` methods for the Array class):

```
function accumulate(combineFn, A, initVal,X) {
  var res = initVal;
  for(var i=0; i<A.length; i++) res = combineFn(res, A[i], X);
  return res;
}
```

Adding a Feature to wordList; 2-Dimensional Arrays

Before we move on to another big topic, we'd like to add a feature to our `wordList` application. It will improve the application's output; it will give us practice with two-dimensional arrays, and it will show another advantage of the step-by-step data massaging: adding another step is easy.

The step we're contemplating is splitting the word list into sub-arrays, each containing words beginning with the same letter. The word list will become an array of arrays, which is how JavaScript implements two-dimensional arrays. (This will be familiar to the practitioners of C, C++ or Java.) If `res` is the name of our array of arrays, we refer to the first subarray as `res[0]`, the first item of the first subarray as `res[0][0]`, and the third item of the fifth subarray as `res[4][2]`. Each subarray will become a single line of output.

In terms of program design, what we need is another line in the main function, right after the word list is sorted. It should say something like:

```
W = subArrays(newStart,W);      // separate into subarrays, one per letter
```

We imagine the function `subArrays()` as going through `W` and copying its words into a subarray until it detects the beginning of a new letter. At that moment, it quits the current subarray and starts a new one. How does it detect the beginning with a new letter? Using a predicate that we'll pass in as an argument. Here's the code:

```
function subArrays(pred,A){           // the pred detects new first letter
  var res = new Array();              // res is array of arrays
  if(A.length == 0) return res;       // make sure A is not empty
  res[0] = new Array(); res[0][0] = A[0]; // start first subarray, copy first word
  for(var i = 1; i < A.length; i++){  // loop through the rest of A
    var rN = res[res.length-1];       // rN is current subarray
    var rNL = rN.length;              // rNL is its length
    if(!pred (rN[rNL-1],A[i]))        // pred returns false
      rN[rNL] = A[i];                 // continue current subarray
```

```
    else{
      var aN = new Array();              // create new subarray
      aN[0] = A[i];                      // copy current word to it
      res[res.length] = aN;              // make it current subarray of res
    }
  }
  return res;
}
```

Now, let's define the predicate that detects a new first letter. It will be passed as an argument to `subArrays()`:

```
function newStart(a,b){     // true if first characters of a and b are different
  return a.charAt(0).toUpperCase()!= b.charAt(0).toUpperCase();}
```

Now that our word list consist of subarrays, we have to arrange for showing it one subarray per line. Right now, the word list is put on screen by a line of code that assumes that each item in the `wordlist` array is a string:

```
document.body.innerHTML = W.join("<BR>");
```

We are going to keep this line intact, but insert just one more line of code right before it which will convert each subarray into a string. Clearly, we want to write a function that will convert one subarray into a string and map it over the array of subarrays. That function just tells each subarray to convert itself to string by using its `join()` method. The right way to do it is to write another general utility, `mapmethod`, which maps a method rather than a function over an array of objects of some kind, but we leave this to the reader.

```
function joinWords(arr,separator)
{
  return arr.join(separator);
}
```

The new main function, in `wdlist2.js`, is the same as in `wdlist1.js`, except for two new lines:

```
function wordList(txt)
{
  var W = txt.split(" ");              // separate the words
  W = map(initLetters,W);              // trim punctuation marks and the rest
  W = filter(nonTrivialWord,W);        // ignore trivial words
  W = remDuplicates(W);                // remove duplicates
  W.sort(strLessThan);                 // sort alphabetically, accounting for case
  W = subArrays(newStart,W);           // separate into subarrays, one per letter
  W = map(joinWords,W,", ");           // make each subarray a string
  document.body.innerHTML = W.join("<BR>");
}
```

With remarkably few changes, we can massage this sequence into an application that lists for each word its frequency in the text. All we need is a couple of lines that would count the duplicates before removing them. However, such counting is much easier to do if you have an associative array to play with, and we will, later in this chapter. So, frequency count is definitely a promise, before this chapter is over.

Try It Out

The new and improved word list application is in `wdlist2.htm`. As promised, it breaks the list into sublists and shows it one sublist per line.

Functions as Objects

Creating Functions on the Fly

The perceptive reader will have noticed that some of our examples of the use of `map`, `filter` and `accumulate` have a flaw. We're talking about such examples as the following:

```
function even(n) {return n%2 == 0;}      // even is a predicate
var evens = filter(upto(51),even);       // evens == [0,2,4,...50]
function plus(x,y) {return x + y;}
var sum = accum (plus, ar, 0);
```

In these examples, we define a truly trivial function only to pass it as an argument to the higher-order function that does the work. It is as if every time we wanted to use the number 17 we first had to give it a name by assigning its value to a variable, then use the named variable. Fortunately, we don't have to. Just as the more mundane data types, functions have the right to remain anonymous. All we need is an expression that will evaluate directly to a function, just as expression "42" directly evaluates to number 42. As you can guess from the rhetorical build-up, such an expression is readily available. We illustrate by rewriting the piece of code that doubles every number in an array. Instead of:

```
function mul(x,y) {return x * y;}
var d = map(mul, seq, 2);         // seq is the array of numbers to be doubled
```

we say simply:

```
var d = map(new Function("x,y", "return x * y;"), seq, 2);
```

In a similar fashion, we can rewrite `sum` (which adds together all numbers in an array) as:

```
var sum = accumulate(new Function("x", "y", "return x + y;"), seq, 0);
```

What's going on here? If you analyze the text of the definition of the function `mul()`, you'll see that it contains the following information, from left to right:

❑ this is going to be a function
❑ its name is "`mul`"
❑ it has two arguments, "`x`" and "`y`"
❑ its body, enclosed by braces { and }, consists of the following text: "`return x * y;`"

All this information, minus the name, is packaged into the `new Function` expression. The Function constructor can take any number of arguments, all of them strings. All but the last one are the formal parameters of the anonymous function being defined. (You can also list all the parameters as a single comma-separated string: there's no difference between "`new Function("x, y",…)`" and "`new Function("x", "y",…)`".) The last argument is the code of the new function. So, an expression that evaluates to a function that averages two numbers would be:

```
new Function("x", "y", "return (x + y)/2;")
```

We can of course give the value of this expression a name, e.g., 'average', by saying:

```
var average = new Function("x", "y", "return (x + y)/2;");
```

This defines, as you might guess, a function, and is completely equivalent to saying:

```
function average(x,y) {return (x + y)/2;}
```

Functions as Returned Values

As you can see, functions are objects for which `Function` is a constructor. One could say that functions form a primitive data type for which `Function` is a wrapper class, just as `Number` is a wrapper class for numbers. However, the ECMA standard doesn't say that, and so we won't either. We're going to look at the opportunities provided by the mechanism that builds functions out of strings. One of them is that, as we said, we don't have to pollute the global name space by giving names to trivial functions. Another one is that we can write functions that return functions as their return values. The usefulness of this feature may not be immediately obvious, but you'll see it appear in several later chapters. For instance, when we write the Calculator application in Chapter 4, we'll use a `binop()` function a lot, to define the functions of the calculator:

```
function binop(op)
{
  return new Function("x,y", "return x" + op + "y");
}
var k = binop("*")(3,5);     // k == 15
```

Using `binop(*)` this way is just a verbose way of multiplying two numbers, but mapping it over an array results in economy of expression:

```
map(binop("*"),upto(5),10)  // produces the array [0,10,20,30,40]
```

Properties of Functions

Since functions are objects, and objects have properties, functions have properties. The only twist is that those properties are transient: they are available only when the function is running. For instance, every function object has an `arguments` property, which is an array of the function's arguments. We cannot, out of the blue, go to a function and ask it to show its arguments because a function, in its dormant state, doesn't have actual arguments. However, during the function call we can manipulate `f.arguments` the way we manipulate any other array. This opens the possibility to have functions of an arbitrary number of arguments. For instance, we can rewrite our average function so that it finds the average of however many arguments are given it.

```
function average()
{
  var len = average.arguments.length;
  var sum = accumulate(plus,average.arguments,0);
  return sum/len;
}
```

The other properties that a function has are `caller` (the function that called this function, null if it's a top-level call) and all the function's arguments and local variables. Consider:

```
function pickySquare(x)
{
  if (pickySquare.caller == null) return x * x;
  else return "I will not be called by your kind, especially with " +
    pickySquare.x + " as the argument";
}
```

We're not sure how useful this particular feature is. It has not been standardized, and works differently in NC4 than in IE4 or earlier versions of the Netscape browser.

Adding Properties to Functions

As with any other object, you can add your own properties to functions. This feature can be used to reproduce, in JavaScript, the functionality of static local variables. Static variables (this is C/C++ terminology) are local in scope but global in temporal extent. They're local in the sense that their names are not visible outside the function in which they are declared. They're global in the sense that their values persist from one function call to another. A very common use of a static variable is a counter that keeps track of how many times the function has been called. In C++, one would write:

```
void count() {
  static int counter = 0;
  cout <<                 // this is how you print to standard output in C++
      "I have been called " << ++counter << " times\n";
  return;
}
```

A similar effect can be achieved by giving a JavaScript function a `counter` property:

```
function countedSquare(x) {
  alert("You've squared " + counter + " number(s).");
  countedSquare.counter++;
  return x*x;
}
countedSquare.counter = 1;
```

In later chapters, we frequently use this feature to add properties to constructor functions for the classes we define.

Arrays and the Copying Problem

You've seen enough arrays by now to be convinced that arrays are objects. There are three constructors: the default constructor, a constructor with an integer argument that specifies size, and a constructor that takes a list of comma-delimited arguments and makes them into an array. There's a length property and the `sort()`, `join()` and `reverse()` methods. You pretty much have seen them all:

```
var a = new Array(5, 3, 7);
a.sort(); a.reverse(); alert(a.join("**"));      // shows 7**5**3
```

Surprisingly, there's no copy constructor for arrays. If you say:

```
var aCopy = new Array(a);
```

you will get an array of 1 element that contains an object (not a string!) that shows as 7,5,3 in the alert box. If you say `alert(typeof(aCopy[0]));` the alert box will show "object". Hmmm... it looks like there is a data type `Object` in JavaScript. Indeed, there is, and we'll give it a thorough treatment in the next section. For now, all we need to know is that one of its methods is `toString()` which we can use as follows:

```
var strACopy = aCopy.toString();
```

We can finally get something like a copy of the original array by saying `strACopy.split()`. (What we actually get is an array of string representations of the original array's elements, in this case numbers.) To get a real copy, you should take the straightforward route of creating a new array of the same length as the original and copy each element in a loop. We leave it as an exercise to write a global function `arrayCopy()` and an `Array.copy()` method which create a totally new copy of a given array.

But wait a minute, some of you might say, why can't we simply use assignment? We can, but there is a catch illustrated below:

```
var aa = new Array("a","b","c");
var ab = aa; alert(ab.join());
aa[1] = "newbie"; alert(ab.join());
```

We haven't touched `ab`, and yet the second alert shows "a,newbie,c" instead of "a,b,c". This phenomenon is called "reference semantics" (as opposed to value semantics) and deserves an explanation.

References and Values

Compare the code above with the following:

```
var x = 3;
var y = x; alert(y);
x = 17; alert(y);
```

As you would expect, the two alerts will show the same value. When the assignment is made, the variable y gets a little memory of its own, stores the **value** of x in it, and from that moment on x and y lead separate existences. Put differently, the name of the variable points, in this case, to the memory space where the actual value of the variable is stored, and this value is copied to the new variable. When the new variable is changed, the old one remains unaffected.

With numbers, copying the value is not such a big expense, one or two memory cells. With arrays, this sort of commitment can quickly break your memory bank. (Remember that JavaScript arrays are resizable, so it would be literally an open-ended commitment.) The way it works with arrays is that the name of an array points to the memory space where the address of, or a **reference** to, the actual array is stored. This space is, again, not very large, whatever it takes to store a memory address. When the value of one array variable is assigned to another one, what gets copied is a reference to the array value, not the value itself. The two array variables thus share the same body of data, which is why this arrangement is sometimes called "structure sharing." When you make changes to one variable, the other one gets changed also, as you saw in the example above. This can result in extremely nasty bugs.

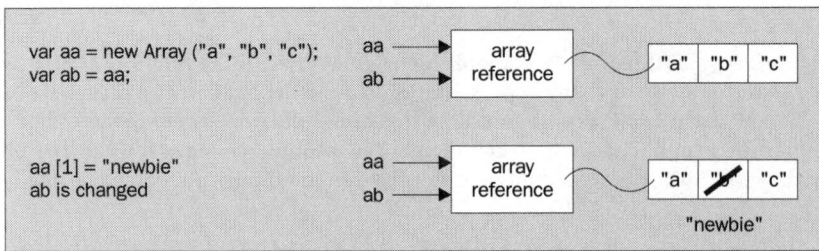

Assignment is one of three contexts where the difference between value and reference semantics shows up. The other two are comparisons and function calls. In comparisons, the question is whether you compare objects themselves or references to them. Consider:

```
var aa = new Array("a","b","c");
var ab = aa;            // ab is another reference to the same array
var ac = arrayCopy(aa); // ac is a new array with the same elements as aa
alert(aa == ab);        // true or false? True
alert(aa == ac);        // true or false? False
```

Arrays, we can see, are compared by reference. What about strings? Here the situation is complex: literal strings are compared by value while `String` objects (and, in fact, any objects) are compared by reference. We illustrate:

```
var sa = new String("same content");
var sb = sa;
var sc = new String("same content");
alert(sa == sb);            // True
alert(sa == sc);            // False
```

However:

```
var lita = "hello peter" + " how are you";
var litb = "hell" + "o peter how are you";
alert(lita == litb);        // True (literal strings are compared by value)
```

Finally, in passing parameters to functions a kind of assignment takes place: the values of the actual parameters are assigned to the formal parameters of the function. If the assignment is by reference, any changes made to the parameter inside the function will have side effects outside the function:

```
function f(aa)
{
 if(aa[0] != "new value") aa[0] = "new value";
 else aa[0] = "totally new value";
}
var outsideArray = new Array("a","b","c");
f(outsideArray);
alert(outsideArray.join());       // shows "new value,b,c"
```

As always, reference semantics calls for extra care and understanding.

The Object Object and Associative Arrays

There's a class of objects in JavaScript called `"Object"`, the mother of all classes, from which all others are descended. Here's an `Object`:

```
var theDict = new Object();
```

You rarely deal with `Object` directly: there's little use for something so generic. In a later chapter, we would certainly declare `theDict` as an object of a more specific class that we would have defined ourselves. However, it is adequate for our purposes here, and it is important to familiarize yourself with `Object`'s properties and methods because they are shared by all other objects. (This is what we mean by saying that all other objects are descended from `Object`: they inherit `Object`'s properties and methods.)

The special methods of `Object` are `toString()` and `valueOf()`. The first of them converts the contents of an object to a string. It is this method that gets invoked when automatic type conversion to string is done, as in:

```
var msg = "Your sentence is " + 3 + " years of easy labor."
```

Behind the scenes, the number 3 is converted to a `Number` object and its `Number.toString()` method is called. The interesting thing is that you can overwrite the built-in definition with your own:

```
function ar_toString()
{
var len = this.length; var str = "";
for (var i=0; i<len; ++i) str += "index: " + i + " \tvalue: " + this[i] + "\n";
return str;
}
Array.prototype.toString = ar_printArray;
var aa = new Array("a","b","c");
alert(aa.toString());
```

The alert box will show:

```
index: 0    value: a
index: 1    value: b
index: 2    value: c
```

This may be useful for debugging, especially with objects in classes you define yourself. (Coming up in Chapter 4!)

Objects as Associative Arrays

The truly interesting fact about JavaScript objects is that they're implemented (and can be used) as associative arrays. Associative arrays are lists of items that are not indexed by numbers but by something more human and "associative." For instance, you can define an associative array person as:

```
person["height"] = 6;        // in feet
person["eyeColor"] = "brown";  // or blue or whatever
person["age"] = 19;          // in years
```

Now, suppose you define a JavaScript object as follows:

```
var person = new Object();
person.height = 6;
person.eyeColor = "brown";
person.age = 19;
```

It turns out that the object person can be thought of, and used, as the associative array person: it is good JavaScript to say:

```
person["age"] ++;        // time for a birthday party
person["height"] += 0.1;  // he's still growing!
```

...and so on, you get the idea.

One advantage of using a string index, as in person["age"], rather than a property identifier, as in person.age, is that a string can be created or constructed dynamically when the program is running, while identifiers have to be there from the start. We'll use this to our advantage to find the frequency count of every non-trivial word in a text. Recall that we already know how to create a list of such words:

```
function wordList(txt)
{
  var W = txt.split(" ");          // separate the words
  W = map(initLetters,W);          // trim punctuation marks and the rest
  W = filter(nonTrivialWord,W);    // ignore trivial words
  ...
```

Now, before we remove duplicates, we're going to count them, using an object, er... an associative array, indexed by the words in our text. Remember that you don't have to declare a property of an object (or a category in an associative array) before using it. So, let's say we have an object C (for Count) and a word wrd; we look up C[wrd] in our associative array. If it's undefined we set it to 1. If it is defined, we increment it by 1. This is the function incFreq():

```
function incFreq(C,wrd)
{
  if(!C[wrd]) C[wrd] = 1; else C[wrd] ++; return C;
}
```

We want to do this to every word on our list... quick, which one of our array utilities should we use? (The answer is in the *How It Works* section below.) This pretty much takes care of frequencies except for one minor annoying detail: case-sensitivity again! For frequency purposes we want to count "fly" and "Fly" as the same word, but our C object will think of them as different. The simplest way around is to convert everything to lower case before counting; so we insert one more line, right before running `incFreq()`:

```
W = map(new Function("s", "return s.toLowerCase()"), W);
```

Try It Out

Frequency count is included on the same page with the other text processing applications. Point your browser at `txtUtils.htm`, and you will see a text and a few buttons at the bottom. (We'll review this file when we go over the dictionary application later in the chapter.) Click on the button that says FrequesCounts. You will see the familiar word list, but following each word is its frequency in the text.

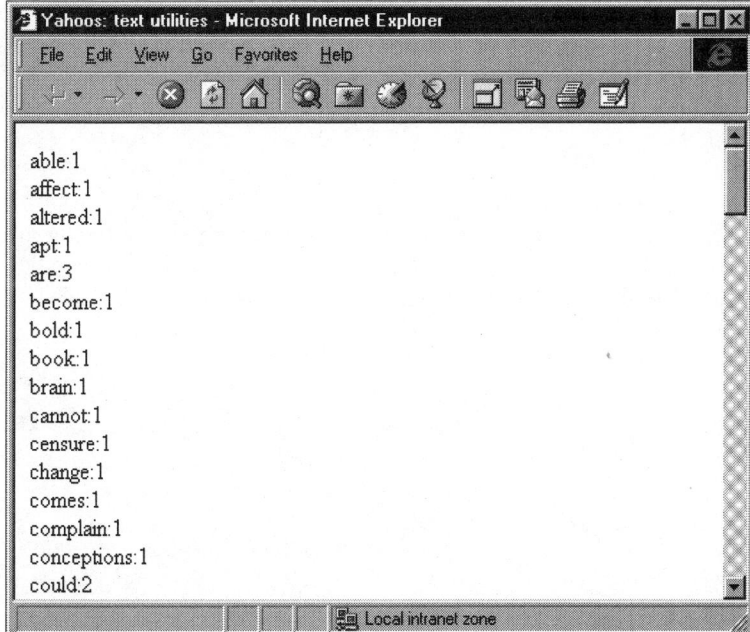

As long as you're on this page, you may also want to look at what the other buttons are doing. For explanations on how to set it all up, see the next *Try It Out* section.

How It Works

The main function for the frequency application is `freq.js`. The highlighted lines are those that are added to the word list application. To provide a little variety, we've rewritten `incFreq()` using a function object constructor. We collect (accumulate!) all the frequencies in the `Freq` object using the `accumulate()` array utility. We map the `labelFreq()` function over the word list to produce the desired output, and make it the innerHTML of our page.

```
function makeWordFreqCountList(txt)
{
  var W = txt.split(" ");              // separate the words
  W = map(initLetters,W);             // prune punctuation marks
  W = filter(nonTrivialWord,W);       // ignore very short words
  var incFreq =
      new Function("C,wrd", "if(!C[wrd])C[wrd] = 1; else C[wrd]++; return C;");
  var Freq = accumulate(incFreq, W, new Object());
  W = remDuplicates(W);               // remove duplicate words
  W.sort(strLessThan);                // sort alphabetically, accounting for case
  var labelFreq = new Function("w,C","return w + ':' + C[w]");
  W = map(labelFreq, W, Freq);
  document.body.innerHTML = W.join("<BR>");
}
```

For...In... Loop

As is common with associative arrays, JavaScript provides a for...in... statement to iterate through all the elements of an associative array (i.e., through all the properties of an object). We give several examples of its use. The first will show you the properties of the document object in client-side JavaScript (the end of this chapter is getting close and it's time to start thinking about the next one.) In the next section, we use the for...in... construction in the dictionary application.

Try It Out

The document object has many interesting properties that are exposed to JavaScript, and to preview them all you can use the following simple page. Notice that the page has no body: it's all constructed by a JavaScript function call. The call itself takes place in the so-called event handler, onload, which is automatically triggered by the event of loading the page.

```
<!DOCTYPE HTML PUBLIC "-//W3C//DTD HTML 3.2//EN">
<HTML>
<HEAD>
 <TITLE> Document Properties </TITLE>
<SCRIPT language = "JavaScript">
 function showDocProps()
 {
 var props = "<H2> Document Properties </H2>";
 for(prop in document) props += prop + ": " + document[prop] + "<BR>";
 document.write(props);
 }
</SCRIPT>
</HEAD>
<BODY onload = "showDocProps();">
</BODY> </HTML>
```

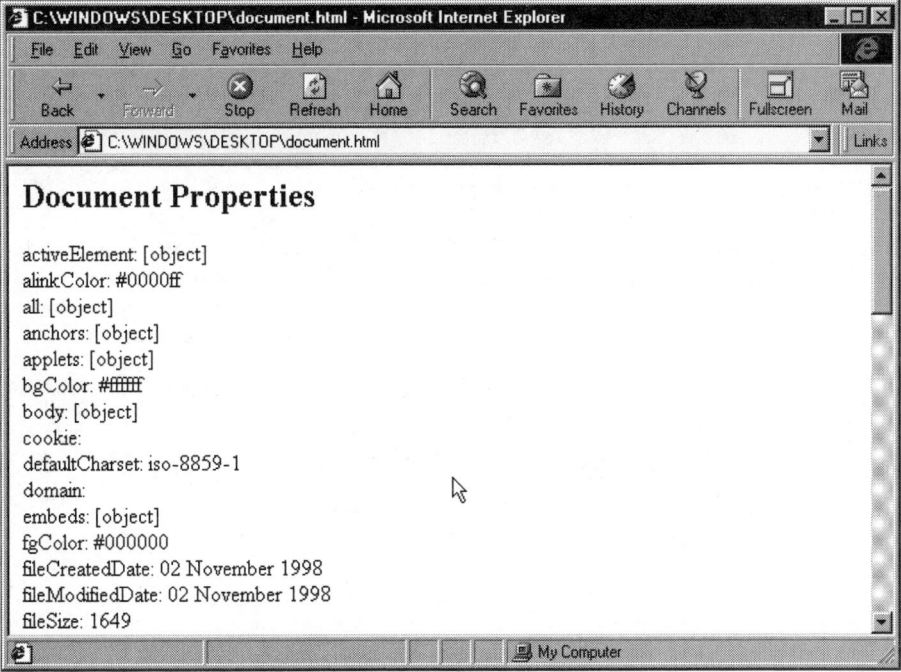

Some of them may appear puzzling but an experienced HTMLer will immediately recognize the body, bgColor, anchors, the URL, and many other elements of the page that you have come to know and love. Now you can manipulate them all dynamically, after the page is rendered, in response to user actions, using JavaScript.

A Dictionary Application

In the remainder of this section, we will work with objects as associative arrays to implement a dictionary application. Our design will remain very simple. We'll assume that the dictionary is also in the same window as the text, separated from it by three colons (: : :). (Recall the "lettuce" examples in the beginning of the chapter.) So, if we split the innerText of the page using " : : : " as a separator, we'll get an array, whose first element is the text, and the second element the dictionary. We can get them into variables using these lines of code:

```
var T = document.body.innerText.split(":::")[0];    // the text
var D = document.body.innerText.split(":::")[1];    // the dictionary
```

What shall we do with them once we have them? We'll write two functions. One will make all the defined words in the text into hyperlinks, and clicking on such a word will bring up the definition in an alert dialog box. The other will show the entire dictionary in alphabetical order.

Try It Out

The code files for the txtUtils.htm application are many because we're putting all our text applications on this page. Here's the list, copied from the page verbatim:

LIVERPOOL HOPE UNIVERSITY COLLEGE

```
<SCRIPT src="../utils/arrUtils.js"> /* array utilities */ </SCRIPT>
<SCRIPT src="../utils/strUtils.js"> /* string utilities */ </SCRIPT>
<SCRIPT src="../utils/subArrs.js"> /* utils for wdlist2 */ </SCRIPT>
<SCRIPT src="../utils/freq.js"> /* freqList function */ </SCRIPT>
<SCRIPT src="../utils/dctUtils.js"> /* dictionary utilities */ </SCRIPT>
<SCRIPT src="wdlist1.js"> /* wdlist1 function */ </SCRIPT>
<SCRIPT src="wdlist2.js"> /* wdlist2 function */ </SCRIPT>
<SCRIPT src="dict1.js"> /* show dictionary */ </SCRIPT>
<SCRIPT src="dict2.js"> /* add dict to text */ </SCRIPT>
```

The page consists of three parts, separated by ":::". The parts are: a text to work on, a dictionary in our special format, and five buttons for our five applications. The applications are: two word lists, a frequency count, and two dictionary utilities. The user interface is really skimpy (to get back to the page you have to click the Refresh button) but we'll improve on it in the next chapter.

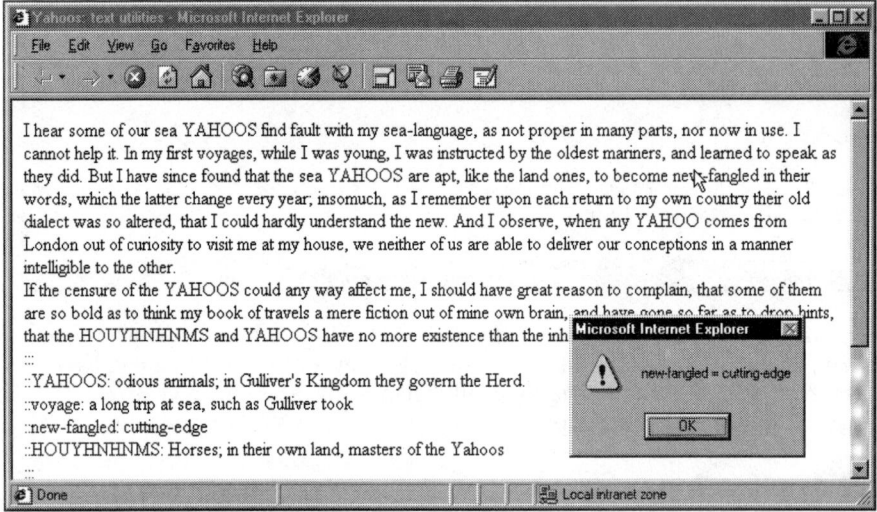

How It Works

Internally, we represent a dictionary, the way we represented the `Freq` object, as a variable of class `Object`. Every word defined in the dictionary will be its property, and the value of that property will be the word's definition. In short, we're again using an object as an associative array, to store values indexed by words.

```
var theDict = new Object();
function addDef1(word,def) {theDict[word] = def;}
function lookUp1(word) {return theDict[word];}
```

After these definitions, we can call on

```
addDef1("avocado","if soft and ripe, eat with a spoon, with a touch of salt");
```

and the `lookUp1()` function will retrieve the right definition.

One problem with `lookUp1()` is that it is case-sensitive. We fix this in `lookUp2()` using the `for...in...` loop. First we try `lookUp1()` and check whether it returns a value. If so, this is the definition we want. If `lookUp1()` fails, we search through the entire dictionary using `strEqual()`. Obviously, this strategy is only feasible for very small dictionaries:

```
function lookUp2(wrd)
{
 var def1 = theDict[wrd];         // just like lookUp1
 if(def1) return def1;
 for(w in theDict)
  if (strEqual(w,wrd)) return theDict[w];
 return "";
}
```

In order to see the entire dictionary in alphabetical order, we provide a `showDict()` function. It uses the `for...in...` loop to store all the properties of the dictionary object in an array, each element of which is itself an array of two items, a word and its definition. We write a compare function, `compEntry()`, which compares two arrays by their first elements and uses it to sort the array. Once sorted, we join it with "`<BR>`" to prepare for display:

```
function getDictArray()
{
 var Pairs = new Array();
 for(w in theDict) Pairs[Pairs.length] = new Array(w,theDict[w]);
 return Pairs;
}
function comPair(a,b){return strLessThan(a[0], b[0]);}
function showDefPair(pair){return pair[0].bold() + ": " + pair[1];}
function showDefPairs()
{
 return map(showDefPair, getDictArray().sort(comPair)).join("<BR>");
}
```

All that's left to do to show the resulting string, is make it into an innerHTML of some document. The function below makes a dictionary, then shows it:

```
function makeAndShowDict(){
  makeDict();
  window.document.body.innerHTML = showDefPairs();
}
```

How does one make a dictionary? It's mostly a matter of splitting the innerText at the right places. Splitting at the "`:::`" marker separates the text from the dictionary; the dictionary becomes the second element of an array. Splitting the dictionary itself at the "`::`" marker separates it into individual word-definition pairs. Each such pair is processed by the `extractDef1()` function. We map that function over the list of pairs, and we're done:

```
function makeDict1()
{
 theDict = new Object();
 var theDefList = document.body.innerText.split(":::")[1];
 if(!theDefList)
 {
  alert("cannot find dictionary surrounded by ':::' markers"); return;
 }
 map(extractDef,theDefList.split("::"),theDict);
}
```

How does `extractDef()` do its work? It finds the index of the first `": "` string (colon followed by space) and extracts two substrings. Note that the definition can contain colons, but the word may not. (It wouldn't anyway, not after we ran `initLetters()` on it.)

```
function extractDef1(S){     // e.g. S == "justice: Truth in action (Disraeli)";
  var N = S.indexOf(": ");
  if (N < 0) return;
                             // in this case, N == 7 == "justice".length;
  var wrd = S.substring(0, N);
  var def = S.substring(N + 2);
  theDict[wrd] = def;        // lookUp1("justice") is "Truth in ... "
}
```

The last question is: how does the user add words and definitions to the dictionary? Using the Notepad user interface: type the words and definitions into the text of the page, just making sure that entries are separated by `"::"` and the word is separated from its definition or definitions by `":"`. It really begins to feel like it's time for a chapter on client-side JavaScript, so we can put the text in one frame, the dictionary in another, and provide a form with a text box and a text area for words and definitions.

Conclusion

We hope this chapter has convinced you that programming with objects is fun. They package all their stuff very nicely together and carry it along wherever you send them. In the next two chapters, we'll take our study of objects into two new directions. The next chapter will show you all the objects of the browser and the web page. It really gives you a good feeling to see that each element of the page is a JavaScript object, and you can refer to it, change its properties, and call on its methods. The chapter after that will show you how to define your own classes of objects. (That gives a good feeling too.)

Let's recapitulate, item by item, what we've covered:

- ❑   objects, properties, and methods
- ❑   classes and their prototypes
- ❑   defining your own properties and methods (for existing objects)
- ❑   native JavaScript classes, especially strings, arrays, functions, and objects (and how to add new methods to them, using their prototypes)
- ❑   functions as data, functions as objects and functions as properties of objects
- ❑   reference and value semantics (we told you not to worry, and you probably agree that it wasn't too bad)
- ❑   objects and associative arrays

In addition to objects, you've also learned good things about patterns of programming with arrays (or any other linear structures). You've learnt about `map`, `filter` and `accumulate`, and how you can use them to transform sequences of items, one step at a time, from an initial condition to a final product. This style of programming is very powerful, and it directs the programmer's mind away from specific problems to general tools that can be re-combined to solve many problems.

Finally, we used our tools to build several text-processing applications that can be useful, and can easily be expanded to become even more useful. We'll do some of the expanding in the next chapter.

3

JavaScript in the Browser

Introduction

Chapter 2 has exposed you to a great deal of object talk, which should make it easy to approach client-side JavaScript. The main principle is that the browser window, the document that appears in it, and various elements of the window and the document, are JavaScript objects with properties and methods. Much of this will be familiar, both from the earlier chapters and from your knowledge of HTML. A major new feature of client-side JavaScript, which core JavaScript objects don't have, is **event handling**. Many window and document elements are visible and can thus be the target of the user's actions, such as a mouse click. To respond to user actions, JavaScript objects have special properties called **event handlers**, with self-explanatory names like onmouseclick. To learn client-side JavaScript is to learn which elements are exposed to scripting, how to refer to them, what properties and methods they have, and what events they can handle.

Of all these skills, knowing how to 'refer' is perhaps the most important. Once you can identify the element you want to deal with, you've won half the battle. So, after an overview section, we spend a whole section learning the names of things. The section after that will be about events and event handlers. HTML forms deserve a separate section. Finally, we'll cover frames and other objects outside the HTML document.

The material of this chapter overlaps with the phenomenon called **Dynamic HTML** (DHTML). DHTML is really a commercial term which packages several technologies together for the purposes of advertising and promotion. These technologies include HTML 4.0, Cascading Style Sheets (including positioning on the page), and tools for browser scripting, especially the Document Object Model. As we said in the introduction, we assume that you're familiar with HTML and style sheets; for information on those subjects, we refer you to DHTML books such as *Instant IE4 Dynamic HTML* (IE4 Edition, Wrox Press, ISBN1-861000-68-5) and *Instant Netscape Dynamic HTML* (NC4 Edition, Wrox Press, ISBN1-861001-19-3). In this chapter we're going to focus on client-side JavaScript. As in previous chapters, we do not aim for exhaustive coverage. If you want every single detail, consult the appendices, or get yourself the Dynamic HTML books and McFarlane's *Instant JavaScript*. In this chapter, we concentrate on the main principles and most important features for understanding objects in the browser, and we provide applications that let you go out and experiment on your own. (See especially `travdoc.htm`, which allows you to move around the document in the browser window, exploring its structure.)

In outline, the chapter will cover:

❑ the tree structure and its terminology
❑ recursive functions, especially on trees
❑ the HTML document tree
❑ the main idea of HTML 4.0 and Dynamic HTML
❑ changing the contents of the document
❑ rules of referring to objects in the web page: absolute and relative reference
❑ programming with events and event handlers
❑ the global event object
❑ interactive forms and form elements
❑ form validation using regular expressions
❑ multiple frames
❑ the `Location` and `History` objects

The applications in this chapter are mainly designed to help you understand the document tree. The form validator, however, is a powerful tool that is easy to extend and customize.

Definitions and Overview

Recall the diagram from the introductory chapter that showed the relationship between three languages: HTML 4.0, CSS/CSSP, and JavaScript. In this chapter we're going to dive into that diagram and remain there until we can move around it with confidence and ease.

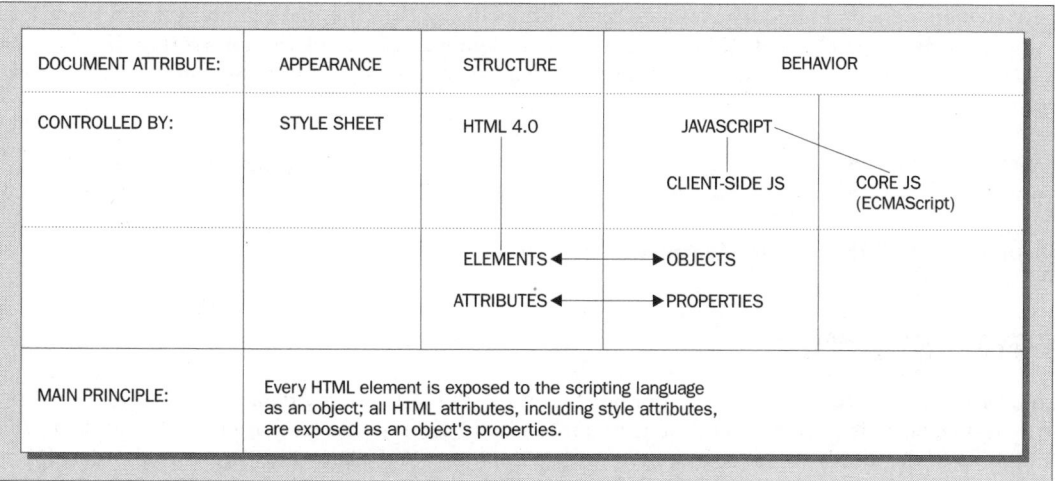

DOCUMENT ATTRIBUTE:	APPEARANCE	STRUCTURE	BEHAVIOR	
CONTROLLED BY:	STYLE SHEET	HTML 4.0	JAVASCRIPT	
			CLIENT-SIDE JS	CORE JS (ECMAScript)
		ELEMENTS ◄──────► OBJECTS		
		ATTRIBUTES ◄──────► PROPERTIES		
MAIN PRINCIPLE:	Every HTML element is exposed to the scripting language as an object; all HTML attributes, including style attributes, are exposed as an object's properties.			

Let's begin by establishing a common terminology. The HTML language uses markup **tags** to partition a **page** into **elements**. Elements fall into **classes**. A class of elements is defined by its tag. A paragraph is an example of an HTML element; it's defined by the <P> tag. Elements have **attributes**, some of them specific to a given element class, others shared by many other classes of elements. These common attributes include the **style** attribute and **event handlers**.

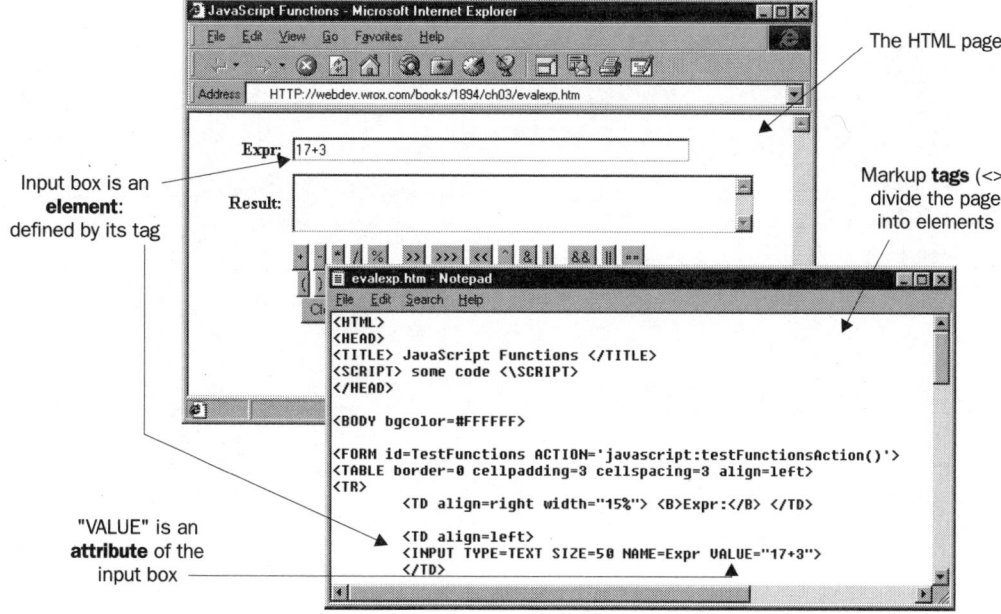

The HTML page

Input box is an **element**: defined by its tag

Markup **tags** (<>) divide the page into elements

"VALUE" is an **attribute** of the input box

Many elements are delimited by the opening and the closing tag. The material in between those tags forms the body of the element. It may contain other elements. Elements cannot overlap: if <A> is one tag and <B> is another, the first line below shows legitimate markup, and the second illegitimate markup:

```
<A> ... <B> ... </B> ... <A>        // tag <B> correctly contained in <A>
<A> ... <B> ... </A> ... </B>       // this overlapping is incorrect
```

What this means is that HTML elements form a tree.

The Tree Structure

A **tree** is a data structure, i.e., a way of organizing data. There are many data structures out there (array is one, stack is another), but tree is unquestionably our favorite (and arguably the best). First it reminds us of the family tree. Second, it controls complexity and establishes an internal order. (Many important organizations, from a small company to the US Army or the Catholic Church, have a tree structure.) Third, they are like sentence diagrams. Suppose you take a sentence and divide it into phrases and subphrases; if you make each phrase into a node you'll get a tree.

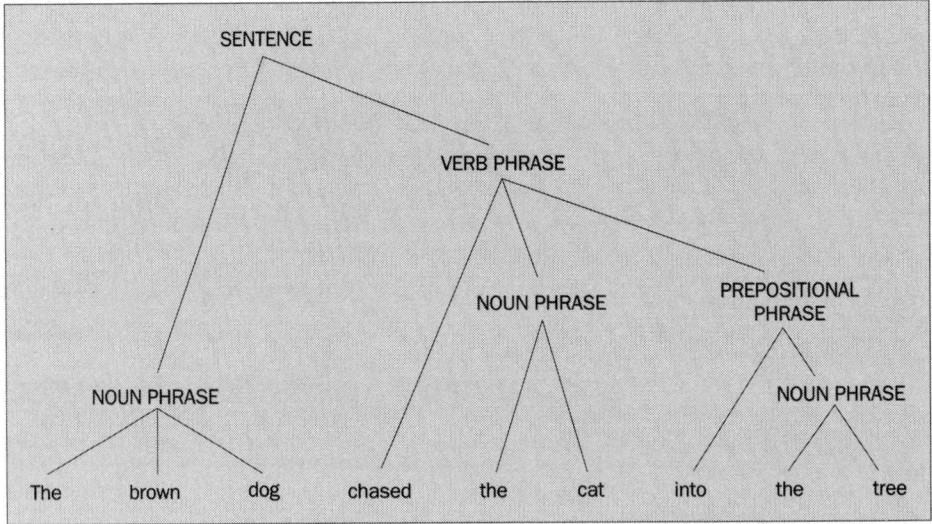

Every time you divide a linear sequence into parts that don't overlap and don't leave gaps, you get a tree. But that's precisely what HTML markup does: it divides a page into elements that don't overlap and don't leave gaps. A web page naturally gives rise to a tree.

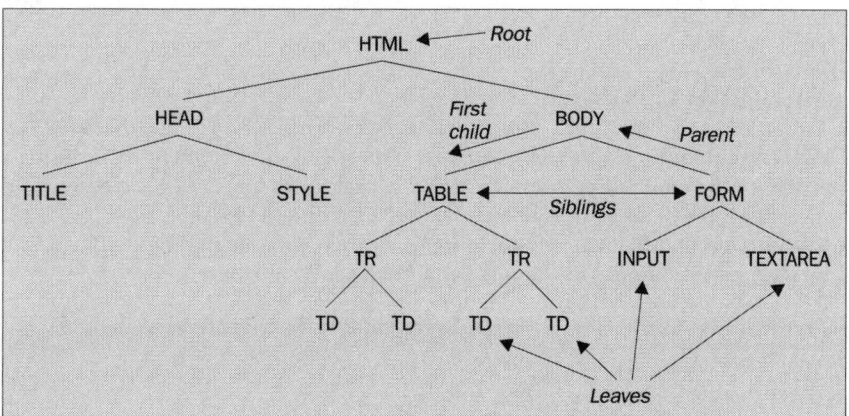

Tree Terminology, Including Recursion

Since we're going to talk a lot about trees we should become familiar with the tree vocabulary. It mostly comes from two metaphors, hopelessly mixed: the family tree and the natural tree. From the natural tree come the root, branches and leaves. The **root** of every HTML tree is the <HTML> element which contains everything else. It has two children... that's the other metaphor. The first **child**, which is also the left **branch** of the tree, is the <HEAD> element. The second child (also the right branch or the <HEAD>'s sibling) is the <BODY> or the <FRAMESET>, depending on whether we have one frame or more. Either way, the <HTML> is their **parent** element.

Both the <HEAD> and the <BODY> elements are themselves trees, and this is perhaps the main reason why the tree is so much loved by programmers. It is a recursive data structure, defined in terms of itself: a tree is either a single node with no children (a **leaf node**), or a node that has one or more children, each of them a tree. This makes it easy to write functions that do things to trees. You use something like this:

```
function doSomethingWith (theTree){
  do what you want to do to the root
  for each child of theTree, doSomethingWith (theChild))
}
```

This is called "a recursive function". It works by calling itself again and again until all the work is done. You'll see many of them in this chapter and later in the book. Here's an example:

```
function showTree(ob,S){        // show the tag of ob and all its descendants
  var R = "<BR>" + S + " = " + ob.tagName;
  for(var i=0; i<ob.children.length; i++)
   R += showTree(ob.children[i],S + "." + (i + 1));
  return R;
}
```

This little function builds a multi-line string. Each line begins with `<BR>`, followed by the "tree number" of an HTML element, followed by its tag. A tree number (or a tree address) is a string like `root.3.2.4`, meaning "the fourth child of the second child of the third child of the root". (You see strings like that in outlines, and indeed, an outline is another example of the tree structure.)

Try It Out

We put this function into an application (`http://webdev.wrox.com/books/1894/Chapter03/showTree.htm`) that allows you to specify an HTML element and view its tree structure. You specify the element by entering a reference to it in the input box of the controlling form. Initially, it's set to be the `<BODY>` element, so you can see the entire document tree. The form also has two buttons, one to run the `showTree()` function, the other to run a function that lists the `ID` attribute of all the elements that have it. In HTML 4.0 (implemented by IE4) every element in the page can have an `ID` attribute.

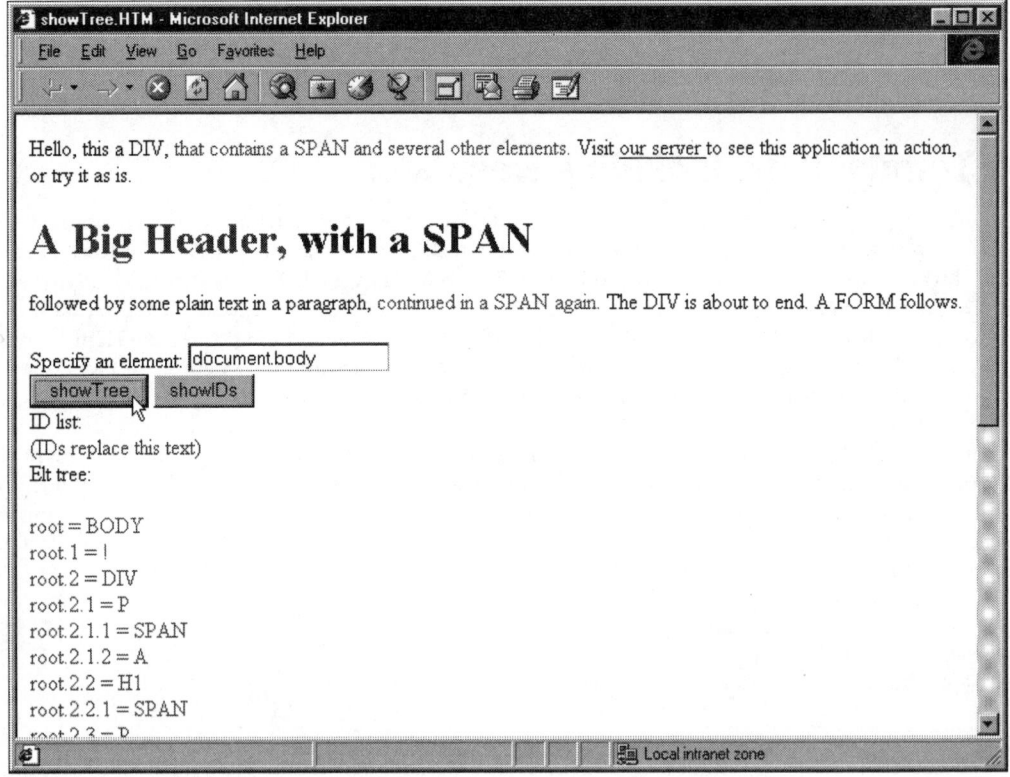

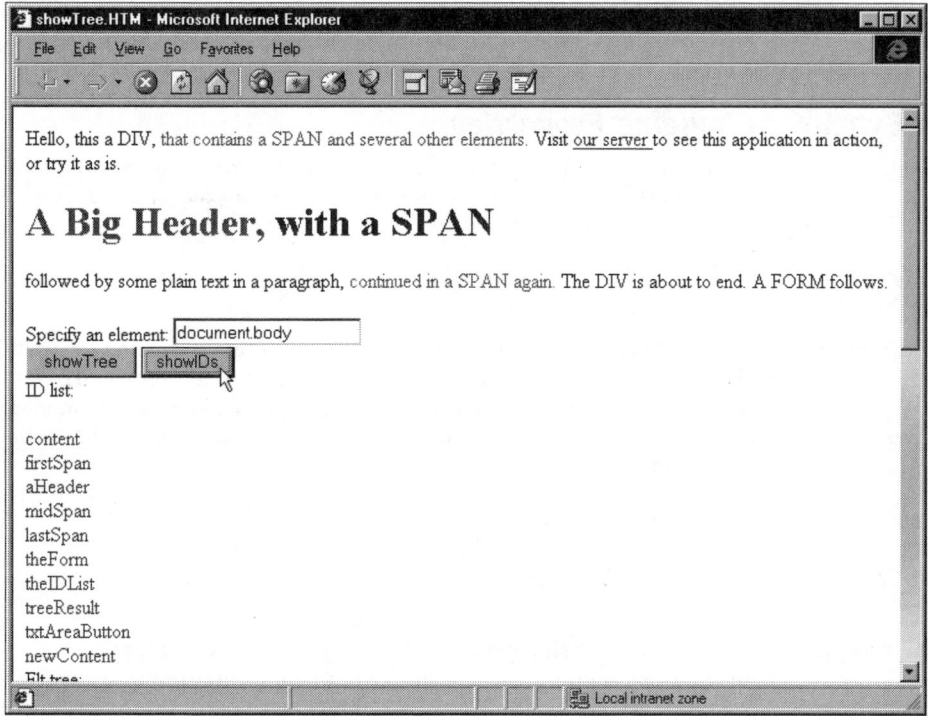

If you inspect the tree and the IDs, you'll see that the page consists of three large chunks: a <DIV> whose ID is content, the controlling form, and another <DIV> that contains a textarea and a button. The purpose of the last two items is to make it easier for you to experiment with the tree structure of the page. A good way to experiment is by replacing the content of the first <DIV> with your own, and see the tree structure of the content you have created. You can do this simply by editing the page and clicking Refresh, or you can also enter any HTML and text you wish into the textarea and click the NewCont button. The content of **content** will be replaced with what you've typed. If you're not in the habit of typing raw HTML, create some HTML in a specialized editor, switch to the HTML view, and copy the HTML you want into the **textarea** in our application.

How It Works

The code for this application is very simple. You've already seen the showTree() function earlier in this chapter. We'll show you the rest after introducing one big idea and a few details.

The Big Idea

The Big Idea of HTML 4.0, CSS/CSSP, JavaScript 1.2 and the whole "Dynamic HTML" is this: all HTML elements in the web page should be JavaScript objects, and most of their attributes, including the style attribute, should be properties of those objects. As a result, any element of the page can be constructed in JavaScript as the page is loading, and can be called or changed with JavaScript after the page has loaded. Currently, IE4 is much closer to achieving this goal than NC4, but the goal has been endorsed by W3C and the fifth generation browsers are expected to comply to a single, consistent object model for HTML.

In what follows, we'll frequently have to talk about "an HTML element and the properties of the corresponding JavaScript object", or "a JavaScript object and the attributes of the corresponding HTML element". Don't hold it against us if we simplify the language on occasion and talk about "the properties of an HTML element".

A Simple Example: Changing Properties

You know that the <BODY> element has the BGCOLOR attribute. This attribute is exposed to JavaScript as the bgColor property of the document object. If you want your entire document to turn light blue in response to a mouse click, you say:

```
<BODY onclick = "this.bgColor = 'aliceblue'">
```

Note the capitalization patterns: HTML is case-insensitive but is traditionally written in capitals. JavaScript is case-sensitive, and bgColor shows a typical capitalization pattern for an HTML attribute in JavaScript. Apart from capitalization, the JavaScript property name is the same as the HTML attribute with two exceptions: CLASS becomes className in JavaScript, and FOR becomes htmlFor. (We don't use FOR and htmlFor in this book.)

The same code in stylesheet-speak comes out as:

```
<BODY onclick = "this.style.backgroundColor = 'aliceblue'">
```

Notice the capitalization pattern again: stylesheet's background-color becomes backgroundColor. Following this simple pattern (remove hyphen, capitalize the second word), all the attributes of style are exposed to the scripting language. You can see how this opens interesting possibilities. It's very easy, for instance, to make an element disappear: just set its style.display property to "none".

Replacing the Content of Existing Pages

The content of every HTML element is exposed to JavaScript through these four properties: innerText, outerText, innerHTML and outerHTML. The first two return the same string, the text of the element, without any HTML tags. The difference between them is in assignment. If you assign a value to innerText, the text of the element is replaced but its surrounding tags are preserved; if you assign to outerText, everything, including the surrounding tags, is gone, replaced by plain text. If you include HTML markup in the replacement, it will show as text.

The other two properties, innerHTML and outerHTML (the first of them should sound familiar from Chapter 2) return the text with all markup included. The difference between them is exactly as you would expect: innerHTML excludes the element's own tags, keeping any tags nested in the content, while outerHTML includes them. In assignment, if the assigned string contains markup, it will be rendered correctly.

As you can guess, assignment to innerHTML is used in showTree(). We'll look at the code after we learn how to refer to elements on the page.

Adding to Documents as They are Loading

The preceding section showed how to modify the contents of an existing document that has already been parsed, loaded and rendered. It is also possible to add material to a document as it is loading, using the write() method. For instance, you can pop up a prompt dialog, ask the user for his or her name, and insert a friendly message into the HTML page:

```
<SCRIPT>
var uName = prompt("What's your name, stranger?");
document.write("Hello, " + uName + "! Welcome and feel at home.")
</SCRIPT>
```

If the document is loading in a different window from where your code is, you can create the entire document from scratch. (After all, an HTML document is just one long text string.) You will see many examples of this technique later in the book.

Referring to Page Elements

The Global Object

As we mentioned in Chapter 1, everything that looks like a global variable in JavaScript is, in fact, a property of the global object, and in browser JavaScript, the global object is the main browser window. It doesn't have a name, but it has properties that refer back to it. One such property is top. In a single-frame situation, you can also refer to it as window or self. If you have a multi-frame situation, window and self refer to the frame containing the code. You test to see whether you're in the main window by saying: if(top==self). (There is a section on frames later in the chapter.)

Consider a short HTML page. It has two functions defined in the header and one in the body, and it has a <SPAN> element with an id attribute. Its main attraction is that if you click on the button, the name in the text box gets replaced with a randomly selected item from nameList. We use it to illustrate references to the global object:

```
<HTML>
<HEAD> <TITLE>Hello.htm</TITLE>
<SCRIPT>

// getWord("a b c",0) returns "a"
function getWord(S,i){return S.split(" ")[i];}

// randInt(3,8) returns a random integer 3..8 inclusive
function randInt(lo,hi){return lo + Math.floor((hi-lo+1) * Math.random());}

</SCRIPT>
</HEAD>

<BODY>
My favorite name is <SPAN id=favoriteName> Mary </SPAN>.

<FORM> <INPUT TYPE=BUTTON VALUE="Select a name"
  onclick="top.favoriteName.innerHTML = top.nextName()">
</FORM>

<SCRIPT>
var nameList = "Anne Betsy Carol Dorothy Ellen";
function nextName(){return top.getWord(top.nameList,top.randInt(0,4));}
</SCRIPT>

</BODY> </HTML>
```

The main point of this example is that all the occurrences of `top` are redundant and can be removed. You only need references to `top` in a multi-frame situation, when you have an event handler in one frame and you want some action performed in a different frame.

For another example, each Frame and Window object has the `document` property, which refers to the HTML document loaded into the window or frame. You can refer to it simply as `document` (as in the many examples of `document.body.innerText` that you've seen) or as `window.document`, or as `self.document`, or as `top.document`. You only have to do any of these if you want to refer to a document in a different frame.

Absolute References

References can be relative and absolute. The difference is familiar from everyday use of language. **Absolute references** are those that don't change when you move. It's like a full postal address, or the latitude-longitude pair. **Relative references** are relative to where you are, as in "the house across the street" or "this object here". You go to another street and the reference changes.

In browser JavaScript, absolute references begin explicitly or implicitly with the global window object (just as full postal addresses implicitly begin or end–depending on the country–with "the Planet Earth"). Within the global context, you refer to an individual element either by using its tag and an array index, or by its `ID`.

Finding Individual Elements in Arrays

In addition to the document tree, several important types of HTML elements are collected into arrays, called **collections**, which are properties of the document object. The array index (0-based!) reflects the element's position on the page. To refer to the second form on your page, you say `document.forms[1]`, or, in full, `window.document.forms[1]`. To process in some way each form on your page, you say:

```
var N = document.forms.length;
for (var i=0; i<N; ++i) process(form[i]);
```

Other built-in arrays are `anchors`, `applets`, `images`, `links` and `scripts`. These arrays are also associative arrays whose properties include the `ID` or `NAME` attributes of the HTML elements. (HTML 4.0 allows an `ID` attribute for every element.) If you give that form we just mentioned an `ID` of "myForm2", then you can also refer to it as: `document.forms["myForm2"]` or `document.forms.myForm2`. You'll notice that the second syntax demonstrates explicitly that the form is an object.

The All Array and its Subarrays

IE4 also provides an `all` array which lists all the elements in the page in order. You can refer to each one of them by index or, in the associative array manner, by its `ID` or `NAME` property. So, you can refer to the same form as: `document.all["myForm2"]` or `document.all.myForm2`.

The main value of the `all` array is that you can create your own arrays of tag-specific elements. To get an array of all paragraphs, you'd say `document.all.tags("P")`. As you can see, `tags()` is a method that "filters" the `all` array to return only elements with a specific tag. It's a simple but useful exercise to pretend that the `tags()` method is not available and write your own. All you need to know is that an element's tag is exposed to JavaScript as the `tagName` property, and, as we said in the introduction, a suggested solution can be downloaded from our website.

The Best Way: Using IDs and NAMEs

We've saved the best way for the end. The element's ID attribute is the global name of the corresponding JavaScript object. You can refer to that second form simply as `myForm2`, as long as you are in the same frame or window.

Instead of the ID attribute, or in addition to it, some elements may have a NAME attribute. This is an older usage, and sometimes frowned upon. NAME is mostly used with the control elements of forms.

Try It Out

Go back to `showTree.htm` and practice referring to various elements of the page using their ID. Enter the reference in the text input box and view the tree structure of the element. For instance, enter "content" into the text box and view only the tree structure of the first `<DIV>` element, whose ID is "content".

Relative References

Relative references arise when you have an element in the focus of attention and you want to make references to other elements relative the element currently in focus. Most commonly, this situation arises in response to events, such as a mouse click. The clicked element is in the focus of attention, and you can refer to it as `this`. To refer to its parent in the HTML tree you use the `parentElement` property, and to refer to its children, you use the `children` array.

The Code of showTree

We can now work through some of the code of `showTree.htm`. Here's the page in outline:

```
<HTML>
<HEAD> <TITLE> showTree.HTM </TITLE>
<SCRIPT>

function showTree(ob,S)
{
// definition of showTree()
}
function idList()
{
// definition of idList()
}

</SCRIPT>
</HEAD>

<BODY style = "background-color: #ffffef" >

<DIV ID = "content">
 plain html, replace with your own for experimentation
</DIV>

<FORM id = theForm>
 control elements and event handlers
</FORM>
```

```
<DIV id = "txtAreaButton">
 text area and button
</DIV>

</BODY> </HTML>
```

The showTree() Function, Again

We have already shown a shortened version of showTree(). It's time to see the complete code:

```
function showTree(ob,S)          // show the tag of ob and all its descendants
{
 if(typeof ob.tagName == "undefined")
  return "<BR>" + S + " !no tag!";
 var R = "<BR>" + S + " = " + ob.tagName;
 for(var i=0; i<ob.children.length; i++)
  R += showTree(ob.children[i],S + "." + (i + 1));
 return R;
}
```

The new lines do a routine checking; the rest of the function traverses the tree underneath the ob element. The element is specified in the text box of the form, from where it is retrieved by an event handler. That line of code deserves a detailed discussion.

An Onclick Event Handler

The event handler is an attribute of a button within the same form that holds the text box. Here's the code for both, a mixture of HTML and JavaScript:

```
<FORM id = "theForm">
Specify an element:<INPUT TYPE="TEXT" NAME="Ob" VALUE="document.body"> <BR>
<INPUT TYPE=BUTTON  value="showTree"
onclick =
"treeResult.innerHTML = showTree(eval(this.parentElement.Ob.value),'root');">
```

The text input element has a NAME and a VALUE attribute. The value is what holds the string in the text box; it is initially set to document.body. The name is used for referring to the text box, so that its sibling, the button element, can find the box and the input. The reference, inside the eval() function, goes from the button up to its parent form, then down to the text box, using its name: this.parentElement.Ob.value.

While all the children of the form can refer to the form itself as parentElement, they can also say simply this.form, meaning "the form I'm in". This is a remnant of older times when forms and their descendants were about the only elements exposed to JavaScript. Although dated, this is a convenient form of reference.

Another notable thing in this line of code is the use of eval(). It evaluates the argument that it's given. Note that we couldn't use the JavaScript + operator to build the desired result, as in the following buggy line of code:

```
onclick = "treeResult.innerHTML = showTree(" + this.form.Ob.value + ",'root');">
```

The reason is that we're not, at this moment, talking to the JavaScript interpreter. This piece of code is in an event handler in the middle of HTML, which doesn't know what "+" means.

The final observation is about assignment: the result of the function call on showTree() becomes the innerHTML of treeResult. What's treeResult? A little further down in the file, we have this line:

```
<SPAN id = treeResult style = "color:green"> tree structure goes here </SPAN>
```

Now you can see what's going on. The string constructed by showTree() becomes the innerHTML of the <SPAN> element specifically created for the purpose and given an ID, for ease of reference.

The idList() Function and Its Caller, an Event Handler

Since you're getting much better at reading JavaScript code, we can comment on the idList() function in much less detail.

```
function idList()
{
 var S = "";
 with(document)
   for(var i=0; i<all.length; i++)
     with(all[i]) if(id)S += "<BR>" + id;
 return S;
}
```

Just as showTree(), this function builds a string which eventually becomes the innerHTML of a <SPAN> element. It goes through the document.all array of all elements in the page and says: "if you have an ID attribute, I'll add it to the string, after a
". The only mildly tricky aspect of the code is the use of embedded with statements. Without them, we'd have to repeat document.all too many times.

The corresponding button, its onclick attribute, and the <SPAN> receptacle are all familiar:

```
<INPUT TYPE=BUTTON value="showIDs" onclick="theIDList.innerHTML = idList()"> <BR>
ID list: <BR>
<SPAN id=theIDList style="color:purple"> IDs go here </SPAN>
```

The Textarea and Its Button

Finally, the textarea element has a small peculiarity of its own: the text you type into it does not become its value property, but rather its innerText.

```
<TEXTAREA id="newContent" cols=60 rows=4> </TEXTAREA> <BR>
<BUTTON onclick="content.innerHTML=newContent.innerText"> NewCont </BUTTON>
```

The identifier content is the ID of the <DIV> element whose content gets replaced by what you type into the textarea. Congratulations! We've completed our first in-depth discussion of a browser JavaScript application.

Event Handling and the Event Object

You've already seen the basics of event handling. To process an event that happens to an element, you give that element an attribute that begins with the letters "on", followed by the event's name. The value of the attribute is the code that gets activated when the event occurs. If the code is brief you can spell it out right there. If it's more than one line, you wrap everything you want to do into a function in a `<SCRIPT>` section somewhere and make a call on that function the value of the attribute. You've seen it in `showTree.htm` and elsewhere. The rest is details, and there are a lot of them. In this section, we delve into the subject a little deeper.

What Kind of Events are There?

Mouse and Keyboard Events

These are prototypical user events. We're going to get a listing of them from an unusual place, the HTML 4.0 specification called the **Document Type Definition**, or DTD for short. It's a text written in SGML (Standard Generalized Markup Language), which is really a language for defining languages. It was developed by the publishing industry in the 1980s for the purposes of electronic publishing but with no anticipation of its Internet use. Tim Berners-Lee used it to define HTML, and with each successive version, HTML's definition is getting closer to SGML specifications. The so-called "strict DTD" for HTML 4.0 is an impeccable SGML document. We'll present one small sample:

```
<!ELEMENT BODY O O (%block;|SCRIPT) ++ (INS|DEL) -- document body -->
<!ATTLIST BODY
  %attrs;              -- %coreattrs, %i18n, %events --
  onload      %Script;  #IMPLIED -- the document has been loaded --
  onunload    %Script;  #IMPLIED -- the document has been removed --
  >
```

Some of this is probably obscure, but we're not going to bother you with the details, especially since XML (a simplified version of SGML supported by the fifth generation browsers) is more likely to be relevant to you than SGML. What you see here is the definition of the `<BODY>` element and its `ATTLIST` (attribute list). Within attributes, those items that begin with a % are abbreviations for a list of "real" attributes. Such abbreviations are called "entities" in SGML. The `ATTLIST` definition says that `<BODY>` has all the standard attributes listed in `%attrs`, plus `onload` and `onunload`. The comment (between -- and --) explains that `%attrs` consist of `%coreattrs`, `%i18n`, and `%events`. It's the `%events` that we're interested in. Here's the listing:

```
<!ENTITY % events "
  onclick     %Script;  #IMPLIED -- a pointer button was clicked --
  ondblclick  %Script;  #IMPLIED -- a pointer button was double clicked--
  onmousedown %Script;  #IMPLIED -- a pointer button was pressed down --
  onmouseup   %Script;  #IMPLIED -- a pointer button was released --
  onmouseover %Script;  #IMPLIED -- a pointer was moved onto --
  onmousemove %Script;  #IMPLIED -- a pointer was moved within --
  onmouseout  %Script;  #IMPLIED -- a pointer was moved away --
  onkeypress  %Script;  #IMPLIED -- a key was pressed and released --
  onkeydown   %Script;  #IMPLIED -- a key was pressed down --
  onkeyup     %Script;  #IMPLIED -- a key was released --" >
```

It pays to learn how to read a DTD. It's the ultimate documentation for HTML, and it's an important part of XML that will soon become a very important language of the Web. To find out more about XML, please refer to *Professional XML Applications*, ISBN 1-861001-52-5, from Wrox Press.

Other Events

As you can see from the DTD, the `<BODY>` element has the attributes `onload` and `onunload`, in addition to attributes for mouse and keyboard events. We only use `onload`, but we use it a lot. This event handler is triggered when the document is parsed, but not necessarily fully loaded. This limits its usefulness. To check for complete load, you can't rely on that event, so you have to use special-purpose tools which we cover in excruciating detail in Chapter 5 and again in Chapter 8.

Other notable events include:

Name	Condition that triggers the event
onblur	an element loses focus
onfocus	an element gains focus
onerror	error occurs during loading a document or image
onchange	the contents of a select or text control element change
onsubmit	a form's submit button is clicked or the Enter key is pressed
onreset	a form's reset button is clicked

The first two are window events that can also occur on frames, control elements and applets. They always come in pairs: when an element gains focus, somebody else has to lose it. The focused window is simply the active window; in Windows, the one with the blue bar at the top. The user can switch focus by clicking on a different window; within a control element, the user can switch focus by tabbing through the options.

The last three events occur on form elements, and we'll discuss them in the section on forms later in this chapter.

The `onerror` event handler is designed to intercept error messages from the browser and give us a chance to handle the error more gracefully. We've found it not completely reliable, and do traditional error checking in the code.

The Event Object

There are important properties of events that are not captured by event handlers. Which key has been pressed? Is it the right button or the left button that's been clicked? What's the absolute reference of the element on which the event occurred (so I can pass it to another function)? To answer these questions, an `Event` object is created every time an event occurs, whose properties carry information about the event. Both IE4 and NC4 define an `Event` object, but in completely incompatible ways. We describe the IE4 model.

Try It Out

Point your browser at `showEvnt.htm`. It's a slightly modified version of `showTree`, in which the `showIDs` button has been renamed as `showEvent`. If you click on it, all the properties of the event object appear in the textarea at the bottom. Most of them are never used in this book, but since our application shows them, we list all available properties in the table below, grouped by meaning:

Properties	Data type	Description
type	String	name of event; same as event handler name, without "on"
altKey ctrlKey shiftKey	Boolean	modifier key status (pressed or not)
button	Integer	which button is pressed
cancelBubble	Boolean	bubble the even up or not?
clientX, clientY	Integer	horizontal and vertical coordinates of event within the browser window
offsetX, offsetY	Integer	horizontal and vertical coordinates of event within the element
screenX, screenY	Integer	horizontal and vertical coordinates of event within the screen
x, y	Integer	horizontal and vertical coordinates of event within the <BODY> element or a positioned element
fromElement, toElement	Object	for mouseover and mouseout events, the elements from and to which the mouse has moved
keyCode	Integer	keyboard character code of a keyboard event
reason	Integer	status of a data transfer event in data binding
returnValue	Boolean	value returned by the event
srcElement	Object	default element intended to receive the event
srcFilter	Object	filter object that triggered a filter event

How It Works

The event handler for the showEvent button is a two-liner:

```
function showEvent(E)
{
 var S = ""; for(x in E) S += x + "=" + E[x] + "\n";        // alert(S);
 newContent.innerText = S;
}
```

We call it by saying:

```
<INPUT TYPE=BUTTON value="showEvent" onclick="showEvent(event)">
```

As you can see, event can be used as if it were a global variable, because it is a property of the window. Every time an event occurs, a new event object is created. Try putting an onkeypress attribute, with the same value, into a text input element and experiment by pressing unmodified and shift keys (e.g., a lower case and upper case 'A'): the shiftKey property will switch accordingly. (Getting control and alt keys into a text input requires a special effort.)

The Source Element

The `srcElement` property of the event object is a reference to the element on which the event occurred. To store it in a variable `currOb` for further manipulation, you say:

```
var currOb = event.srcElement;
```

Suppose you have a number of images in your page, each contained in a <DIV> element, together with an explanatory paragraph of text which is hidden until the user clicks on the image; clicking on the visible text hides it again. (This admittedly is a contrived example; things of this sort are better done with frames, but we're trying to do without for a moment.) You can achieve the desired result thus (only the relevant snatches of code are shown):

```
<STYLE> P.hidden {display:none} </STYLE>

<SCRIPT>
function showTxt(e){e.srcElement.parentElement.children[1].className = "";}
function hideTxt(e){e.srcElement.className = "hidden";}
</SCRIPT>
...
<DIV> <IMG src= ... onclick="showTxt(event)">
   <P onclick="hideTxt(event)">...</P>
</DIV>
```

Event Bubbling

Continuing with this example, suppose you have defined an `onclick` handler for the entire body, which contains all your <DIV>s with images and paragraphs, plus some introductory text. When the user clicks on that text, you want a window to pop up, with the standard information about the author, copyright, and the best place to buy the hard copy. However, you only want it to happen when the user clicks on that text or some whitespace area but not when the user clicks on the image or on the paragraph to be hidden. This requires special arrangements because the event registers itself not only with the element on which it occurred but with each one of its ancestors in the document tree, all the way up to the window. This is called "event bubbling". If any of the ancestors has a handler for the event, it will be triggered, unless you "cancel the bubble". In our example, you'd make this addition:

```
<DIV> <IMG src=...; onclick="showTxt(event); event.cancelBubble=true;">
   <P onclick="hideTxt(event); event.cancelBubble=true;">...</P>
</DIV>
```

Overriding Defaults

Some elements have pre-programmed default behavior in response to some events. The most familiar example is the <A> element, which follows its hyperlink in response to a mouse click. If you want to change this behavior and provide your own `onclick` handler, you have to return a boolean value from it. You return `false` to cancel the default behavior, and `true` to let it proceed. (If your function is sloppy enough to return no value, true is assumed and the event proceeds.) You will see examples in the section on forms, where we'll override the default behavior of the button.

Note that `cancelBubble` and `returnValue` are two different properties of the Event object, and can be controlled independently. To override the default behavior of an event handler somewhere up the tree, it is not enough to cancel the bubbling of the event; you also have to make sure to return `false`.

Interactive Forms

The form element was the first object to be exposed to JavaScript, and it retains special significance as the home for interactive controls. You can put all the event handlers you want on a paragraph or even on a horizontal rule, but if you want to collect the user's typed input and have it trigger some action on the server, you need the form.

Form Elements

By their function, form elements fall into three groups. **Hidden** elements, if present, store a value for internal use. **Visible** elements, such as text boxes or buttons, serve to collect and manipulate data from the user. Two special buttons, the Submit and Reset buttons, require a little more explanation. The Submit button performs the action specified in the ACTION attribute of the form, usually sending the collected information to the server. The Reset button clears the data-collection elements from user input, resetting them to default values.

Formally, most form elements are `<INPUT>` elements with a type attribute: `<INPUT TYPE=X>`. The possible types are: `hidden` (for hidden elements), `submit` and `reset` (for Submit and Reset buttons), and a number of types of control elements for user input: `button`, `checkbox`, `radio`, `text`, `password`, `filename`. In addition, also for user input, there are `<BUTTON>`, `<SELECT>`, and `<TEXTAREA>` elements. They are properly discussed in an HTML book, such as *Instant HTML: a Programmer's Reference* from Wrox (ISBN 1-861001-56-8). As far as JavaScript is concerned, they are just objects with name and value properties and various event handlers. We do comment on them selectively in the rest of the section.

Names and Values

With one exception, data-collection elements have a NAME and a VALUE attribute. When a form is submitted, the name-value pairs are collected from the form's elements into one string, which is sent to the server, to be parsed and acted upon. (We describe this process in more detail in Chapter 6.) The one exception to this arrangement is the `<SELECT>` element. It has a NAME attribute, but no VALUE. The value of a `<SELECT>` element comes from the `<OPTION>` elements it contains.

The naming convention for radio buttons deserves mention. They serve, as you know, to choose one and only one of a set of possible values. For each value, there is a separate button in a group of buttons, but they all must have the same name. This name is paired with the value of the selected button.

Referring to Elements

Since most elements have names, you can refer to them simply by name. Be aware that forms create their own name spaces, so it's possible to have two forms that have an element with the same name. It's better to refer to a form's element through the form itself. A form's name must of course be unique within a document.

The form object has an `elements` property, which is an array of all its elements in the order in which they appear in your code. So, if your form's name is `theForm`, and it has two buttons, named `b1` and `b2`, and a text input named `t1`, you can refer to them as:

```
b1:  theForm.b1, theForm["b1"], theForm.elements[0], theForm.elements["b1"]
b2:  theForm.b2, theForm["b2"], theForm.elements[1], theForm.elements["b2"]
t1:  theForm.t1, theForm["t1"], theForm.elements[2], theForm.elements["t1"]
```

Referring to radio buttons is a bit different because there are several of them with the same name. What happens is that an array of radio buttons is returned. If we added three radio buttons to our form as the last element, with the name `pickOne`, we'd refer to the second of them as:

```
theForm.pickOne[1] or theForm.elements[3][1]
```

with `[3]` being the position of the radio buttons within the array of elements, and `[1]` being the array index of the button chosen.

Select and Options

The object corresponding to a `SELECT` element is the only one that contains another object, an `options` array. You refer to individual options using the array notation: `theForm.mySelect.options[3]`. The elements of the `options` array are objects of the `Option` class, and can be created using the `new` operator. To add an option to `mySelect`, you'd say:

```
with (theForm.mySelect)
{
 options[options.length] =
  new Option("the latest option","lastOpt",[true,false]);
}        // the booleans mean: selected by default or not currently selected
```

The options array has two features to make it easy to delete options at runtime. If you decrease the length of the array, items are deleted from the end of it. If you set the value of an option to null, it is deleted from the array and the elements that follow it are shifted to fill the gap.

Form Validation

The most common use of JavaScript in client-side form processing is for validating user input. Users, as we know, make mistakes, and the programmer's task is to catch them before they make too much damage or waste too much time and bandwidth. Since the variety of possible user mistakes is endless, there will always be need for more form validators. So, we decided to create an authoring system for them, or a template validator that is easy to customize for specific needs. We sometimes call it "the mother of all validators".

Intercepting the Mistake

Most user mistakes have to do with keyboard input in a text or textarea field. (If there is a wrong value on a radio button or option element, that's the programmer's mistake, not the user's.) There are situations when a mistake is in submitting incompatible values from several fields, but we're not dealing with those.

With keyboard input, there are several stages at which the user mistake can be captured. The first line of defense is the `keypress` event. If you're asking for a number and the user presses a question mark, you can detect it and put out an alert message, or simply cancel the event, so the offending character doesn't appear no matter how hard the user presses the key. Many people will probably find this approach intrusive, over-protective and paternalistic.

The second line of defense is the `onchange` event which is triggered when the user moves on to the next field of the form. At this moment, you can inspect the input and pass judgement. It can be expressed as an alert box, or you can use the style property (which every input element has) and color its background blue or red, to express approval or disapproval. This is a very common strategy. The validator we develop doesn't follow it but can easily be modified to do so.

The last line of defense is when the user submits the form. This generates an `onsubmit` event. At this moment, we can go through the entire form, check every element of it, and either proceed with submit or cancel it and produce a message. This is what we do in five examples that follow. They start with a simple example but get more and more complex. The last version is both the most powerful and the most challenging; don't be discouraged if you have to skim it on first reading and come back.

The Simplest Validator

The first example (**formval1.htm**) doesn't really do any serious validating. It only checks to see that the input box is not empty, but it shows how you cancel the default action of the submit button.

```
<HTML> <HEAD> <TITLE> formVal.HTM </TITLE>
<SCRIPT>
function showForm(theForm)
{
 alert("hi, this is the form " + theForm.id + "\nperforming its Action");
}
function validateForm(theForm)              // return true if all is well
{
 if(theForm.tBox.value! = "") return true;
 alert("you didn't put anything in there!");
 return false;
}
</SCRIPT>
</HEAD>

<BODY> <P>
This is a simple exercise in form validation
<FORM id=theForm onSubmit="return validateForm(theForm)"
  Action="javascript:showForm(theForm)">
Input Box (try it empty and nonempty) :
<INPUT TYPE=TEXT name=tBox value="a value"> <BR>
<INPUT TYPE = SUBMIT>
</FORM>
</BODY> </HTML>
```

To test a form validator, we need some action in case the form content is valid. We didn't want to get the server involved for a client-side exercise, so we gave our form a JavaScript action. The action is of the simplest kind: the `showForm()` function that just puts an alert box out, declaring the action performed.

The `validateForm()` function returns true if we want the submission to succeed and false if we want it canceled. The value is returned to the `onsubmit` handler of the form. You can test the page with `tBox` empty and non-empty, to see that different alerts are produced.

The Power Tool: a Regular Expression

In our second example (**formVal2.htm**), we added two more text boxes to check for more conditions. The first box has the same "be non-empty!" condition. The second box must have a string that begins with a consonant. The third box must have only digits. The big news is that we express all those conditions as regular expressions. To store those expressions in a convenient place, we add a `validator` property to those form elements that we want to validate (all of them in our example). The value of the property is the regular expression that the string in the text box must match in order to pass muster. (Just as, in Chapter 2, we added our own properties to core JavaScript objects, you can add properties to client-side JavaScript objects.)

```
The NonEmpty Box (try it empty and nonempty):
<INPUT TYPE=TEXT  name=nonempty  value="a value"  validator="/./"> <BR>
The Vowel Starter:
<INPUT TYPE=TEXT  name=cons  value=None  validator="/^[aeiou]/i"> <BR>
The digit Sequence:
<INPUT TYPE=TEXT  name=digiSeq  value=help  validator="/^\d+$/"> <BR>
```

The rest of the body of the page is exactly the same, but the code in the <HEAD> is very different. Let's look at the `validateForm()` first:

```
function validateForm(theForm)            // return true if all is well
{
 var elArr = theForm.elements;
 for(var i=0; i<elArr.length; i++)
  with(elArr[i]){                         // for each element of the form...
   var v = elArr[i].validator;
   if(!v)continue;                        // no validator property, skip
   var pair = patPat.exec(v);             // break reg exp into pattern and modifier
   var thePat = new RegExp(pair[1],pair[2]);
   var gotIt = thePat.exec(value);
   if(!gotIt)
   {
     alert(name + ": failure to match " + v + " to " + value); return false;}
   }
 return true;
}
```

We go through the elements of the form checking for the `validator` property. If an element doesn't have it, we skip to the beginning of the loop and continue. If the property is there, we apply the global `patPat` to it. This is a regular expression that analyzes regular expressions and breaks them into the pattern part and modifier part. (You'll see it in a moment.) Recall from Chapter 1 that the `exec()` method returns an array whose first element is the entire string to match and the rest are the components of the string. In our case, `pair[1]` is the pattern and `pair[2]` is the modifier, and we pass them as arguments to the `RegExp()` constructor. The rest is fairly obvious.

Our `validator` function breaks the loop and returns with an error message as soon as a single malformed field is found. It's a simple but useful exercise—with the solution available from the homepage of this book, at `http://www.wrox.com/Store/Details.asp?Code=1894`—to rewrite it so that it always checks all the fields, adding error messages, if there are any, to a string. In the end, if the string is empty it returns true, otherwise it displays the string and returns false.

To complete the picture, here's the `patPat`:

```
var patPat = / ^\/ (.*) \/ ([^/]*) /;       // a pattern to match patterns
// alert(patPat.exec("/pattern/modifiers").join("\n"));
```

Stepping through the pattern, we see that it asks for a string that begins with the "/" character (escaped in the pattern). Following the slash, there can be any number of any characters other than newline. That's the . * part, in parentheses, which becomes a component of the returned array. Then we have another "/", followed by, in parentheses, any number of anything other than "/". That second parenthetical expression becomes another component of the returned array. If you uncomment the alert, it will show three lines corresponding to three elements of the array returned by `exec()`:

```
pattern/modifiers
pattern
modifiers
```

A More Efficient Version

This is pretty good but our validator is very inefficient: it does the same thing over and over again. Let's say our form is about money. We wrote a pattern that matches all and only currency expressions like $12,000.00. We attached it as the validator property to every field that has money in it. Every time a field like that is validated, the same regular expression is parsed before being applied to the string in the field. What we want to do is to name our validating patterns and keep them, parsed into `RegExp` objects, in a dictionary. The first time we come across a pattern, we parse it and store in the dictionary. After that, we retrieve it from the dictionary by its name. Here's the revised `validateForm()`:

```
function validateForm(theForm)              // return true if all is well
{
 var elArr = theForm.elements;
 for(var i = 0; i < elArr.length; i++)
  with(elArr[i])
     {
     var v = elArr[i].validator; if(!v)continue;
     var thePat = patternDict(v);
     var gotIt = thePat.exec(value);
     if(!gotIt)
        {
        alert(name + ": failure to match " + v + " to " + value); return false;
        }
     }
 return true;
}
```

All the new action is in the `patternDict()` function. It can take two arguments. The first is a name to give to a pattern, the second is the pattern itself. If only one argument is given, it has to be a regular expression which is also its own name:

```
function patternDict(Name,Pat)       // two arguments are given
{
 if(Pat)
  {
    var p = patPat.exec(Pat); if(!p)return null;
    return patternDict[Name] = new RegExp(p[1],p[2]);
  }
 var p = patternDict[Name];          // one argument; try to retrieve pattern
 if(p)return p;                      // if retrieved, return it
 p = patPat.exec(Name);              // check the argument against patPat
 if(!p)return null;                  // if failed return null
 return patternDict[Name] = new RegExp(p[1],p[2]); // compile and put in dict
}
```

Note the two return statements which are also assignments; the assigned value is returned.

Version 4: Friendly Names

Here we're getting even more complicated. Our validator property now can have the form "=" + name + regular expression. In other words, we can use a validator as before, or we can prepend an "=" followed by an arbitrary name to it, as in:

```
The NonEmpty Box (try it empty and nonempty):
<INPUT TYPE=TEXT  name=nonempty  value="a value"
validator = "=notEmpty/./"> <BR>
```

It is compiled the first time it is used, and after that can be referred to simply by name, as in:

```
Another NonEmpty Box (try it empty and nonempty):
<INPUT TYPE=TEXT  name=nonempty  value="another value"  validator="notEmpty">
```

To achieve this new functionality, we only need a new pattern to complement patPat, and a few minor changes in patternDict(). Here's patPatDef:

```
var patPatDef = / ^= (\w+) \/ (.*) \/ ([^/]*) /;    // pattern for pattern defs
```

We add two new lines to the very end of patternDict():

```
p = patPatDef.exec(Name);
if(p)return patternDict[p[1]] = new RegExp(p[2],p[3]);
```

Try it in formval4.htm.

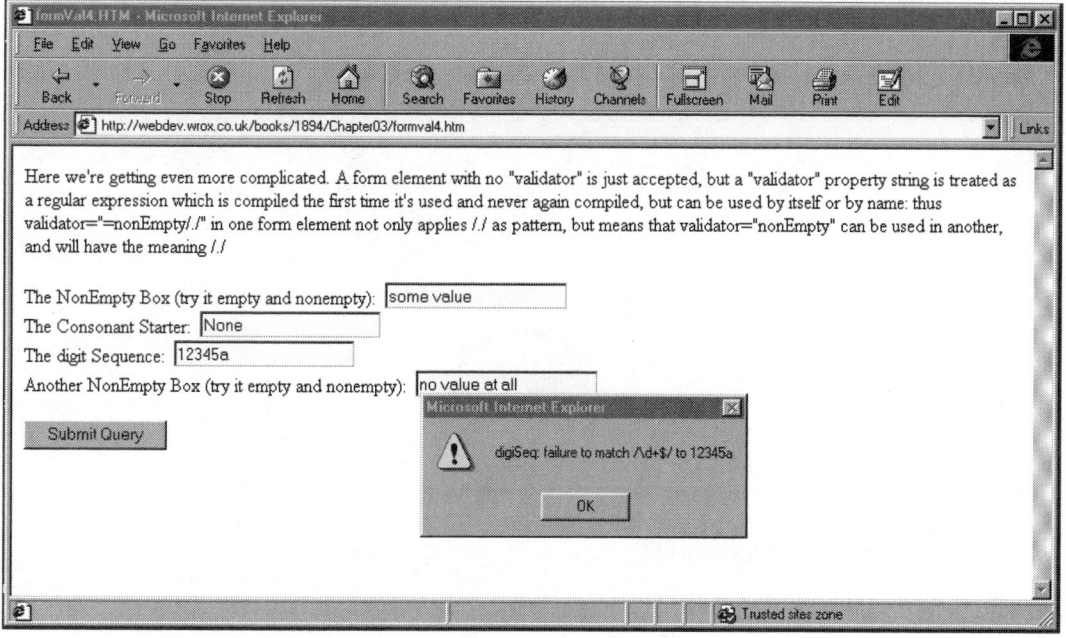

The Final Version

In addition to a `validator` property, we can give each element of the form a `validatorFn` property. Its value can be an arbitrary function to be run on the element. If we need other arguments to give it, we can add them as the element's properties. Validators are stored as properties of `patternDict`, as before, while validator functions are stored as properties of the `validatorFns()` function. The activity of form validation is reduced to the activity of accumulating patterns and functions that express desired constraints. The patterns and functions can be added to the global `patternDict` and `validatorFns()` in a separate initializing function, before any forms are processed:

```
function initPatternDict()
{
 patternDict("Date",
 "/(Jan|Feb|Mar|Apr|May|Jun|Jul|Aug|Sep|Oct|Nov|Dec) (\.|) +" +
 "(\\d|\\d\\d), * (\\d+)/i");
 validatorFns();
}

function validatorFns()
{
 validatorFns["intFn"] = isIntFn;
}
```

Here `isIntFn()` is a function that checks a form element to make sure its value is an integer between `lowLim` and `hiLim`. The limits can be specified as properties of the element; if they are not, they're given default values of 0 and 1000000.

```
function isIntFn(theFormElt)
{
   if(0 > theFormElt.value.search (/ ^*(-|) \d +*$ /))
     {
     alert("the form element " + theFormElt.name + " must be an integer");
     return false;
     }
   var lowLim = theFormElt.validatorLowLim, hiLim = theFormElt.validatorHiLim;
   if(!lowLim) lowLim = 0; else lowLim = parseInt(lowLim,10);
   if(!hiLim) hiLim = 1000000; else hiLim = parseInt(hiLim,10);
   var val = parseInt(theFormElt.value,10);
   if(val < lowLim || hiLim < val)
     {
     alert("the value of " + theFormElt.name +
         " should be between " + lowLim + " and " + hiLim);
     return false;
     }
   return true;
}
```

The final version of `validateForm()` makes use of both `patternDict` and `validatorFns()`:

```
function validateForm(theForm)                    // return true if all is well
{
 var elArr = theForm.elements;
 for(var i=0; i<elArr.length; i++)
   with(elArr[i])
     {
```

```
      var f = elArr[i].validatorFn;
      if (f) return validatorFns[f](elArr[i],theForm);
      var v = elArr[i].validator; if(!v)continue;
      var thePat = patternDict(v);
      var gotIt = thePat.exec(value);
      if(!gotIt)
         {
         alert(name + ": failure to match " + v + " to " + value); return false;
         }
      }
   return true;
}
```

The full version, called (unsurprisingly) `formval5.html`, looks like this:

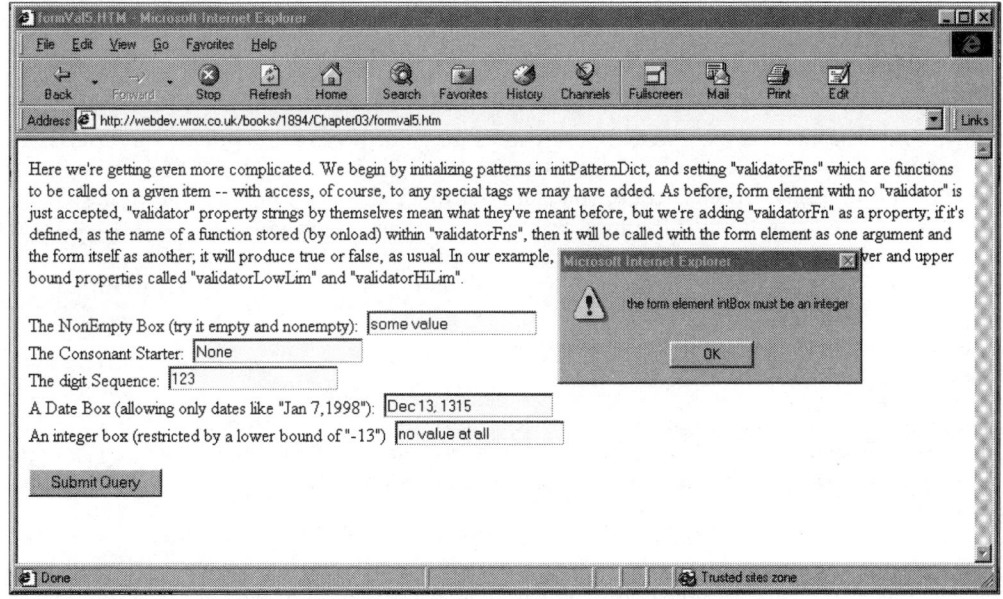

As usual, the file is available from our website, at `http://webdev.wrox.co.uk/books/1894/Chapter03/formval5.htm`.

In conclusion, we find this approach to form validation promising because of its modularity of design. It's easy, and makes a good exercise for the reader, to add regular expressions and functions to two global objects, perhaps in a separate `.js` file; should you need help, point your browser at this book's home page, `http://www.wrox.com/Store/Details.asp?Code=1894`. When a form needs validation, include the file and start using your library of validating tools.

Beyond the Document: Windows and Frames

It's time to broaden our perspective beyond a single document within a single frame. Let's not forget that the document is just a property, albeit an important one, of the window. What other "object" properties does the window have? Here's a partial list; for complete coverage, refer to Appendix C and to our standard references (*Instant JavaScript* and *Instant IE4 Dynamic HTML*).

```
window, self, document, event, frames, parent,
top, location, history, navigator, screen
```

Be aware that window properties and methods are no more standardized than the Document Object Model. Eventually, W3C will get to work on them also, but only after DOM is standardized.

Of the properties listed, you've already seen the first four. `window` and `self` refer to the window itself. `document` and `event` have been discussed earlier in the chapter. This brings us to `frames`.

Multiple Frames

The `frames` property of the window is an array of frames. It's a flattened list of all the child frames of the window. Frames also form a tree of their own; a frame can refer to its parent window as `parent`, and to the top window as `top`. If there is only one window, then `top`, `parent`, `window`, and `self` all refer to the same single window. To test whether you're in the top window, say: `if(self==top)....` To see if your window has any children frames, say: `if(frames.length>0)...`

Usually, you refer to frames by name. Suppose you've put your JavaScript code in the top frame (i.e., in the `<FRAMESET>` document), and you have two frames, called `tDoc` and `tCtlframe` (a document frame and a control frame). In your code, you can refer to an object `Ob` in the `tDoc` frame as `tDoc.Ob`. If you need to refer to it from the `tCtlframe` frame, you'd say `parent.tDoc.Ob`. As usual, instead of the object-property syntax, you can use the associative array syntax and say `parent["tDoc"].Ob`. Finally, you can use array notation: `parent.frames[0]`, where `tDoc` is the first member of the array.

Try It Out

We've put together one more application (`travdoc.htm`) to explore the tree structure of the HTML page. It consists of two frames. The top frame has a document, any document. (After you've played with ours, replace it with one of your own.) If you click anywhere on it, the smallest surrounding element turns pink.

The bottom frame has a form with buttons, text boxes, and a textarea. The up, next, prev and down buttons take you to the parent, right sibling, left sibling and first child of the currently selected element. The text boxes show various HTML attributes of the selection. The textarea shows the selected element's complete innerHTML.

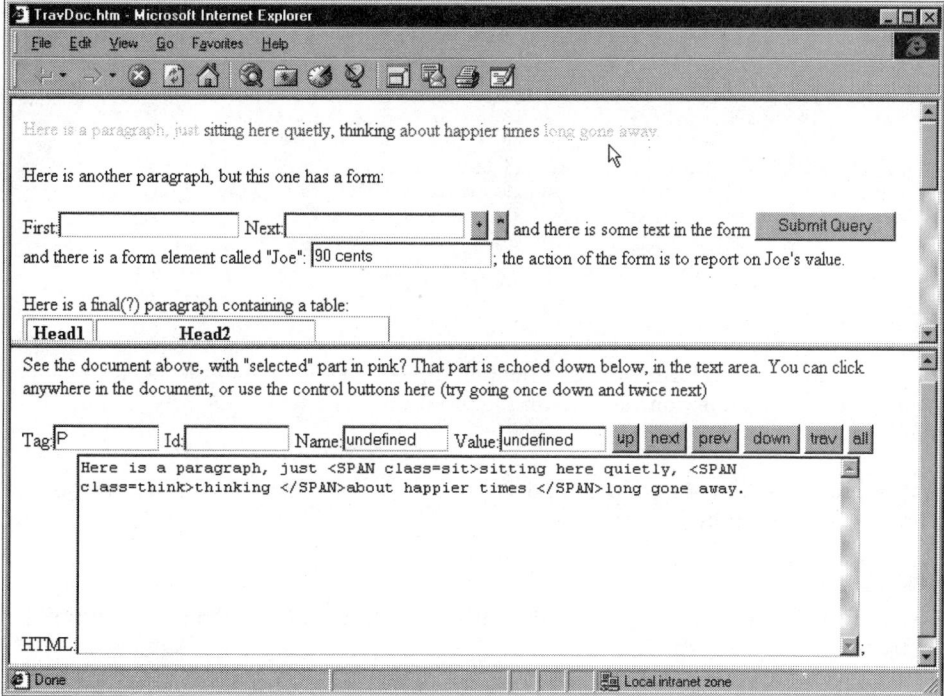

How It Works

The overall structure of the application is just as we described: a frameset page that contains all the code, a document frame and a control frame. The frameset page, in outline, is like this:

```
<HTML>

<HEAD> <TITLE> TravDoc.htm </TITLE>
<SCRIPT> the application's code </SCRIPT>
</HEAD>

<FRAMESET rows="50%,50%"  onload="doOnLoad()">
 <FRAME name="tDoc"  src="tdoc.htm">
 <FRAME name="tCtl"  src="tctl.htm">
</FRAMESET>

</HTML>
```

The page in the `tDoc` frame can be any page, and it's best explored through the application itself. The page in `tCtl` has a form with control elements:

```
<HTML>
<HEAD> <TITLE> TravDoc.htm </TITLE> </HEAD>

<BODY>
<FORM id=TravControl  ACTION="javascript:parent.upOb()">
Tag: <INPUT TYPE=TEXT  name=theObTag  size=10>,
Id: <INPUT TYPE=TEXT  name=theObId  size=10>,
```

```
Name: <INPUT TYPE=TEXT  name=theObName  size=10>;
Value:<INPUT TYPE=TEXT  name=theObValue  size=10>;
<INPUT TYPE=BUTTON  value="up"  onclick='parent.upOb()'>
<INPUT TYPE=BUTTON  value="next"  onclick='parent.nextOb()'>
<INPUT TYPE=BUTTON  value="prev"  onclick='parent.prevOb()'>
<INPUT TYPE=BUTTON  value="dn"  onclick='parent.downOb()'>
<INPUT TYPE=BUTTON  value="trav"  onclick='parent.travNext()'>
<INPUT TYPE=BUTTON value="all"  onclick='parent.traverseAll()'> <BR>
HTML:<TEXTAREA name=theObHTML  rows=10  cols=80> </TEXTAREA>;
</FORM>
</BODY>

</HTML>
```

The text input elements of the form will have the tag, id, name and value of the selected element. The buttons, when clicked, call functions defined in the top frame. The textarea holds the innerHTML of the selected object.

We'll look at some of the functions of the application, both to see examples of using frames and as a review of earlier sections of this chapter.

Setting Things Up

First, we set up two global variables, one for the currently selected object, the other for the root of the tree:

```
var theBrowserOb = null, topBrowserOb = null;
```

All of the action begins with `doOnLoad()`, called from the `onload()` handler of the frameset:

```
function doOnLoad()
{
  setBrowserOb(topBrowserOb = tDoc.document.body);
  topBrowserOb.onclick = setClickedOb;
}
```

This does three things in two lines of code:

```
topBrowserOb = tDoc.document.body;      // set topBrowserOb
setBrowserOb(topBrowerOb);              // call setBrowserOb with that value
topBrowserOb.onclick = setClickedOb;    // set its onclick to setClickedOb
```

That `setClickOb()` function is a one-liner that calls `setBrowserOb()` with the source element of the click. Note that the `event` object is a property of the frame in which the event occurs:

```
function setClickedOb()
{
  setBrowserOb(tDoc.event.srcElement);
}
```

To "set" a browser object means simply to discolor the currently selected object and to color the newly-selected one. (The task is simple because every object has a style property.) Then we call `showOb()`, to update information in the control frame:

```
function setBrowserOb(ob)
{
 if(!ob) return;                // this line is needed in nextOb()
 if(theBrowserOb) theBrowserOb.style.color = "";
 theBrowserOb = ob;
 theBrowserOb.style.color = "red";
 showOb(theBrowserOb);
}
function showOb(Ob)
{
 with(tCtl)                     // the name of the frame
  with(TravControl)             // the name of the form
  {
// prefix all references to form fields with tCtl.TravControl.
    theObHTML.value = Ob.innerHTML;
    theObTag.value = Ob.tagName;
    theObId.value = Ob.id;
    theObName.value = Ob.name;
    theObValue.value =Ob.value;
    Ob.scrollIntoView(true);    // scroll the doc frame so Ob shows
  }
}
```

Navigating a Document Tree (a Review Session)

The navigation functions explore the familiar themes of parents, children and recursion. Moving up and down is trivial:

```
function upOb()
{
 if(theBrowserOb! = topBrowserOb)
   setBrowserOb(theBrowserOb.parentElement);
}
function downOb()
{
 if(theBrowserOb && theBrowserOb.children.length > 0)
   setBrowserOb(theBrowserOb.children[0]);
}
```

Moving to a sibling is trickier because you have to know where you are in your parent's children array. We call it "the kid number", kidNum for short. Once you have that, moving to the next and previous child is easy:

```
function kidNum(ob)
{
 if(!ob || ob.tagName == "BODY")return -1;
 var B = ob.parentElement;
 for(var i=0; i<B.children.length; i++)
  if(B.children[i] == ob)return i;
 return -1;
}
function nextOb()
{
 var N = kidNum(theBrowserOb);
 if(N >= 0) setBrowserOb(theBrowserOb.parentElement.children[N + 1]);
}          // if N + 1 == childern.length, theBrowserOb returns without complaint
function prevOb()
```

```
  {
  var N = kidNum(theBrowserOb);
  if(N > 0)setBrowserOb(theBrowserOb.parentElement.children[N - 1]);
  }
```

Finally, complete traversal. To do it all in one go is easy; you've seen the showTree(ob,S) function twice. We also provide a function that traverses the document one step at a time, moving from one element to the next in the "depth-first" order. This means that the "next" element after the current one is its first child, if any; otherwise, its next sibling, if any; otherwise go up to its parent and try again.

```
function travNext()
{
 if(theBrowserOb.children.length > 0)
  return setBrowserOb(theBrowserOb.children[0]);
 while(true)
  {
  if (theBrowserOb == topBrowserOb)
   return setBrowserOb(theBrowserOb.children[0]);
  var mom = theBrowserOb.parentElement;
  var sibs = mom.children.length;
  var N = kidNum(theBrowserOb);
  var sisNum = N + 1;
  if (sisNum < sibs) return setBrowserOb(mom.children[sisNum]);
  setBrowserOb(mom);
  }
}
```

Text utilities, a framed version

As promised, we have also put together a version of txtUtils.htm from Chapter 2 that uses frames. You will find it at http://webdev.wrox.co.uk/books/1894/Chapter03sdict/txtFrame.htm. The page has exactly the same functionality as txtUtils.htm, but it keeps the text, the dictionary, the control buttons, and the output of its applications in different frames.

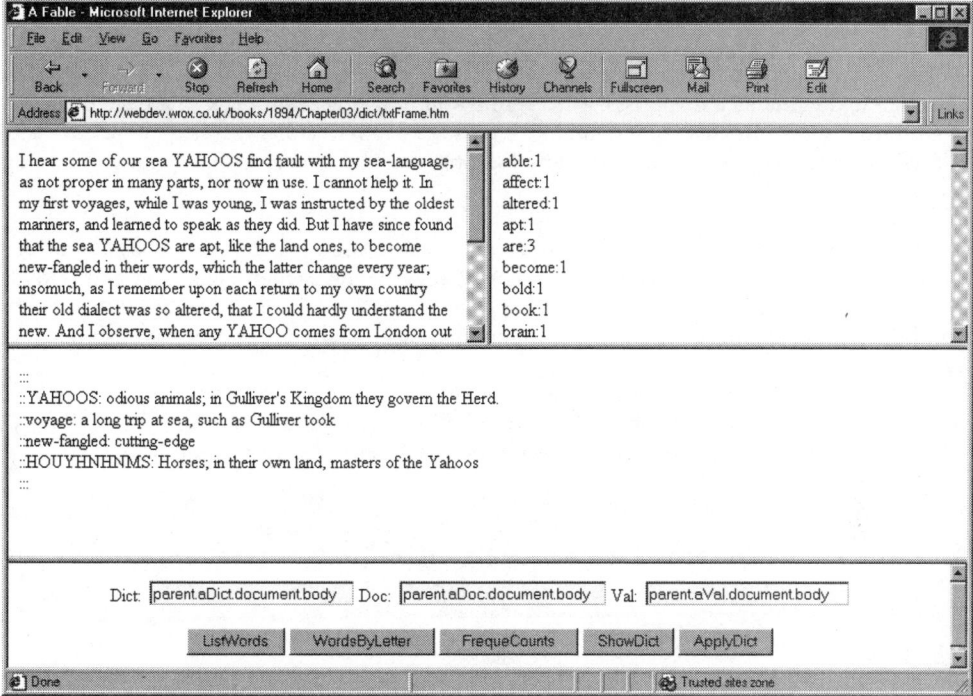

Location and History

Both `window.history` and `window.location` are themselves objects with properties and methods. `History` is an array of URLs the browser has visited, one of which is current. The methods `back()` and `forward()` change the current URL, and the method `go()`, if given the argument 0, sends the browser to the current URL. A call on `go()` with a non-zero argument sends the browser a specified number of steps backward or forward in its history. Either of the two lines below tells the browser to revisit the URL that is three steps in the past:

```
history.go(-3);
for(var i=0; i<3; ++i) history.back(); history.go(0); }
```

The `history` property is read-only, so you cannot purge or rewrite it.

The `location` object has properties and methods for working with the current URL. Recall that the URL has the following structure (many parts of which are optional):

```
protocol://hostname:port/pathname?search#hash
```

Correspondingly, the `location` object has the properties of `protocol`, `hostname`, `host` (which is `hostname` + `port`), `pathname`, `search` and `hash`. It also has the `href` property which is writable; if you want to move to a new place that is not on your history list, assign its URL to the `href` property:

```
location.href = "http://www.newhome.newserver.com"
```

The window object also has an `href` property which is really an alias for `location.href`, so you can simply say `href=...`, assuming that you mean your current frame.

Revisiting the `go()` method of the history object, it has the following minor peculiarity: if you go back to a page that contains a form, IE4 will assume you're trying to go back to a page out of the cache, and dutifully ask "Repost form data?" The only way to overcome this is by explicitly setting the `href` property to the desired page, thereby loading a new instance, without thereby loading a new, blank, instance of the form.

The `location` object has two methods, `reload()` and `replace()`. If given an argument that does not evaluate to false (true would work), `reload()` disregards the cached document and reloads from the server. If given no argument, `reload()` checks whether the document has been changed on the server, and if not, reloads from cache. If your document has included files that have been changed, you have to force reload from the server.

The `replace()` method changes the URL without adding it to history, which is useful when you want to redirect visitors to another URL but keep their **Back** button operational:

```
<HTML> <HEAD>
<SCRIPT>
function redirect(uri) {location.replace(uri)}
</SCRIPT> </HEAD>
<BODY onload = "redirect('myNewHomePage.htm');"> </BODY> </HTML>
```

If you used assignment to `href`, clicking on the **Back** button would keep you in an infinite loop.

Conclusions

We've tried to compress into a single chapter the material of a large book. Our goal was to give you enough background to go out and explore on your own. The rest is really a lot of details. You will find some of them in the appendix dealing with the browser object model in IE4, Appendix C, and most of the others in many excellent reference books, such as the two Dynamic HTML titles from Wrox Press (*Instant IE4 Dynamic HTML*, ISBN 1-861000-68-5; *Instant Netscape Dynamic HTML*, ISBN 1-861001-19-3) and McFarlane's *Instant JavaScript* (Wrox Press, ISBN 1-861001-27-4).

As we promised, the chapter has covered:

- ❑ the tree structure and its terminology
- ❑ recursive functions, especially on trees
- ❑ the HTML document tree
- ❑ the main concepts of HTML 4.0 and Dynamic HTML
- ❑ changing the contents of the document
- ❑ rules of referring: absolute and relative reference
- ❑ programming with events and event handlers
- ❑ the global event object
- ❑ interactive forms and form elements
- ❑ form validation using regular expressions
- ❑ multiple frames
- ❑ the `location` and `history` objects

This concludes the introductory chapters of the book. From now on, we'll be in the business of defining and using our own classes of objects, following the ideas and techniques of object-oriented programming.

4

Object-Oriented Programming

Introduction

Chapters 2 and 3 have shown how to program with objects in JavaScript. However, a language that programs with objects is not necessarily an object-oriented programming language, i.e. one that is properly equipped to do object-oriented programming (OOP). OOP is a way of organizing large programs as a collection of autonomous but inter-related objects. This book argues that OOP is good for you, and that you can do OOP in JavaScript. In fact, a JavaScript program of any substantial size *should* use OOP. Why, you may ask? For at least three reasons. First, because OOP programs are easier to design before they're written, and easier to maintain after that. Second, various components of such programs (definitions of classes of objects) are easy to reuse in other contexts. Third, OOP provides tools and techniques for reusing components in building new components that are more powerful or more specific to a task. Frequently, you further develop your program by further developing the components that it's built from.

Beginning with this chapter, our programming examples will run on two tracks: examples of reusable components (definitions of classes) and examples of applications that are put together using those components. The components developed in this chapter are `Stack`, `DisplayStack` and `Calculator`.

`Stack` is a very general data structure that is widely used in computing. We'll give three examples of its use in applications: reverse a linear sequence, traverse a tree, and remove recursion using your own stack of function calls. The last example will be developed in the context of a well-known puzzle called "the Towers of Hanoi". While less obviously useful than our other examples (one can even accuse it of being kind of amusing), the Towers of Hanoi program illustrates extremely important issues in programming in general and JavaScript programming in particular. The techniques it develops will be used throughout the rest of the book.

`DisplayStack` illustrates two very general and important issues in programming. First, it shows how to take an existing component (the `Stack`) and expand its functionality. `DisplayStack` is, in a very precise sense, derived from `Stack`, inheriting all its properties and adding to them. What `DisplayStack` adds to `Stack` is a visual representation, or view. `DisplayStack` is our first example of a computational object that contains, as one of its properties, an HTML element that shows the contents of the computational object and changes when those contents change.

The `Calculator` class develops this theme further, showing two-way communication between a computational object and its view: the `Calculator`'s visual representation not only shows the contents of the calculator object, but also lets the user enter data for the object to work on.

In summary, this chapter will cover:

- ❑ the principles of OOP and how they can be put into JavaScript practice
- ❑ the `Stack` class and its uses, including a traversal of the HTML document tree
- ❑ the `DisplayStack` class, which is an extension of the `Stack` class
- ❑ the inner workings of a function call, including a recursive function call
- ❑ how to make your program pause, either for the user to inspect it or for the program itself to wait for some condition
- ❑ how to implement a class, and how to derive one class from another
- ❑ how to establish communication between a computational object and its view

In the last section of the chapter, we develop a `Calculator` class and a `Calculator` application. To use it, simply add its URL (`http://webdev.wrox.co.uk/books/1894/Chapter04/Calc.htm`) to your favorite bookmarks.

Principles of OOP

OOP is based on three principles. Each one of them makes perfect sense but comes with a long and difficult name, which is probably why people sometimes think that OOP is a ploy by PhD academics to mess up what real programmers do. We do mention those names (and we are burdened with a PhD each) but we hope to persuade you that OOP makes sense for everybody, including real programmers.

We're going to illustrate our discussion of the principles with a well-known data structure called `stack`. A stack is basically an array whose elements are not positioned horizontally, in a row, but vertically, in a column (hence, a stack), and all operations on that array take place at its top. (The inspiration for that data structure, or at least its name, came from a stack of plates in a cafeteria supported by a spring mechanism, such that at any time only the top plate can be seen or removed.) In other words, instead of array-style unrestricted access to any element, a stack has the operations `push()`, which adds an element or several elements to the top of the stack; `top()`, which returns the top element, and `pop()`, which removes the top element and also returns it. These are the only operations you use in programming with stacks, according to the first of the OOP principles.

Principle 1: Separate Public Interface from Implementation

The scholarly word for separating the public interface from implementation is **encapsulation**. In its general form, it has always been part of good programming. OOP's specific angle on it is that you provide public methods to access and modify the properties of objects. "Real" OOP languages, like C++ and Java, have facilities to enforce encapsulation: special words in the language declare some methods and properties **public**, others **private**, and whatever is private is not accessible from outside the object. So, an object might have a private property called `size` and public methods called `getSize()` and `setSize()`, and the only way to get the value of `size` or to change it is to call the public method. An attempt to get or set it directly by saying, for instance, `object.size = 17` would be an error caught at compile-time by the language processor. JavaScript is a smaller language with more flexibility and fewer restraints, and the programmer has to rely on her inner resources and self-discipline to enforce encapsulation. (So, as you build good programs in JavaScript, you also build character and resistance to bad habits.) In our practice, we put implementation into a `.js` file and the interface into a prominently displayed comment. For instance, a web page that uses the Stack class would have this line of code in its header:

```
<script src = "stack.js">  /* implementation of Stack class*/  </script>
```

Either in the same page or at the top of `stack.js` we'd put the following comment:

```
/* the public interface of the Stack class:
  Stack()                returns a new, empty stack with methods
  Stack.isEmpty()        returns true if stack is empty, else false
  Stack.push(x...)       pushes arguments on stack one at a time, left to right
  Stack.top()            returns value of most recently pushed item
  Stack.pop()            same as top, but also removes the top item
  Stack.toString()       returns stack items as strings, concatenated
*/
```

In this chapter, we program for a long time using this public interface before we take a look at the implementation.

Principle 2. Provide for Code Sharing Between Classes of Objects.

The two principal mechanisms for code sharing are inheritance and aggregation. **Aggregation** is easier to understand: it simply means that one object can contain another object, and the container can implement some of its methods by reusing the corresponding methods of the contained object. For instance, the `Stack()` constructor would have this line:

```
function Stack() {
  this.A = new Array();...
```

The array would hold the contents of the stack. The definition of the `Stack.toString()` method would simply say: `return this.A.toString()`.

Aggregation is also easy to implement: it does not put any special requirements on the language, beyond the reasonable expectation that properties of objects may themselves be objects.

JavaScript Objects

Inheritance is more difficult, both to understand and to implement. The concept of inheritance is based on an analogy with the "is-a-kind-of" relationship in the real world. For instance, when we say that "dog is a kind of mammal," we presumably mean that the class of dogs has all the properties of the class of mammal, plus some additional, more specific properties that differentiate it from, e.g., the class of cats. Using the term non-technically, we can say that, in the tree hierarchy of the natural kingdom, the class `dog` inherits (from up the tree) all the properties of the class mammal, and adds some of its own. This analogy has been carried over to the design of programming languages.

Inheritance does impose certain requirements on the language—namely, the ability to say that a class D is going to have all the properties and methods of a class B plus perhaps some more. In addition, some of the methods of B may be implemented differently in D. In this situation, B is called the base class and D a derived class, and we say that D **inherits** its properties and methods from B, and perhaps **overrides** (i.e., implements differently) some of those methods.

In C++ you express inheritance by saying:

```
class D : public B { ...
```

and in Java it comes out as:

```
class D extends B {
```

JavaScript doesn't have either special syntax or a special keyword for inheritance, but you achieve the same result by setting the prototype of the derived class to be an object of the base class— check back to Chapters 1 & 2 for a refresher on the prototype. So, after defining D() as the constructor for the derived class, we'd say:

```
D.prototype = new B(...);
```

To continue with our example, for the `Stack` class we would say:

```
Stack.prototype = new Array();
```

Aggregation and Inheritance Contrasted

Does one need both inheritance and aggregation? If both are available, which one is better, and when? One commonly-held opinion is that the choice between these two mechanisms for code reuse should reflect the relationship between the classes involved. Remember that we think of our objects as somehow modeling objects in the real world. Suppose you work for AT&T and write programs that model telephones. A portable phone is a kind of phone, so you would derive the `PortablePhone` class from the `Phone` class and add features specific to the portable phones (e.g., `batteryLife` and `recharge()`). On the other hand, a phone has a microphone inside, or a microphone is a part of, not a kind of, a phone, therefore you would make the `Mike` class a property of the `Phone` class.

We think that this is too subtle. The time to distinguish between the "is-a-kind-of" and "is-a-part-of" relationships is at the design stage. A class D "is a kind of" class B if they have a lot of identical or similar properties and methods, and D has more of them, while B is more "basic" or "abstract". We capture this observation by giving those identical or similar properties and methods the same names in both classes. Whether we then import all the properties from one class to another, or re-implement them by delegating from one class to another is a question of implementation rather than semantical content. It is true that if we use inheritance we don't have to write one-liners like:

```
function stk_toString(){return this.A.toString();}
Stack.prototype.toString = stk_toString;    // we explain this code shortly
```

On the other hand, when you use aggregation, you can be selective about which properties and methods of the base class are transferred to the derived class. With inheritance, you have to accept them all, which is frequently not what you want to do. One influential book (*Design Patterns* from Addison-Wesley, 1994) simply says "Favor object composition over class inheritance" (p.20), and we're inclined to agree. However, we provide examples of both. In particular, to test the integrity of our encapsulation principles, we provide two implementations of the Stack class as derived from the Array class, one using aggregation, the other inheritance. In every program of the book, one implementation can be replaced with the other, and the program wouldn't notice.

Principle 3. An Object Should Know How to Do Things to Itself.

This is known as **polymorphism**, or dynamic binding of methods to objects. Suppose you have an array of graphical objects, such as rectangles, ovals and polygons, and you want to draw them on screen. Each one of those objects presumably has a draw() method, differently implemented in different classes of objects. It should be possible for the programmer to write a simple loop whose body is something like: ar[i].draw(). This in effect tells each object in the array to go and draw itself, without the programmer's telling it how. Two language features are required for this to happen. First, different classes should be able to have methods of the same name. Second, the decision as to which of those methods should be invoked is made dynamically, at runtime, depending on the class of the object involved. Both features are standard behavior in JavaScript. In fact, you saw both of them in operation in Chapter 2, in the section on why methods are better than global functions.

Examples Using Stack

We repeat the public interface of Stack here for convenience:

```
Stack()                  returns a new, empty stack with methods
Stack.isEmpty()          returns true if stack is empty, else false
Stack.push(x...)         pushes arguments on stack one at a time, left to right
Stack.top()              returns value of most recently pushed item
Stack.pop()              same as top, but also removes the top item
Stack.toString()         returns stack items as strings, concatenated
```

The implementation of the class is in the file stack.js, but we're not going to look at it for a while. What we're going to do is use the class by programming to its public interface. We solve three typical tasks in which stacks come in very handy: reversing linear sequences; traversing a tree; and removing recursion from a program. The first one is also the simplest, and we'll dispense with it without any preliminaries.

Safe Reverse

In order to reverse a linear sequence, we push its items in order on the stack, then pop the items into a fresh copy, and they come out reversed. (Railroad depots use a similar technique to reverse a sequence of railroad cars.)

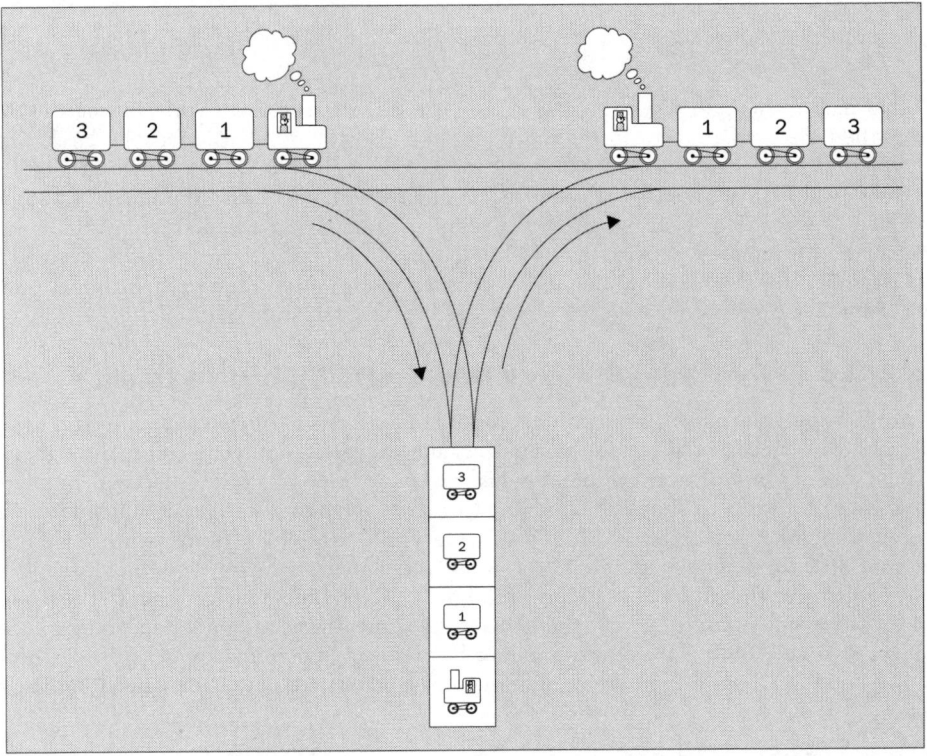

Our trusted reliable sequence is, of course, the Array class. It comes with a reverse method, but that method reverses the array in place, destroying the initial content. Let's write safeReverse() which returns a fresh copy, reversed.

```
function ar_reverse()
  {
  var len = this.length;
  var A = new Stack();
  var res = new Array(len);
  for (var i=0; i<len; ++i) A.push(this[i]);
  for (var i=0; i<len; ++i) res[i] = A.pop();
  return res;
  }
Array.prototype.safeReverse = ar_reverse;
```

The function testReverse() checks it out:

```
function testReverse()
{
  var A = new Array(1,2,3,4,5);
  var B = new Array();
  B = A.safeReverse();
  alert("before: " + A.join() + " after: " + B.join());
}               // shows "before: 1,2,3,4,5 after: 5,4,3,2,1"
```

Tree Traversal

We told you in the last chapter how much we like trees. Our second-most favorite data structure is the stack, precisely because of its intimate relationship with trees. Most generally, the relationship is as follows: if your sentence structure is a tree then you can parse it using a stack. We're not going to cover parsing but we will definitely do a lot of tree traversals in which you walk around the tree visiting each node. A stack provides a simple strategy for doing that: put the root of the tree on the stack and go into a loop that repeats two actions: (1) pop the top element off the stack and "visit it"; (2) put the children of the popped element on the stack so the first child is on top. The loop terminates when the stack is empty. What we do when we "visit" a node depends on the task at hand; in the example below, which traverses document trees, we simply show the node's HTML tag. (Remember showTree() from the preceding chapter? This is another way to do it, without recursion.)

```
function traverseDoc()
{
 var A = new Stack();
 A.push(document.body);
 while (!A.isEmpty)
 {
  var A = A.pop();
  alert(A.tagName);
  for(var i=A.children.length-1; i>=0; i--) A.push(A.children[i]);
 }
}
```

If you drop this function into your web page and run it from an event handler, you'll see the tags of all the elements of your document tree. You can vary the order in which you traverse the tree by changing the way you add the children of a current node to the list of nodes to visit. The way we just did it is called "depth-first" because the traversal route takes you all the way to the bottom of the first subtree before starting on the next one. Another common traversal pattern is called "breadth-first": you visit all the first-generation descendants of the root before you go to second-generation descendants; visit all of them before starting on the third generation, and so on. We leave it as an exercise to implement a data structure called queue, in which all the new arrivals go to one end (the rear) while all the removals take place at the other end (the head of the queue). If you use a queue instead of a stack in the traversal function, you will be doing a breadth-first traversal. As usual, a suggested solution for this exercise is available from this book's home page, at http://www.wrox.com/Store/Details.asp?Code=1894.

Watching the tags go by is instructive and may be fun the first time around, but we can certainly do something more useful. Remember that we have access to the contents of each node through such functions as innerText() or outerHTML(). As a simple example, we provide a tool that imitates a well-known columnist in San Francisco who had every other paragraph in his column printed in boldface. Let's write a little function to do that; most of its code, except for the highlighted lines in the while loop, is the same as in traverseDoc():

```
function boldEveryOther()
{
 var A = new Stack(); var count=0;
 A.push(document.body);
 while (!A.isEmpty())
 {
  var A = A.pop();
```

```
    if(A.tagName == "p" || A.tagName == "P")
     if (++count%2 == 0)              // increment count then check if it's even
      A.innerHTML = "<B>" + A.innerHTML + "</B>";
    for(var i=0; i<A.children.length; i++) A.push(A.children[i]);
  }
 }
```

Since `traverseDoc()` and `boldEveryOther()` share so much of their code, there's clearly a generalization to be made here. In the next chapter, we will define a `Tree` class and give it a `traverse(func)` method that will visit all the nodes of its owner object and apply the supplied function to each.

An Extended Example: Towers of Hanoi

Our next problem comes from an old puzzle about three Buddhist monks in Hanoi who are engaged in moving golden disks from one diamond pin to another. They started with 64 golden disks of different sizes, arranged in a pyramid on a diamond pin. There are two more such pins, initially empty. The task is to move all the disks from the initial pin to another one using the third as a temporary storage. The constraint is that at no time can you place a larger disk on top of a smaller one. When the monks are done, the world will supposedly come to an end. Fortunately, it can be shown that the number of required moves grows exponentially with the number of disks, so to move a pyramid of 64 disks, the monks will have to make 2^{64} moves. A simple calculation shows that if the monks work 24 hours a day (three 8-hour shifts) and spend a minute on moving each disk, then it will take them about 35 trillion years to do the job; if they speed up and spend 30 seconds on each move, that figure will be cut in half to 17.5 trillion years.

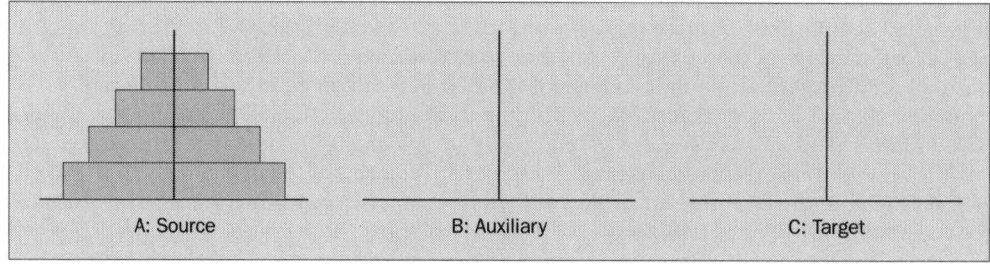

A: Source   B: Auxiliary   C: Target

Recursive Solution

Solving the Towers of Hanoi directly, even for 4-5 disks, is difficult, but a recursive solution is quite easy. We reason as follows:

Let's say we have to move N disks from the `Source` pin to the `Target` pin using an `Auxiliary` pin for temporary storage. If N is 0 then we're done. Otherwise, let's assume that we know how to move N-1 disks. (That's the recursive way of thinking.) We use that knowledge to move top N-1 disks from `Source` to `Auxiliary` using `Target` for temporary storage. We move the remaining largest disk from `Source` to `Target`, and we never move it again. We again use our assumed knowledge (i.e., a recursive call) to move N-1 disks from `Auxiliary` to `Target` using `Source` as temporary storage.

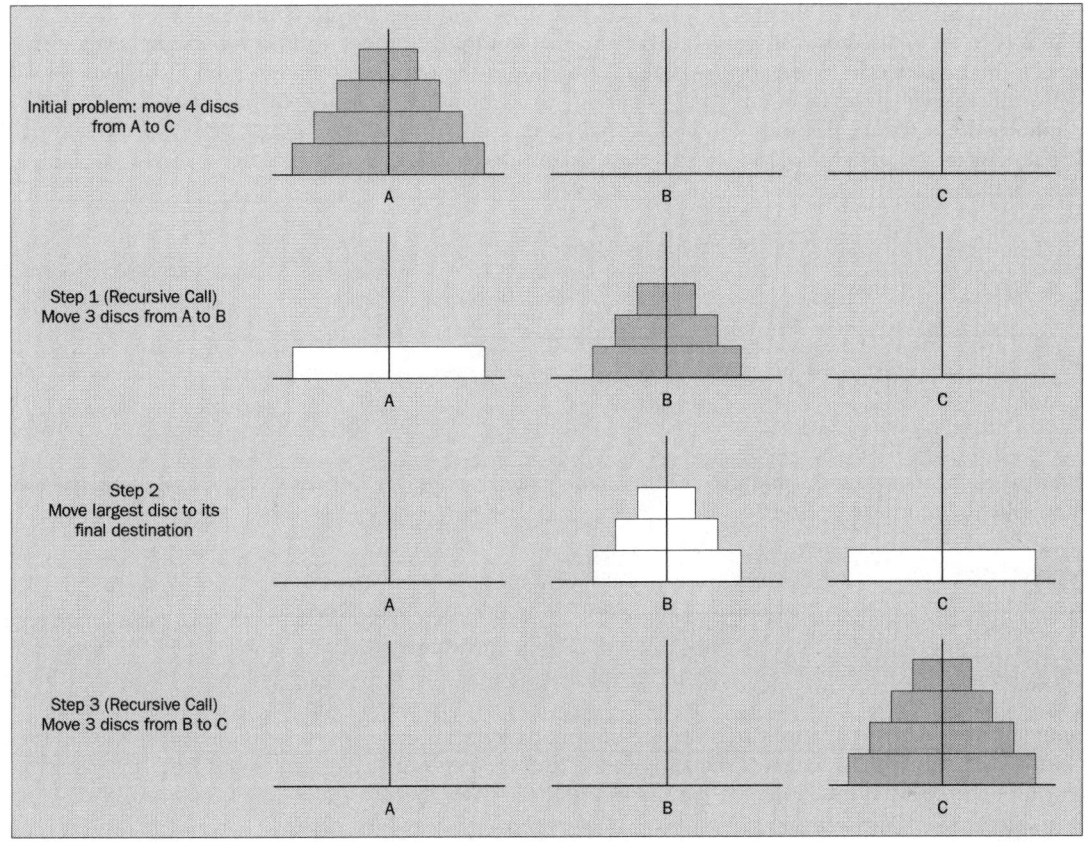

In JavaScript, this comes out as:

```
function h1(N,A,B,C)      // move N disks from A to C using B as auxiliary
{
 if(N==0)return;          // the "base case" of recursion
 h1(N-1,A,C,B);           // move N-1 disks from A to B using C as auxiliary
 moveTop(A,C);            // do the actual move
 h1(N-1,B,A,C);           // move N-1 disks from B to C using A as auxiliary
}
```

where:

```
function moveTop(sA,sB)
{
 var d = sA.pop();
 sB.push(d);
}
```

How do we know that this works? If we simply initialize three stacks and run the program, it will do something and return in silence. It would be nice if we could see the disks moving. We will not go all the way to an animation with golden disks and diamond pins, but we will do something visual: disks will be represented by numbers 1 through N (the larger the number, the larger the disk), and we will show numbers moving from one pin to another, by associating each pin with a one-column HTML table. In other words, our pins will be internally represented by objects of the DisplayStack class. That class is very much like the Stack class except that it contains a reference to an HTML table, in the form of its ID attribute:

```
function Hanoi1(N,ATableID,BTableID,CTableID)
{
var A = new DisplayStack(ATableID,N);
var B = new DisplayStack(BTableID,N);
var C = new DisplayStack(CTableID,N);
for(var i=N; i>0; i--) A.push(i);
h1(N,A,B,C);
}
```

Functions h1(N,A,B,C) and moveTop() are exactly as before because DisplayStack has the same public interface as Stack.

Try It Out

Point your browser at the file Chapter04/Hanoi1.htm. The code files for the page are stack.js, dispstk.js, and Hanoi1.js. The body of the file mostly consists of a table that holds three stacks. We also provide a form with a text box to specify the number of disks and a button that starts the program. In case the user presses the Enter key, which submits the form, we give the form an action, an alert dialog telling the user to click the button. The onclick() event handler of the button calls Hanoi1(). Hanoi1() collects the arguments from the rest of the page: N comes from the same form's text box, and the names of the stacks are the IDs of the three one-column tables. With arguments initialized, Hanoi1() calls h1() shown on the previous page:

```
<HTML>

<HEAD> <TITLE>Towers of Hanoi</TITLE>
<STYLE>
  TD.S {background:lightblue; width:30; font-size:8;font-family:courier;}
  TD.SS {background:lightgreen; width:200; font-size:8;font-family:courier;}
</STYLE>

<SCRIPT src="stack.js">/* stack implementation */</SCRIPT>
<SCRIPT src="dispstk.js">/* DisplayStack implementation */</SCRIPT>
<SCRIPT src="hanoi1.js">/* recursive Hanoi */</SCRIPT>
</HEAD>

<BODY>
<P> To play, click the startHanoi1 button. </P>
<TABLE>
  <TR> <TD VALIGN=TOP width=100>
  <FORM>
  Number of Disks: <INPUT TYPE=TEXT VALUE="4" ID=NumDisks size=2>
  <INPUT TYPE=BUTTON VALUE="startHanoi1"
   ONCLICK = 'Hanoi1(this.parentElement.NumDisks.value,"A","B","C")'>
  </FORM>
  </TD> <TD VALIGN=TOP>
```

```
        <TABLE id=A BORDER>
        </TABLE>
      </TD> <TD VALIGN=TOP>
        <TABLE id=B BORDER>
        </TABLE>
      </TD> <TD VALIGN=TOP>
        <TABLE id=C BORDER>
        </TABLE>
      </TD> </TR> </TABLE>
    </BODY>

  </HTML>
```

A screen shot of the page appears below. Click the **startHanoi1** button. The initial problem will appear, together with a confirm dialog. Click OK. After each move, the problem will pause to put the same confirm dialog on the screen. You can use the pauses to try and predict the next move. Watch how the program first moves 1, then 1-2, then 1-2-3, 1-2-3-4 and finally 1-2-3-4-5.

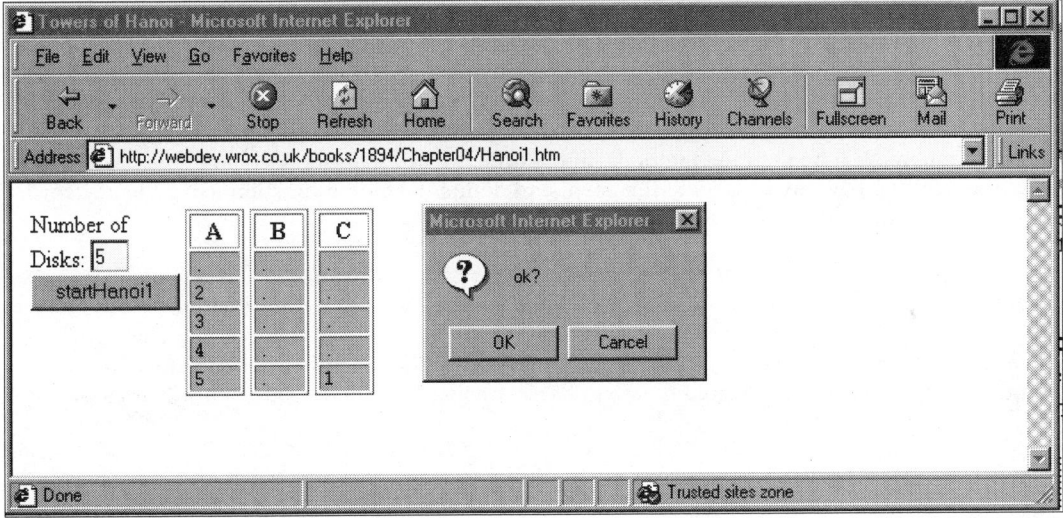

How It Works

The code for this application is in three files: `stack.js`, `DispStack.js`, and `Hanoi1.js`. The *Recursive Solution* section above shows all the code of `Hanoi1.js`, except for three lines that put a confirm dialog on the screen and give the user a choice to proceed or to cancel. (Without those lines the program would simply proceed from the initial to the final state without showing any intermediate stages.) The real gist of the application is in two reusable classes, `Stack` and `DisplayStack`. Their implementation is presented in the next two sections. Although the code is relatively simple, these sections are very important because they suggest a general methodology for doing OOP in JavaScript. You may adopt our methodology or invent your own, but it is extremely important for you to have a set of procedures that you consistently follow. Remember what we said about self-discipline: JavaScript will not enforce your methodology for you, and programming without an established methodology puts a heavy burden both on the programmer and on the entire team. (We have learned and re-learned this lesson, the hard way, even in our small team of two.)

Implementing the Stack Class

Since this is the first class we implement, we'll summarize the procedure in a separate section.

Procedure and Naming Conventions for Defining a Class

To define a class is to define its constructors and methods. A constructor is just a function, defined like any other function. It differs from "normal" functions in how it is used:

- ❑ we add properties and methods to the prototype property of the constructor function
- ❑ we use the constructor function with the `new` operator, to create objects

You add methods to your own classes in exactly the same way you add methods to existing classes. In other words, you follow the same steps that were described, explained and illustrated in Chapter 2, in the section on adding your own methods to existing classes. We repeat the steps from Chapter 2:

- ❑ define a global function that does the same thing to one of its arguments as the method will do to its "owner" object
- ❑ rewrite the function using the word "`this`" to refer to that argument
- ❑ make the revised function a property of the prototype

In Chapter 2, we said: "Since this is our first try, we'll go through the steps very carefully. In Chapter 4 and later, where we'll be defining methods all the time, we'll usually skip the first one". We really meant it. Beginning now, we'll skip the first step, and define the global function using the keyword `this` to refer to the object on which the method operates.

In going through the steps, we follow certain naming conventions. Names of constructors are always capitalized (and no other function names are). The names of global functions that are method definitions always consist of two parts, as in `Stack_pop()`. As you can see, the first part is the name of the class, frequently shortened (as in `dispStk_pop`), and the second part is the name of the method. The two parts are connected by the underscore character, and we don't use that character in any other function names.

The Stack Class

As you would expect, `Stack` reuses much of the functionality of the `Array` class. In this example we use aggregation to reuse code: each `Stack` object will contain a property that is an object of the class `Array`. Our first inclination was to create an `Array` object in the constructor:

```
function Stack(){this.A = new Array();}
```

However, this got us into trouble later, when we derived a `DisplayStack` class from out `Stack`. We'll explain the nature of the trouble in the section on `DisplayStack`; for now, just note the solution, because it represents a common technique. We give our `Stack` class a method, `initStack()`, that creates an `Array` object for a `Stack` object. This method is called from the constructor:

```
function Stack(){this.initStack();}
```

Apart from creating an array, our `initStack()` doesn't do any other initializations, but it could. It is common practice, resulting in more modular software, to separate construction from initialization in this way. (The well-known Microsoft Foundation Classes (MFC) library uses it often.)

We can now present the entire code that implements the `Stack` class:

```
// step 1 of class definition: define a constructor, always capitalized
function Stack(){this.initStack();}

// step 2, define methods as global functions using "this" keyword
function Stack_initStack(){this.A = new Array();}
function Stack_IsEmpty(){return this.A.length == 0;}
function Stack_length(){return this.A.length;}
function Stack_Top(){return this.A[this.A.length - 1];}
function Stack_Pop()
  {
  var N = this.A.length - 1;
  var X = this.A[N];
  this.A.length = N;
  return X;
  }
// the classical push, pushes one item only
function Stack_Push(A)
  {
  var N = this.A.length;
  this.A.length = N + 1;
  this.A[N] = A;
  }

// a more powerful push, so S.push(A,B,C) pushes A, then B, then C
function stk_push()
  {
  for(var i=0; i<stk_push.arguments.length; i++)
    this.A[this.A.length] = stk_push.arguments[i];
  }
function Stack_toString(C)
  {
  if(!C) C = ",";
  return this.A.join(C);
  }
function Stack_toArray(){return this.A;}
          // dangerous: returns a reference to the internal array

// we can use functions as arguments, for instance to find stuff within a stack:
function Stack_indexOf(X,f)       // f is the function that compares for identity
  {
  for(var i=this.A.length-1; i>=0; i--)
    if(f(X,this.A[i])) return i;
  return -1;
  }

// step 3: install the methods as properties of the prototype:
Stack.prototype.initStack = Stack_initStack;
Stack.prototype.isEmpty = Stack_IsEmpty;
Stack.prototype.top = Stack_Top;
Stack.prototype.pop = Stack_Pop;
Stack.prototype.length = Stack_length;
 // Stack.prototype.push = Stack_Push;
 // commented out in favor of the more powerful one
```

```
Stack.prototype.push = stk_push;
Stack.prototype.toString = Stack_toString;
 // Stack.prototype.toArray = Stack_toArray;
 // commented out because dangerous and violates encapsulation
Stack.prototype.indexOf = Stack_indexOf;
```

All this code hardly needs explaining. However, we hope that you read it carefully, because we use this very simple example to show the procedures and conventions for defining a class in JavaScript. The next example is more complex. It also illustrates two extremely important programming issues, and proposes a methodology for dealing with them.

Implementing the DisplayStack Class

The first issue that `DisplayStack` illustrates is code reuse through inheritance. `DisplayStack` is a kind of stack. The `DisplayStack` class extends the `Stack` class. It ought to be able to inherit all the properties of `Stack`. This is exactly what happens when we set the prototype of `DisplayStack` to be an object of class `Stack`. (Since all the properties of the `DisplayStack` prototype are copied to every `DisplayStack` object, every such object inherits all the properties of the `Stack`.) We then override the `push()` and `pop()` methods, incorporating the additional features of `DisplayStack`. (Recall that to **override** a method of the base class in a derived class means to give the derived class a method with the same name but a new definition.)

Computational Objects and Their "Views"

The additional features of `DisplayStack` illustrate another very general programming issue: how to establish communication between a computational object and its visual representation, or **view**. In the case of a `DisplayStack` in the Towers of Hanoi problem, this communication is one-way: the computational object needs to be able to inform its view of any changes that happen to it. (For instance, if an item is pushed on a `DisplayStack` object, it has to inform its view, so that the item appears in the associated table.) We will return to this issue in the `Calculator` example later in this chapter, where the computational objects have to process user input, and the communication is both ways. For now just take a note of how the communication from the object to the view is established: the `DisplayStack` constructor receives, as its first argument, the corresponding table's `ID`. Armed with this piece of information, it can refer to its view as:

```
var T = document.all[this.theTableID];
```

The Constructor

Speaking of the constructor's arguments, you may be surprised to discover that it has four of them:

```
function DisplayStack(theTableID,numRows,initFill,cellStyle){...
```

In `Hanoi1()`, you may recall, the lines that construct `DisplayStacks` have only two arguments, `theTableID` and `numRows`:

```
var A = new DisplayStack(ATableID,N);
```

This is a very common situation in JavaScript: you can supply fewer arguments than in the definition, and provide defaults for the missing arguments. How do you supply defaults? One technique would be to test the length of the arguments array. (Recall the discussion of the `arguments` property of the Function object in Chapter 2.) Another technique, which we use in the code of `DisplayStack`, relies on the fact that `undefined`, `null`, and the `empty string` all evaluate to false in the conditional test, so you can write code as follows:

```
this.initFill = initFill ? initFill : ".";
```

This says: if the `"fill"` string is supplied, use it as the value of the `initFill` property of the object; otherwise use the default value of `"."`. In this way, the constructor below provides the default number of rows for the table and the default style for its cells. Time to look at the constructor's code in full:

```
function DisplayStack(theTableID,numRows,initFill,cellStyle)
{
  this.theTableID = theTableID;       // no default for this argument
  this.numRows = numRows?numRows:8;   // if argument is not supplied, set to default
  this.initFill = initFill?initFill:"."; // same comment
  this.cellStyle = cellStyle?cellStyle:"A"; // same comment
  this.initStack();                   // create an array for the DisplayStack object
  this.init();                        // create the HTML table
}
DisplayStack.prototype = new Stack();   // inheritance!
```

As explained, the constructor begins by setting its properties, starting with `theTableID`, from the parameters it receives. All parameters except the first one are optional, in the sense that if these parameters are not specified, reasonable default values for the corresponding properties are provided. Once the properties are set, we call the `initStack()` method, which is inherited from `Stack`, and `DisplayStack`'s own `init()` method. The syntax is the same whether the object calls its own or inherited method.

The initStack() Method

A call on `initStack()` at this point is useful in two ways. The first is modularity of code. As we know, `initStack()` only sets the member variable A to be a new `Array`, but it could easily set other member variables of the `Stack` class for use by inherited `stack` methods. At the `DisplayStack` level, we wouldn't need to be aware of these. The value of `initStack()` is that it protects `DisplayStack` from having to know all the details of `Stack`, which may change in the future. Without such an initialization function, `DisplayStack` might have to be updated every time you added something clever to `Stack`.

Secondly, we need `initStack()` in order to give each `DisplayStack` object an array of its own. Note that right after defining the `DisplayStack()` constructor, but before the first time it's run, we set the prototype property of `DisplayStack` to a new stack. This gives the prototype all the properties of a stack, including an internal array A. However, we cannot depend on that array A because it is the same for every `DisplayStack` object. (The prototype object is unique for the class.) So, if we had to use the `Array` object in the prototype, it would be shared by every `DisplayStack` created by the constructor, and we couldn't have more than one `DisplayStack` per page. This is why we arranged for an `Array` object to be created by running `this.initStack` every time the constructor is called.

You may well ask why we don't have a similar `initDisplayStack()` method for setting all the member variables of `DisplayStack`. We would if we had any plans to derive other classes from it. We don't; but you may still want to write it as an exercise. If you do write an `initDisplayStack()` method, have it initialize all the local variables and also give it all the functionality that we've put in the `init()` method, which constructs the HTML table.

Why do we construct the table in the code rather than directly in HTML? The reason is that we want the size of the table to match the size of the Hanoi problem, specified by the user. We could omit the `init()` method if we established an arbitrary limit on the size of the problem and created an HTML table of that limit size directly in the page.

The init() Method

The `init()` method does a fairly common thing: builds a string that contains complete HTML code for the table it wants to construct, then sets the outerHTML of the table to be that string. Before it can be done, the method has to get a reference to the table. This is where `theTableID` property comes into play (see the last two lines of the code).

```
function dispStk_init()                              // initialize table
{
 var tblHTML = "<TABLE border=" + T.border + " id=" + T.id + ">\n";
 tblHTML += "\n<TBODY>";
 tblHTML += "<TH>" + this.theTableID + "</TH>\n";
 for(var i=0; i<this.numRows; i++)
  tblHTML += "\n<TR>\n<TD class=" + this.cellStyle + ">" +
             this.initFill + "<\/TD><\/TR>";
 tblHTML += "<\/TBODY><\/TABLE>";
 var T = document.all[this.theTableID];        // get its ID from the constructor
 T.outerHTML = tblHTML;
}
```

An aside and a warning: when we define "border" this way, we do assume that the page's HTML code is created with `"<TABLE border id=stkName>"` or perhaps `"<TABLE border=0 id=stkName>"` for a stack display with no borders. If you call this with no BORDER property, e.g. with `"<TABLE id=stkName>"`, you'll get an error because `"T.border"` will be undefined. We could avoid this by setting the border property for all tables in a stylesheet, or by using `((T.border)?1:0)`.

push() and pop()

Finally, we redefine `push()` and `pop()`, and assign the newly redefined methods to the corresponding properties of the prototype. Consider `push()` first:

```
function dispStk_push()                         // push arguments on stack, update table
{
 var T = document.all[this.theTableID];
 for(var i=0; i<dispStk_push.arguments.length; i++)
 {
  var x = dispStk_push.arguments[i];
  this.A[this.A.length] = x;
  var R = T.rows.length - this.A.length;
  if(R > 0)                                     // R==0 would be the header row
  {
   var theCell = T.rows[R].cells[0];
```

```
        theCell.innerHTML = x.displayName ? x.displayName() : x.toString();

    }
  }
. }
```

This code is largely self-explanatory, except perhaps for the last line. Its purpose is to create a text string representing object x on the stack, and place that string in the table cell. In the case of DisplayStacks A, B and C, our "object x" is just a number, and simply applying the toString() method to it would yield an appropriate string. However, it may happen that a DisplayStack will contain large objects, such that applying toString() to them would yield long strings, inappropriate for display in the table. In fact, the global DisplayStack S in Hanoi2 and Hanoi3 (coming up next) provides an example: in addition to numbers and strings, it contains DisplayStacks A, B and C. Our convention is that, in such situations, a displayName() method should be defined, which produces a compact textual representation of the objects that are put on the stack and displayed in the DisplayStack's table. In our program here, we have to give such a method to DisplayStack itself:

```
function dispStk_DisplayName()
{
  return this.theTableID;
}
DisplayStack.prototype.displayName = dispStk_DisplayName;
```

That's all there is to know about push(). The code for pop() is similar but simpler:

```
function dispStk_pop()
{
 var T = document.all[this.theTableID];
 var N = this.A.length - 1;
 var x = this.A[N];
 this.A.length = N;
 var R = T.rows.length - (N+1);
  if(R>0 || R==0 && !this.theTableID)            // was displayed
  {
  var theCell = T.rows[R].cells[0];
  theCell.innerHTML = this.initFill;
  }
 return x;
}

DisplayStack.prototype.init = dispStk_init;
DisplayStack.prototype.push = dispStk_push;
DisplayStack.prototype.pop = dispStk_pop;
```

This completes our first extended example of a class that is derived from another class and has a view attached to it, i.e. an HTML page element that serves as the visual representation for objects of the class. Another, more complete example is the Calculator class in the final section of this chapter. Readers who have seen enough of stacks and diamond pins may proceed directly to that section. Readers who would like to get a better feel for the internal workings of programs (how they call functions and why they sometimes run out of stack memory) are invited to work through the next section. Among other things, it will show you how to control the execution of your programs (slow them down, speed them up, stop and restart) which may be useful in writing animations. In short, the next section's material is admittedly tricky, but in productive ways.

Do-it-Yourself Recursion with Stack and setTimeout

Our Towers of Hanoi program is set up by default to do four disks. To do larger problems, specify the number of disks in the input text box, but don't get carried away: even a very fast computer with a lot of memory will take years to do a problem of size 64. On a personal computer, you will probably run out of patience and hit `Control-C` or `Command-.` at size 12. Chances are, you will run out of memory even before that because there will be too many recursive calls waiting on stack.

Did we say "stack"? Well, yes, deep down inside, every time a program makes a function call, whether recursive or not, information about it goes into an area of memory that operates as a stack: items are removed in the 'last-in-first-out' order. Why a stack? Because function calls within a program form a tree. It's the same idea of a linear sequence with sub-sequences and sub-sub-sequences that divide the main sequence without gaps or overlaps, except in this case the sequence unfolds in time, not in space. The running time of a program consists of function calls. If there is a function call within a function call, we suspend the mother function, put the information about the new call on the stack and stay with it until it returns; at that moment we pop its information off the stack. Running a program is like tree traversal: we start by putting the very first function call on the stack (it will be the `main()` function in a C program) and traverse the tree of procedure calls.

To prove that some such design will work, we're going to do a little experiment: we'll rewrite the Hanoi function so that its recursive calls, instead of passing arguments to each other, will put them on a stack, together with the instructions on what to do next when the call returns. These instructions, in our case, will be a text string, the text of instructions to carry out. When the function does return, we submit those instructions to a mechanism that can execute them. What kind of mechanism is it? In the case of compiled languages, this would be the CPU itself, whose job it is to execute the binary codes of a compiled program. In our interpreted language, we're dealing with the text of commands and language-internal constructs to put them into action. JavaScript has two such constructs, `eval()` and `setTimeout()`. (There's also `setInterval()`, but we don't use it in the book.) Both take a text string as an argument and run its contents:

```
var i = eval("15+10");            // i gets the value 25, a number
var j = setTimeout(1000,"15+10"); // after a second's wait, j gets the value 25
```

As you can see, `eval()` takes one argument, a string, and evaluates it as if it were part of a JavaScript program. `setTimeout()` does the same, but after waiting a specified number of milliseconds. Which one shall we choose for our program?

Well, our real purpose in rewriting Hanoi is to investigate different ways of controlling the program's execution. `Hanoi1()` used the crudest possible way of control: interrupt the execution with a confirm dialog. In this second version, we will use `setTimeout()` to slow things down so the user can watch the program's progress. We don't need a confirm dialog any more because we manipulate the stack of function calls ourselves, and therefore have a more intimate control over the program's execution. In the third and final version, we'll develop a construct that will let the user interrupt the program at will, and inspect the contents of the stack.

Hanoi 2

So this is what we're going to do. First, we declare a global variable for a stack that will hold function call information. The variable is declared outside any function calls and initialized in the main `Hanoi2()` function:

```
var S;          // will become a global stack displayed within "sTable"
```

The function `Hanoi2()` begins, as before, by creating DisplayStacks and initializing them. `DisplayStack A` is initialized, as before, to hold numbers 1 through N. `DisplayStack S` is initialized to hold the arguments for the initial call to `h2()`, and the action to perform when the initial call returns, which is `alert('done!')`. Finally `h2()` is called:

```
function Hanoi2(N,aTable,bTable,cTable,sTable)
{
  S = new DisplayStack(sTable,6*N," ","SS");        // for recursive calls
  var A = new DisplayStack(aTable,N);               // pin A, source
  var B = new DisplayStack(bTable,N);               // pin B, auxiliary
  var C = new DisplayStack(cTable,N);               // pin C, target
  for(var i=N; i>0; i--) A.push(i);
  S.push("alert('done!')",C,B,A,N);                 // arguments, in REVERSE ORDER
  h2();                         // was h1(N,A,B,C) in the recursive version
}
```

In order to understand what has happened and what's about to happen, it's useful to have the previous version in front of you. We repeat it here, with lines numbered and without the `confirm('ok?')` call:

```
(0) function h1(N,A,B,C)      // A, B, and C are DisplayStacks, N is number of disks
    {

2)     if(N==0) return;
(3)      h1(N-1,A,C,B);
(4)      moveTop(A,C);
(5)      h1(N-1,B,A,C);
    }
```

Every time `h1()` is called and before it exits, three calls on `h1()` are active: the original call, and two recursive calls in lines 3 and 5 that the original call generates. Correspondingly, there will be three calls on `h()` in the code that follows. Let's give them names so our discussion can keep them apart: we'll refer to them as `call-0`, `call-1` and `call-2` (lines 0, 3 and 5, respectively). In our new implementation, `h2()` no longer gets its arguments from the function that calls it. Instead, `h2()` has to get its arguments from the stack, and that's the first thing it does:

```
function h2(){                          // this is the implied call-0
  var N = S.pop();
  var A = S.pop(); var B = S.pop(); var C = S.pop(); // args from stack
  var ret = S.pop();
```

Once the arguments are available, `call-0` proceeds to check whether N is 0. If so, it runs the action stored in the variable `ret`, and returns. This will happen when all the other calls have been popped off the stack and the only thing left is the initial `alert('done!')` at the very bottom of the stack:

```
  if(N==0) { setTimeout(ret,100); return;}
```

Otherwise, `call-0` puts its arguments back on the stack, for eventual use by `call-2`, and gets into a sequence of actions equivalent to lines (3)-(5) of the recursive version. That sequence falls into two parts. The first is `call-1`, a call by `h2()` on itself with a different set of arguments (line 2). The second is the equivalent of lines (4)-(5), and constitutes the "action upon return" for the first part. We'll put the return action of `call-1` into a separate function, `h2b()`, and present its code in a moment. In the meantime, we put `h2b()` and the arguments for `call-1` on the stack:

```
S.push(ret,C,B,A,N);        // push arguments back for reuse in call-2
S.push("h2b()",B,C,A,N-1);  // push arguments and return action for call-1
```

The contents of the stack at this point are, from top down:

```
N-1,A,C,B,"h2b()",      N,A,B,C,ret, ...            rest of stack
[arguments for call-1]  [arguments for call-0]
```

This determines the order of computational events: before you can run the return action of the current call on h2(), you have to dispose of the (N-1,A,C,B) bunch of arguments, and run h2b(). The last line of h2() does exactly that:

```
setTimeout("h2()",100);
// this is call-1, which will use the arguments on top of the stack
```

This sets off another round of the same activity with a different set of arguments after a hundred milliseconds, but we don't have to follow it through. Sooner or later it will return (after moving a lot of disks around), and at this point h2b() will be called. What's h2b()? Let's take a look:

```
function h2b()              // h2() has returned from "h2(N-1,A,C,B)"
{
var N = S.pop();var A = S.pop();var B = S.pop();var C = S.pop();

// Note: these are the initial arguments of call-0; ret is now
// at the top of the stack
// Note: we DO NOT pop the ret action

moveTop(A,C);              // finally do some actual work
S.push(C,A,B,N-1);         // push arguments for call-2

// Note: we DO NOT push the ret action

setTimeout("h2()",100);    // this is call-2; it will return to wherever call-0
                           // would return
}
```

The difference between the way we treat two recursive calls, call-1 and call-2, is instructive. The first recursive call returns to some point in the middle of its mother-function. We therefore have to give it a fresh set of arguments and a return action, equivalent to the rest of the mother-function's code. The second recursive call is "tail-recursive": after it returns there's nothing left for the mother-function to do. It can therefore use the mother-function's arguments and return action, without any growth of the stack.

Try It Out

The code for this application uses the same two classes defined in stack.js and DspStack.js; the only new file is hanoi2.js, replacing hanoi1.js. To run the application, point your browser at hanoi2.htm, and click on the **startHanoi** button. To slow it down or speed it up, change the second argument to setTimeout() in all three places where it's called. Note that changes in delay time are not in proportion to the actual running time of the program, because of the overhead. In our testing, a ten-fold increase in delay time resulted in quadrupling of the running time.

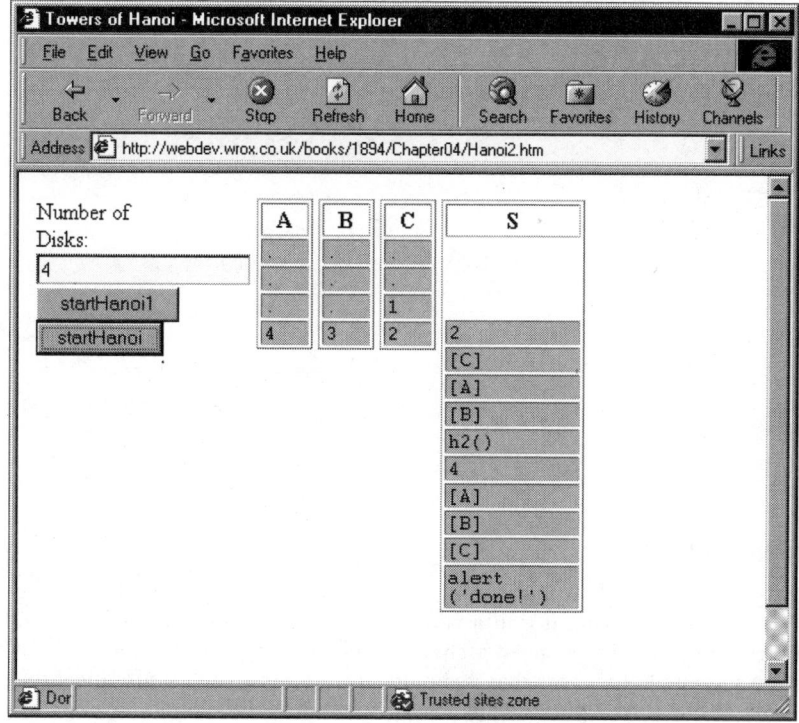

The program will work even if you set delay time to 0, because even with zero delay, the action of setTimeout() is delayed until other non-delayed actions are carried out. You will see this use of setTimeout() many times in later chapters, when we need to delay an action on a document until the browser has downloaded it completely.

How It Works

We've pretty much explained how this application works in the *Hanoi 2* section above. All that's left is to show the code in its entirety:

```
var S;        // GLOBAL stack displayed within "tallTable"

function Hanoi2(N,aTable,bTable,cTable,sTable){
 S = new DisplayStack(sTable,6*N," ","SS");     // for recursive calls
 var A = new DisplayStack(aTable,N);            // pin A, source
 var B = new DisplayStack(bTable,N);            // pin B, auxiliary
 var C = new DisplayStack(cTable,N);            // pin C, target
 for(var i=N; i>0; i--) A.push(i);
 S.push("alert('done!')",C,B,A,N);              // arguments, in REVERSE ORDER
 h2();                                // was h1(N,A,B,C) in the recursive version
}
function h2(){
 var N = S.pop();
 var A = S.pop();
 var B = S.pop();
 var C = S.pop();               // args
```

```
      var ret = S.pop();
      if(N==0) { setTimeout(ret,100); return;}

            // otherwise pushback args for use after call and return:

      S.push(ret,C,B,A,N);          // h2 is continuation after "h" returns.
                                    // so now we get ready to call "h" recursively:
      S.push("h2()",B,C,A,N-1);
      setTimeout("h()",100);
    }
    function h2(){                  // h has returned from "h(N-1,A,C,B)"
      var N = S.pop();
      var A = S.pop();
      var B = S.pop();
      var C = S.pop();
      moveTop(A,C);                 // finally do some actual work
      S.push(C,A,B,N-1);            // push arguments for call-2; DO NOT push ret action
      setTimeout("h()",100);        // this is call-2; it will return to wherever call-0
                                    // would return

    }
```

An Even Better Hanoi

`Hanoi2()` has a better control structure than `Hanoi1()`, but it's still far from perfect. As we promised, we're going to see what it would take to let the user interrupt the program, inspect its condition, and resume. Clearly, we need a channel of communication: the user clicks on a button, and the program somehow discovers that it should stop. In order for communication to be successful, the program must continuously poll the channel to see if the interruption message has arrived.

Our communication channel will be a property of the `Hanoi3()` function itself. The property, `delayTime`, will serve a dual purpose. If it is non-negative, it will specify the delay time for our calls on `setTimeout()`. A negative `delayTime` will serve as a signal for the program to stop.

The function that will continuously poll the value of `delayTime` to whether it's negative or not is called `hDelay()`. It takes one argument, a piece of code to be executed. If `delayTime` is non-negative, the `hDelay()` function will call `setTimeout()`, with two arguments: its own argument as the code to run and `delayTime`. If `delayTime` is negative, `hDelay` will simply put its argument on the stack, to be executed when the user restarts the program. In effect, `hDelay` simply refuses to proceed with a meaningless `delayTime` value.

How does the program get restarted? We use the same communication channel: the user clicks on a button, and two things happen: `delayTime` gets reset to a non-negative value, and the piece of code that's been waiting on the stack is popped and executed. In this case, we use `eval()` rather than `setTimeout()` because the user presumably doesn't want any more delays.

Try It Out

The code files for `hanoi3.htm` are the same as before, except that `hanoi3.js` replaces `hanoi2.js`. To try out this new version we added two new buttons, **stopHanoi** and **restartHanoi**. Otherwise, the page looks the same. Run the program, stop it at will, inspect the stack to satisfy your curiosity, then restart again. As a simple exercise, consider what would be needed to let the user either stop the program or quit it altogether without waiting for all the disks to reach their final destination.

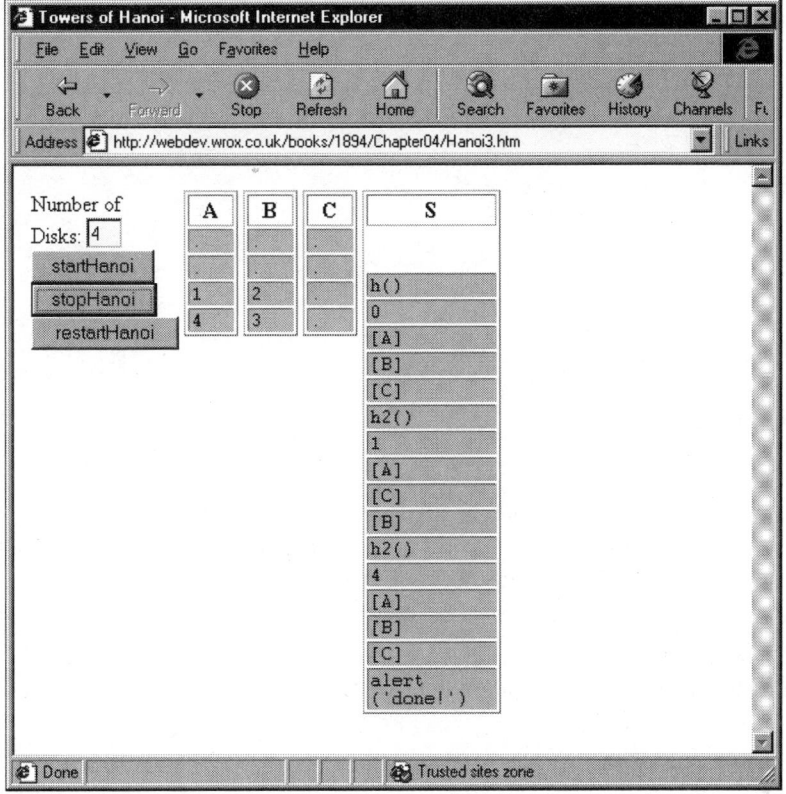

How It Works

The code for Hanoi3() is given below. For what it manages to achieve, it is remarkably simple and similar to the preceding version. We highlight the changes:

```
var S;    // GLOBAL stack displayed within "tallTable"
```

```
function hDelay(action)
{
 if(Hanoi3.delayTime >= 0) setTimeout(action,Hanoi.delayTime);
 else S.push(action);
}
function restartHanoi()//assigned to onclick handler of "restartHanoi" button
{
  Hanoi3.delayTime = 100; eval(S.pop());
}
```

```
function Hanoi3(N,aTable,bTable,cTable,sTable)
{
 S = new DisplayStack(sTable,6*N," ","SS");
 var A = new DisplayStack(aTable,N);
 var B = new DisplayStack(bTable,N);
 var C = new DisplayStack(cTable,N);
 for(var i=N; i>0; i--) A.push(i);
S.push("alert('done!')",C,B,A,N);
```

```
      Hanoi3.delayTime = 100;
      h();
    }
    function h3()
    {
      var N = S.pop(); var A = S.pop(); var B = S.pop(); var C = S.pop();
      var ret = S.pop();
      if(N==0) { hDelay(ret); return;}
      S.push(ret,C,B,A,N);
      S.push("h3b()",B,C,A,N-1);
      hdelay();
    }
    function h3b()
    {
      var N = S.pop();var A = S.pop();var B = S.pop();var C = S.pop();
      moveTop(A,C);
      S.push(C,A,B,N-1);              // the return address is underneath C;
      hDelay("h3()");
    }
```

Can the technique of this section be used elsewhere? The answer is yes. All we need is two variables to make it work: a place to store the variable that serves as a channel of communication, and a place to put the suspended code when the program is stopped.

This concludes our discussion of stacks for now. We're going to see stacks again in later chapters, when we do tree traversals of documents. A great deal of client-side web programming can be done by traversing the document tree and modifying or replacing its nodes.

Calculator

The final example of this chapter is the calculator. It imitates the functionality of the familiar hand-held device, except that you click on buttons with your mouse rather than push them with your fingers. It tries to look like a regular calculator, too, but if you don't like the way it looks, it's very easy to change. The calculator's appearance is controlled by a style sheet, its structure is an HTML table within an HTML form, and its behavior is determined by the methods of the `Calculator` class.

The Calculator Class

The public interface for the `Calculator` class consists of a constructor and several methods:

```
/*
Calc(cF)            // construct a calculator with the given HTML form
Calc.addFn(type,name,def)
                    // add function to the calculator;
                    // type can be Fn0, Fn1 or Fn2;
                    // type specifies the number of arguments: 0, 1 or 2
Calc.doKey()        // convert captured key press to string, send to doStr()
Calc.doClick()      // convert captured mouse click to string, send to doStr()
Calc.doStr()        // process information from doKey() and doClick()
Calc.reset()        // reset calculator to initial condition; everything cleared
*/
```

We ask (and answer) two questions about the calculator: "What can it do?" and "How does it do it?". The first question is about the computational capability: what functions does the calculator know about? We provide a method, addFn(), to add functions to the calculator, and use that method within the constructor to build the minimal initial functionality. The same method can be used outside the constructor, to add functionality to individual, customized calculators.

The second question is about processing: how does the calculator process the user's input? In brief, the doKey() and doClick() methods capture the input, convert it to string, and pass it on to doStr(), which does all the work. All this processing machinery is completely independent of the functions that make up the computational capability of the calculator: you can replace all the functions without changing anything in doStr().

The remaining reset() method initializes the properties that support the operation of doStr(). We present these properties as we go through the code, beginning with the constructor. The constructor goes through four steps:

- ❑ initializes the form and name properties;
- ❑ calls reset() to prepare for processing;
- ❑ initializes lists of functions;
- ❑ calls addFn() to add functions to those lists.

We present them in order.

Form and Name Properties

```
function Calc(cF)          // the view of a calculator is an HTML form
{
  this.calcForm = cF;      // the form becomes a property of the calculator
  Calc[cF.id] = this;      // the calculator itself can be found as Calc[cF.id]
```

These initial lines of the constructor set up the relationship between an internal object and the view it presents to the user. Either partner in this relationship needs to be able to refer to the other one. The object needs to refer to the view in order to obtain user input and show the results of calculations. The view needs to refer to the object because it's the view that captures the user events and sends them in for processing. For instance, the HTML form for our first calculator has this opening tag:

```
<FORM id=SimpC onkeypress="return Calc.SimpC.doKey()">
```

The event handler has to call the appropriate method of the object for which this form is the view, so it has to make a reference to that object. In the absence of pointers, this reference has to be the name of the object. What name should it be, and in what namespace? The pattern we use, whenever there is a one-to-one correspondence between the object and the view is: use the same name as the ID attribute of the view, stored on the property list of the constructor. So, if the calculator form's ID is "SimpC", its event handlers refer to the calculator object as Calc.SimpC. (This assumes that the calculator object and its view are in the same window or frame.)

JavaScript Objects

Reset and Function Lists

Returning to the constructor, the next two lines reset the calculator and initialize the list of functions it supports:

```
this.reset();              // set prevVal and curVal to 0, prevFn, etc.
this.Fn2 = ":"; this.Fn1 = ":"; this.fn0 = ":";      // lists of functions
```

The call on `reset()` sets up the properties used in processing the user's input; we'll get to them in a moment. For now, we concentrate on setting up the functions. A function, you recall, consists of a name, a list of arguments, and a definition. The arguments to calculator functions are provided by the user, with the following restrictions: each function takes a specific number of arguments and that number can only be 2, 1 or 0. The calculator object maintains three properties, `Fn2`, `Fn1`, and `Fn0`, which are colon-separated lists of functions of the corresponding type.

Adding Functions to the Calculator: Binary Operators

To add functions to the calculator, we give it an `addFn` method. It takes three arguments: the function type (`Fn2`, `Fn1` or `Fn0`), the function name, and the function definition. It adds the function name to the appropriate list and also associates that name with the definition:

```
function calc_addFn(type,name,def)
{
 this[type] += name + ":";
 this[name] = def;
}
Calc.prototype.addFn = calc_addFn;
```

Functions of two arguments include "+" and "*"; functions of one argument include "SqRt"; functions of no arguments include "Clear". We give one-argument functions precedence over two-argument functions, so that "5 + 4 SqRt =" will produce 7, not 3.

To work through an example, for the "+" operator, we would insert this line in the constructor:

```
this.addFn("Fn2","+",new Function("x,y","return x+y"));
```

At this moment, you may recall that we have, among the utilities of Chapter 2, a `binop` function that takes a binary operator as an argument and returns a JavaScript function that takes two arguments, applies the operator to them and returns the result:

```
function binop(op){return new Function("x,y","return x " + op + " y;");}
```

We can therefore simplify our calls on `addFn` as follows:

```
this.addFn("Fn2","+",binop("+"));
this.addFn("Fn2","*",binop("*"));
this.addFn("Fn2","-",binop("-"));
this.addFn("Fn2","/",binop("/"));
```

The operator that terminates a string of calculations and returns the result is "=". The meaning of this operator in the "Calculator language" is quite different from its meaning in JavaScript, and for this reason we don't define it using `binop()` (although we could, and it would work). We still have to define it as an `Fn2`:

```
this.addFn("Fn2","=",new Function("x,y","return y"));
```

Why can't we define it as an `Fn1`?

```
this.addFn("Fn1","=",new Function("y","return y"));
```

It would make more sense, but the peculiar rules of the "calculator language" make it impossible. In that language, all the unary operators are executed immediately, before any binary operators. So, with the `Fn1` definition, a sequence like 5+4= would produce 4, not 9. We want our "=" function to be evaluated after the preceding operator; in order for this to happen, it has to be an `Fn2`.

Functions of 1 and 0 Arguments

Our example of a one-argument function shows how to bring in the facilities of the `Math` object:

```
this.addFn("Fn1","SqRt", new Function("x","return Math.sqrt(x)"));
```

To make this into a scientific calculator, you would add many more mathematical functions using the methods of the `Math` object.

Finally, we add a zero-argument `Clear` function which resets everything to the initial condition by calling `this.reset()`.

```
this.addFn("FnClr","C",new Function("","this.reset()"));
```

Notice that we place the call on `reset()` in the body of a new Function definition, as if the new Function object is a method of our calculator. Well, if you inspect the code of `addFn()` you'll see that by the time the function is called, it will indeed be a method of the `Calculator` object, and can call its other methods.

This completes our discussion of the constructor. Let's now look at the object in operation. We begin by trying it out.

Try It Out

The stylesheet file for the calculator application is **calc.css**; the JavaScript files are `calc.js` and `arrUtils.js` (for `binop` only). In the body of your page, place the following code:

```
<FORM id=SimpC onkeypress="return window.Calc.SimpC.doKey()">
<INPUT TYPE=TEXT id=curVal VALUE="0" class=Entry> <BR>
<TABLE id=theCalcTable onclick="window.Calc.SimpC.doClick()">
<TR> <TD class=Num> 7 </TD> <TD class=Num> 8 </TD>
  <TD class=Num> 9 </TD> <TD class=Fn2> + </TD> </TR>
<TR> <TD class=Num> 4 </TD> <TD class=Num> 5 </TD>
  <TD class=Num> 6 </TD> <TD class=Fn2> - </TD> </TR>
<TR> <TD class=Num> 1 </TD> <TD class=Num> 2 </TD>
  <TD class=Num> 3 </TD> <TD class=Fn2> * </TD> </TR>
<TR> <TD class=Num> 0 </TD> <TD class=Fn0> C </TD>
  <TD class=Eq> = </TD> <TD class=Fn1> SqRt </TD> </TR>
</TABLE>
</FORM>
<SCRIPT> new Calc(SimpC); </SCRIPT>
```

As you can see, the calculator is a fairly straightforward form, with an input text box and a table of cells to click on. Your page should look similar to the one below, testable from our website:

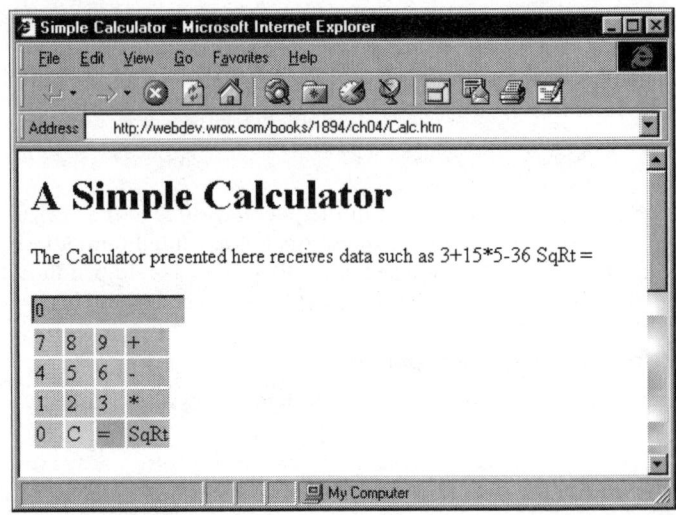

Try entering a sequence of numbers and operators, e.g., 2 + 3 * 4 =. Everything including the last = can be either clicked in using the mouse or typed from the keyboard. The result for this expression will be 20, because our calculator does what all calculators do: evaluates expressions with binary operators from left to right, without regard for precedence. (Nor can you use parentheses to indicate grouping; our calculator doesn't know parentheses.) However, if you try 25 - 9 SqRt =, the result should be 22: SqRt, like all unary functions, is evaluated first.

How It Works

Since we have already discussed the constructor and the addFn() method, we'll go straight to the next function, which is reset(). To understand reset(), consider what the calculator needs to know in order to process the simplest input, 2 + 3. The values of 2,"+", and 3 have to be stored somewhere so that if the user continues with "=", the sum of 2 and 3 can be computed and entered as the result. On the other hand, the program has to know not to do any calculations yet because the user may continue with another digit. In other words, the program doesn't yet know the value of the second argument to "+", but it does know the first argument because that sequence of digits was already terminated by the function name.

It looks as if we have identified four items (and so we need four variables):

- ❏ previous value: the value that has already been determined but not yet used in calculation
- ❏ previous function: a binary operator that is waiting for its second argument
- ❏ current value: the value that appears in the text box of the form
- ❏ mode: are we in the middle of numeric data input, or ready for new numeric data

Of these, the current value appears in the text box of the form and can be kept in the JavaScript variable for that text box. The other three will be properties of the Calculator object. All four appear in the reset() function.

```
function calc_reset()
{
  this.prevValue = 0;        // previous value is set to 0
```

```
    this.prevFn = "=";              // previous function is set to "=";
                                    // everything's cleared
    this.calcForm.curVal.value = "0"; // value of the HTML form element.
    this.mode = "newIn";            // we're ready for new input
    this.calcForm.curVal.focus();   // set focus where the user wants it
    }
    Calc.prototype.reset = calc_reset;
```

Now, let's set it all in motion. As far as the calculator is concerned, there are just two events that matter, a mouseclick and a keypress. In either case, an event object is generated, a property of the window. What we need from that event object is a string, either a one-character string that corresponds to the pressed key, or the string that's sitting in the clicked-upon table cell. Once we get the string, we pass it to doStr() and get out.

```
    function calc_doKey(){          // pass a keyboard key on to calc_doStr
     var kc = window.event.keyCode;
     this.doStr(String.fromCharCode(kc));
     return false;
    }
    Calc.prototype.doKey = calc_doKey;

    function calc_doClick(){        // pass an HTML keyclick key on to calc_doStr
     var e = window.event.srcElement;
     if(e.tagName!="TD"){alert("clicked on a "+e.tagName);return true;}
     this.doStr(e.innerText);
     return true;
    }
    Calc.prototype.doClick = calc_doClick;
```

This code is pretty much self-explanatory. Obviously, programmers have to do this sort of thing often, and the designers of the language thoughtfully put all the machinery in place. For a keypress, we get the event's keyCode property and pass it to the right String method. For a mouseclick, we get to the source element of the event and retrieve its innerText property. The only complication is that the user's finger may twitch and the click will fall on the border between two cells. What's the program to do? Well, a click on the border is not a click on any particular cell (it's considered a click on the table), so we can check for the tag name of the clicked element, and if it's not TD, we'll exit right away.

Actually, there is one more complication that the previous paragraph is trying to gloss over (but we won't let this happen). For some reason, doKey() returns false while doClick() returns true. Why the difference? Because in the case of doKey() we want to stop the event from bubbling up the document tree, and that's what returning false does. In IE4-specific code you would say, more transparently, cancelBubble=true. We use that mechanism elsewhere in the book, but Calculator is otherwise cross-browser, and we decided to keep it that way.

But the question remains: why do we want to stop event bubbling in the case of doKey() but not doClick()? Notice that calc_doClick is only attached to theCalcTable within theCalcForm, and is not activated by a click on the input text box. calc_doKey, however, is attached to the form as a whole; it is activated by a key directed at the table or at the input box. If you change calc_doKey to return true, you'll see that a keypress directed at the table still works (click on the table to direct focus, then press a key), but digits typed directly into the input box appear twice each, once via calc_doKey and once via the default handler. Having calc_doKey return false avoids this.

With `doKey()` and `doClick()` explained, we can finally work through `doStr()` which does all the real work. Basically, it inspects the string that it gets from `doKey()` or `doClick()`, checks the condition of the calculator object, and dispatches the right action. Here's the code:

```
function calc_doStr(S)
{
 var SS = ":" + S + ":";               // if S is a function, :S: is on a function
list
 var fV = this.calcForm.curVal;
 with(this)
  {
  if(0 <= Fn2.indexOf(SS))             // a binary function, like "+"
   {
   prevValue = this[prevFn](prevValue,parseFloat(fV.value,10));
   fV.value = "" + prevValue;
   prevFn=S; mode="newIn";
   }
  else if(0 <= Fn1.indexOf(SS))        // a unary function, like "SqRt"
   {
   fV.value = "" + this[S](parseFloat(fV.value,10));
   mode = "newIn";
   }
  else if(0 <= Fn0.indexOf(SS))        // a 0-argument operation
   {
   this[S]();
   }
  else                                 // data: a digit or a "."
   if (mode == "addIn")                // previous input was data also
     fV.value += S;
   else {mode = "addIn"; fV.value = S;}
  }
}
Calc.prototype.doStr = calc_doStr;
```

The big question is whether we're dealing with a function or a data item (`digit` or `"."`). Remember that all the functions of our calculator are kept on three colon-separated lists. So, we check our string against each list in order, and if it is found, we dispatch the appropriate function call. (This is where you should appreciate the convenience of treating functions as first-class objects: when you need them, you retrieve them from the data structure in which they are stored, and make your call.) If the string is not a function, then we check the mode: if it's `addIn`, we append the new input, otherwise we set the value of `curVal` to be the new input, and set the mode to be `addIn`.

Here's the `Calculator` class code all together, for your reading pleasure:

```
function Calc(cF)           // every calculator has an associated calcForm
 {
 this.calcForm = cF;        // the form on which the calculator works
 this.name = cF.id;         // if the form's id is A1,
 Calc[cF.id] = this;        // "onclick" handlers call me Calc.A1
 this.reset();              // set prevVal and curVal to 0, prevFn &c
 this.Fn2=":"; this.Fn1=":"; this.Fn0=":";     // lists of functions

 // use addFn, defined later, to add functions to the calculator
 this.addFn("Fn2","+",binop("+"));
 this.addFn("Fn2","*",binop("*"));
 this.addFn("Fn2","-",binop("-"));
 this.addFn("Fn2","/",binop("/"));
 this.addFn("Fn2","=",new Function("x,y","return y"));
```

```
  // a one-argument function using the Math object
  this.addFn("Fn1","SqRt", new Function("x","return Math.sqrt(x)"));

  // add a "Clearing" function of no arguments
  this.addFn("Fn0","C", new Function("","this.reset()"));
}

function calc_reset()
{
  this.prevValue = 0;                    // properties of a function
  this.prevFn = "=";
  this.calcForm.curVal.value = "0";  // value of an HTML form element.
  this.mode = "newIn";                   // we're ready for new input
  this.calcForm.curVal.focus();
}
Calc.prototype.reset = calc_reset;

function calc_addFn(cl,name,def)
{
  this[cl]+ = name + ":";
  this[name] = def;
}
Calc.prototype.addFn = calc_addFn;

function calc_doKey()               // pass a keyboard key on to calc_doStr
{
  var kc = window.event.keyCode;
  this.doStr(String.fromCharCode(kc));
  return false;
}
Calc.prototype.doKey = calc_doKey;

function calc_doClick()             // pass an HTML keyclick key on to calc_doStr
{
  var e = window.event.srcElement;
  if(e.tagName != "TD"){alert("clicked on a "+e.tagName);return true;}
  this.doStr(e.innerText);
  return true;
}
Calc.prototype.doClick = calc_doClick;

function calc_doStr(S)
{
  var SS = ":" + S + ":";           // if S is a function, :S: is on a function list
  var fV = this.calcForm.curVal;
  with(this)
  {
  if(0 <= Fn2.indexOf(SS))          // a binary function, like "+"
    {
    prevValue = this[prevFn](prevValue,parseFloat(fV.value,10));
    fV.value = "" + prevValue;
    prevFn=S; mode="newIn";
    }
  else if(0 <= Fn1.indexOf(SS))     // a unary function, like "SqRt"
    {
    fV.value = "" + this[S](parseFloat(fV.value,10));
    mode = "newIn";
    }
  else if(0 <= Fn0.indexOf(SS))
```

```
    {                              // a "clear" operation
  this[S]();}
  else if (mode == "addIn")        // data; probably a digit or a ".".
  fV.value += S;
  else {mode = "addIn"; fV.value = S;
  }
  }
}
Calc.prototype.doStr = calc_doStr;
```

Extending the Calculator

To extend the calculator, you need to add functionality to the `Calculator` object and the corresponding visual elements to the HTML form. In this section, we will do some extending ourselves, after that you're free to experiment on your own. We add two kinds of functions: a mathematical function and two evaluating functions. What's an evaluating function for? We want the user to be able to type any well-formed JavaScript expression into the calculator and have it evaluated. So, we add another input box to the calculator for typing expressions in, and a button that calls `eval()`. Unlike the initial input box, you can type any legal JavaScript in the new one, including function calls.

We also thought it might be educationally instructive if we provide a `calcEval()` function that evaluates the way calculators do: from left to right, without regard for operator precedence. So, in addition to a "V" button that calls the built-in `eval()`, we provide a "CV" button that calls `calcEval()`. Now you can type any arithmetic expression (without parentheses!) into the new input box, and see how its values differ depending on the evaluating function.

Finally, we provide a new mathematical function, `factors()`, which takes one argument and finds its prime factors. Since we have a new text box, we arrange to have the result of factorization placed into that box, separating the factors by the "*" character. If you then press the "V" or the "CV" button (doesn't matter in this case) you will see the initial number back in the `curVal` input box.

Try It Out

The new calculator needs three things:

- new functions defined and added to `calc.js`
- a new form in the body of the page
- a couple of lines of JavaScript code following the new form, to create the `Calculator` object and add new functions to it

If you're not a function-code-writing type, ask your programmer friend to do it for you, but we hope that you can add the lines in the body of the page yourself. (In fact, a good way to interact with your programmer friend may be for you to decide what you want first, produce the page the way you want it, then tell your programmer friend to go and write those functions.) Here is what the form and accompanying code look like.

0				
0				
7	8	9	+	C
4	5	6	-	V
1	2	3	*	CV
0	.	=	SqRt	F

```
<FORM id=C2 >
<INPUT TYPE=TEXT id=evalStr VALUE="0" class=Entry> <BR>
<INPUT TYPE=TEXT id=curVal VALUE="0" class=Entry
     onkeypress="return window.Calc.C2.doKey()"> <BR>
<TABLE id=theCalcTable onclick="window.Calc.C2.doClick()"
       onkeypress="return window.Calc.C2.doKey()">
<TR> <TD class=Num> 7 </TD> <TD class=Num> 8 </TD>
  <TD class=Num> 9 </TD> <TD class=Fn2> + </TD> <TD class=Fn0> C </TD> </TR>
<TR> <TD class=Num> 4 </TD> <TD class=Num> 5 </TD>
  <TD class=Num> 6 </TD> <TD class=Fn2> - </TD> <TD class=Fn0> V </TD> </TR>
<TR> <TD class=Num> 1 </TD> <TD class=Num> 2 </TD>
  <TD class=Num> 3 </TD> <TD class=Fn2> * </TD> <TD class=Fn0> CV </TD> </TR>
<TR> <TD class=Num> 0 </TD> <TD class=Num> . </TD>
  <TD class=Eq> = </TD> <TD class=Fn1> SqRt </TD> <TD class=Fn1> F </TD> </TR>
</TABLE>
</FORM>

<SCRIPT>
 new Calc(C2);           // the name of the calculator is the ID of the form
 Calc.C2.addFn("Fn1","F",factors);
 Calc.C2.addFn("Fn0","CV",calcEval);
 Calc.C2.addFn("Fn0","V", JSEval);
</SCRIPT>
```

How It Works

Since we have not installed the new functions into the prototype, they have to be added after the form is created. The rules for creating the calculator and adding the functions are as follows. First, you create a new calculator object, with the same name as the ID of the form. Second, you add functions using addFn(). The three arguments to addFn() are:

- ❑ Fn2, Fn1 or Fn0, depending on whether the new function takes 2, 1 or 0 arguments
- ❑ the label of the table cell for the new function
- ❑ the name of the new function

The code for the new functions we have added is given below:

```
function factors(N)
{
 var A = new Array();
 while(N%2==0){A[A.length]=2; N=N/2;}
 var lim = (Math.sqrt(N));
 for(var i=3; i<=lim && N>1; i+=2)
   while(N%i==0)A[A.length]=i; N=N/i;}
 if(N>1)A[A.length] = N;
 this.calcForm.evalStr.value = A.join("*");
 return N;
}
function calcEval()
{
  var V = this.calcForm.evalStr;
  var A = V.value; this.reset();
  for(var i=0; i<A.length; i++)this.doStr(A.substring(i,i+1));
  this.doStr("=");
}
function JSEval(){with (this.calcForm) curVal.value = eval(evalStr.value);}
```

The `factors()` function does its mathematical thing and puts the prime factors into an array. We then join the contents of that array with the `"*"` character, which gives us exactly the expression we want.

The `JSEval()` function is a one-liner that sends the contents of the `evalStr` text box to the built-in `eval()`, and stores the result in the `curVal` text box.

The `calcEval()` function uses a simple trick: it takes the string that's in the `evalStr` text box and pretends to enter it character by character. In other words, it submits that string, one character at a time, to the `doStr()` function. Note that this only works with digits and single-character operators like `"*"`; you couldn't enter `"SqRt"` this way. (It's a good exercise to try and fix `doStr()` so that you could.) In the end, `calcEval()` calls `doStr()` with the `"="` argument, forcing the evaluation.

Summary

In this chapter, we have made a very important advance: we've learnt what OOP is and how to do it in JavaScript. You can now argue for or against inheritance in contradistinction to aggregation, and debate the virtues of polymorphism and dynamic binding. More importantly,

- ❑ you now have a toolkit of procedures for building reusable components (classes)
- ❑ you have learnt how to extend a component (class) to build a more specialized component (derived class)
- ❑ you now have two simple but useful components, `Stack` and `DisplayStack`, and you've learned how stacks are used in computing
- ❑ you have learnt how to establish a connection between an internal computational object (an instance of a class) and its view, i.e., its visual representation in the web page
- ❑ finally, you now have a simple calculator that you can extend to suit your mathematical needs

We're well-positioned to begin building larger classes and more substantial applications.

5

Tree-Structured Data and the Tree Controller

Introduction

This chapter will be about trees, tree-structured data, and tree controllers. Tree-structured data is anything that's organized as a tree hierarchy. In Chapter 3, we mentioned family trees, classification trees, and the tree of elements in an HTML page. To these we now add tree-structured directories and document outlines. The applications you will work with in this chapter all start by collecting some tree-structured data into a tree object. Once the tree is constructed, the application associates a tree controller with it. A tree controller is a GUI (**Graphical User Interface**) element for convenient access to tree structured data. One example of a tree controller is a directory browser such as the Macintosh Finder or the Windows Explorer. Another example is the outline view of a MSWord document that contains several levels of headers. In fact, our first application will automate the process of constructing an outline for HTML documents with several levels of header elements, H1 to H6. Our second application will automatically show the directory structure of local links within a web site map.

In summary, these are the main topics of the chapter:

- ❑ trees and tree addresses;
- ❑ design of the `TreeController` class;
- ❑ the Table of Contents application;
- ❑ implementation of the `TreeController` and `Tree` classes;
- ❑ programming issues: recursion and timing;
- ❑ the SiteMap application

In terms of tangible results, we will develop two general classes, `Tree` and `TreeController`, and several more specific classes that can be customized in various ways. We'll do a lot of tree traversals, decorating the nodes with HTML markup. Our old friend the `Stack` will be constantly at our side. We will build two applications: **Table of Contents (TOC)** and **SiteMap**. The emphasis will be on good class relations and code reuse.

Try It Out

Point your browser at `http://webdev.wrox.co.uk/books/1894/chapter05/toc1.htm`. You will see a page with two frames in it. The right frame contains a document with subdivisions. The left frame contains a table of contents for that document. The table of contents was constructed on the fly when you opened the page. If you replace the document with another one, the table of contents will reflect the new document, as long as you use `<Hn>` tags (where n = 1 . . 6) for marking your section headers.

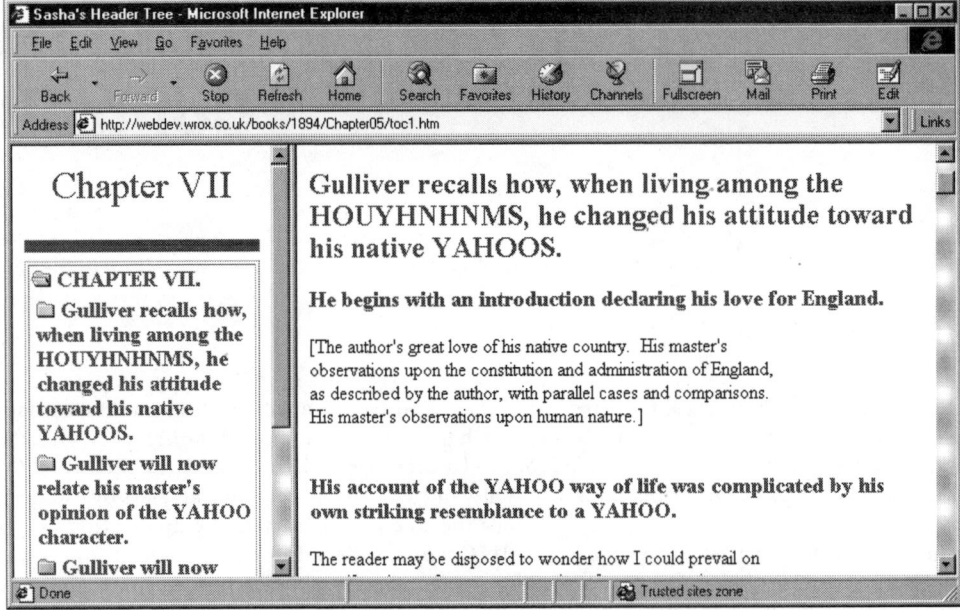

Tree Controller

A tree controller allows you to expand or collapse tree nodes by clicking on them. Each node also contains a brief title which serves as a link to the corresponding node in a body of tree-structured data somewhere. The point of a tree controller is that it gives you an overview of and convenient access to tree-structured data.

Examples of Tree-Structured Data and Applications

Where would the data come from? Well, once you start looking, you'll see tree-structured data all over the place-from the contents page of this book through to your own family tree. One obvious case is a list (a <UL> element in the page) that has sublists, and sublists of sublists. If you have such a structure in your web page, you can associate it with a tree controller, so the user can expand or collapse sublists. Or you can put your tree controller into a separate frame and make every node in it a link to the corresponding sublist in the document frame. The user can jump to the right place in the document frame by following a link in the tree controller. This is beginning to look like a table of contents for your list of sublists, and indeed, our next application will be a table of contents, with an important twist: the table of contents will be automatically generated.

Suppose you're writing a long text that consists of sections, subsections and sub-subsections - up to six levels deep. Each section and subsection will have to have a number or a title, perhaps both. Let's assume that the tags for the titles come from the <Hn> family of tags, where n is 1 to 6. Our application will extract the tree structure of the table of contents from your document, associate with a tree controller, and place it in a separate frame. This will automate the process of creating and maintaining a table of contents.

Our second application will be a site map generator. It will only work on well-organized sites, of the kind that are all contained in one directory, with subdirectories for various departments, divisions and subdivisions. (They may be virtual subdirectories but this is unimportant for our purposes.) Our application will extract all the links in your site and separate external links to other sites from local ones, within the site. The local links, sorted, will give us a listing of pathnames that reflects the directory structure of the site, which is, of course, a tree. This is the tree that the application will build and associate with a tree controller. Clicking on a node in the tree controller will take the user to the corresponding file or directory on the site.

The applications we've described all have a similar structure. A data collection process recursively traverses a body of tree-structured data and collects it into a tree object. Once the tree object is constructed, the application associates a tree controller with it which contains links to the original data. The only data-specific parts of the application are those that have to do with the data collection routine and the onclick handlers that connect the controller to the data. The rest of the application should (and will) be in reusable classes, so that new such applications can be easily constructed.

HTML Design

In terms of code, a tree control will be an automatically generated HTML page that contains nested <UL> elements. The nested <UL>s will recreate the tree structure of the data for which they serve as an outline. Each <UL> element in the tree controller page, together with the associated title, will represent a tree node in the data. We will talk about such a title-<UL> pair as **a node in the tree controller**.

Tree Controller Nodes

In more detail, each node in the tree controller will have the following structure:

- ❑ a title, i.e., some textual label which is also a link to the data. Let's assume it's H4.
- ❑ an image that will toggle between the "open" and "closed" condition.
- ❑ for non-leaf (end) nodes, an arbitrary number of children, similarly structured.

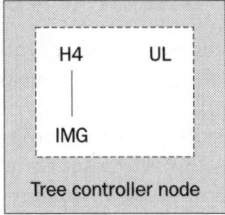

Tree controller node

Note that the <UL>s will not contain any list items (<LI> elements), only titles and embedded <UL>s. In other words, we're not using the <UL> tag in its direct function, but solely because of its "recursive ability": a <UL> element can contain other <UL> elements. This is precisely what we need in order to represent tree nodes whose children are also tree nodes.

Tree Controller Nodes and HTML Elements

Note the tricky mismatch between tree-controller nodes and the tree structure of the HTML elements of the page. Each tree controller node consists of two elements that are **siblings** in the HTML tree. Consider a small tree and the corresponding tree of tree-controller nodes. (To reduce clutter, <IMG> elements inside <H4>s are not shown.)

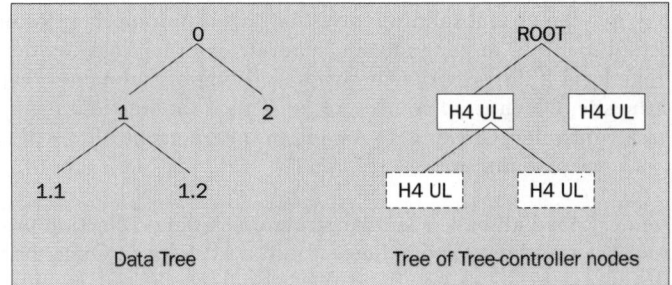

Data Tree   Tree of Tree-controller nodes

In terms of HTML structure, the tree controller looks like this:

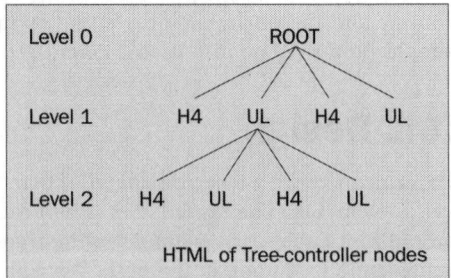

HTML of Tree-controller nodes

We will return to this diagram in the next section, after we present the complete HTML code for the page. Right now, we'll address the question of why things are set up in such a way. Why couldn't we put the title node inside the matching <UL> node and have the tree-controller structure mirror the HTML structure in a more transparent way? The answer is that we want to be able to click on the image inside the title and have matching <UL> close, so that its contents become invisible–but we want the title and the image to remain visible. Therefore the title has to be a sibling, not a child, of its matching <UL>.

Open and Closed Nodes

When we close a node, its children will have to disappear, and reappear again when the node is opened. To make this happen, we give the following style specifications to `<UL>`:

```
UL.open {display:block}
UL.closed {display:none}
```

The Title and Image

The title will be a text element of some sort. It doesn't particularly matter what element the title is because its appearance will be controlled by a stylesheet; it could be a paragraph or any of the `<Hn>` elements. For now, as we said, we'll be putting all our titles into `<H4>`s. The image will be contained within the title, so, the node for section 1, in its closed state, will have this HTML markup:

```
<H4 ...>
 <IMG SRC='close.gif' ...>
 Title of section 1
</H4>
<UL class=closed ...> ...children nodes... </UL>
```

Event Handlers

Both the title and the image need an `onclick` event handler. Clicking on the text of the title should result in a hypertext jump somewhere: to a nested list, to an anchor in the document, or a page in the web site. Clicking on the image toggles the condition of the node between open (expanded) and closed (collapsed). Looks like we'll need two functions, `clickHdr()` and `toggle()`, to handle the clicks. (Coming up soon!)

In order for a tree controller to do its job, every element of the node needs to know the node's position in the tree. The image needs to know the position of the node it is associated with, so that the onclick handler of the image can find the node's list of children and tell it to show or hide itself. The list of the node's children needs to know the node's position so that it can be found by the onclick event handler. The title needs to know the node's position so it can find the corresponding node in the tree structure of the data, and tell it to scroll into view. We have to develop a way to refer to nodes in a tree as easily as we can refer to elements in an array, so the first methods we'll look at for our Tree class will be for moving around from one node of a tree to another.

Tree Addresses

You can think of an array as a function or mapping from integers 0, 1, ... to values stored in the array: you give the array an integer, it gives you back a value. Trees are not linear, so we need more than a single integer to identify a node in a tree. What we need is a way to represent a path from the root to a node. We'll adopt the same kind of period-separated sequences of numbers that are used for numbering sections in a multi-level outline: the first child of the root is given number 1; the second child of the third child of the root is numbered 3.2, and so on. We call such numberings **tree addresses**. The "numbers" in tree addresses are not, of course, numbers: in terms of data types, a tree address is a string. However, it's easy to take it apart and extract numbers from it. Once the numbers are extracted, various tree-related tasks can be easily performed. Here are a few examples:

Parents, Children, Siblings

Given a tree address of a node, how do you find the address of its parent and its nth child? Easy: you just have to remember that `substring()` takes as its second argument the position right after the desired substring. In our case, it's the position of the last occurrence of "." in the tree address:

```
function parentAddr(addr)
{
  return addr.substring(0,addr.lastIndexOf("."));
}

function nthChildAddr(addr,n){ return addr + "." + n;}
```

How do you find the "child number" of the node? This is a little more work because we have to convert a string to an integer:

```
function chNum(addr)
{
 var chA = addr.split(".");
 var N = chA.length;
 return parseInt(chA[N-1],10);
}
```

We can combine these little utilities to get the tree address of the next sibling of a node:

```
function nextSibAddr(addr)
{
 var nextSibNum = chNum(addr)++;
 return parentAddr(addr) + "." + nextSibNum;
}
```

Get Subtree at a Given Address

We've been going from address to address, but how do you get the node itself, if you know its address? Here's how; all the tools we need are by now familiar:

```
function getSubTree(ob,addr){           // get subtree at a given address
  if(addr == "") return ob;
  addr = addr.split(".");               // split string into array: "1.2" => ["1","2"]
  for(var i=0; i<addr.length; i++)
   addr[i]=parseInt(addr[i],10)];       // convert strings to decimals
  for(var i=0; i<addr.length; i++)
   ob = ob.children[addr[i]];           // walk down the tree
  return ob;
}
```

We can make the code more compact (and more opaque) by combining the two `for` loops in it into one, as follows:

```
function getSubTree(ob,addr)            // get subtree at a given address
{
 if(addr == "") return ob;
 addr = addr.split(".");                // split string into array
            // walk down the tree converting strings to decimals as you go
 for(var i=0; i<addr.length; i++)
   ob = ob.children[parseInt(addr[i],10)];
 return ob;
}
```

This function, rewritten as a method of the `Tree` class, will be used a great deal in all `TreeController` applications.

Tree Addresses in the Tree Controller

Suppose we're building a tree control for a tree that has four nodes, in addition to the root. The tree numbers are 1, 1.1, 1.2 and 2; think of them as:

Chapter 1
Section 1.1
Section 1.2
Chapter 2.

How can we build into a "node" of the tree controller the tree address of the corresponding node in the tree? We'll use the id attribute of the `<H4>`, `<IMG>` and `<UL>` tags in the node. If the node's address is 1.2, then the id of its title element will be `hd1.2`, the id of its image will be `im1.2`, and the id of its list of children will be `ul1.2`. To extract the tree address from an id, we take its `substring(2)`, i.e., everything from the third character on. Given the tree address of a node and a global reference to the tree, we can get to the node and do something with it: color it red or make it scroll into view.

The HTML code

We can now show the HTML for our small tree controller in all its detail.

```
<BODY>
<H4 name='hd1' onclick='clickHdr(this)'>
 <IMG name='im1' SRC='close.gif' onclick='toggle(this,event)'>
 Title of section 1
</H4>

<UL class=closed id='ul1'>

  <H4 id='hd1.1' onclick='clickHdr(this)'>
   <IMG id='im1.1' SRC='close.gif' onclick='toggle(this,event)'>
   Title of subsection 1.1
  </H4>
  <UL class=closed id='ul1.1'> </UL>

  <H4 id='hd1.2' onclick='clickHdr(this)'>
   <IMG id='im1.2' SRC='close.gif' onclick='toggle(this,event)'>
   Title of subsection 1.2
  </H4>
  <UL class=closed id='ul1.2'> </UL>

</UL>

<H4 id='hd2' onclick='clickHdr(this)'>
  <IMG id='im2' SRC='close.gif' onclick='toggle(this,event)'>
  Title of section 2
</H4>

<UL class=closed id='ul2'> </UL>
</BODY>
```

The HTML tree structure of the page is shown below, together with the fully decorated tree of tree-controller nodes. Note that the second tree needs a dummy root, because we assume that the document is divided into main parts by `<H1>` headers. Each one of them will become the root of a tree, but they themselves need a root. We'll revisit this detail in the section where we implement the tree controller class.

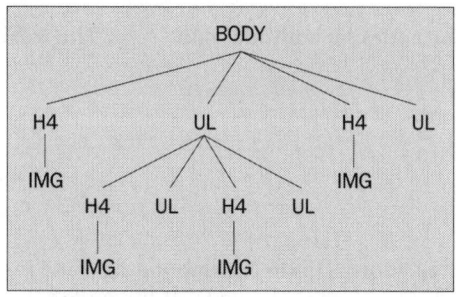 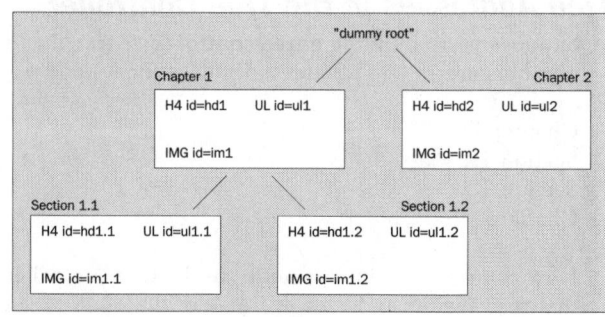

Generating HTML code

The HTML code for a tree controller is extremely repetitive. Writing this sort of code by hand is a boring task prone to errors. We're going to automate it. Notice the recursive structure of the code: to build a tree controller for a tree, you write down the controller node corresponding to the root (including the image and the title), then open the `<UL>` tag and (recursively) construct controller nodes corresponding to the children of the root before the closing `</UL>` tag. We'll do exactly that in our `consControl()` function described shortly. But first we have to get ourselves some tree to work on.

A Simple Demo

In our two main applications (TOC and SiteMap), the tree structure is hidden in the HTML code of the page, in the arrangement of header elements or the text of local links. Before we can construct a tree controller for it, we have to extract the tree structure from HTML text and place it into a tree object. For our Simple Demo, we'll construct a tree controller for a page that is itself structured very obviously as a tree, so that we can postpone writing a tree extraction routine and the `Tree` class. In other words, the HTML page for which we'll construct a tree controller will itself consist of nothing but nested `<UL>`s, with a paragraph of text added here and there. The main reason we're putting additional text inside the `<UL>`s is to make the document longer than a screenful; this will let us show how embedded elements at the bottom are scrolled into view. (But read that text anyway, it tries to be helpful.)

Try It Out

Point your browser at `simpdemo.htm`. When the page opens, you'll see a table of one horizontal row with two cells. The cell on the right has a nested unordered list, with titles and some content. The cell on the left is initially empty except for a button that says "Analyze". Click on the button, and the program will create an outline of the data in the right cell. The outline is a tree controller. Clicking on the icons opens and closes subnodes; clicking on a title makes the corresponding subnode red and scroll into view.

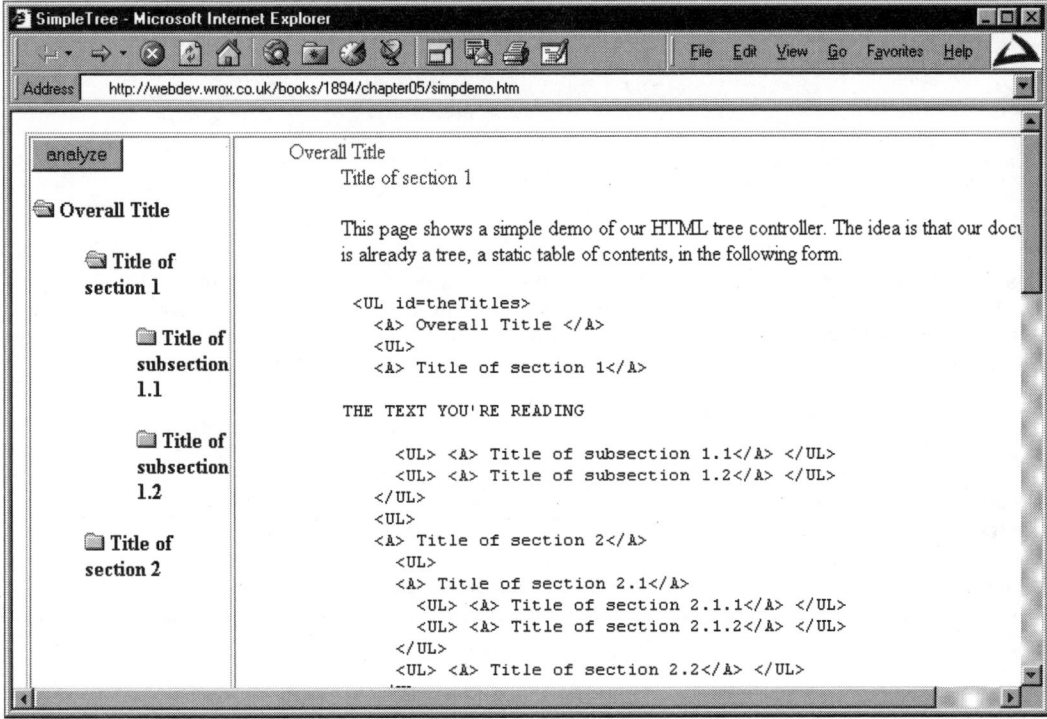

How It Works

The left cell of the table in the Simple Demo page contains an `<A>` element whose name is
"`theStruct`". Initially, it has no content except for a short notice that says that its contents will be
replaced by the `analyze()` function. The function, triggered by a button in the same cell, is a two
liner. The first line builds the HTML code for a tree control, the second makes that code
`theStruct`'s innerHTML:

```
function analyze()
{
  var S = consControl(document.all['theTitles'],''); // build tree control
  document.all['theStruct'].innerHTML = S;            // show it in "theStruct"
}
```

As you can see, all the work is done by the `consControl()` function that "constructs" the control. It
is one of those functions, very common in JavaScript, that return a long string of HTML code to be
inserted into a web page. Putting together a long string with quotes within quotes can be a messy and
confusing affair. We're trying to reduce the messiness by following a simple principle: break the
string to be constructed into meaningful parts and compose each part separately, and then,
concatenate the parts. In the case of `consControl()`, we have to construct an HTML text similar to
the sample that we created by hand. It consists of code for the title element (containing an image and
the text of the title) and the list of children. Our function will construct three strings, one for the
image, one for the title, and one for the list of children. Its overall structure is like this:

```
function consControl(ulOb,tAddr)
{
// first some preparatory steps, then:
var imStr =... // construct code for image
var hdStr =... // construct code for title containing code for image
var ulStr =... // construct code for list of children
var S = hdStr + ulStr; return S;
}
```

The "preparatory steps" mentioned in the comment place the children of ulOb into an array chA, put the length of that array into N, and return the empty string if N==0. Constructing imStr and hdStr is completely straightforward, just be careful with single quotes within double quotes. Constructing ulStr requires a recursive call within a for loop, to construct the code for the children. We're ready to look at the entire function, broken into parts corresponding to the outline above:

```
function consControl(ulOb,tAddr){    // recursively build controller for UL
var chA = ulOb.children;             // array of the node's children
var N = chA.length;
if(N == 0) return "";                // returns innerHTML for ulOb
var tag = "H4";                      // or any other text tag
```

This ends the preparatory steps; imgStr next. Recall that if the node's address is 1.2, then the id of its title element will be hd1.2, the id of its image will be im1.2, and the id of its list of children will be ul3.2. For the imgStr, we construct the id attribute, then SRC, and finally onclick:

```
var imgStr="<IMG id='im"+tAddr+
    "' SRC='close.gif' onclick='toggle(this,event)'> ";
```

For hdStr, we begin by constructing its tag (such as <H4>), followed by the id and onclick attributes. We then insert the imgStr, followed by the innerHTML of the first child of our node:

```
var hdStr=" <"+tag+" id='hd"+tAddr+"' onclick='clickHdr(this)'> "+
    imgStr+
    chA[0].innerHTML + " </"+tag+">\n ";
```

The ulStr is perhaps the trickiest of them all because it includes a for loop which includes a recursive call on consControl() to construct a tree controller node for each of the children:

```
var ulStr = "<UL class=closed id='ul"+tAddr+"'>\n ";       // start UL
for(var i=1; i<N; i++)          // recursively consControl nodes for children
  ulStr += consControl(chA[i],tAddr ? tAddr + "." + i:"" + i); ulStr += "</UL>\n
";          // close UL
```

Finally, put everything together and return:

```
var S = hdStr + ulStr;
return S;
}
```

The rest of our **Simple Demo** consists of three functions that are common to all tree controller applications: getSubTree() which finds a subtree given its tree address, and the onclick handlers for the image and the title. We've already seen getSubTree(); time to inspect the handlers.

The Event Handlers

Both handlers begin by finding the tree address of their "node." The first handler, `clickHdr()` needs it to get to the corresponding data. Once there, the handler makes the data turn red and scroll into view:

```
function clickHdr(hdr)                    // get from tree controller to tree
{
 var tAddr = hdr.id.substring(2);
 var ob = getSubTree(document.all['theTitles'],tAddr);
 ob.children[0].className = "clicked";   // make it red
 ob.children[0].scrollIntoView(true);    // scroll it into view
}
```

The `toggle()` function needs its tree address to get to its own `<UL>` partner within the tree controller. Once the partner is found, toggling the class name and the image source is trivial, but there's one more thing to do. We don't want the click to bubble up to the title element that contains the image, so we cancel the bubbling of the event. (This is why `toggle()` has an event argument.)

```
function toggle(imageObj,ev)
{
 ev.cancelBubble = true; var tAddr = imageObj.id.substring(2);
 var ul = document.all['ul'+tAddr];
 if(!ul) {alert("help, no list for image " + imageObj.id); return;}
 if(ul.className == "closed")
   {ul.className="open"; imageObj.src='open.gif';}
 else
   {ul.className="closed"; imageObj.src='close.gif';}
}
```

This concludes our discussion of the **Simple Demo**. Many of the pieces you have seen in this section will repeat, almost without any changes, in the classes and applications that follow.

The Table of Contents Application

Our **Simple Demo** has helped us develop some of the tools we'll need for our real goal, a table of contents application. It will use the `Tree` and `TreeController` classes and some application-specific code. We will present application-specific code first, by tracing its operation. We will look at the complete interface and the implementation of the classes after we work our way through the code that uses them.

Try It Out

In this section, you can try a different version of the **TOC** application in `toc2.htm`. It shows a document in a single frame, with a title and multiple headers. If you click on the title or on the line underneath the title, the window will split into two frames and the left frame will show the document's table of contents. Clicking on the title or on the green line again, in either frame, will restore the single-frame view.

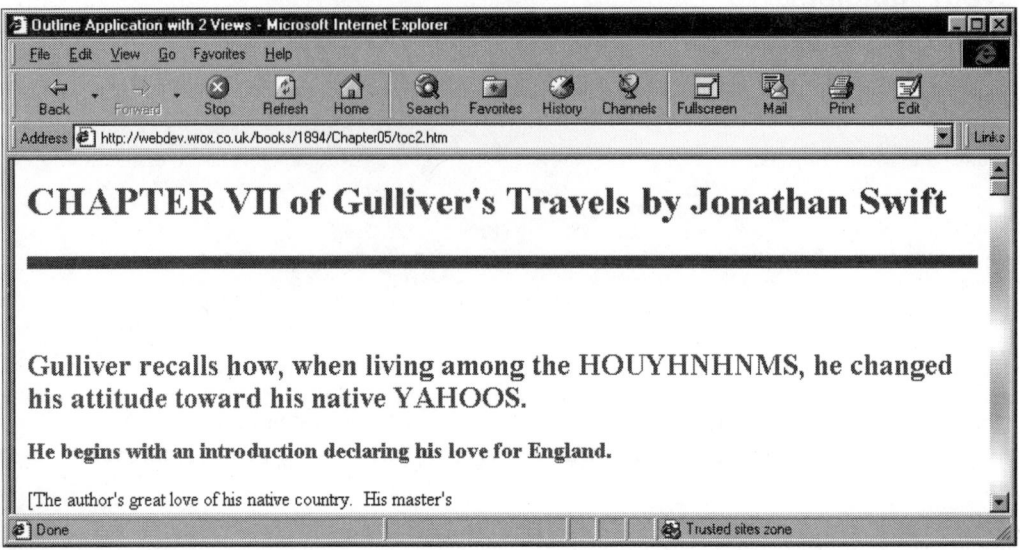

In order to use this interface with a document of your own, you need to do two things. First, open the file `toc2.htm` and replace the source for the **dframe** with your document. Second, make sure that some element at the top of your document (it can be a horizontal line or a button or a paragraph) has the following attribute:

```
onclick="top.switchFrames();"
```

Clicking on that element will toggle between the single frame and the outline views. If you'd like to see a visual clue, as we have done, you can give the same element a style attribute:

```
style="cursor:hand"
```

How It Works

Explaining how this application works will take a couple of sections. First we will explain the workings of the HTML and JavaScript of the interface. Then we'll look at application-specific code that collects a tree of headers and sets up a tree controller. Finally, we'll look at the interface and implementation of the `Tree` and `TreeController` classes.

The Interface and Possible Customizations

The application consists of three HTML files, three code files, and three image files to show open nodes, closed nodes and leaf nodes without children. The HTML files are `toc2.htm`, `tocframe.htm` and `docframe.htm`.

The Frameset File

The first of these is a frameset page with frames for the document and its table of contents. It also contains JavaScript code for switching between single-frame and outline views. The frameset part of the page is totally unremarkable, except that it initially allocates 0% to the tree control frame on the left.

```
<FRAMESET cols="0%,100%">
  <FRAME name="cframe" src="tocframe.htm">
  <FRAME name="dframe" src="docframe.htm">
</FRAMESET>
```

Switching between views is accomplished by switching the column widths of the two frames between `"0%,100%"` and `"35%,*"`. Here is the JavaScript code:

```
function switchFrames()
{
 var config = top.document.body.cols;
 if(config == "0%,100%")
 {
  if(switchFrames.firstTime)
  {
   headerController(
     top.cframe.document.all['hdrControl'],
     top.dframe.document.body);
   switchFrames.firstTime = false;
  }
  top.document.body.cols = "35%,*";
 }
 else (top.document.body.cols = "0%,100%");
}
switchFrames.firstTime = true;
```

Notice that we use a static variable, `switchFrames.firstTime`, to avoid recreating the table of contents every time the user switches frames. (Refer back to Chapter 2 for a discussion of static variables that preserve value across function calls, in the section concerning Functions as Objects.) That computation is done only once, in the call to `headerController()`. We'll get to that function after we finish with the HTML files.

The function `switchFrames()` is embedded in the HTML code of `toc2.htm` as shown below:

```
<HTML> <HEAD> <TITLE> Outline Application with 2 Views </TITLE>
<SCRIPT SRC = "../utils/stack.js">  /* stack class */  </SCRIPT>
<SCRIPT SRC = "dumtree.js">  /* simple tree class */  </SCRIPT>
<SCRIPT SRC = "treecon.js">  /* tree controller class */  </SCRIPT>
<SCRIPT SRC = "Shdrtree.js">  /* header tree code */  </SCRIPT>
<SCRIPT>
function switchFrames(){
/* see code above */
}
switchFrames.firstTime = true;
</SCRIPT> </HEAD>
/* see FRAMESET above */
</HTML>
```

Four code files are included. The first three contain the code for our old friend `Stack` and our two new friends, `Tree` and `TreeController`. These files have no application-specific code, and are therefore reusable, while all the specific code is contained in `hdrtree.js`. (This is where `headerController()` lives.)

The Document Frame

The `docframe.htm` file contains your document. As we said in the *Try It Out* section, it needs a visual element that would serve as a toggle between views. We provided two such elements. (Remember that virtually every HTML 4.0 tag has event-handler attributes.)

```
<HEAD> <TITLE> Document with Headers </TITLE>
<STYLE>
 H1 {color:red}
 H2,H3,H4 {color:brown}
</STYLE> </HEAD>
<BODY>
<P style = "text-align:center;font-size:x-large"
   onclick = "top.switchFrames();"> The Long Title </P>
<HR style = "height:10;color:green;cursor:hand"
   onclick = "top.switchFrames();">
```

We are using the `<P>` tag rather than `<H1>` for the title because we wanted to use `<H1>` for major divisions of the text, and we didn't want the title as a major division. Fortunately, `<P>`, like most other tags, has a style attribute, and we can make it look as good as an `<H1>` or even better.

Note that the onclick event handler refers to its function as `top.switchFrames()`. This assumes that the document and the tree control live in sibling frames, one level below the top frame. If this assumption is incorrect, you'll have to revise the reference. The code for the tree controller uses a user-supplied variable, `fDepth` (frame depth), to construct an absolute reference to the tree controller.

The Control Frame and Its Style Sheet

The main requirement on the control frame document is that it must contain an HTML element whose ID is used in the call on the `headerController()`:

```
headerController(
    top.cframe.document.all['hdrControl'],
    top.dframe.document.body);
```

We chose that ID to be `hdrControl` but it can be anything as long as the function call refers to the element correctly. It is that element that will contain the table of contents. You can use any text tag for it. In this application, we use plain `<DIV>`:

```
<DIV id=hdrControl showTAddrs=0 titleTag=H3>
  table of contents goes here </DIV>
```

The attributes we give to the element that will hold the tree controller specify the details of its appearance. Do you want tree addresses shown together with section titles? If so, set `showTAddrs` to 1, otherwise set it to 0. Do you want any specific tag for section titles? Make that tag the value of the `titleTag` attribute. If you leave that attribute out, the titles will show in the same header tags in which they appear in the original document. You can, of course, provide a style sheet for those tags to make them look the way you want them, which may be different from the browser default or from the style you set for them in the top frame.

Another use for the style sheet is to control the appearance of the `<UL>` elements in the outline. The default leaves large spaces between; we personally prefer a tighter placement within a table cell with a border. Change our margins if you wish, to match your taste and screen resolution.

Application-Specific Code

Enough delays and promises: it's time to discuss the real JavaScript internals of the application. We'll start by watching them in motion, as we untangle the sequence of actions triggered by the call on `headerController()`. Recall that the `headerController()` function was called in `toc2.htm` (and `toc1.htm`) with two arguments:

```
headerController(
    top.cframe.document.all['hdrControl'],
    top.dframe.document.body);
```

The first argument is the object that will contain the tree controller, and the second argument is the object that contains the text to be analyzed. That text doesn't have to be the entire document, as in `toc2.htm`. If you want an outline only for a part of your document, make that part into, for instance, a `<DIV>` element, give that element an ID attribute (e.g., `myTxt`), and change the second argument to `headerController()` to be:

```
top.dframe.document.all['myTxt']
```

So, what does `headerController()` do?

The Function headerController() and Supporting Cast

It should be no surprise to you by now that the function is defined with more arguments than the two you've seen:

```
function headerController(controlOb,srcDoc,fDepth)
{
  if(headerController.arguments.length < 3) fDepth = 1;    // set default
  var hTree = getTopHeaderTree(srcDoc);
  var TC = new TreeController(controlOb,hTree,clickHdrTree,fDepth);
}
```

The third argument, `fDepth`, specifies whether the document, its outline and the application code are in the same frame or in different frames. If you set it to 0, they will all live in the same frame. If you set it to 3, the code will be three frame levels up from the document and its outline. The default is 1, as in `toc2.htm`, with the code in the frameset header and two frames for the document and outline.

After taking care of the default value for `fDepth`, the function does its job in two lines of code, as transparently as we could make it. The first line extracts the `Tree` object from the document using the application-specific `getTopHeaderTree()` function. The second line constructs a `TreeController` object. And that's it, we're done.

The constructor for the `TreeController` takes four arguments. Two of them come from the arguments to `headerController`: the object in which the controller will live, and `fDepth`. The other two are the newly-constructed tree and an onclick handler. The handler is almost the same as in the **Simple Demo**. The only change is that the data element of the document is found in the tree node property called label, and it's that element that we scroll into view. (We decided not to change its color.)

```
function clickHdrTree(h){        // passed to TreeController constructor
 var tAddr = h.name.substring(2);
 var T = this.theTree.getSubTree(tAddr);
 T.label.scrollIntoView(true);
}
```

Clearly, there's more to say about the constructor for the `TreeController` class, but let's finish with the application-specific code first.

Tree Collection Code

Tree collection is a recursive process. It's a kind of a tree traversal. At every moment, there is the current node that we have to build a subtree for. As long as it has children, we (recursively) build their subtrees and add them to the tree for the current node. When there are no more children, we return the finished subtree. This is done in the `makeHeaderTree()` function. Its only argument is a traverser object `HG` (HeaderGetter). It has a property called `current` that holds the current node of the emerging tree. We start the tree collection process by storing `HG.current` in a local variable `item` and creating a new `Tree` object with `item` as root.

```
function makeHeaderTree(HG)
{
// build subtree for header HG.current and its children
 var item = HG.current;
 var T = new Tree(item);
```

The next line calls for a little suspension of disbelief because we haven't yet seen the code for the `TraverserOb` class, but clearly it has a method `getNext()` that somehow extracts the next `<Hn>` element from the text and makes it the current one. (You will see the code for `TraverserOb` later in the chapter.)

```
HG.getNext();    // find next header, make it the value of HG.current
```

Now we have to decide whether that next element is a child of the `item` or not. How do we decide? The children of `<H1>`s are `<H2>`s, the children of `<H2>`s are `<H3>`s, and so on. The design decision we have to make is whether we should allow the user to skip a level and, for instance, have an `<H4>` immediately following an `<H1>`. If we do allow such "level skipping," then the test of whether the current header is a child of item is simply:

```
while(hdrLevel(HG.current) > hdrLevel(item))
```

Otherwise, it would be:

```
while(hdrLevel(HG.current) - hdrLevel(item) == 1)
```

In any event, we need a function that extracts the "level" of the header. Since it's a one-liner, we'll give it right here, before returning to `makeHeaderTree()`:

```
function hdrLevel(ob){return (!ob)?-1:parseInt(ob.tagName.charAt(1),10);}
```

Resuming `makeHeaderTree()`, you can see from the code below, we decided it was unreasonable to insist on a rule that many users would find overly restrictive:

```
  while(hdrLevel(HG.current) > hdrLevel(item))
    T.addChild(makeHeaderTree(HG));
  return T;
}
```

As long as the next header is a child of the item, we recursively call `makeHeaderTree(HG)` to build a subtree for it and add it as a child to the new tree `T` we're building. In the end, we return `T`. Note that so far we have not made many assumptions about the `Tree` class, only that it has a constructor and an `addChild()` method which takes a tree and attaches it as the rightmost child to the tree object that calls the method.

Here is the code for `makeHeaderTree()` all together:

```
function makeHeaderTree(HG){
// build subtree for header HG.current and its children
  var item = HG.current;
  var T = new Tree(item);
  HG.getNext();          // find next header, make it HG.current
  while(hdrLevel(HG.current) > hdrLevel(item))
// while HG.current is child of item, build a subtree for it
    T.addChild(makeHeaderTree(HG));
  return T;
}
```

Starting off the Collection Process

That's all well and good, you can say, but our main function, `headerController()`, did not call on `makeHeaderTree()`, it called on `getTopHeaderTree()`. Yes, that's true, and the reason is that we have to create all the props for our recursive process before we can start it off. There are two props involved. One is a new traverser object that does the hard part, looking for the next header element in the HTML page. The other prop is a dummy root of the tree. Our assumption is that the document is divided into main parts by H1 headers. Each one of them will become the root of a tree, but they themselves need a root. So, we create a totally fictitious new object called `dummy`, we give it a `tagName` property, as if it's an HTML tag, and we set it to H0. Then we make it the current node of the traverser object. (The next section explains the role of the current property of the traverser object.)

```
function getTopHeaderTree(ob){
// return tree of headers under dummy root H0
  var HG = new TraverserOb(ob,isHeader);      // HeaderGetter
  var dummy = new Object();
  dummy.tagName = "H0"; HG.current = dummy;
  var T = makeHeaderTree(HG);
  return T;
}
```

The TraverserOb Class

The traverser object has only one purpose in life: find the next header element within the HTML object that is given it, and make it the current header. So we give it a single method called `getNext()`. Every time `getNext()` is called we get into an infinite loop (but we provide two escapes from it). We start the loop by asking: "Is your stack empty yet?". If the stack is empty, there's nothing else to do, and there's no node to make current, so we set current to null and return that. (When you return an assignment expression, what you return is the assigned value.)

```
  if(this.Stk.isEmpty())return this.current = null;
```

If the stack is not empty, we pop the top element and put its children on stack, in right-to-left order so that the leftmost child is on top. Then we inspect the popped element: is it a header? If it is, then it becomes the current one and we return it. Otherwise, we start on the top element of the stack, if any.

```
function travOb_Next()
{
 while(true){
   if(this.Stk.isEmpty())return this.current = null;
   var x = this.Stk.pop();
   for(var i=x.children.length-1; i>=0; i--)
     this.Stk.push(x.children[i]);
   if(this.p(x))return this.current = x;
   }
}
```

The only thing left is a traverser constructor. The traverser needs three items: an HTML object to work on, a predicate to do the checking, and a stack. The first two are arguments to the constructor. The stack is created new, and the starting object is pushed on it.

```
function TraverserOb(ob,p)
{
  this.Stk = new Stack();
  this.Stk.push(ob);
  this.p = p;
}
TraverserOb.prototype.getNext = travOb_Next;
```

That's all there is to the traverser object. Although we've discussed it in the context of the headers application, it is not really application-specific because its "application-specificity" is entirely contained in the predicate argument to its constructor. It can thus be used to construct any tree out of the elements of an HTML document. It would make a good exercise to reuse the traverser object in an application that constructs a tree of embedded <DIV> elements, and as usual, a suggested solution is available from our website.

To finish up, we do need an application-specific predicate that would check whether a given HTML object is a header. This is best done using a regular expression match:

```
function isHeader(ob)
{
  if(!ob) return false;          // null is not a header
  return ob.tagName.match(/^[hH][1-6]$/);
// match "beginning, then 'h' or 'H', then '1'..'6', then end"
}
```

The TreeController Implementation

Our next big project is to implement the TreeController class. As we work through the implementation of `TreeController`, refer back to two earlier sections. One is the **Simple Demo** section in this chapter. The onclick handlers and the function that constructs the innerHTML of the controller are discussed there in a simpler context. The other is the sections on `DisplayStack` and `Calculator` in Chapter 4. `TreeController` is a view class, providing a GUI to a computational object. Everything we said in Chapter 4 about the problems of communication between a computational object and its view applies to the case of `Tree` and `TreeController`, and the solutions we use here are very similar to those we developed in Chapter 4.

The Constructor and Initalization

The constructor for the `TreeController` class receives up to five arguments. The first of them is the HTML element whose innerHTML will be the `TreeController` object under construction. As in `DisplayStack`, the ID attribute of that HTML element becomes the name of the `TreeController` object, and the object itself is stored under that name as a property of the constructor. This happens in the first three lines of the constructor:

```
/* treecontroller class */
function TreeController(theOb,theTree,clickFn, fDepth,showTop){
  this.theOb = theOb;

// must have "ID" property, may have showTAddrs=1, titleTag=...

  this.name = theOb.id;
  TreeController[this.name] = this;
```

The reason, as before, is that the event handlers will need to find the tree controller object, and so we need its name stashed away where we can easily find it. Watch how this happens in the calls on `toggle()` and `consControl()`.

In addition to the ID property, `theOb` may have its `showTAddrs` property set to 1 and its `titleTag` property set to some HTML tag to format the title. You've seen them at work in the **TOC** application.

Proceeding with the constructor, the rest of the arguments are simply copied to the properties of the object. A default is provided for `fDepth` in case it is not specified. That default, as you remember from the **TOC** application, means that the tree controller will live in a frame one level below the top.

The default for `showTop` is false, so no special provisions are necessary. (If the argument is not provided, its value is undefined, which evaluates to false in conditional contexts.) What's `showTop` for? If it's false, it means that there is a dummy root node which will not be shown, as in the **TOC** applicaton. If it's true, the user must provide a title for the root node. Again, see `consControl()` for how this argument is used. Here's the rest of the constructor:

```
  this.theTree = theTree;
  this.clickFn = clickFn;
  if(TreeController.arguments.length == 3) fDepth = 1;      // default
  this.fDepth = fDepth;              //frame-depth for controller HTML
  this.showTop = showTop;           // false if dummy header is used
  this.init();                      // build controller, add info to tree.
}
```

JavaScript Objects

The last line of the constructor calls on the init() method which does the real hard work of initialization. This consists of building an absolute reference to the controller and the controller itself:

```
function tc_init()
{               // builds path and controller
  this.path = '';
  for(var i=0; i<this.fDepth; i++)this.path += 'parent.';
  this.path += "TreeController." + this.name + ".";
  var TC = this.consControl(this.theTree,"");
  this.theOb.innerHTML = TC;
  this.setULs(this.theTree,this.theOb);
}
```

The absolute reference, constructed in the first three lines, finds the tree controller by its name, buried in a frame fDepth levels deep. The innerHTML for the tree controller is then constructed by a call on consControl(). Finally, we call on yet another initializing function, to set up communication from each node of the tree to the corresponding "node" of the tree control:

```
function tc_setULs(tree,ob)
{
  tree.ul = ob;              // a UL element of 0 or more Hd-UL pairs
  for(var i=0; i<tree.numChildren(); i++)
    tc_setULs (tree.getNth(i),ob.children[1+2*i])
}
```

This is one of those transparently recursive functions that make trees so easy to work with. It says, very simply: "do something to the root, then recursively call me on all the children so I can do the same to each child and their children if any, until all are done". In this case, what we do to the root is set its ul property to be the HTML object of the tree controller. To do the same to the children means to find each child of the root in the tree and the corresponding <UL> element of the controller. We use getNth(i) method of the tree to find the ith child. In the controller, we reach for the child number [1+2*i] in the HTML tree. To see why child number i in the tree corresponds to child number [1+2*i] in the tree controller, consider a diagram similar to those in the section on the HTML design of the tree controller.

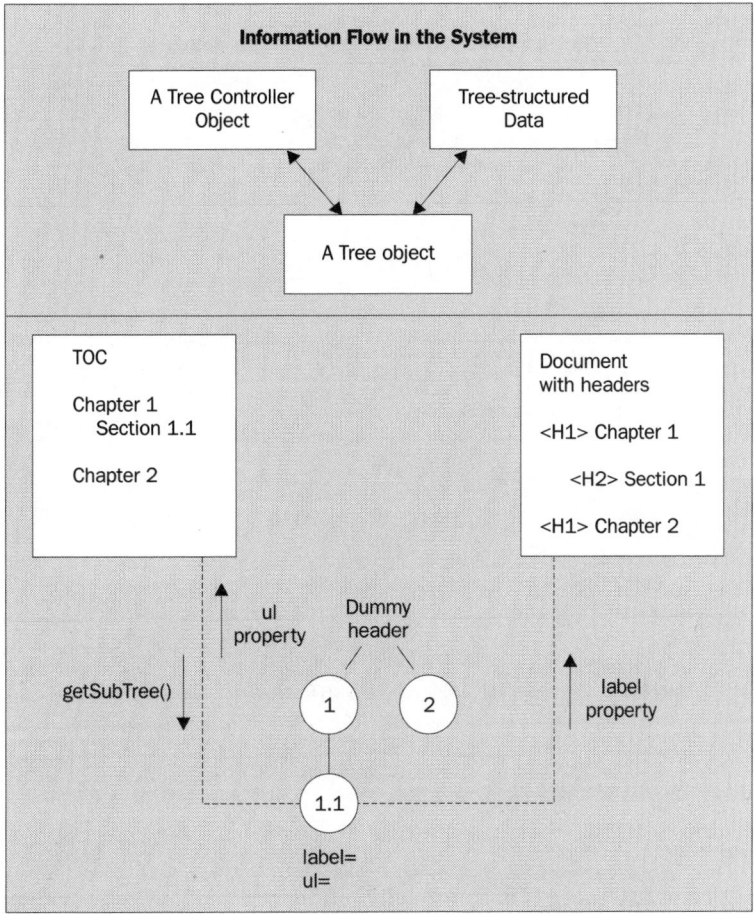

Note that we number the nodes in the data tree and the tree controller beginning with 1, but the elements of the HTML children array are numbered from 0. So, the <UL> element for the first child node is children[1], and you add two for each subsequent node.

The HTML Code and the Handlers

We're sort of done, but we really aren't because the main part of constructing a TreeControl object is to construct its HTML, together with whatever snippets of JavaScript it has to contain. This is all done in the consControl() method which parcels out some of its work to consTitle(). Before we take them apart, let's recall the big picture of the flow of information between tree structured data, the tree, and the tree control.

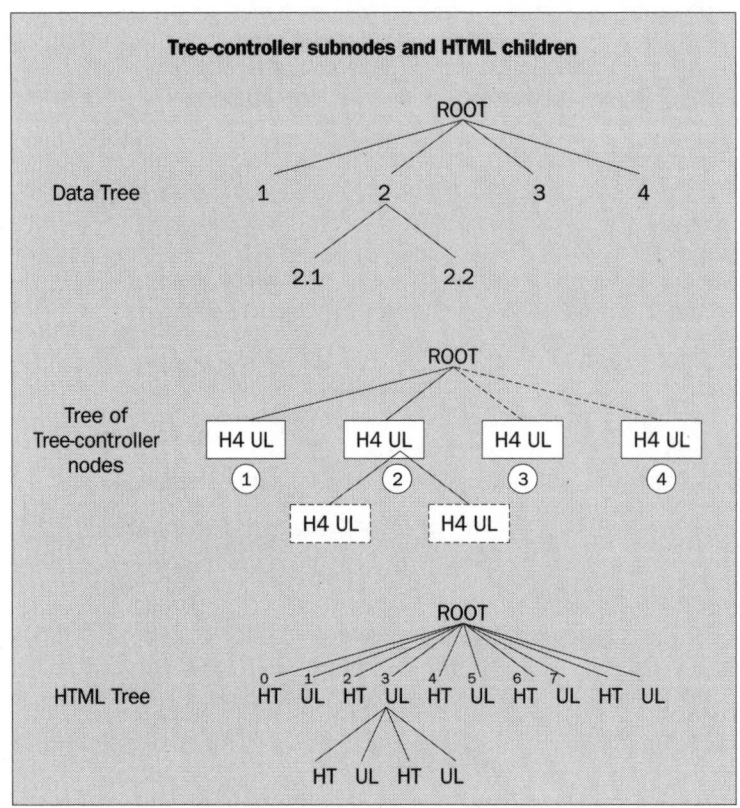

The Big Picture

You and the `Tree` class have not yet been formally introduced, but you've seen glimpses of it here and there. You know that a tree consists of nodes. Each node has a `ul` property which refers to the corresponding `<UL>` element of the tree control. This is how information about the tree's structure flows from the tree to the control. Each node also has a label property which holds the element of the data that the node represents. (In the **TOC** application, that property holds a reference to the corresponding header in the document.) This is how information flows from the tree to data. Each node also has a numbered list of children, and it gets its nth child by saying `getNth(n)`.

So far so good, but what we really need is to get from the control to data, in response to a mouse click, for instance. Half of this problem has already been solved because if we can get from the control to the tree, then we can use the label property to get to the right place in the data. How do we get from the control to the tree? Look back in the **Simple Demo**! Each HTML element of the control—the title tag, the image and the `<UL>`—have ID attributes which contain the tree address of the corresponding node of the tree. In addition, the tree control as a whole has a reference to the tree as a whole: it came as the second argument to the constructor. So, to get from the control to the tree node, you extract the tree address of the node from the ID and use the `getSubTree()` method.

Now we're ready to look at `consControl()` and `consTitle()`.

Outputting the HTML for the Control

The task of outputting the code for the tree controller is handled by the `consControl()` method, with part of the job parceled out to `consTitle()`. Both methods perform the meticulous work of building HTML strings, using recursion whenever appropriate.

The consControl() Method

The `consControl()` method would be a bit simpler if we didn't have to worry about the dummy header. It often happens that tree-structured data is really forest-structured: it has many trees that are not brought together under a single root. So, as in the TOC application, we have to create a dummy root that requires special treatment because it doesn't have any HTML representation. If it weren't for this nuisance, the method would have a very clear recursive structure:

```
function tc_consControl(tree,tAddr){
  // initial stuff: check that tree is not empty, initialize local variables
  // construct title and opening UL tag
  for(var i=0; i<N; i++){
    // call consControl on children
  }
  // construct closing UL tag and return
}
```

As it is, the for-loop with recursive calls has to be repeated twice, with small variations: once for the dummy header and once for the general case. In the dummy header situation, we allow for the possibility that the user may want to provide a label for that header (so it's not such a dummy after all); this is indicated by the `showTop` argument to the constructor. Here's the code for the initial part and the dummy header:

```
function tc_consControl(tree,tAddr)
{
  if(!tree)return "";
  var N = tree.numChildren();
  tree.tAddr = tAddr;
  if(!this.showTop && tAddr == "")                    // dummy header case
  {
    var S = "";
    for(var i=0; i<N; i++)
      S += this.consControl(tree.getNth(i),"" + (i+1));
    return S;
  }
}
```

The method receives two arguments, a tree and a tree address in that tree. (We need the second argument for recursive calls.) After the preliminaries, we check to see whether or not we're dealing with the dummy header, and if so, we initialize S to `""` and construct the HTML for the control. Notice the usual off-by-one banana peel: `getNth()` uses a 0-based count, but tree addresses of children are counted beginning from 1.

The code for the general case is very similar, but S is initialized to have the HTML for the title and the opening `<UL>` tag:

```
var S = this.consTitle(tree.label,tAddr,N>0);
S += "<UL class=closed name='ul "+tAddr+"'>\n ";        // opening UL tag
for(var i=0; i<N; i++)
  {
```

```
    S += this.consControl(tree.getNth(i),tAddr + "." + (i+1));
    }
    return S + "</UL>\n";            // add the closing UL tag and return
}
```

Everything in this code should be familiar to you. To construct the title, a separate function is called and given `tree.label` as its first argument, the tree address `tAddr` as its second. The tree address is, of course, inserted in the `<UL>`'s name attribute. It is also used to construct the tree addresses of children in recursive calls.

The consTitle() Method

The code of `consTitle()` proceeds through these steps:

- ❑ construct the tag
- ❑ construct the event handler for clicking on image
- ❑ construct the HTML for the IMG element
- ❑ put it all together into a string and return it.

We'll present each part in turn, beginning with the tag. The default value of the tag is `<Hn>`, where n is the tree level of the node, but it can be overridden by giving an alternative value to the `titleTag` property:

```
function tc_consTitle(label,tAddr,hasChildren)
{
 // calculate level from address
 var Lvl = tAddr==""?0:tAddr.split(".").length;
 var tag = Lvl>6?"H6":"H"+Lvl;  // the default tag is H1..H6, by tree level
 if(this.theOb.titleTag)
   tag = this.theOb.titleTag;   // override default
```

Next we construct an `imclickStr` that contains the onclick handler. The only tricky part here is to alternate the quotes as necessary:

```
 var imclickStr = " onclick='" + this.path + "toggle(this,event)'";
```

Next is `imStr`, the code for the image. We only put out the image if the node has children; otherwise, the image has really nothing to do:

```
 var imStr = "";
 if(hasChildren)      // put image in only if the node has children
  imStr = "<IMG id='im"+tAddr+"' SRC='close.gif'"+ imclickStr+"> ";
```

Finally, we put everything together:

```
 var S = " <"+tag+" id='hd"+tAddr+"' " +
     "onclick='"+this.path+"clickFn(this)' > " +
     imStr + (this.theOb.showTAddrs=="1"?" "+tAddr+" ":"") +
     label.innerHTML + "</"+tag+">\n ";
 return S;
}
```

The toggle() Method

There are two onclick event handlers that a tree controller needs. One of them, `clickHeader()` is passed in as an argument because it is application-specific. The other is to toggle the node condition between open and closed, and you saw a self-contained version of this function in Simple Demo. Here's the method:

```
function tc_toggle(imageObj,ev)
{
 var tAddr = imageObj.name.substring(2);
 var T = this.theTree.getSubTree(tAddr);
 var ul = T.ul;
 if(!ul){alert("help, no list for image " + imageObj.name); return;}
 if(ul.className == "closed")
 {
  ul.className = "open"; imageObj.src = 'open.gif';
 }
 else
 {
  ul.className = "closed"; imageObj.src = 'close.gif';
 }
 ev.cancelBubble = true;
}
```

You can really see lines of communication in action here. The method knows the image that received the click. (It's the source element of the event.) We use the image name to extract the tree address, and use that to get to the right node of the tree. Once there, we use the node's `ul` property to get back to the right <UL> element of the tree controller.

This concludes our discussion of the `TreeController` class. We'll see it again, unchanged, in the SiteMap application. But let's look at the `Tree` class first.

The Tree Class Interface and Implementation

We have developed two substantial applications using the `Tree` class and its methods, without ever presenting the class in any organized way. The reason we could get away with it is that the class uses very few methods, all of them clear, intuitive and task-related to trees. You will be able to see for yourself, because in this section we will give the class the treatment it deserves. We'll present its interface first, then an implementation. Our implementation is deliberately small and compact, but adequate for the applications at hand. We have developed two more implementations that support a wider array of methods (e.g., node deletions), but we'll leave them as an exercise for the reader.

The Minimal Interface

If you look through the code of the TOC application, you'll see that we have been very modest in our assumptions about what a tree object can do for us. Here's the interface so far used:

```
/*
Tree(item)          constructor; return a tree object with item as root
numChildren()       return number of children of the tree object
getNth(i)           return i-th child of the tree object
addChild(item)      add item as rightmost child
getSubTree(tAddr)   find subtree at a given address
*/
```

To be completely honest, we also have a `toString()` method for debugging purposes, but that's all. One important feature of this interface is that it provides no facilities for inserting or deleting "middle" children: all insertions are at the right end, and there are no deletions at all, although deleting the rightmost child wouldn't be difficult to add. It turns out that, as long as you don't expect to do deletions or insertions in the middle, the `Tree` class can be implemented with very little code.

A Simple Implementation

In the implementation we present, each node is an array whose first element, at index 0, contains the data (or "label") of the node, and the rest contain the children. The implementation is very compact, taking less space than a constructor for some of the later classes. A couple of methods are so short that we don't even have to define them separately as global functions with names: we simply create new Function objects and assign them as properties to the prototype. The reason for the compactness is the flexibility of the `Array` class that can hold values of different data types, and expands on demand:

```
function Tree(item)              // the constructor
{
 this.A=new Array(); this.A[0]=item; this.label=item;
}
function tree_addchild(sub) {this.A[this.A.length] = sub;}
function tree_getSubTree(addr)
{
 if(addr == "")return this;
 var ob=this; addr=addr.split(".");
 for(var i=0; i<addr.length; i++)
  ob = ob.getNth(parseInt(addr[i],10)-1);      // off-by-one again!
 return ob;
}
Tree.prototype.numChildren = new Function("n","return this.A.length - 1");
Tree.prototype.getNth = new Function("n","return this.A[n+1]");
Tree.prototype.addChild = tree_addchild;
Tree.prototype.getSubTree = tree_getSubTree;
```

We'll need two more methods for the **SiteMap** application but they don't do any operations in the middle of the children list and can be easily added to this implementation. What if you do want to include those "difficult" operations? Then an array-based implementation would become a bit awkward because after each deletion in the middle you'd have to shift all the younger children to the left in order to close the gap, and before each insertion you'd have to move some children to the right to make room for the new arrival. We could fill another chapter with several possible implementations of the tree class for all occasions, but instead we'll fill a small subsection, in this chapter, with suggestions on how it can be done and leave them as an exercise for the reader. Right after that, we're going to move on to the **SiteMap** application because, ultimately, classes are there to build applications with.

Alternative implementations

In this section we suggest two more possible implementations of the `Tree` class, based on traditional and language-independent ways of implementing the tree data structure. (The implementation described above is somewhat dependent on the properties of the `Array` object in JavaScript.) The first possibility is `nodeTree`, in which each node knows how to refer to its parent, first child and next sibling:

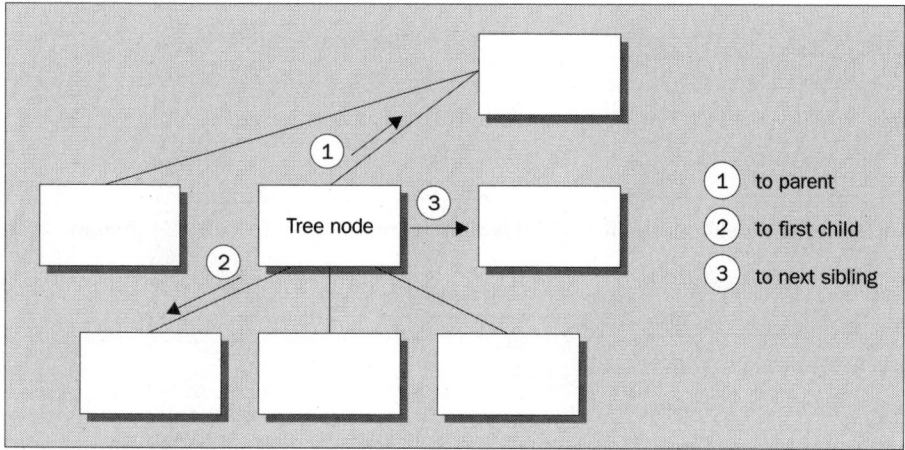

In a language with pointers, `parent`, `firstChild` and `nextSibling` would be pointers to the corresponding nodes. In JavaScript, a node in a `nodeTree` implementation is an object with the properties `parent`, `firstChild` and `nextSibling` (and perhaps others, such as `label`):

```
function nodeTree(l,p,f,n)          // a constructor
{
  with(this)
  {
    label=l; parent=p; firstChild=f; nextSibling=n;
  }
}
```

Notice that in this implementation, adding a new `firstChild` is easy:

```
function nt_newFirst(T)        // add tree T as new first child of "this"
{
  T.nextSibling = this.firstChild;
  this.firstChild = T;
}
```

The other common implementation of tree shows its recursive nature more transparently, and so we call it `recTree` (for recursive tree). In the `recTree` implementation, each tree node contains a list of its subtrees. The list can be implemented as a linked list (to make insertions and deletions easier) or as an array:

```
function recTree(L)            // a constructor
{
  this.label=L; this.subTrees=new Array();
}
```

Some methods are easier in this implementation than in `nodeTree`:

```
function rt_getNth(N){return this.subTrees[N];}
function rt_length(){return this.subTrees.length;}
```

In `nodeTree`, these methods would require loops, e.g.:

```
function nt_length()
{
  var N = 0;
  for(var T=this.firstChild; T; T=T.nextSibling) N++;
  return N;
}
```

However, inserting and deleting the first child is more complicated in `recTree` than in `nodeTree`:

```
function rt_newFirst(T){          // add tree T as new first child of "this"
    for(var i=this.subTrees.length; i>0; i--)
      this.subTrees[i] = this.subTrees[i-1];
    this.subTrees[0] = T;
}
```

There are pros and cons to either implementation, some of them quite subtle. For instance, if B is a `recTree`, you can do:

```
B.newFirst(A); B.newFirst(A); alert(B.length());
```

However, if B is a `nodeTree`, you'll find yourself in an infinite loop because A has become its own sibling. We're not going to continue on this tangent any further; if you're interested, consult one of many excellent books on data structures and algorithms. We do recommend that you complete both implementations, providing all the methods in our implementation, plus methods for insertion and deletion. Ultimately, you should be able to replace our `simptree.js` file with your `nodetree.js` or `rectree.js`, and the applications that depend on it will continue to function without a hiccup-demonstrating, once again, the ease with which you can expand and improve object functionality without breaking the code that relies upon it.

The SiteMap

The idea of the SiteMap application is fairly straightforward. You start from an HTML file on your local machine that has links to other local files. The most likely starting point would be the homepage for a project. You load the file, collect all the links in it, filter out non-local links, and repeat the process for all the local links. As you (recursively) search for more links, you make sure that you don't repeat the same link more than once, otherwise you'd go collecting links forever. Eventually there will be no new local links. The list of links you've accumulated is really a list of directory paths, so they form trees and subtrees. You use a tree control object to show the directory structure of the site, and you get something potentially useful, especially if each title in the tree controller is a link to the corresponding file, so you can view the files by clicking on the titles. As an extra embellishment, you can combine the SiteMap with the TOC application, so that if you view a document with a header structure in it, you'll get to see both the document and its outline.

Try It Out

Point your browser at `smonly.htm`. A form will appear asking you for the starting URL. You can specify either a `file:` URL or an `http:` URL, as long as it's on the local machine. If you want to view only files within a specific directory (e.g., files for a specific project rather than the entire site) you can also specify the path to that directory, otherwise leave it blank. We've provided a couple of simple test links on our website; it's hardly a complex structure, but will give you some idea of the tool's potential. Click on the Do It button and watch the links being collected. You should end up with a site map in the left frame, the currently selected file in the right frame, and an outline for it (if any) in the middle frame.

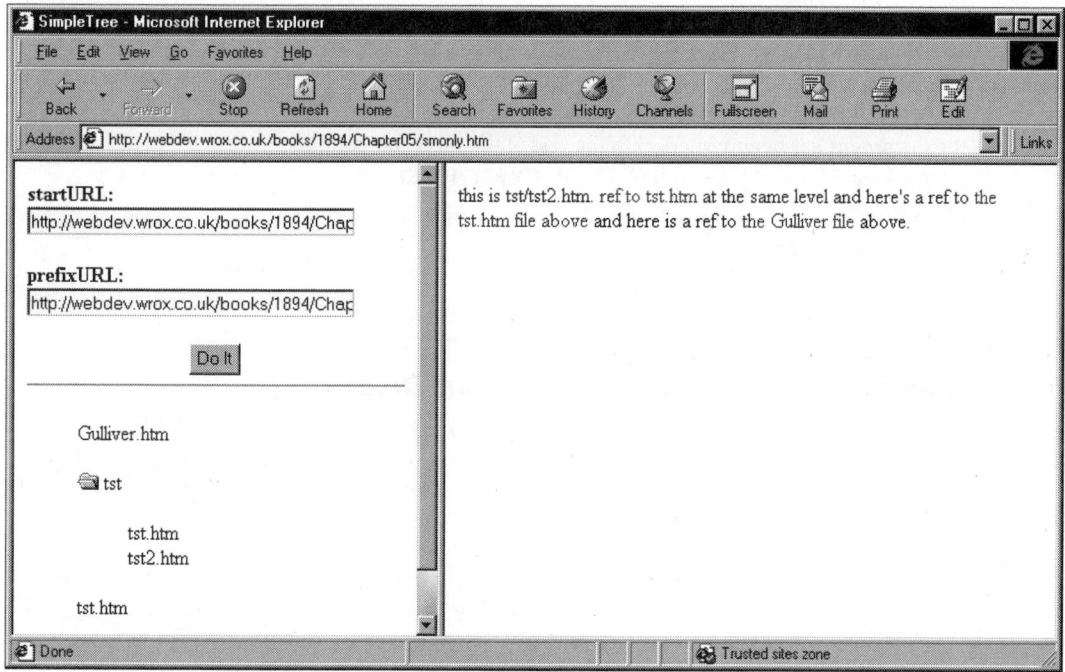

How It Works

The structure of the application is similar to what you saw in TOC. There is a main function and an application-specific class for the tree collection process called `TraverserDocs`. The main structural difference occurs where a tree control is constructed. In TOC, the main function dispatched `TraverserOb` to collect the tree, then called `TreeController` to construct the tree control. In SiteMap, the tree control is constructed by the same `TraverserDocs` object that collects the tree. The reason is that `TraverserDocs` cannot really return a tree to the main function because when it starts out it cannot know when the tree is going to be ready. The tree data is spread over many documents each of which has to be loaded into the browser before its links can be collected. Once you start loading and unloading files, delays are unavoidably introduced. If you ask for the links in the file before it is fully loaded, you'll get an error. So, you have to check, and if the file is not ready you have to set a timeout and call the loader again when it expires. This theme of waiting for the document to load before processing it is a very common one in JavaScript programming, and the techniques we introduce in this section will serve you in many applications.

Data Collection

Algorithm for Data Collection

If it weren't for delays and timeouts, the algorithm for data collection would be really easy. As usual, we'll want a stack to keep a list of files to be visited. We'll also need some way of keeping track of the files that have already been visited so we don't visit them again. This is very easy to do with an object used as an associative array. Every time we find a new file, we make its name a property of the object and set the value of that property to true. Before we put a file name on stack we check to see whether it's registered with the object.

To start the process, we push the starting URL on stack and repeat until the stack is empty:

- ❏ pop the top document off the stack
- ❏ if the document has been visited, skip the rest of the loop and continue
- ❏ load the document into a frame (DANGER: EXPECT DELAYS)
- ❏ add the document to the "known" object
- ❏ add a node for the document to tree
- ❏ pull out its links
- ❏ for each link, if the link is local and is not known push it on stack

A Simple Implementation for a World Without Delays

To flesh it out, let's write a bit of fictitious code that could only work if document loading were instantaneous. However, we'll structure the code so that it has convenient slots for plugging in required additions. In particular, we'll spread the loop over two methods, run() and waitLoad() that will call on each other:

```
function td_run()
{
 while(!this.S.isEmpty())
  {
  var x = this.S.pop();
  if(this.known[x])continue;       // ignore old URLs
  this.frame.location = x;         // found a new one, load it
  return this.waitLoad();
  }
 this.finish(this.acc);           // stack empty; construct tree controller
}
function td_waitLoad()
{
 var x = this.frame.location.href);
 this.known[x] = true;
 this.acc = this.combine(this.acc,x);   // add node to tree
 var L = this.frame.document.links;     // pull out links
 for(var i=0; i<L.length; i++)
  {
  var u = L[i].href;
  if(this.filter(u) && !this.known[u])  // link is local and not known
   this.S.push(u);
  }
 this.run();
}
```

Note how the loop is divided up between the two functions: the first three actions, up to the loading of the file, are performed in run(). The last thing run() does is start the loading process. The rest of the loop, which depends on its successful completion, is dispatched to a different function. We can now have this function check to make sure that loading has been successful; if not, it will call itself again after a timeout.

A Small Nuisance and a Fix For It

There is one more fix to the current code that we'll need. It really is a fix, a function (not a method) called fixURL(), which makes sure that the local URLs are in the standard format. That format stipulates that the name of the drive should be followed by the "|" character, but IE4 sometimes inserts ":", as in Windows. This has to be standardizedso our comparison functions work correctly. The function also checks to see whether the URL is followed by a "#" for anchors inside documents, or a "?" to separate the URL from a query string.

```
function fixURL(S)
{
    if(S.match(/^file:\/\/\/.:/))      // match "file:///C:...", for instance
      S = S.substring(0,9) + "|" + S.substring(10,S.length); // "file:///C|...
    var srch = S.indexOf("?");
    if(srch > 0)S = S.substring(0,srch);
    var hash = S.indexOf("#");
    if(hash > 0)S = S.substring(0,hash);
    return S;
}
```

To generalize, our purpose here is to ensure that if two URLs, u1 and u2, point to the same document then fixURL(u1)==fixURL(u2). We haven't made it one hundred percent perfect, but it's pretty close. We leave it as an exercise for you to think of possible improvements and to implement them. For instance, if you have a web server on your machine and its root directory is C:\webshare\wwwroot, also known as http://localhost, then file:///C|webshare/wwwroot/default.htm and http://localhost/default.htm point to the same document.

The Real Code for the Real World (With Delays)

We can now look at the complete code for run() and waitLoad():

```
function td_run()
{
  while(!this.S.isEmpty())
    {
    var x = this.S.pop();
    if(this.known[x])continue;       // ignore old URLs
    this.frame.location = x;         // found a new one, load it
    return setTimeout(this.path + ".waitLoad()",100);
    }
  this.finish(this.acc);             // stack was empty
}
function td_waitLoad()
{
  if(this.frame.document.readyState != "complete")
    return setTimeout(this.path + ".waitLoad()",100);
  var url = fixURL(this.frame.location.href);
  this.known[url] = true;
```

```
    this.acc = this.combine(this.acc,url);
    var L = this.frame.document.links;
    for(var i=0; i<L.length; i++)
    {
     var u = fixURL(L[i].href);
     if(this.filter(u) && !this.known[u])this.S.push(u);
    }
    this.run();
   }
```

The most important change from the first version is that all calls on waitLoad() are replaced with setTimeout(this.path + ".waitLoad()",100). This happens both in the first call from run(), and in the "recursive" loop in the beginning of waitLoad() that waits for the readyState property of the document to become complete. The second change is that all URLs are fixed before they are used. (See fixURL() above.)

The acc Property

Before we leave run() and waitLoad(), we should spend a little time puzzling over two lines of code that are not related to the recursive task of document traversal in search of new links. Both of them have to do with the acc property of the TraverserDocs object. It must be a very important property because, when the stack gets empty and we're finally out of the loop that searches for new links, the run() method has only one more line:

```
    this.finish(this.acc);      // stack was empty
```

Clearly, acc contains everything the program needs to finish its task, which is to construct a tree controller. (This is the only action performed by finish(), a call on the constructor.) What does the program need to construct a tree controller? Well, a tree, of course. The tree is constructed in the other line with acc, in waitLoad():

```
    this.acc = this.combine(this.acc,url);
```

Looks like every new URL is somehow incorporated into acc by the combine() method, so that acc accumulates a tree of document nodes, constructed incrementally by the same loop that finds the data for the tree.The rest of the application mostly consists of support for these two lines, one that builds the tree, and the other that sends the completed tree off to be outfitted with a controller.

TraverserDocs Class

This is the final class we define in this chapter. Its purpose is to encapsulate the application-specific task of traversing the data and building the application-independent tree. It works recursively, in a manner similar to a web crawler, first collecting and filtering the links found on the current page, then visiting the as-yet-unvisited links.

The Constructor for TraverserDoc

Let's start with a large-scale picture. In order to do its work, a TraverserDocs object needs to know:

❑ its own name, in order to construct an absolute reference to itself
❑ the frame to use for loading documents
❑ the starting URL

These are the arguments to the constructor. It also needs, as properties, a stack, an object to keep track of visited files, and yet another object to store two items of information supplied by the user. They are: the prefix URL to specify the directory the user is interested in, and the HTML object that will contain the tree controller when it's finally built. So, the constructor is as follows:

```
function TraverserDocs(name,frame,startURL)
{
 TraverserDocs[name]=this; this.path="TraverserDocs." + name;
 this.frame = frame;
 this.S = new Stack(); this.S.push(startURL);
 this.known = new Object();    // !known[URL] == we haven't checked URL yet
 this.user = new Object();     // userData, to be used by methods
}
```

Methods of TraverserDocs

In addition to the run() and waitLoad() methods that we saw, TraverserDocs has three more: filter(), combine() and finish(). (You've seen all of them used in the code.) Before giving them application-specific definitions, we're going to try and give them default values such that even if no other definitions are given, TraverserDocs would produce something meaningful. For the SiteMap to work, these definitions, of course, have to be overridden. Since they are defaults, we put them in the prototype, together with the acc property in which, as you recall, the tree is accumulated:

```
TraverserDocs.prototype.acc = null;
TraverserDocs.prototype.filter = new Function("x","return true");
TraverserDocs.prototype.combine =
     new Function("a,x","alert('doc ' + x); return null");
TraverserDocs.prototype.finish =
     new Function("a","alert('doc traversal done')");
```

The actual definitions of the methods are not much longer than the defaults and can be given "inline" in the main function. This is because much of their functionality comes from the TreeController constructor and general methods of the Tree class, some of them new. So, as we go through the main function, you'll have to suspend your disbelief again, but very briefly.

Other Possible Uses

Although we've presented TraverserDocs in the context of the SiteMap application, it can be used for a variety of other project management tasks at your web site. In most cases, adopting it to other uses requires minimal changes to one or two methods. Suppose that you wanted a list of all the links from your project to the outside, except those at site gamble.com, in the folder named secret. Solution: change the filter function in waitLoad() that decides which URLs to keep. Suppose that you wanted a list of all the images in your project which are not in folders named image. Solution: replace document.links with document.images in waitLoad() and provide the appropriate filter. Suppose that you wanted to replace all occurrences of "disintermediation" in your project with something simpler, like "layoffs". Again, use TraverserDocs to traverse your documents, pull out the innerHTML of each, and use the appropriate string methods to do the replacement. Each of these is a routine bookkeeping task, if you have only one document. Imagine a project using many files in many deeply nested subfolders, where old versions and trial pages for future versions may be kept together with the current material. This is where TraverserDocs can be helpful. It does have limitations, the biggest of which is that it isn't particularly clever. It doesn't deal well with JavaScript URLs (as in javascript://), and it doesn't consider the fact that a page may contain document.write statements which cause it to vary from one run to another. It doesn't even know how to deal with frameset pages, because it only pushes window.links on stack, missing all frame.location.href links. Within those limitations, it does give you a good start on your bookkeeping tasks.

Building the Tree and Tree Controller

Now that all the classes are in place, together with their methods, we can put it all together to construct the application. We'll start with a "main function", where the execution begins. (Those who are familiar with C, may think of it as similar in intent to the `main()` function in that language.) The main function constructs a `TraverserDocs` object and calls its `run()` method. The `run()` and `waitLoad()` methods together collect the data and build the tree. When they're done, they call `finish()` to construct the tree controller. As we unwind this story line, we'll also define a couple of new `Tree` methods, to insert labeled nodes into the tree.

The Main Function

```
function siteMapController(theController,theFrame,startURL,prefixURL)
{
var TD = new TraverserDocs(theController.id,theFrame,fixURL(startURL));
 TD.user.pU = fixURL(prefixURL);
 TD.user.tC = theController;
 TD.filter = new Function("u","return u.indexOf(this.user.pU)==0");
 TD.acc = new Tree(new docNode(TD.user.pU,TD.user.pU));  // initialize acc
 TD.acc.theFrame = theFrame;      //this property is used by clickSiteMapTree
 TD.combine = insDocTree;         // function to combine nodes
 TD.finish = new Function("t",
        "new TreeController(this.user.tC," +      // the HTML object
        "t.sort(cmpNode)," +                       // the tree, sorted
        "clickSiteMapTree," +                      // the onclick function
        "1,false)");                               // fDepth and showTop
 TD.run();
}
```

This looks like a mouthful, but actually is not too bad. Let's go line by line. The function is given four arguments, of which we've already seen three: `theFrame`, `startURL` and `prefixURL`. What's `theController`? That's the HTML object that will hold the resulting tree controller. As such, it must have an ID attribute, which we can just as well also use as a name for the `TraverserDocs` object. That object is what the main function spends most of its time building. Once it is built, the main function sets it running and quits.

Create and initialize TraverserDocs

We create a new `TraverserDocs` in the first line, and methodically fill in its properties and methods. `TD.user` gets the prefix URL and the HTML object to put the tree controller in. `TD.filter()` is a single-line string-manipulation function that checks to see whether the URL it is given begins with the prefix URL. Finally, we initialize `TD.acc` to be a new tree whose root is a new `docNode`, and that's where things become more interesting. What's a `docNode`?

The docNode

As the name suggests, a `docNode` is a tree node that contains a reference to a document. That reference is the document's URL. However, when we display the node in a tree controller, we don't want to annotate it with the complete absolute URL, including the prefix; we just want to display the name of the corresponding file or folder. So, a `docNode` receives two arguments and stores them in two properties:

```
function docNode(innerH,fullURL)
{
this.innerH = innerT;     //innerH is string to display in tree controller,
this.fullURL = fullURL;}  //fullURL is full path, for loading.
```

Once the `acc` property is initialized, the stage is set for building the tree. This is done, as you recall, in the `waitLoad()` method, when we say:

```
this.acc = this.combine(this.acc,url);
   // url is a new doc that passed all tests
```

Clearly, we somehow combine the already accumulated tree and the new document, but how? The answer is: call the function `insDocTree()`. (Presumably, in some other applications you'd call another function. We suggest possible other applications later in the chapter.) And what does `insDocTree()` do? The short answer is that it builds a new subtree for the current URL. The long answer is that it's time for an example, and a new section.

The insDocTree() Method and New Tree Facilities

Suppose you encounter a URL among the links that starts with your URL prefix, and if you cut the prefix off, you're left with `x/y/z.htm`. You want to incorporate the new URL into the tree. This means that you need tree nodes for the x folder and the `x/y` folder, in addition to the new leaf node `z.htm`. The folder nodes may already be there (if you have already encountered files from them), or they may need to be constructed. In either case, when you're done, the part of the URL that is left after the prefix is cut off is like the tree address of the new node. The node contains, as its data, the complete initial absolute URL and the short name, `z.htm`, for display in the tree controller.

We can now start untangling `insDocTree()`. It receives two arguments, a tree and a new URL. The first line cuts off the URL's prefix and splits the rest into an array of strings using "/" as the separator. In our example, you'd get an array `["x","y","z.htm"]`. These are short node labels for display in the tree controller. The remaining code creates a function that builds a `docNode` and sends it, together with the URL and the array of strings to `t.insLabel()`.

```
function insDocTree(t,url){
   // use as the "combining" method of TraverserDocs
   var pathStr = url.substring(1 + this.user.pU.length);
   var pathArr = pathStr.split("/");
   var f = new Function("u,Ai","return new docNode(Ai,u)");

   // insert url via sequence pathArr with f as node-building function
   var TT = t.insLabel(url,pathArr,f);
   return TT;
}
```

Since `t` is a tree, `t.insLabel()` must be a new general tree method. Indeed, it is. It works together with a little partner called `indexOf()`, on analogy with the string method of the same name. It takes an item and a comparison function and returns the "index", or the number of the child for which the comparison function returns true. If no such child is found, `indexOf()` returns -1:

```
function t_indexOf(x,f){           // alert("indexOf on tree " + this);
  for(var i=0; i<this.numChildren(); i++)
   if(f(this.getNth(i),x))return i;
  return -1;
}
```

The `insLabel()` method assumes that we have a "labeled" tree which holds its node information in the label property. It uses `indexOf()` to see whether a new node needs to be created for a given label. Its code is transparent, but you ought to be impressed (again and again) by the flexibility and power resulting from treating functions as first-class objects:

```
function eqLabel(theTree,theLabel)      // supporting func for insLabel
{
  return theTree.label.innerHTML==theLabel;
}
function t_insLabel(x,A,f){                   // traverse tree,
  // looking for labels A[0],A[1] etc; addChild(f(x,A[i])) if missing
  var t = this;
  for(var i=0; i<A.length; i++){
    var k = t.indexOf(A[i], eqLabel);    if(k<0){
      k = t.numChildren();
      t.addChild(new Tree(f(x,A[i])));
    }
    t = t.getNth(k);
  }
  return this;            // for convenience, return at root of insertion
}
```

This completes our coverage of how the tree is constructed. In summary, the tree is a tree of docNodes. Each docNode carries its complete URL and a short label—a file or folder name—to display in the tree controller. Every time a new URL is processed (after it's popped off the stack), it's added to the acc tree by the `combine()` method which ultimately calls on `insLabel()`. The resulting tree will be passed to the constructor for `TreeController` and post-edited in the process, as we'll discover when we get there.

Constructing the Tree Controller

We're down to defining the last method, `finish()`. Once it's defined, the main function calls `run()`; `run()` and `waitLoad()` together collect the data and build the tree, and when they're done, they call `finish()`. What's left to finish? Constructing the tree controller, of course. That's all that `finish()` does. In the process, it uses an onclick function and the `sort()` method of the tree class which we will present immediately after this section.

This is how we could define `finish()`:

```
function simpleFinish(t)
{
  // sort t and collapse non-branching nodes if any
  var theTree = t.sort(cmpNode);
  new TreeController(this.user.tC,      // the HTML object
            theTree,
            clickSiteMapTree,          // the onclick function
            1,false);                  // fDepth and showTop
}
TD.finish = simpleFinish;
```

We could do the same thing in one step, constructing the text of `simpleFinish()` on the fly (this is the version shown in the "Main Function" section above):

```
TD.finish =
  new Function("t",
    "new TreeController(this.user.tC," +      // the HTML object
    "t.sort(cmpNode)," +                       // the tree
    "clickSiteMapTree," +                      // the onclick function
    "1,false)");                               // fDepth and showTop
```

To understand `finish()`, you only have to understand where the arguments to the `TreeControl` constructor come from. The first argument is the HTML element to house the control, which came from the user. The second is the tree that was collected in `acc`, subjected to a couple of transformations (shown in a moment). The third is the click function which we still have to write. The last two are `fDepth` and `showTop`, which here have the default values and could, in fact, have been omitted.

This completes the discussion of `siteMapController()`, except for sorting and the click function. The click function is much more compact, so we'll do it first.

The Click Function

There's really nothing new here:

```
function clickSiteMapTree(h)
{
  var tAddr = h.name.substring(2);
  var T = this.theTree.getSubTree(tAddr);
  this.theTree.theFrame.location = T.label.fullURL;
}
```

As before, the communication goes from the clicked title to the tree, using a tree address; once the tree node is found, its full URL is extracted and loaded into the frame `theFrame`, which we have very thoughtfully stored as a property of `this.theTree`.

Sorting the Tree

Since `sort()` is a general tree utility, we define it as a method of the tree class:

```
function t_sort(f)          // sort the tree using f, which compares trees
{
  var N = this.numChildren();
  if(N == 0) return this;
  var A = new Array();
  for(var i=0; i<N; i++) A[i] = this.getNth(i).sort(f);
                              // sort the children
  A.sort(f);                  // sort thyself
  for(var i=0; i<N; i++) this.setNth(i,A[i]);
  return this;
}
```

This is a straightforward recursive affair, with one small twist. We don't want to write a sorting routine, so we copy the children to an array, use the array's sorting facility, then insert the children back into the tree using the new (and trivial) `setNth()` method. But wait, you could say, we already have our children implemented as an array, why do we have to copy them to a new one. Ah, but we want to be implementation independent! (Remember encapsulation?) So, we'd rather do a little extra work but preserve the abstraction barrier between the implementation and the interface.

The actual sorting order is determined by the sorting function that we pass in as a parameter. There are at least two possibilities: plain alphabetical sort or, as in Windows Explorer, all folders first, followed by files. We'll do the plain one because it's easier, and leave the hard one for you as an exercise. (Hint: how many children does a non-folder have?)

```
function cmpNode(a,b){
  // compares two nodes whose innerHTML fields hold URLs
  var aU = a.label.innerHTML.toUpperCase();
  var bU = b.label.innerHTML.toUpperCase();
  return aU < bU ?-1: aU == bU ?0: 1;
}
```

A Couple of Extras

The application is practically finished. We could easily have stopped the chapter here; if this section were removed nothing would have to be changed in the conclusions. However, we wanted to provide two additional features, one to make the application a bit more user-friendly, the other to give it some additional functionality. If you feel that you have spent enough time on this chapter, consider skipping this section, reading the conclusions and moving on. (You can always return later.) If you would like to see some more tree traversals that use a function argument to do something to each node, or more code that tests to see whether a document has been fully loaded into a frame, press on.

The two additions we'll make are:

❑   if the user has not provided the prefix URL, have the program calculate it
❑   combine the TOC and the SiteMap applications so that if the document loaded by SiteMap has a tree structure of headers, the SiteMap will place its outline in a new frame provided for the purpose.

Calculating the Prefix URL From Directory Paths

Suppose the prefix URL is an empty string, i.e., the user hasn't specified any. In that case, the root of our tree will be the protocol name followed by the host name, e.g., file://C|. Each path will begin at the root. We can figure out what the prefix URL is by inspecting the paths. If the root of the tree has only one child whose label is a, and a has only one child whose label is b, and b has only one child whose label is c, and c has more than one child, then the common prefix is file://C|/a/b/c.

There are two places in the program where we can figure out the common prefix, using two completely different sets of tools. The first place is in the array of paths: we can find the longest common prefix that ends in "/" using the methods of the String object. The other place is after the tree is already constructed: to determine the prefix URL, we go through the tree beginning at the top and collapse together all the nodes that don't branch.

We present the second solution because it's closer to the main theme of this chapter; the other one is left as an exercise to the reader.

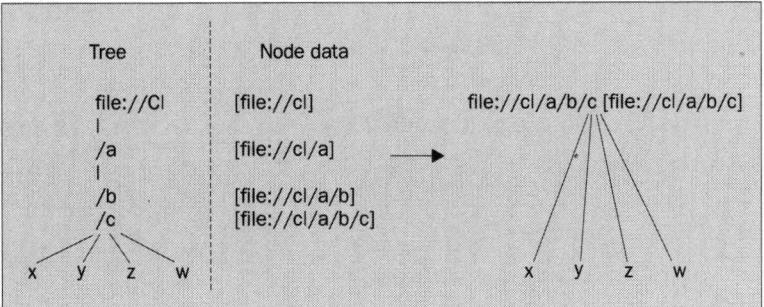

The diagram above shows what we want to do to our tree. Each node in the tree has two fields: a brief label to display and the node's complete data (the complete path from the root in the SiteMap application). The label doesn't need to be changed, but the complete data does. In the case of SiteMap application, we could simply copy the complete path from the first branching node (/c in the diagram) to the root, but we wanted to provide a more general tree utility, implemented as a method of the tree class. So, we update the root's data incrementally, as we move down through the non-branching nodes, and we encapsulate the required incremental changes in a function that's passed as an argument to the collapseTree() method:

```
function t_collapseHd(f)           // collapse common headers into one header
{
  // "f(lbl,sublabel)" adds info of sublabel to "lbl".
  if(this.numChildren()!=1) return this;
  var L = this.label;
  var t = this.getNth(0);
  while(t.numChildren()==1){
    f(this.label,t.label);
    t = t.getNth(0);
  }
  var N = t.numChildren();
  this.setNumChildren(N);             // NOT: this.A.length = t.A.length
  for(var i=0; i<N; i++) this.setNth(i,t.getNth(i));
  return this;
}
```

(Note, as an aside, how we're again doing our best to preserve encapsulation: instead of saying, in an implementation-dependent way:

```
this.A.length = t.A.length
```

we define a new method, setNumChildren()*, and hide the details of the implementation within it. The payback is that we can replace the implementation of the basic methods of the* Tree *class without touching the code of* collapseHD()*.)*

To incorporate collapseHD() in siteMapController(), only one line needs to be changed, within the definition of finish():

```
TD.finish = new Function("t",
      "new TreeController(this.user.tC," +        // the HTML object
      "t.sort(cmpNode).collapseHd(addInnerT)," + //tree sorted, collapsed
```

```
            "clickSiteMapTree," +              // the onclick function
            "1,false)");                       // fDepth and showTop
    TD.run();
}
```

The function parameter, `addInnerT()`, does the right thing:

```
function addInnerT(a,b)
{
 // add innerHTML of b to that of a, with "/" in between
 a.innerHTML += "/" + b.innerHTML;
}
```

Now you can really try it out. Point your browser at `smonly.htm`, fill in the starting URL and, if desired, the prefix URL, and view the files and folders in your projects.

Combining the SiteMap and the TOC Applications

In our final addition to SiteMap, we'll give it an extra frame, and if the loaded document has a tree structure of headers, the New and Improved SiteMap will place its outline in the new frame. This will presumably happen in response to a click on the title of the document in the tree control, so our natural first impulse is to add a line of code to `clickSiteMapTree()`:

```
function clickSiteMapTree(h)
{
 var tAddr = h.name.substring(2);
 var T = this.theTree.getSubTree(tAddr);
 this.theTree.theFrame.location = T.label.fullURL;
 headerController(theHFrame.hdrControl,theDFrame.document.body,1)
}
```

The highlighted line says: construct a header controller for the document in the document frame and put it in the new "header frame" as the innerHTML for `hdrControl`. This code has a problem, the usual one (... pause, to give you time to think and figure it out by yourself). The line right before it loads a document into a frame. The new line assumes that the document has already been loaded. We need a time cushion in between. Let's call that cushion `doAfterLoading()`, and give it two arguments: the text of code to execute and the frame to wait for:

```
function clickSiteMapTree(h)
{
 var tAddr = h.name.substring(2);
 var T = this.theTree.getSubTree(tAddr);
 this.theTree.theFrame.location = T.label.fullURL;
 doAfterLoading(
   "headerController(theHFrame.hdrControl,theDFrame.document.body,1)",
   theDFrame);      // wait until theDFrame loads, then make hdrController
}
```

The `doAfterLoading()` function will pass the waiting loop to a generic `dAL()` function which will test the `readyState` property and call itself again and again until the property becomes true:

```
function doAfterLoading(expr,frame){
  dAL.expr = expr; dAL.frame = frame; setTimeout("dAL()",100);}
function dAL(){
  if(dAL.frame.document.readyState == "complete") eval(dAL.expr);
  else setTimeout("dAL()",100);
  }
```

With this final fix, the combined **SiteMap** and **TOC** application is ready (at `smhdr.htm`), and we hope you will never again be thrown off balance by a document that has not loaded on time.

Conclusions

What you've learned in this chapter falls into three (at least) different categories:

❑ about trees and how to use recursion in programming with trees, how to implement a tree class, how to traverse a tree doing useful things to its nodes, how to collect tree structured data into a tree object;

❑ about computational objects and their views and how to establish communication between them;

❑ about the timing issues in JavaScript programming and how to make sure that you don't start poking a document until it's completely loaded;

❑ about class design and interactions between classes, especially between structure classes (like the tree), view classes (like the tree controller), and traverser classes (like the document traverser).

And, even more importantly, you've worked your way through two substantial applications that you can use, experiment with, customize, develop further, and explain to your friends. Where does one go from here? To even more challenging applications that work together to create an integrated working environment. This is the project that we will embark on in the next chapter, and continue through the remainder of the book.

6

Persistent Storage and Database Applications

Introduction

All our applications so far share one property: they don't know their past. Every time our calculator or the TOC application is run, it starts afresh, without any memory of its previous appearances. Clearly, there are applications that couldn't function in that way. Imagine an appointment book: it wouldn't be worth much if you couldn't add to it, or mark some of its items as done. Whenever you need to be able to update your data, you want it to persist from one application run to the next. Database applications (an appointment book, a project schedule, or inventories of various kinds) are primary examples of persistent data.

In order to make your data persistent, it has to be stored on a hard drive somewhere. There are three logical possibilities:

- ❑ the client machine that a JavaScript application is visiting as part of a web page
- ❑ the server that the application came from
- ❑ some other computer on the Internet

With the help of Java, a JavaScript application can do all three, and we'll show you how in Chapter 9. Without such help, JavaScript is severely limited in what it can do, for obvious security reasons. It can do cookies, of course, but otherwise it cannot write anything to the client's hard drive. Core JavaScript (ECMAScript) doesn't even have any facilities to manage files. (Microsoft's JScript does have such facilities, but even though we're using JScript's DOM, we have not used any of JScript's extensions to the core language; `FileSystemObject` and the other objects are covered in Appendix C.) The only hard drive unconditionally available to a JavaScript application is the server that it came from. You have to send the data back there and ask the web server to save it. The server will use the services of some other program (which you have to provide) to save the data and to retrieve it on request.

Very often, the other program that saves and retrieves data for the web server is a database program. If you've never worked with databases, this chapter explains the basic principles and tools of a relational database. In the meantime, let's just say that a database lets you store, retrieve, sort, search, edit, add, and delete structured data items called records. In a very common arrangement, the web server would use an intermediary program to communicate with a database and store data submitted from the browser (via an HTML form), or display database records in the browser, in an HTML table.

We're going to do something different: implement a small database engine in JavaScript, and keep the database records in HTML tables. In our arrangement, a database is loaded, in its entirety, with the web page, and the user can sort, search, etc. on the client side, without bothering the server any more, except to save the changes to the database. The database is saved as a plain text (HTML) file, and retrieved as one long string.

What's the point, some of you may ask. Why not simply use the "professional service" of a database program on the server? Such a service would include features that our little engine cannot provide, e.g., security and the ability to handle multiple simultaneous interactions. Well, databases are used in a variety of contexts, and to see the motivation for ours, we suggest that you think about the database facilities in Excel (and other spreadsheets). They are limited in size, their query facilities are far less powerful than those of any reasonable database engine (including ours!), they offer very little security and no synchronization features; but people (including us) find them useful, even when database engines are readily available. Why are they useful? We suggest that they are more "open", easier to start up when you're not really sure what you're doing, less resistant to casual redesign in the early stages of a project's development, and we want to use HTML tables in the same way. We already find ourselves writing collections of HTML tables which look like databases; we want them to behave like databases, but to retain their HTML openness (and edit capability) as long as possible. As a project grows, it may grow beyond the HTML (or Excel) tabular-database model, either because there's too much data or because there are too many users who might update the same table. In such cases, a conventional database is needed, and may be used as a replacement or a supplement just as tends to happen with Excel.

We hope that "supplement" will become more and more common as time goes on: if you look for information at your favorite web searcher (Yahoo, AltaVista, DejaNews, whatever) or look for books at Amazon.com, you'll find yourself with a database query output which is still a whole lot of stuff to wade through by hand. Tools like ours, tools for working with HTML tables of information, could help a lot. It's not just that local queries can be faster than server queries, even though the server is a faster machine and is running compiled code. As you'll see in the next chapter, it's easy to apply the Chapter 5 tools to make tree controllers for different views of the same database...and wouldn't you like a choice of three or four tree-controllers for the thousand hits you just got on your web query? If you're designing a shopping-cart system, wouldn't you like to turn around and give your user some automatically generated tree-controllers for the virtual supermarket aisle defined by her last query?

The user would do what people in supermarkets often do: get quickly to the right aisle, then slowly browse, looking at labels and comparing prices. With our JavaScript database engine, users will be able to browse through, search and sort the contents of an aisle, using a fast, local, in-browser computation. (In the MoreApps folder, you'll find a working Shopping Cart application, in which individual store aisles and customers' orders are implemented using our database engine.)

In this book, we will not provide much server-side intelligence: our examples get complex enough without that. We will go no further than giving you two quite different ways to save and load data: one based on CGI, the other based on the Java tools explained in Chapter 9. In each of these, the "save" action in the browser sends a page to another process, and the "load" action receives a page from that process. Our implementations simply save a page as a file, and load the page from a file. However, if you want to interpret some "saved" pages as customer orders and reinterpret "load" requests as database queries to some conventional database, that's up to you - we can't fit it in this book, but we approve. Meanwhile, we're working on a few projects where this sort of small, open, editable database, in which JavaScript functions can be freely written, is just what the client wants.

In summary, this chapter will cover:

- ❑ negotiations with the server
- ❑ the CGI protocol and alternatives
- ❑ elements of database theory
- ❑ a minimal set of database operations
- ❑ an example of a database application
- ❑ using the database as an authoring tool
- ❑ design and implementation of a database class

Try It Out

This chapter develops a database program that shows snippet web pages (a line of text and a photograph) of the faculty and staff of an imaginary college. The faculty of this college is peculiar in certain ways, most obviously because their photographs show more peace and tranquility than one usually finds in a faculty picture book. The photos and names are, of course, easy to change. A more serious constraint is that the application can only work on relatively small databases. (A thousand items would probably push it too far, depending on the speed of the server and the browser.) In later chapters, we use our database class for completely realistic educational applications. In this chapter, our goal is to learn several new concepts (CGI protocol; database operations) and create a database class in the context of a small application.

We actually present two versions of the database, a minimal one (minDB.htm) for pedagogical purposes, and a slightly more elaborate one (tmplDB.htm) that can serve as a template for similar applications. An even more elaborate version is developed in the next chapter. The screen shot below shows the template version.

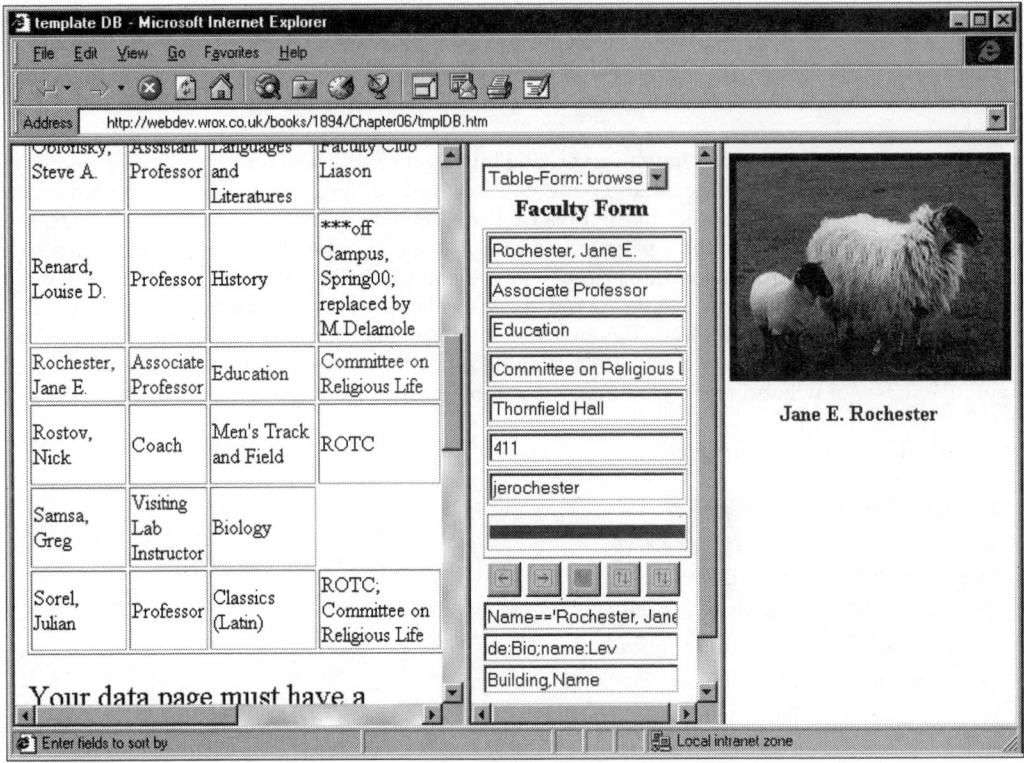

Three Applications In One

As you try it out, be aware that every database application is really three different applications, providing different capabilities for different categories of users. The capabilities are: browse the data, edit the data, and define the data. The distinction between browsing and editing has to do with levels of access: users who have only read access can only view the data, while users with the read/write access can both view and edit. The distinction between both browsing and editing on the one hand and defining the format of the data on the other, is the difference between using an existing application and creating one of your own. In database terminology, browsing and editing is **data manipulation**, while creating your own tables and forms is **data definition**. If the database is used for creating educational software (see Chapter 8), its data-definition capability can provide **an authoring tool** for creating applications of your own.

In our application, whether you view or edit the data, you're provided with a `Select` element at the top that allows you to switch between browsing, editing, and data definition modes. The difference between them is in the number of command buttons and control forms that are visible to the user. The browsing mode hides, and the editing reveals, the buttons for adding, deleting or editing existing records, as well as buttons for saving the database on the server and loading it from there. The data definition mode, in addition, shows a data definition form that allows you to specify the names of the tables and the name of the overall application.

A Possible Scenario

Here's one possible scenario of how it may all unfold, from conception to deployment and use. A college professor receives a small grant to develop a "picture book" for a literature course: a body of visual materials that supplement the textbook. The course consists of several topics, each topic covers several authors, for each author there are several texts, and each text can be appropriately illustrated by a photograph and some commentary. The professor creates an HTML table that has the following headers (<TH> elements): topic, author, text, URL, (the URL contains the image and the commentary). She may also fill in several rows in the table, or she may add them later using the Add button. The main task at this stage is to create the applications, one for each assignment.

Let's assume that the professor wants to create two assignments for the course. One is passive: the students simply browse the materials prepared by the instructor, look at paintings and read the commentary. The other gives students a more active role: they must themselves find two appropriate paintings for each text, provide links to them, and write a brief commentary explaining the connection between the text and the painting. The names of the assignments are 'Assgn1' and 'Assgn2'; the name of the course is 'French 366'.

To create an assignment, the professor fills in the dbInfo form, in which she specifies the ID of the table she has just created, the name of the course and assignment (Fren366/Assgn1), and her username and password. Assuming that she has made all the necessary arrangements with the system administrator, she saves the new application on the server.

Every instructor who teaches the course creates a list of usernames and passwords for the students. (The details of how this can be done are discussed in Chapter 8, and further details are available from our website.) In this list, the instructor specifies the assignments available for the course and the level of access (browse, edit, define) that the students have in that assignment. That's it, the materials are ready to use. We have, in effect, described the data definition facilities of our database application: all you need is the authority to edit the HTML file that contains the dbInfo form and the basic tables. The second major section of this chapter is a tutorial that will take you through the process step by step.

Browsing, Searching and Editing

Let's say you're a student in that imaginary course. When you start the application, you see a table, a form, and a number of buttons. Each row of a table forms a **record**. You can cycle through the records by using the Next and Previous buttons, or you can search for specific records by using the search or the query facility. At any time, one of the records is the current record, highlighted in the table. Its contents appear in the form and can be edited there, but in order for the changes to stick, you have to be in the editing mode.

In the editing mode, you can change the database, through the services provided by the Add, Delete and Replace buttons. The Delete button deletes the current record. Both Add and Replace put the edited contents of the form into the table as the current record, either adding it to the end of the table, or replacing the currently selected record. All these changes are happening in the HTML table on the loaded page. To make them persistent, you click on the Save button. The next time you want do the same assignment, you click the Reload button and resume your work from where you left it.

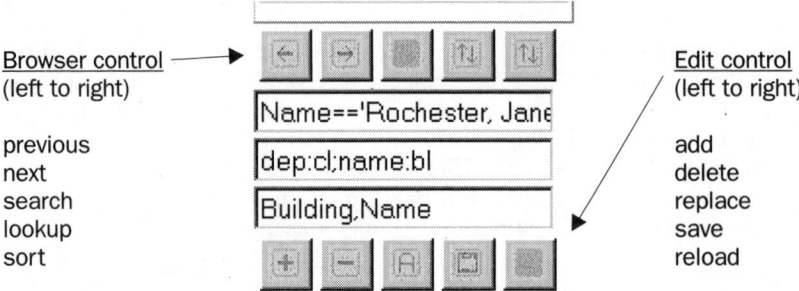

Browser control →
(left to right)

previous
next
search
lookup
sort

Edit control
(left to right)

add
delete
replace
save
reload

The application actually has three search facilities. The one named Search asks the user to enter a valid JavaScript expression, such as `Building=='McGregory' && Office>=400`. (In English: find all faculty in McGregory on floors 4 and above.) The LookUp facility is less demanding; you can make errors and abbreviations. Finally, the Query facility is the most general of the three because it allows you to combine material from more than one table. Read about all three later in the chapter.

Another Outline

Clearly, there's quite a bit of stuff to absorb before we can fully understand how this application works. But don't worry, it all consists of manageable pieces, which we're going to slice thin into sections and subsections, and serve with plenty of verbal dressing.

In outline, our first major section will deal with theoretical preliminaries. These fall into two parts: browser-server interactions, and elements of relational database theory.

The second major section, "Database Applications," is a tutorial on how to build database applications using our database class. It assumes only a reasonable knowledge of HTML and a careful reading of the first section.

Finally, the third major section will go through the implementation of the database class. Some possible back-end arrangements on the server are discussed in Chapter 9.

Theoretical Preliminaries

Negotiations With the Server

A web server may strike you as an amazing, and amazingly complex, piece of software, but in essence it is very simple. (Its complex behavior arises from the truly amazing framework in which it operates.)Most of the servers spend most of their time responding to two commands they receive from browsers, GET and POST. In either case, what they do is send a specified sequence of bits back to the browser, either as text or as binary data. The sequence of bits may come from a file or constructed by another program and given to the server to send. The commands and the specifications as to whether the data is text or binary are part of the HTTP protocol. (HTTP stands for Hyper-Text Transfer Protocol; it was invented, together with HTML, by Tim Berners-Lee.)

The Basics of HTTP

As usual, in order to understand HTTP, let's look at it in motion. What happens when you start your browser, type in a URL and press Enter? A URL consists of at least three parts: the protocol, the hostname, and the path to a file or directory. If the protocol is http, the host is cs.colgate.edu, and the path is /cslabs/cs303/default.htm, the following sequence of events takes place. First, the browser connects to the HTTP port on the specified server using the telnet protocol. Once the connection is established, the browser sends (roughly) the following text:

```
GET /cslabs/cs303/default.htm HTTP/1.0
From: ...
User-agent: ...
more information about itself, including a list of recognized file types;

a blank line to indicate the end of request
```

The web server fetches the specified file and sends it as text because the file is of type text/html. If the requested file were myImage.gif, of type image/gif, it would go as binary. All the interpretation of the bits is done by the browser.

There are small variations, familiar to you from experience. If the file is not found, the server will send an error message. If the path ends with a directory name, the server will look for a default file in that directory. The possible names of default files are specified in a list that the server consults; usually, the list includes index.html or default.htm or another couple of common names. If none of those are found, and directory browsing is enabled, the server will send the listing of the directory. If directory browsing is not enabled, the server will tell you so.

You may remember from Chapter 6 that the path part of the URL can be followed by either a "#" or a "?" character, followed by additional information. The "#" case does not concern the server at all: it sends the page as usual and the browser scrolls it to the specified position. The case of "?" mark is different: the server is asked to do something with the information that follows. Since the server doesn't know what to do with it, it seeks help.

The CGI Protocol

In order to get help, the web server has to communicate with another program at its end, rather than the client's, pass information to it, and receive information back. There are several ways to do that, of which the oldest and still most commonly used is the CGI (Common Gateway Interface) protocol. This is how it works. The server needs two pieces of information: the name of the program to ask for help, and the information to pass to that program. Both pieces come from the browser. The name of the program is specified in the path section of the URL. In other words, if an interaction between a server and another program is intended, the path doesn't specify a web page or an image or some other content to be sent back, but rather a program that will provide that content to the server, perhaps constructing it on the fly.

The information for the server to send to a CGI program is a text string in a specific format called "the URL encoding". You must have seen it occasionally when communicating with a search engine or an internet vendor. It's basically a sequence of attribute=value pairs, separated by the "&" character, with blanks replaced by the "+" character. So, if you're asking the server to approach the program /cgi-bin/animals to find out what dogfood collies like the best, your URL might end up looking something like this:

```
http://somehost.somewhere.com/cgi-bin/animals ? breed = collie &
                                         query = favorite + food
```

It is then up to the `animals` program to parse and interpret the URL-encoded string, fetch the requested information, compose a web page with that information in it, and give the page to the server.

Sending Information to the Server

Information is always sent to the server as a URL-encoded string but it can be sent through two different channels. One is shown in our example: the string is appended to the path, after the "?" character. The browser sends the URL as usual, after a GET command. The server realizes that it's a request to run another program when it reaches cgi-bin in the path part of the URL, and the file name at the end whose extension is not .html. Having realized that, the server detaches the query string that comes after the ? and sends it off to the specified program. From the user's perspective, the string can simply be typed in, but this is tedious and error prone. It's much easier to use an HTML form.

The other channel uses the POST rather than the GET command. In this case, the browser's message to the server looks like this:

```
POST /cgi-bin/aProgram.pl HTTP/1.0
From: ...
User-agent: ...
Content-length: length of content to follow;
more information about itself, including a list of recognized file types;
a blank line to indicate the end of request;
the URL-encoded string containing the data to be sent to the program;
```

In this case, the server understands that this is a request to run another program, and it sends the URL-encoded string directly to that program, as input. It's up to the program to decide what to do with it, and how to construct the required web page.

We can now review the components of the HTML form, to see how they feed into the flow of information between the browser, the server, and the supporting program.

- ❑ The ACTION attribute of the form specifies the URL of the supporting program.
- ❑ The METHOD attribute of the form specifies whether the browser sends a GET or a POST command to the server
- ❑ The names and values of the form's input elements provide the attribute-value pairs to send.

Alternatives to CGI

One significant drawback of CGI is that it can be computationally quite expensive to start another program in addition to the web server. Another drawback is that CGI programs use a language that is totally different from JavaScript, usually Perl. Several alternatives have been developed. All of them give a little (or a lot) extra intelligence to the server itself, so it can run programs or scripts. One alternative is Active Server Pages (ASP) from Microsoft. These look like ordinary HTML pages, but have the .asp extension. You can place ordinary JScript (or VBScript) scripts directly into ASP pages, within specific delimiters. When the server is asked for an ASP page, the server itself scans through the page and executes all the scripts before sending the results back to the browser. ASP pages initially worked only with Microsoft servers, but they've been, or are being ported to other servers as well, including Unix and Sun.

Another alternative is to use Java servlets, from Sun Microsystems. These are Java programs that are, again, compiled and run by the server itself. Initially, only Sun's own Java Web Server knew the Servlet protocol well, but it has been vigorously supported by many third-party companies, including IBM, so by now you can run servlets with virtually every server, including Apache.

Our Plan of Action

This is a book on JavaScript, not CGI programming. We're going to restrict our CGI activity to the barest minimum by pushing as much intelligence and hard work as we can onto the client. That minimum, which cannot be pushed on the client, is persistent storage: our supporting program or script has to do the work of saving on the server and retrieving the saved data for input into a web page. Everything else will be done by the client. Since whatever the server sends to the client has to become an HTML page, this is exactly what we're going to save and retrieve. Remember that an HTML page is just a long string of characters which the browser knows how to interpret.

In more precise terms, our interactions with the server will be restricted to two forms on the client side and two programs on the server side. The first form will send a file name and a text string to the server, and the server will write the string to the specified file. The second form will send a file name to the server, and the server will send back the contents of the file as an HTML page.

(In truth, the picture is more complex because of arrangements for user access. The name of the file and the directory path will be constructed out of the name of the project, the name of the assignment within the project, and the username and password of the current user. How precisely the user name and password determine the file name, is up to the CGI program on the server. The sole promise is that if a "virtual file" for a given username and password was accepted, the same user can retrieve it later.)

What about our promise of a database application, or several such applications? Well, we'll put the functionality of a database on the client side, in a JavaScript class. That class will use the incoming HTML information to construct a database object that will do database work for us. Looks like we're again designing an intimate relationship between a computational object in JavaScript and an HTML object of a related structure. However, we're adding a new twist to the relationship: the HTML object is used not only for user interface, but also for storage.

What's a Database?

The applications in this and the next two chapters will use a `Database` class. It will not have all the capabilities of a real relational database, but enough to make useful applications possible. It will support many operations on a single table, and two types of inter-table operation, the inner join and the query. If these terms are new to you, read the rest of this section, otherwise you can probably skip to the next one.

Tables, Records, Fields

This is a very quick introduction to the main concepts and terminology of relational database theory. A database is a collection of **tables**. A table consists of rows and columns. Each row of a table forms a database **record**. Each column in a database has a name, which is the name of the corresponding **field** in each database record. For instance, if your table is about cars, then the top three rows of your table (the field names and the first two records) may look like this:

Model ID	Make	Model	Year	Cylinders	Doors	Category	Comment
1	Acura	Gran diosa	2002	6	2	Sports car	Very fast
2	Alfa-Romeo	GLX 2Q	2003	6	4	Luxury sedan	Very cool

This is the **tabular view** of a database table. It is often useful, especially for data entry or editing, to have a more spacious **form view** which usually flips rows and columns around.

Make	Acura
Model	Grandiosa
Year	2002
Cylinders	6
Doors	2
Category	Sports car
Comment	Very fast

In either case, you want to be able to cycle through the records, going from the current record to the next or previous one. (Thinking ahead, we'll need a `Next()` and a `Prev()` methods for our database class.) You also want to be able to find a record by its **key**. (This sounds like a `Search()` method.) A key may consist of a single field (the ModelID), or several fields (Make, Model and Year in our example, assuming that all cars of a given make, model and year come with the same number of doors and cylinders).

Instead of one record, you may want to review a group of records that satisfy some condition. (Find all cars that have a 6-cylinder engine.) This operation is called **selection**, because it selects a group of rows in the table. Sometimes, you don't want to see the entire record but only part of it. (Show make, model and category of all cars.) This operation is called **projection**; it selects a group of columns in the table. Selection and projection can be combined. (Show make, model and category of those cars that have a 6-cylinder engine.) The important thing is that any combination of projections and selections produce a table, so if we know how to show a table, we can always show the result of those operations.

So far, we've been talking about a single table; what if our database has several? As long as our tables don't have identical fields (i.e., columns that have the same data), we can work with each table separately. If our tables do share fields, all sorts of new possibilities arise. Let's push our example a little further, to explore them.

Inner Join and Virtual Tables

Once you have more than one table, you have to give them names. Let's call the table we have developed "Car Models," because it doesn't really describe individual "car objects," but rather classes of cars. Individual cars have an identity, a color, and a price. So, we might want to add another table called "Inventory" which lists actual items we have on the floor and in the parking lot.

ItemID	ModelID	Color	Interior	Price
1	1	Red	Leather	67,500
2	1	Green	Vinyl	63,000
3	2	Beige	Leather	72,000

Notice that the only information repeated from the first table is the ModelID. Everything else can be reconstructed from this unique identifier. If you want to know the number of cylinders of our inventory item 1, look up its ModelID, go to the Cars Models table and trace the appropriate row with your finger until you come to the cylinders column.

Clearly, this is not an occupation for a human being. The situation is quite common and the procedure is completely mechanical. We have two related tables that share a field, and not just a field but a key that uniquely identifies a row in one of the tables. (The terminology is that ModelID is the **primary key** of the Car Models table and a **foreign key** in the Inventory table.) We want to join the information from the two tables together, to get complete rundown on all the cars in our inventory. The result will be a table that has all the columns from both tables, without repetition. In the illustration below we've left out the Category and Comments fields to fit the result on the page:

ItemI ID	Model ID	Make	Mo- del	Year	Cylin ders	Doors	Co- lor	In- terior	Price
1	1	Acura	Grand iosa	2002	6	2	Red	Leather	67,500

Even if our page were infinitely wide, we frequently want to be selective about what we see. Cutting extraneous stuff out makes the rest easier to see. Suppose we're interested only in the Make, Model and Price of all cars that have 6 cylinders. The creators of the database cannot anticipate all the possible tables that the users will ask for. They need a general mechanism to produce such tables on demand, in response to the users' queries. This mechanism is just an ability to combine the join, selection and projection operations. The query we just cited can be satisfied by three steps:

- join the Cars and Inventory tables on the ModelID field
- select those rows that satisfy the predicate Cylinders==6
- project only Make, Model and Price columns

The result is a **virtual table** that exists temporarily to answer a query.

As you can see, splitting your data among two or more tables gives you economy and flexibility, but at a price. You have to make sure that your multiple tables are in agreement. It's easy to corrupt your database by entering an inventory item with a ModelID that does not exist in the Cars table. A typical remedy, found in database programs and readily available in JavaScript, is to use a SELECT OPTION element in your data entry and editing form. Make the element of the form where the user enters ModelID into a SELECT element whose options are legitimate IDs.

We have accumulated enough theory to get a reasonably clear idea of the methods that our database class will need for its internal operation. But how will it show itself to the user? Even before that, how will a database object be created? Who will be creating those objects? It is time to start thinking about how the database class will fit in the context of a web application. This is an important moment of major design decisions, when we have to look at a broader picture. Our theoretical preliminaries are over. If you would like to learn more about databases (we have barely scratched the surface of the subject) consult one of the many excellent books on the subject, such as *Database System: a Practical approach to Design, Implementation and Management* from Addison-Wesley, or Wrox Press's forthcoming *Database Design and Implementation*, by Susan Perschke.)

Database Applications

What's a Database Application?

A fully-fledged database application consists of tables, forms, queries and reports. We're not going to bother with reports: just use HTML and style sheets. Tables, forms and queries are the essentials, without which a database application cannot function. (However, you can have a usable database without multiple-table queries, and we will initially live without them, until later in the chapter.) Tables are the data, forms are the control structure to view and modify the data, and queries are the mechanism to locate the data to view or edit. The query mechanism is the same for all databases; to create a new database application is to define its tables and forms.

Notice that there are two levels of creative activity here. Let's say we want to create a database of all dogs in the village of Hamilton, providing, for each dog, the name, breed, roaming area, and general disposition. We want to be able to click on a street corner on a map of Hamilton and see a listing of all dogs who regularly leave their marks there. This is the activity of creating a database application. You have to specify tables (dogs and breeds in one table; dogs and their areas in the other) and forms (what do you want to see and how?). Once the application is created and made public, many other villages will probably want a similar database. This is a second level of creative activity: using existing tables and forms but filling them with a different content.

To take a more serious example, a common scenario in the educational context is that the instructor will design an application (by creating tables and forms), and the students will fill it with content. Our main design goal is to make sure that everybody who is reasonably fluent in HTML can create a database application, and everybody who knows how to use the browser can create content for it. Neither the designer nor the content creator needs to know anything about databases that is not found in this chapter. This is the reason why we have developed a `database` class: to make the creation of database applications accessible to those who don't know or want to work with a database program.

With this design goal in mind, let's see how we can build an HTML interface for the `database` class.

HTML Input to the Database Constructor

To make our goal more precise, let's concentrate on the following question: what information is required for the constructor to create a database and populate it with initial data? Once we have a clear picture of the requirements, we'll figure out how that information can be provided in HTML.

The constructor needs to know the names of the tables, and, for each table, the name of the fields. It also needs to know which tables should have corresponding forms to view and edit the data. (There may be supporting tables that the users never change or even see.) How can this information be provided to the constructor? The answer is almost obvious from the terminology. Remember that the tables and forms of our requirements statement are **database** tables and forms. But of course, there are tables and forms in HTML. Looks like a match made in heaven. However, there is a minor hitch.

Until now, our computational objects could be matched to a single HTML object: a stack was matched with a one-column table, and a tree was matched with a nested UL. A database is matched with several HTML elements: a table or several tables, and a form or several forms. How can we conveniently pass them all as arguments to the constructor? We could make the constructor analyze its argument list and identify table and form names, but it's probably easier to put them all in a frame or two frames, and have the constructor work on them. This will be our approach.

Once our database is constructed, revising and adding to it will be just the matter of pushing buttons that will trigger the right methods of the **database** class. The difficult part will be making all the necessary arrangements on the server. At this point, the database designer will have to contact the server administrator to make sure that all the programs are in place, and all directory permissions are set correctly.Fortunately, this needs to be done only once. In Chapter 9, we provide all the necessary tools and explain how to use them, but be aware that you need a server to install them on. If you don't control a server yourself, you'll need the consent of the server administrator to install the tools, and this may be the trickiest part of the process.

Creating a Database Application

This is going to be a hands-on tutorial section. We recommend that you roll up your sleeves, plunk yourself in front of a computer, and follow our instructions to create an application of your own choice. We'll try to make it flexible, so that you can really put together something of your own choosing, perhaps even something that you may find some use for.

The Main Page

We're going to assume that every database application will be a frameset document with at least three frames. The default names for the frames will be **dbData**, **dbControl** and **dbMsg**.

The **dbMsg** frame is often invisible and used only as the recipient of error messages from the CGI programs on the server. In most cases, all the activity will be in the data and control frames, but additional frames may be needed for some application. If your database is a collection of commentaries and annotations to some document, as ours will be in a later chapter, then you can put your document in a **dbDoc** frame.

Incidentally, you may change the names to your liking if you feel strongly about those things, but then you'll have to provide the new names as arguments to the constructor. Assuming that you go along with the default, the main page of your application will look as follows:

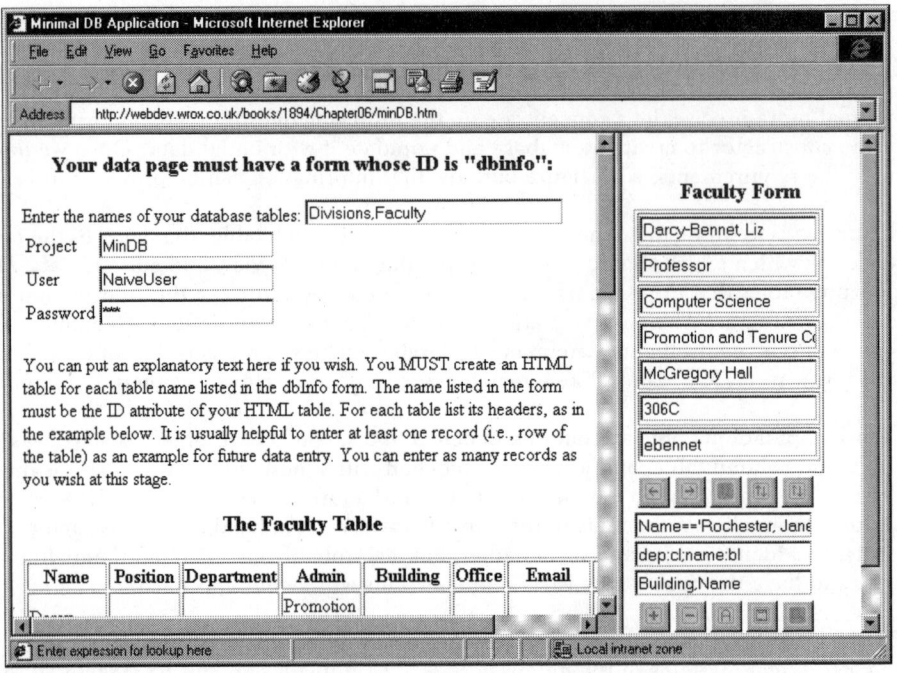

```
<HTML> <HEAD> <TITLE>TemplateDB.htm</TITLE>
<SCRIPT SRC='../class7/dbob.js'>  /* Database class */   </SCRIPT>
<SCRIPT SRC='../utils/arrutils.js'>  /* array utils */   </SCRIPT>
<SCRIPT SRC='../utils/strutils.js'>  /* string utils */   </SCRIPT>
<SCRIPT> function setupDatabase(){
 var D = new Database();
}
</SCRIPT>
</HEAD>
<FRAMESET onload="setupDatabase()" cols="45%,55%,0%">
  <FRAME NAME=dbData   SRC="tmplData.htm">
  <FRAME NAME=dbControl   SRC="tmplCtrl.htm">
  <FRAME NAME=dbMsg   SRC="about:blank">
</FRAMESET>
</HTML>
```

What needs to be changed in this template in order to create your own application? Very little, really. First, if you don't like our arrangement of frames, design your own. Second, provide correct links to your data and control pages. It will be in those pages that all the database design activity takes place.

The Data Frame

The minimal document loaded in the data frame has the following components:

- ❏ a style sheet for the data frame
- ❏ a form called `dbInfo`
- ❏ sample tables
- ❏ forms for interactions with the server (invisible)

In addition, the data frame can have HTML elements that serve as receptacles for the results of joins and queries.

The most important part is the `dbInfo` form that provides crucial information about the database. It has four input elements, all of them text boxes. The first element is called `Tables`; that's where you enter the names of your database tables, separated by commas. The remaining three input elements are for the purposes of storage and security. In order to store the database to a disc in a meaningful fashion, it's good to know the name of the database application or "project" and the name of its creator. To provide a measure of security, we're also asking for a password that can be used to restrict access. The CGI (or alternative) programs on the server will use the three inputs—project name, username and password—to store the database on disc and retrieve it from there; the details have to be worked out by those who implement the back end, in accordance with your specifications.

Keep in mind that all the back-end arrangements have to be done by your server administrator, but they need to be done only once. When the back-end code is written and all the directory permissions are set up, new projects can be created by the front-end user like yourself.

Let's look at a sample data frame and its code:

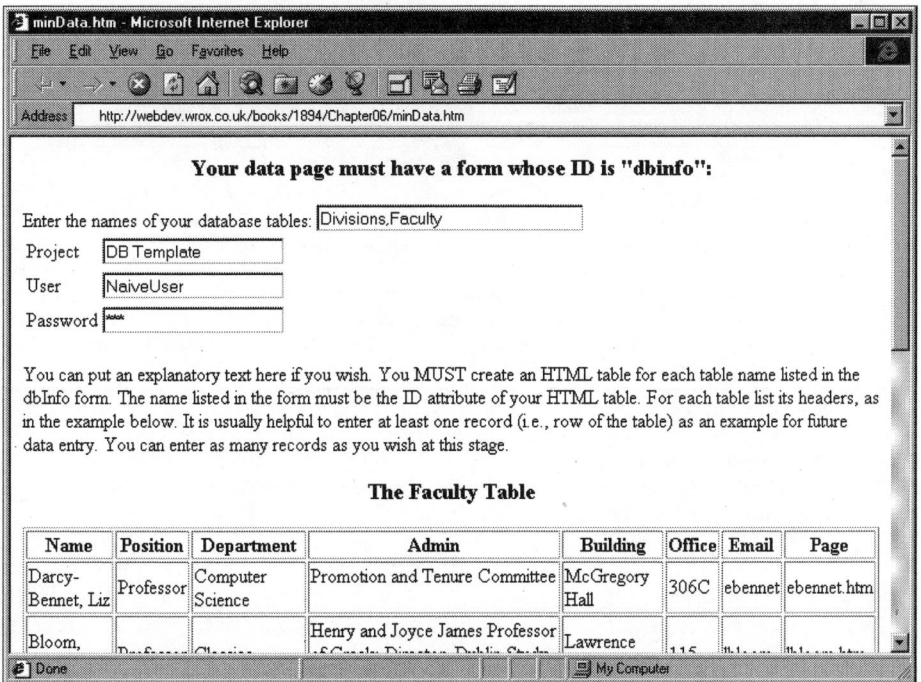

JavaScript Objects

HTML Code for Data Frame

```
<HTML> <HEAD> <TITLE>minData.htm</TITLE>
<LINK REL="STYLESHEET" TYPE="text/css" HREF="../styles/dbdata.css">
</HEAD> <BODY>
<H3 style="text-align:center">
Your data page must have a form whose ID is "dbinfo":</H3>
<form id=dbInfo> <P>Enter the names of your database tables:
<input type=TEXT size=30 name="Tables" value="Divisions,Faculty"> <BR>
<TABLE> <TR>
<TD>Project</TD> <TD><input type=TEXT name="Project" value="DB Template"></TD>
</TR> <TR>
<TD>User</TD> <TD><input type=TEXT name="User" value="NaiveUser"></TD>
</TR> <TR>
<TD>Password</TD> <TD><input type=PASSWORD name="Password" value="pwd"></TD>
</TR> </TABLE> </form>

<P>You can put an explanatory text here if you wish. You MUST create an
HTML table for each table name listed in the dbInfo form. The name
listed in the form must be the ID attribute of your HTML table. For each
table list its headers, as in the example below. It is usually helpful
to enter at least one record (i.e., row of the table) as an example for
future data entry. You can enter as many records as you wish at this stage.

<H3 style="text-align:center"> The Faculty Table </H3>
<TABLE id="Faculty" BORDER >
<TH>Name</TH> <TH>Position</TH> <TH>Department</TH>
 <TH>Admin</TH> <TH>Building</TH> <TH>Office</TH> <TH>Email</TH>
 <TH>Page</TH>
<TR>
<TD>Darcy-Bennet, Liz</TD> <TD>Professor</TD>
<TD>Computer Science</TD> <TD VALIGN=TOP>Promotion and Tenure Committee</TD>
<TD>McGregory Hall</TD> <TD>306C</TD> <TD>ebennet</TD> <TD>ebennet.htm</TD>
</TR> <TR>
<TD>Bloom, Leo</TD> <TD>Professor</TD>
<TD>Classics</TD> <TD>Henry and Joyce James Professor of Greek;
Director, Dublin Study Group</TD>
<TD>Lawrence Hall</TD> <TD>115</TD> <TD>lbloom</TD> <TD>lbloom.htm</TD>
</TR> </TABLE>

<H3 style="text-align:center"> The Divisions Table </H3>
<TABLE BORDER id="Divisions"> <TH>Division</TH> <TH>Department</TH>
<TR> <TD>Natural Sciences</TD> <TD>Biology</TD>
</TR> <TR> <TD>Natural Sciences</TD> <TD>Computer Science</TD>
</TR> <TR> <TD>Humanities</TD> <TD>Classics</TD>
</TR> <TR> <TD>Humanities</TD> <TD>Romance Languages and Literatures</TD>
</TR> <TR> <TD>Social Sciences</TD> <TD>Education</TD>
</TR> <TR> <TD>Social Sciences</TD> <TD>History</TD>
</TR> <TR> <TD>Athletics</TD> <TD>Men's Crew</TD>
</TR> <TR> <TD>Athletics</TD> <TD>Men's Track and Field</TD>
</TR> </TABLE>

<H3> Complete Faculty Database </H3>
can be produced by joining the Faculty and Divisions tables and placed
in the "FullFaculty" DIV element below.
<DIV class="hidden"> <DIV id=FullFaculty>
This space will be filled by a full faculty dbase, produced by join.
</DIV> </DIV>

<H3 style="text-align:center"> Query table </H3>
```

```
There's an invisible DIV element here in which query results are stored.
To use queries, make this element, and the query form in the control frame,
visible.
<DIV id=dbQuery class="hidden">
This space will be filled whenever we try a query
</DIV>
<P> End of tables; start of Load and Save forms
<form NAME='loadDBForm' ACTION='http://cs.colgate.edu/cgi-bin/tommy/dbout'
 METHOD=POST TARGET='dbData'>
<input type="HIDDEN" NAME="fN">
<input type="HIDDEN" name="fV">
<input type="HIDDEN" name="uN">
<input type="HIDDEN" name="pW">
</FORM>
<FORM NAME='saveDBForm' ACTION='http://cs.colgate.edu/cgi-bin/tommy/db'
 METHOD=POST TARGET="dbMsg">
<input type="HIDDEN" NAME="fN">
<input type="HIDDEN" name="fV">
<input type="HIDDEN" name="uN">
<input type="HIDDEN" name="pW">
</FORM>
</BODY> </HTML>
```

To customize for your own application, save this file under a different name. (This will be the name that you used as the source for the dbData frame in the main page.) Then proceed through the page, replacing all application specific details with your own:

❑   Change the values of the input elements in the dbInfo form.

❑   For each table name in the Tables input element, provide a table with headers.

Once the dbInfo form has been filled in, you may want to hide its Tables element, or indeed the entire form, from the users of your application. In order to do that, simply remove the "data definition" select option from the view selection element in the control frame.

Do not change anything in the **Save** and **Load** forms. Otherwise, you can change the styles and edit all the explanatory text outside the dbInfo form, the tables, and the **Save/Load** forms. You can also edit or remove all the non-essential HTML adornments that we put in there, such as a table inside dbInfo form to contain three input boxes. Or you can do these stylistic changes after you finish the substantive work on the control frame.

The Control Frame

The control frame, whose official name is dbControl, consists of HTML forms that serve as view and control forms for the tables of our database. Each form contains:

❑   An input element for each field of the table.

❑   Buttons that correspond to the methods of the database class, divided into browsing buttons (**Next** and **Previous**; **Search, Lookup** and **Sort**) and editing buttons (**Add, Delete** and **Replace**; **Save** and **Load**).

❑   Text boxes to enter the search predicate, the lookup expression (see below on the difference between search and lookup), and the fields to sort by.

JavaScript Objects

Our application contains two tables but only one form, for reasons specific to the application. We assume that the administrative structure of divisions and departments is fairly stable, while faculty data is subject to frequent change.

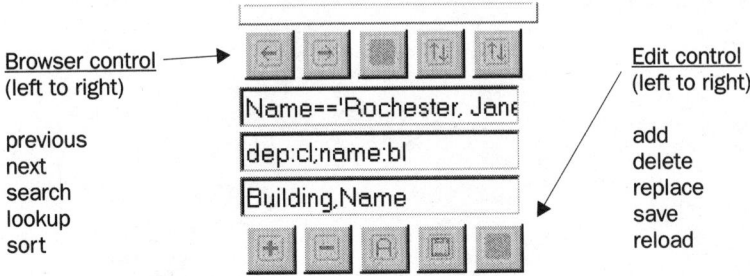

The appearance of each form is, of course, completely up to you. We've arranged the contents in a table but this is optional. You can move things around freely as long as you keep to our naming conventions. The conventions are as follows:

- ❏ The names of the buttons cannot be changed. If you don't provide the names, the values will be used instead, in which case they have to be precisely the same as the names in our default form.
- ❏ The names of the input boxes for the search and lookup expressions cannot be changed.
- ❏ The names of the input boxes for the fields of table records have to be in the following format: the letters "hh" followed by the name of the field. (If the name of the field is "Office," then the name of the text box in the form is "hhOffice.")

Within these (very reasonable) constraints, you're free to arrange your form as you wish. Here's a sample of possible code, with all internal formatting removed. (Our actual pages use BUTTON elements with image buttons rather than <input type=BUTTON...> elements.)

HTML Code for Control Frame

```
<HTML> <HEAD> <TITLE>Control Frame</TITLE> </HEAD>
<BODY>
<form name=frmFaculty> Form for Faculty table; change for your application
<!-- input elements for the fields of Faculty table;
    change for your application -->
<input type=TEXT name=hhName value="zip"> <BR>
<input type=TEXT name=hhPosition value=""> <BR>
<input type=TEXT name=hhDepartment value=""> <BR>
<input type=TEXT name=hhAdmin value=""> <BR>
<input type=TEXT name=hhBuilding value=""> <BR>
<input type=TEXT name=hhOffice value=""> <BR>
<input type=TEXT name=hhEmail value=""> <BR>
<input type=HIDDEN name=hhPage value=""> <BR>
<!-- end of record fields; do not change anything else except formatting-->
<!-- input box for search expressions next -->
```

```
<input type=TEXT name="SearchExpr" value="Enter Search Expression"> <BR>
<input type=TEXT name="LookupFld" value="Enter Lookup Expression"> <BR>
<!-- ************* Start buttons for methods ************* -->
<input type=BUTTON name="Next" value="Next"
   onClick="parent.Database.dbData.clickb(this,event)"> <BR>
<input type=BUTTON name="Prev" value="Previous"
   onClick="parent.Database.dbData.clickb(this,event)"> <BR>
<input type=BUTTON name="Search" value="Search"
   onClick="parent.Database.dbData.clickb(this,event)"> <BR>
<input type=BUTTON name="Del" value="Del"
   onClick="parent.Database.dbData.clickb(this,event)"> <BR>
<input type=BUTTON name="Add" value="Add"
   onClick="parent.Database.dbData.clickb(this,event)"> <BR>
<input type=BUTTON name="Replace" value="Replace"
   onClick="parent.Database.dbData.clickb(this,event)"> <BR>
<input type=BUTTON value="loadDB"
   onClick="parent.Database.dbData.clickb(this,event)"> <BR>
<input type=BUTTON value="saveDB"
   onClick="parent.Database.dbData.clickb(this,event)"> <BR>
</form> </BODY> </HTML>
```

The only changes you need to make are in the top part of the form. First, change the name of the form itself to correspond to the name of your table. Second, change the names of input elements for record fields to correspond to your record structure.

Even though you don't have to change anything else, you may, if you wish, change the appearance of the buttons. If you do, make sure you don't change their name attribute, because it corresponds to the function called by the button's onclick event handler. You will notice that the handler is automatically generated by the clickb() function; that function relies on the button's name for its operation. You can certainly change the value property (which is the text that appears on the button), as well as its color, font, size, etc.

In our template application, we provide two tables but a form for only one of them. If you have more than one table and need more than one form, just make another copy of our form for the Faculty table and edit it for your own purposes.

Moving around in the database

At any given time, one record in the database is "the current record," whose contents appear in the input boxes of the control frame. There are three kinds of facilities for moving around in the database (i.e., for changing the current record). First, there are the Next and Previous buttons. Second, the user can just click on any row of the table in the data frame, and the corresponding record becomes the current one. Finally, the user can search for a specific record or records that satisfy a search condition. If the search is successful, the first record that satisfies the search condition becomes the current record; repeating the search will move the user to the next such record.

Sorting and Searching

The Sort button in a control frame sorts the corresponding table. The Sort() method needs to know the field(s) whose values determine the sort order, and whether that order is ascending or descending. This is the purpose of the input box next to the Sort button: the user can type the field names into it. We set the initial value of that box to Building,Name, which means: sort alphabetically by building, and within each building, sort alphabetically by name. If you want the buildings to be in reverse alphabetical (i.e., descending) order, put a minus sign before the name of the field: -Building,Name. The best thing to do is to try it right now.

For searching, there are two facilities, Search and Lookup. (These are both single-table searches; we later add the Query facility for both single-table and multi-table queries.) Search is more powerful but more demanding of the user; Lookup is more restrictive and forgiving. Search expects a JavaScript boolean expression that uses field names as variables, for instance:

```
Name=='Rochester, Jane E' && Building=='Thornfield Hall'
```

You have to use double equal signs and quotes (can be single or double but have to match), and you must spell the names of the fields in full and correctly.

Lookup takes the attribute-colon-value approach, where the attribute is a field name and the value is the field's value. This, in effect, replaces two equal signs with one colon, so you can say: `Department:Computer Science`.

The colon can be followed by > or <, to indicate "greater than" or "less than": `Office:<400`.

The main advantage of Lookup is that it allows abbreviations (e.g., "Dep" instead of "Department") and errors in capitalization ("dep" is ok, too). Finally, it supplies the quotes if you haven't. Here's an example of a search expression that `lookup()` can understand:

```
name:>N; office:<400; dep:Computer Science
```

This turns into a search for rows such that

```
row.Name > 'N' && row.OfficeNum < 400 && row.Department=="Computer Science"
```

You can ask `lookup()` to display the expanded expression that it has come up with.

Database Queries

If you want your application to have a query capability, so your users could create and view virtual tables, you need two additions: one more form in the control frame and an empty HTML element, to be replaced by the virtual table, in the data frame. Let's look at the form first; it has, as you would expect, input boxes for entering a query and a button to set it in operation.

```
<form id="queryEntry">
Tables:<INPUT TYPE=TEXT NAME=tables value="Divisions,Faculty"> <BR>
Fields:<INPUT TYPE=TEXT NAME=fields value="Name,Dept,Div,Building"> <BR>
Expression:<INPUT TYPE=TEXT NAME=expr
  value="Divisions.Dept==Faculty.Dept && Building!='McGregory'"> <BR>
Output Table:<INPUT TYPE=TEXT NAME=outTab> <BR>
<INPUT TYPE=BUTTON name="withWhere" value="doQuery"
  onclick='parent.Database.dbData.withWhere(this.form)'>
</form>
```

The input boxes are three in number, and each has a name. One is called tables, and that's where you enter the names of the tables on which the query is based. Another is called fields, and that's where you enter the fields that you want to see in the resulting table. The third is called expr, and that's where you enter your query expression. The expression in our example means: join the two tables on the Dept column and select all records whose Building field is not McGregory. Or, in plain English, "show the name, department, division and building of all faculty whose offices are not in McGregory."

There is also an Output Table input box, to specify the ID of the HTML element in the data frame to be replaced by the query-produced virtual table. You can leave it alone; by default, the program will look for an element whose ID is dbQuery. It can be any element because its outerHTML, in its entirety, will be replaced. If the default is ok with you, you can remove the Output Table input box altogether.

Beyond the Bare Minimum

The application you have seen so far is a minimal database, reduced to absolute essentials. Our template application (tmplDB.htm) provides three additional features:

- ❑ a mechanism for making sure the user saves the changes
- ❑ a mechanism for switching views (browsing, editing, data definition)
- ❑ a mechanism to display data items associated with individual records—in our application, faculty personal web pages

We are using the dbMsg frame to show the pages, and so the arrangement of frames is also different.

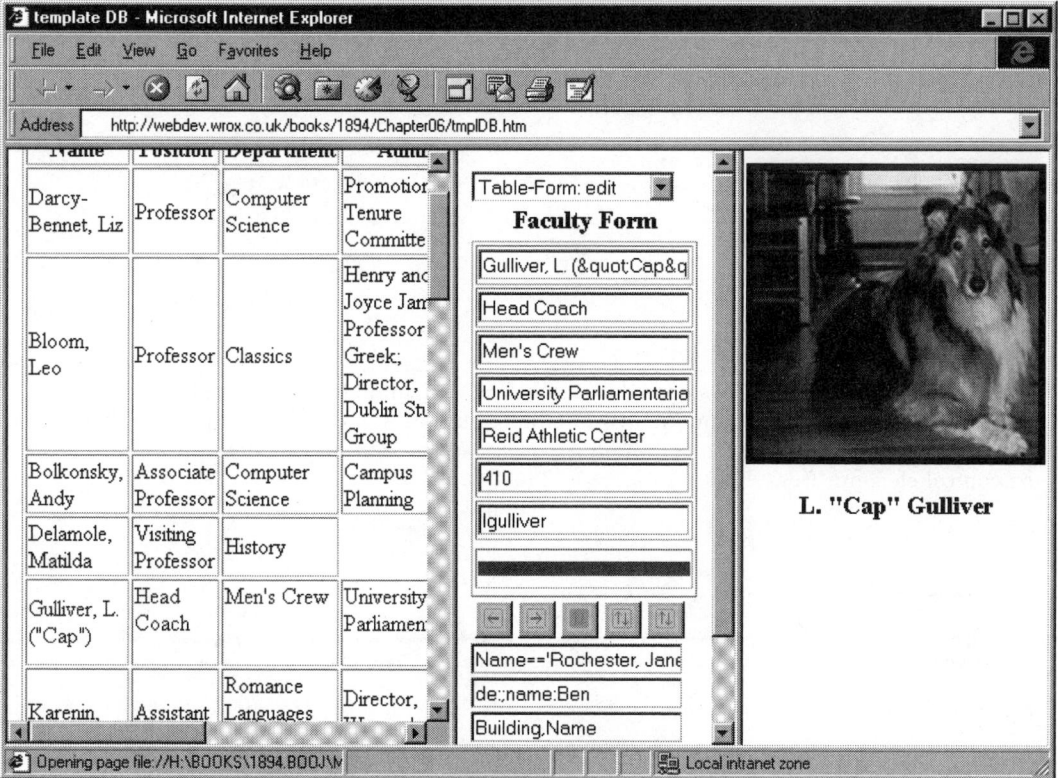

The New Setup Function

To bring in the changes, the `setupDatabase()` function had to become more complex:

```
function setupDatabase()
{
 var D=new Database();
 D.hasBeenChanged=false; // a property used in dbSave and dbLoad
 dbControl.selectView.value='tfe';
 setupView('tfe');
}
```

Two new elements have been added to the minimal setup. First, we set the `hasBeenChanged` property to `false`. The property is used by the program to make sure the user saves the database before quitting. The details can be found in the implementation. Second, we add a mechanism for switching among browsing, editing, and data definition views. This requires another function in the main frameset page, and a `SELECT` element in the control frame.

The switching is done by the `setupView()` function which, once the program starts running, receives its input from a `SELECT` element in the control frame.

Selecting the View

The `SELECT` element is completely self-explanatory. It defines all the right options and calls the `setupView()` function in the main page every time the selected option is changed.

```
<select id="selectView" size=1
 style="position:absolute;margin-top:0;margin-left:70%;font-size:x-small"
 onchange='parent.setupView(this.value)'>
<option value="init" selected>Select View
<option value="tfb">Table-Form: browse
<option value="tfe">Table-Form: edit
<option value="tfd">Table-Form: define
</select>
```

The mechanism of switching views boils down to hiding and unhiding two control elements, the `dbInfo` form in the data frame and the row of editing buttons in the control frame. We define a style sheet "class" called `hidden` whose definition is `{display:none}` and set the `className` property of the control elements from the `setupView()` function.

```
function setupView(view)
{
 if(view=="tfe")                          // table-form edit view
 {
  dbCtrl.editBtns.className = "";         // unhide edit buttons
  dbData.dbInfo.className = "hidden";     // hide dbInfo form
 } else
 if(view=="tfb")                          // table-form browse view
 {
  dbCtrl.editBtns.className = "hidden";   // hide edit buttons
  dbData.dbInfo.className = "hidden";     // hide dbInfo form
 } else                                   // data definition view
 {
  dbCtrl.editBtns.className = "";         // unhide edit buttons
  dbData.dbInfo.className = "";           // unhide dbInfo form
 }
}
```

If you don't want your users to define their own databases (or redefine yours), simply remove the data definition option from the SELECT element.

Showing Pages

The showPage() function is best discussed in the implementation section. It is very similar to the clickb() method of the database class. The reason it's a self-standing function rather than a method is that it contains a couple of application-specific conventions: the pages it shows are all placed in the pages subdirectory, and their filenames are found in the field called "Page." If these conventions are acceptable to you, then you can use it as is; otherwise, minor adjustments to its code will be needed.

From Here

If you have followed the process with us, you're all set to create a database application of your own.Look around, and you will probably find a database you could use, especially since it has a browser interface. In the meantime, here are some applications:

❑ We have already suggested a picture book for a course.
❑ In the next chapter, we'll take our faculty database to the next level of sophistication, while keeping its data definition and editing facilities accessible for users with only HTML skills.
❑ In Chapter 8 we'll use the database class in a text annotating application that keeps definitions and commentaries on a text in a database.
❑ The MoreApps folder contains a Shopping Cart application, in which individual store aisles and customers' orders are implemented using our database engine. That's two databases, each with its own data frame, but sharing the same control frame.

In the rest of this chapter we are going to talk to programmers and show them the insides of the database class.

Implementation of the Database Class

This is the real programming crux of the chapter. As a first step, let's bring together all the methods of the class, grouped together by what they do. A number of them are shown indented, to indicate that they are internal methods used to support user interface methods.

A Complete Listing

```
Database(dataFrame,ctlFrame,msgFrame);        // the constructor
  findControlForms()     // find forms associated with tables; used by constructor
  readTable()       // create database table from HTML table; used by constructor
  writeTable()      // create HTML table from database table;
                    // used by all methods that modify the database

// methods to modify the database
Del()                 // delete row of table
Add()                 // add row to table
Replace()             // replace row with contents of control form
  update()            // used by all functions that change a table or create a new one

join()                // create new table using inner join
  invert()            // create an inverted index; used by join
withWhere()           // create a virtual table based on query
```

```
Sort(fields...)    // sort the database by given fields,
                   // in ascending order unless field is prefixed by "-"
  compareRows()    // used by sort

// methods to move around in the database
Next()             // move to next record
Prev()             // move to previous record
Search()           // move to next record satisfying search condition
lookup()           // same as Search but with simpler syntax for search condition
  setCurRow()      // set current row; used by Next, Prev, Search
  loadRow()        // put contents of a row into form; used by same and others
  // several utilities used by lookup

// methods to interact with the server
saveDB()           // save database to server
loadDB()           // load database from server
  loadNewData()    // used by loadDB in setTimeOut()

// methods to create control elements
clickb()           // create a button with a given name and onclick
```

We're not going to discuss in detail all this code: there's too much of it, and after working your way through Chapter 6 you probably need fewer or less detailed explanations. We do discuss the most important and/or the most difficult parts of the code, and we'll touch upon each group of methods, beginning with the constructor.

The Constructor and Its Support

As we said before, the constructor takes up to three arguments, the names of three frames. The last of the three, for messages from the programs on the server, will probably remain unused in most applications, but we include it for completeness. The other two frames contain HTML tables and forms. They could be all in the same frame (the program, really, doesn't care) but it would become too crowded.

After sorting out the frame names and their default values, the constructor goes through the usual dance between the emerging computational object and its HTML partner. In this case, the partner is the document frame. Its ID becomes the name of the object, the object becomes a global property of the constructor, and so does the frame itself. The other two frames are not used much, and we only store their names:

```
function Database(dataFrame,ctlFrame,msgFrame){
  if(!msgFrame)msgFrame = "dbMsg";
  if(!ctlFrame)ctlFrame = "dbControl";
  if(!dataFrame)dataFrame = "dbData";
  this.name = dataFrame;
  Database[dataFrame] = this;
  this.theFrame = document.frames[dataFrame];
  this.ctlFrame = ctlFrame;
  this.msgFrame = msgFrame;
```

Next, we go into the dbInfo form of the data frame, extract the value of Tables, and split it to get an array of table names. That array becomes the Tables property of the new database. For each name on that array, we create a database table (by calling on readTable()), and set its first row to be the current row. We set the hasBeenChanged property to false. (It will be used by the Save and Load methods to make sure the users don't lose any changes.) Finally, we look through both the data and the control frames for control forms for the created tables. This concludes the construction of the database object (but not quite the constructor function):

```
this.Tables = this.theFrame.document.all.dbInfo.Tables.value.split(",");
for(var i=0; i<this.Tables.length; i++){
 var tab = this.Tables[i];
 this.setCurRow(this.Tables[tab] = this.readTable(tab),0);
 }
this.hasBeenChanged = false;
this.findControlForms(this.dataFrame);
this.findControlForms(document.frames[ctlFrame]);
```

The absolutely last thing we do is install a body.onclick event handler on the data frame. This will allow the user to click on a row in the HTML table and have the corresponding record selected and loaded into the control form.

```
this.theFrame.document.body.onclick =
    new Function("","parent.selectTableRow('"+dataFrame+"')");
}
```

Tables and Forms

The last two lines of the constructor match up each table with the corresponding form, if it exists. The procedure relies on our naming conventions: if a table's name is Tab, the corresponding form's name is frmTab. So, we look for forms that match our table names; if found, the form becomes a property of the table, and the current row of the table is loaded into the form.

```
function db_findControlForms(frame)
{
 if(!frame)return;              // if there's no control frame, return
 for(var i=0; i<this.Tables.length; i++)
  {
  var tab = this.Tables[i];
  var frm = frame["frm" + tab];
  if(frm){this.Tables[tab].form = frm; this.loadRow(tab);}
  }
}
```

Communications Between the Database and HTML Elements

We've come across two functions that move material between HTML and the database. The constructor called readTable() to copy from HTML to the database, and loadRow() was called to copy from a database table to an HTML form. There's nothing fancy to this programming, just careful observing of all the naming conventions. Consider loadRow():

```
function db_loadRow(tab)
{
 var T = this.Tables[tab]; if(!T)return;
```

```
 var H = T.Headers; if(!H)return;
 var r = T[T.currentRow]; var f = T.form;
 if(!f || !r)return;              // we need a form and a row to load in it
 for(var i=0; i<H.length; i++)
{
  var fld = f["hh" + H[i]];
  if(!fld) alert("No field 'hh"+H[i]+"' in controller");
  else fld.value = r[H[i]];}
}
```

In order to load a table row into a form, we need a row and a form. What we're given is the name of the table. First we find the table and retrieve its headers (field names). We also retrieve our row, which is the current row of the table. We retrieve the form as the form property of the table. Finally we copy from the table row to the form, using our naming convention: the name of the form element is "hh" plus the name of the corresponding field.

Internal Representation of Tables

In order to understand `readTable()` and its companion `writeTable()`, you need a clear picture of how tables are represented internally. In overall structure, a database table is an array of records, and each record is an associative array (aka object) of field values, indexed by field names. So, to refer to the value of the `fld` field of the third record of table T, you say `T[2]["fld"]`. The names of the fields are stored in the `Headers` array, which is a property of the table.

In addition to a name, each field of our database tables can have a data type specification, such as `Num` or `Date`. (Deep down inside, we really like the comfortable security of strong typing.) The data type specifications are stored as the `dbKind` property of header elements and transferred to the `Kinds` array, which is another property of the table. (Some or even all elements of `Kinds` may be undefined.)

In addition to `Headers` and `Kinds`, each database table has the properties of `currentRow` (an integer) and `id` (a string equal to the name of the HTML table). We're ready to look at the code of `readTable()`.

readTable() and writeTable()

The `readTable()` method gets an HTML table name as argument and builds a database table in a local variable called `Res`, which it eventually returns. We'll break the code in two parts. The first part builds the arrays of headers and kinds, and sets the properties of the result. The second half copies the data. The first part is completely self-explanatory:

```
function db_readTable(tableName)
{         // HTML table to db table
 var T = this.theFrame.document.all[tableName];
 if(!T || !T.tagName || T.tagName.toUpperCase() != "TABLE")
  return alert("no table named " + tableName);
 var N = T.rows[0].cells.length;
 var H = new Array(N);                   // headers, one per column
 for(var i=0; i<N; i++)
  H[i] = trimSpace(T.rows[0].cells[i].innerHTML);
 var Cl = new Array(N);                  // Kinds of data: Num, Date
 for(var i=0; i<N; i++) Cl[i] = T.rows[0].cells[i].dbKind;
```

The second half has to contend with one minor annoyance: in HTML, the header row of a table is counted as its row[0]. As a result, our data table has one row fewer than the HTML table, and the numbering is off by one. Otherwise, the code is completely straightforward. Note that we're using a string utility, trimSpace(), which trims white space on both ends of a string.

```
    var Rows = T.rows.length - 1;
    var Res = new Array(Rows);
    for(var i=0; i<Rows; i++){
      var Ri = new Object();
      var Ti = T.rows[i+1];
      for(var j=0; j<N; j++) Ri[H[j]] = trimSpace(Ti.cells[j].innerHTML);
      Res[i] = Ri;
      }
    Res.Headers = H; Res.Kinds = Cl; Res.currentRow = 0; Res.id = tableName;
    return Res;
}
```

The code of writeTable() is very similar and we have complete confidence in your ability to work it out by yourself or with a friend. Please do so before moving on, because writeTable() is used by every method that modifies a table in the database or creates a new one. As always, if you do get stuck, the

Methods to Cycle Through and Modify a Table

Supporting Methods

This group of methods consists of the following: Next(), Prev(), Add(), Del(), and Replace(). They use four supporting methods: loadRow(), writeTable(), update() and setCurRow(). We have already discussed the first two of them. The update() method does the bookkeeping: it sets the value of hasBeenChanged to true, and calls writeTable() to transfer changes from the database to the HTML page.

```
function db_update(tblName){
  this.hasBeenChanged = true;
  this.writeTable(tblName);
}
```

Apart from setting the currentRow property of the table, the setCurRow() method changes the style-class attribute of the previously-current and the newly-current rows. It's common practice to make the current row stand out in some way; our simple-minded style specs simply make it turn red.

```
function db_setCurRow(T,i)
{
  if(!T)return;
  if(i<0 || i>=T.length)return;
  var old = T.currentRow;
  T.currentRow = i;
  var theOb = this.theFrame.document.all[T.id];
  if(old>=0 && old<T.length)
    theOb.rows[old+1].className = "baseRow";      // return to normal color
    theOb.rows[i+1].className = "curRow";         // turn red
}
```

The replaceRow() Method

The five methods are similar and quite straightforward in their operation. We'll present the most complicated one, `replaceRow()`, and leave the rest for you to figure out, or view from the source code in the samples you can download from our website.

The task of this method is to replace the current record of the database with the contents of the corresponding form. A record, you recall, is an object whose properties are field names. According to our naming conventions, the elements of the form have the same names plus a constant "hh" prefix. After the usual preliminaries, the method builds a new object from the form's elements and replaces the current record with the new object.

```
function db_replaceRow(tab)
{
 var T = this.Tables[tab]; if(!T) return; if(T.length==0) return;
 var frm = T.form; var H = T.Headers; var N = T.currentRow;
 var A = new Object();
 for(var i=0; i<H.length; i++){
  var fld = frm["hh" + H[i]];
  if(!fld)
  {
    alert("form " + frm.name + " has no field 'hh" + H[i] + "'"); return;
  }
  A[H[i]] = fld.value;
  }
 T[N] = A;
 this.update(tblName);
}
```

Creating Buttons

All the methods in this group are exposed to the user as onclick methods of buttons. That's a lot of buttons and a lot of onclick methods. To make it even worse, they're all the same: all the onclick method does is call a method, whose name may be the same as the name of the button. That method will need an argument, the name of the table, but that's just the name of the form in which the button lives, minus the first three characters ("frm"). So, the whole thing can be automated by a method, `clickb()`. We already mentioned it when we talked about the `facForm.htm` file, because that's the only place where the method is used.

```
function db_clickb(btn,ev)
{
 ev.cancelBubble = true;
 var name = btn.name ? btn.name : btn.value;
 var tab = btn.form.name.substring(3);              // eg "frmFaculty"
 this[name](tab);
}
```

The method takes two arguments, a button and an event. We need the event because we want to stop it from bubbling up the HTML tree. Once this is done, it's all just the matter of playing with names again. First, we assume the naming convention that if the button has a name, it's the same as the name of the method it will call in onclick. If it doesn't have a name then it has to have a value that will give us the name of the method. We use the name of the button's form to get the name of the table to work on, and give it as an argument to the method.

The code for `showCurrent()` in the control frame of our applications is very similar. We leave it as an exercise to rewrite it as a method that calls on `clickb()`. Such a method would be too application-specific to go into `dbob.js`, but it doesn't have to. Methods can be defined and used anywhere, without being added to the prototype.

```
function showCurrent(frmName,ev,fld)
{
// show data field of current rec of corresponding table
 ev.cancelBubble = true;
 var tblName = frmName.substring(3);        // eg "frmFaculty"
 var tbl = parent.Database.dbData.Tables[tblName];
 var recN = tbl.currentRow;
 var url = "pages/" + tbl[recN][fld];
 window.open(url);
}
```

Search and Lookup

The `search()` method is similar to `Next()` and `Prev()` in that it changes (if successful) the current record of the table. You can expect to see our old friends, `setCurRow()` and `loadRow()` in it. The new element is the search expression that specifies what records to search for. The mechanism of `search` is to convert a search expression into a JavaScript predicate that we apply to the records in the table to see whether they satisfy the search condition.

Getting the Search Expression From the User

It's best to work from an example. Suppose the user wants to find the records of all the faculty in Lawrence Hall. Two questions have to be answered: What does the user type in, and where?

Taking up the second question first, clearly the user needs an input element in a form somewhere. For reasons which will become clear in the next chapter (but may be obvious anyway) we want to be flexible about where this form is located. In particular, we don't want to assume that the form is always the control form of the table to be searched. If it is, then we already know how to find it. If it isn't, then we expect to find either the search expression itself, or the form where it is to be found, as an argument to the search method. We could ask for the name of the input element as an argument also, but this is one of those places where a naming convention can simplify things. Let's assume that the name of the input element is always `SearchExpr`.

To summarize, we allow the `search()` method to have one of the following signatures:

```
search(tableName)
search(tableName, stringSearchExpr)
search(tableName, form)
```

In other words, we allow the method to have one or two arguments, and the second argument can be a string (a search expression) or a form (which contains an element called `SearchExpr`, which contains the search expression). If there is only one argument, a table name, we go to the corresponding control form looking for the element called `SearchExpr`.

Some strongly-typed languages allow the same function or method to have several signatures, and call this feature **function overloading**. In such a language, we would write three versions of the function, and the compiler would figure out which one to use on any given occasion. In JavaScript, we do it ourselves, in several lines of code:

```
function db_search(tblName,expFrm){
 var table = this.Tables[tblName]; var frm = table.form; var expr;
 if(typeof expFrm == "string")expr = expFrm;     // expFrm is the search expression
 else if (expFrm && expFrm.SearchExpr)           // second argument is form
  expr = expFrm.SearchExpr.value;
 else if (!expFrm && frm && frm.SearchExpr)      // no second argument, try frm
  expr = frm.SearchExpr.value;
 else{alert("No SearchExpr in form"); return false;}
```

For instance, in our application, the function call:

```
this.search("Faculty","Building == 'Lawrence Hall'")
```

should be equivalent to

```
this.search("Faculty")
```

provided that `this.Tables["Faculty"].form.SearchExpr.value` is the string:

```
Building == 'Lawrence Hall'
```

Or, it would also be equivalent to

```
this.search("Faculty",dbControl.queryForm)
```

provided that `dbControl.queryForm.SearchExpr.value` is the same string.

This is pretty flexible, and we'll use those lines of code in many situations when we want to get input from the user.

Using the Search Expression

Now we have the table and the search expression; what next? Two steps: convert the expression into a predicate, and use the predicate in some sort of a loop that searches through the records of the table.

From Search Expression to Search Predicate: the Splicing Technique

How do we obtain a predicate? It depends on what the search expression is. An easy way out would be for us to ask the user to type in:

```
Building == 'Lawrence Hall'
```

To be honest, this is asking a lot of the users. We're asking them to enter a valid Boolean expression in JavaScript. When that expression refers to a field in the table, the user has to type in the name of the field, and the value of the field also, within matching quotes. If the operator is equality, the user has to remember to put two equal signs next to each other. If the user gets any of those things wrong, the user gets an error. This is not much worse than what most spreadsheet programs ask their users to do in specifying search conditions, but it's not any better, either. We should be able to do better, and we will, but for now let's push the less perfect solution to the end because it greatly simplifies the code. Once we get the simplest (for us, programmers) search going, we'll think of ways to improve it, at the cost of complicating the code.

If we do get raw (but clean) JavaScript from the user, our task is very simple. We splice the Boolean expression that the user gave us into a search predicate:

```
var P = new Function("row","with(row){return "+expr+";}");
```

At first sight, this line may appear cryptic. However, let's continue with the example and substitute our expression for `expr`.

```
var P = new Function("row","with(row){return Building == 'Lawrence Hall';}");
```

This technique can be used every time you need to apply a function to some properties of an object: make the formal parameter of the function refer to that object (`row` in this example), and place the body of the function inside a `with()` expression that uses the same parameter. Inside the `with()` expression, you can freely refer to the properties of the object.

Searching Through the Records

The next thing to do is run the predicate on every record in the table. The question is, starting from where? We could either go from the first record to the last, or from the current record to the end of the table and wrap around. The second version is more common. The actual task of finding the next record satisfying the predicate is relegated to a supporting method `nextP()`. Here's `search()` in its entirety:

```
function db_search(tblName,expFrm)
{
 var table = this.Tables[tblName]; var frm = table.form; var expr;
 if(typeof expFrm == "string")expr = expFrm;
 else if (expFrm && expFrm.SearchExpr) expr = expFrm.SearchExpr.value;
 else if (!expFrm && frm && frm.SearchExpr) expr = frm.SearchExpr.value;
 else{alert("No SearchExpr in form"); return false;}

 if(this.nextP(table,P))return true;
 alert("no records satisfying the condition " + expr);
 return false;
}
```

If no record satisfying the predicate is found, a message of condolence is displayed and the value `false` is returned. If such a record is found, it becomes the current record, and its contents are loaded into the form. This all happens in `nextP()`:

```
function db_nextP(table,P)
{
 var N = table.length;
 for(var i=(1+table.currentRow)%N; i!=table.currentRow; i=(i+1)%N)
  if(P(table[i])){
   this.setCurRow(table,i);
   this.loadRow(table.id);
   return true;}
 return P(table[table.currentRow]);
}
```

Pressing the Search button again resumes the search from the current record, wrapping around when the end of the table is reached. In other words, the method cycles through the recordset of records satisfying the predicate. If the recordset has only one record in it, pressing the button again will return you to the same record: visibly, nothing will change. This is the effect of the last line of nextP().

Improving the Search

In search(), the expression submitted by the user is spliced directly into the predicate, without any processing. The processing is done by the JavaScript interpreter, which is rather unforgiving. The way to improve the user interface is to insert a function between the user input and the search predicate that can try to understand the user better.

There are two kinds of errors the user can make: in JavaScript syntax and in the specifics of field names and values. How can we help? Well, in two ways: by simplifying the syntax, and by making it easier for the user to identify fields and values. There are many approaches one can take, and the lookup() method shows some of them.

The lookup() Method

For syntax, lookup() takes the attribute-colon-value approach, where the attribute is a field name and the value is the field's value. This, in effect, replaces two equal signs with one colon, so you can say: Department:Computer Science. The colon can be followed by > or <, to indicate "greater than" or "less than": Office:<400.

For identifying names and values, lookup() checks to see whether the expression uses shortened field names (e.g., "Dep" instead of "Department"), and it allows for errors in capitalization ("dep" is ok, too). Finally, it supplies the quotes if you haven't. Here's an example of a search expression that lookup() can understand:

```
name:>N; office:<400; dep:Computer Science
```

This turns into a search for rows such that

```
row.Name > 'N' && row.OfficeNum < 400 && row.Department=="Computer Science"
```

You can ask lookup() to display the expanded expression that it has come up with.

How does lookup() do all those things? It inserts a function call between the user's expression and the search predicate; otherwise the code is exactly the same as in search():

```
function db_lookup(tblName,expFrm) // assumes form has "lookupFld" as field;
{
 var table = this.Tables[tblName]; var frm = table.form; var expr;
 if(typeof expFrm == "string")expr = expFrm;
 else if (expFrm && expFrm.LookupFld) expr = expFrm.LookupFld.value;
 else if (!expFrm && frm && frm.LookupFld) expr = frm.LookupFld.value;
 else{alert("No LookupFld in form"); return false;}
 var sExpr = lookupCrit(table,expr); if(!sExpr)return false;
 var P = new Function("row","with(row){return "+ sExpr +";}");
 if (this.nextP(table,P)) return true;
 alert("sorry, no records satisfying condition " + sExpr);
 return false;
}
```

The beginning and end of lookup() are exactly the same as search(). The only difference is in the line that puts the expression through the lookupCrit() function before splicing it into the predicate. That function calls on several others to check for abbreviations, supply quotes, correct capitalization, and convert colons to equal signs. All this takes about fifty lines of code that you're welcome to study and enjoy; it's mostly string processing code.

In some respects, lookup() is more permissive than search() but in some other respects it's more restrictive. It assumes that the search expression uses field names and values in expressions with operators but not functions. There's no way to ask lookup() to find all the faculties whose names begin with 'A', but search(), of course, would have no trouble. The reason is that lookup() uses only a small subset of JavaScript, while search() allows you to enter an arbitrary (Boolean) expression.

Can lookup() be improved upon? Unquestionably so, and you're welcome to try. Be aware, though, that the problem is hard, because we're trying to answer the question: "What does the user mean by this search expression?" Now, understanding what the other person means is a hard problem; even human intelligence frequently fails. In the 1980s, a lot of human effort and money went into developing "natural language front ends to databases," which would allow users to enter queries in English. The results are very modest. We're probably better off with a semi-formal notation of some sort with a lot of error checking.

The join() Method

The join() method creates a new table out of two tables that have a field in common. This is a very limited implementation of the join operation on tables, but it is sufficient for our purposes.

Before looking at the code of the join() method, let's put ourselves in the method's shoes and walk through the steps. We have two tables and the name of a field they have in common. Every time the shared field has the same value in both tables, we retrieve the corresponding records from them and construct a record for the result by copying all fields of the first record and all fields of the second record. The records, you recall, are objects (associative arrays). Looks like we'll be doing a lot of object copying, so before we do anything else let's write a utility for that:

```
function copyOb(A,B){
  if(!B)B = new Object();
  for(x in A) B[x] = A[x]; return B;
}
```

Now, closer to the heart of the matter, how do we find all those values of the shared field that are the same in both tables? One obvious way is to do a for-loop through the first table, and on each turn of the loop go through all the records of the second table and compare the values in the shared field. This would take time proportional to T1.length * T2.length, where T1 and T2 are our tables. We can do better than that if we use JavaScript's associative arrays to create an **inverted index** for each table. An inverted index lets you find things backwards. In our tables, if you know the record and the field name, it's easy to find the value of the field. However, if you know the field name and its value, it's not at all easy to find the record; you have to search through them all. An inverted index will make it easy to go from a field's value to the corresponding record, or records. We do not require the shared field to be a key (i.e., to have a unique value for each different record). A value in the shared field will be associated with an array of records in which it appears; for a key field, all those arrays will be of length 1.

How do we associate a value with an array of records? Using an associative array, of course. We'll create a local variable of type object, and make it into an inverted index. Each value of the shared field will be its property, and the values of those properties will be arrays of records. In addition, the inverted index will have the properties `hhNames`, `hhKinds` and `hhVals`, holding (copies of) the table's arrays of headers, kinds, and the values of the shared field. (To copy an array `H`, we'll use the `slice()` method with arguments 0 and `H.length`.)

We're ready to look at the `invert()` method, which takes two arguments, a table name and a field name, and returns an inverted index. Recall that our database table is an array of records, and each record is an associative array.

```javascript
function db_invert(tab,colName)
{
  if(typeof colName != "string"){alert("invert("+tab+", ... "); return;}
  var T = this.Tables[tab]; var H = T.Headers;
  var col = arrayIndexOf(H,colName);          // find index of colName in H;
                                              // -1 if not found
  if(col<0){alert("no header "+colName+" in "+tab); return null;}
  var Ob = new Object();                      // this will be the inverted index!
  Ob.hhNames = H.slice(0,H.length);           // returns a copy of H
  Ob.hhKinds = T.Kinds.slice(0,H.length);     // returns a copy of Kinds
  Ob.hhVals = new Array();                     // holds the values of colName in tab
  for(var i=0; i<T.length; i++)
    {
    var Ti=T[i]; var key=Ti[colName];         // value of colName field in record Ti
    var obV = Ob[key];
    if(!obV)                                  // new value, not yet recorded in assoc array
      {
      Ob.hhVals[Ob.hhVals.length] = key;
      Ob[key] = new Array; obV = Ob[key];
      }
    obV[obV.length] = Ti;                     // add record Ti to array associated with
key
    }
  return Ob;
}
```

This has been quite a bit of work, and we haven't even started on the `join()` itself. However, with `invert()` and `copyOb()` in place, `join()` is fairly straightforward. The arguments are: two tables to join, a shared field, and the name (actually, the ID) of the HTML object that will be replaced by the new table. We build inverted indices for both tables and use them to check for common values.

```javascript
function db_join(tab1,tab2,colName,newTab) \
{
  var T1 = this.Tables[tab1]; var T2 = this.Tables[tab2];
  var Ob1 = this.invert(tab1,colName);
  var Ob2 = this.invert(tab2,colName);
  if(!Ob1 || !Ob2) return;
  var keys = Ob1.hhVals;             // could be Ob2.hhVals
  var R = new Array();               // this will be the joined table, written to newTab
  var col = arrayIndexOf(T2.Headers,colName);
  for(var i=0; i<keys.length; i++)
    {
    var v = keys[i];
    var R1 = Ob1[v]; var R2 = Ob2[v];
    if(!R1 || !R2) continue;         // skip if only one table has value keys[i]
// common value found; create new record in R by copying all properties
```

```
// from inverted indices
  for(j=0; j<R1.length; j++)
   for(k=0; k<R2.length; k++)
    {
     var Rn = copyOb(R1[j]); Rn = copyOb(R2[k],Rn);
     R[R.length] = Rn;
    }
  }
this.Tables[newTab] = R;
R.Headers = arrayCatAllBut(T1.Headers,T2.Headers,col);
R.Kinds = arrayCatAllBut(T1.Kinds,T2.Kinds,col);
R.id = newTab;
R.currentRow = 0;
this.writeTable(newTab);
}
```

An important question about joins and other derived tables is when they get to be updated. Suppose you create a join of two tables, then revise one of them; what happens to the joined table? In a dedicated database program, you'd have the option of "cascading" your changes in one table through all the tables and queries that depend on it. We haven't implemented any such machinery; the user has to save and reload to update the joins.

Implementing Queries

Our query system creates a new table based on existing tables, a field-list, and a constraint. (Those are the data items that we enter in the query form, remember?) If the constraint is that the values in some field must be equal, then the result of the query is just a join of the tables on that field. The query system can do joins and more, but it's still useful to have a simple common operation of join as a separate method.

Let's again begin by mentally walking through the steps, assuming for simplicity that we have only two tables to work with. We have to look at all possible pairs of rows, one from the first table, the other from the second. For each such pair we do the same thing: check the condition and if it holds, build a row of the result. So, the structure of our method will be like that:

```
function outer(tables, condition)
{         // WARNING: pseudocode follows
  var qres = new Array();      // qres will contain the result of the query
  for(all the rows of first table)
    for(all the rows of the second table)
      check condition; if true, build row in qres;
  return qres;
}
```

It makes sense to outsource the internals of the loop to a separate function

```
function inner(qres,row of table 1,row of table 2)
{                   // given two rows as args
  with(table 1)
    with(table 2)
      if(condition)
        qres[qres.length] = makeRow(fields);
}
```

JavaScript Objects

Finally, we can write some actual code: the `makeRow()` function that builds a row of the result of the query. A row in our database tables is, as you recall, an associative array (an object), indexed by field names. To build a row, our function will need the field names and corresponding values. For simplicity, let's give it the field names all together in one string separated by commas, because that's how we get them from the `queryForm`. This will be the first argument to the function. If we split that string argument using `","` as separator we'll get an array of strings. The remaining arguments to the function are values to be associated with the strings in that array. We'll retrieve them from the array of arguments that is a property of each JavaScript function. (Review Chapter 3 on Function objects, if necessary.) So, we get:

```
function makeRow(fldLst)
{                        // there are more arguments
                         // but we don't know how many until we split fldLst
                         // we'll get them later from the
  var ob = new Object();
  var L = fldLst.split(",");
  for(var i=0; i<L.length; i++)
    ob[L[i]] = makeRow.arguments[i+1]; return ob;
}
```

That was easy because all we had to do is write a function. For our "inner" and "outer" functions, we have a much trickier problem of writing functions that construct their text out of their arguments and some fixed elements. This is perhaps the trickiest piece of code in the entire book, so don't be discouraged if you don't breeze through it at first reading. It's mostly a matter of keeping the quotes and parentheses straight. The code is divided into chunks by our comments; take it a chunk at a time. In outline, the chunks are:

❑ move all input values from the form into local variables
❑ construct the text of the body of the inner function in the string `fnTxt`
❑ define the inner function as `qfn` with the arguments `qres` and the tables from the list; the body is `fnTxt`
❑ construct the text of the body of the outer function in the string `loops`
❑ define the query method as a function with one argument and `loops` as body (this is the outer function)
❑ create the resulting table (this is where all the work is done), set its properties and return it

So, here we go:

```
function db_withWhere(form)
{
// move values from the form into variables
  var tables = form.tables.value;
  var fields = form.fields.value;
  var expr = form.expr.value;
  var outTab = form.outTab.value;
  if(!outTab) outTab = "dbQuery";        //default for outTab
  var tLst = tables.split(",");          // tables to be used;

// start the body of the inner function
  var fnTxt = "with("+tLst.join(")with(")+")\n";     // as many with(..) as needed
  fnTxt += "if("+expr+") qres[qres.length] = makeRow('"+fields+"',"+fields+");\n";
  var qfn = new Function("qres,"+tables,fnTxt);
```

226

Let's take a pause here. Suppose that the contents of the form were:

- ❑ tables: Divisions,Faculty
- ❑ fields: Name,Department,Division,Building
- ❑ expr: Divisions.Department==Faculty.Department && Building!='McGregory'

If at this point you'd put the text of qfn() into an alert box, you'd see this:

```
function anonymous(qres,Divisions,Faculty)
{
with(Divisions)with(Faculty)  if(Divisions.Department == Faculty.Department &&
Building != 'McGregory')
 qres[qres.length] = makeRow('Name,Department,Division,Building',
                       Name,Department,Division,Building);
}
```

(Well, we've cheated a little bit: it would probably not come out so nicely formatted, but the text would be exactly the same.) Resuming our db_withWhere(), the next thing to do is to build the body of the outer function:

```
var loops = "var qres=new Array();\n";
// the "loops" code contains one index variable for each table
 for(var i=0; i<tLst.length; i++)
  {
  var A = tLst[i]; var N = this.Tables[A].length; var V = A + "_i";
  loops += "for(var "+V+"=0; "+V+" < "+N+"; "+V+"++)\n";
  }
 loops += "with(this.Tables)qfn(qres,";
 var lastT = tLst.length-1;
 for(var i=0; i<lastT; i++)
  {          //arguments to Pred are table rows
  var A = tLst[i]; var V = A + "_i"; loops += A + "["+V+"],";
  }
 if(lastT >= 0)
  {
  var A = tLst[i]; var V = A + "_i"; loops += A + "["+V+"]";
  }
 loops += ");"
 loops += "\nreturn qres";
 this.query = new Function("qfn",loops);
```

Again, if you put the text of this.query into an alert box, you'd see this (formatting ours!):

```
function anonymous(qfn)
{
 var qres = new Array();
 for(var Divisions_i=0; Divisions_i<8; Divisions_i++)
  for(var Faculty_i=0; Faculty_i<13; Faculty_i++)
   with(this.Tables)
    qfn(qres,Divisions[Divisions_i],Faculty[Faculty_i]);
 return qres
}
```

We're almost done; the rest is quite simple

```
      var res = this.query(qfn);                // this is where all the work is done
      res.Headers = fields.split(",");
      res.Kinds = new Array(res.Headers.length);
      res.id = outTab;
      res.currentRow = 0;
      this.Tables[outTab] = res;
      this.writeTable(outTab);                  // write HTML
   }
```

As we said, this is the trickiest piece of code so far. It may take a couple of passes over it before it becomes completely transparent.

Conclusions

We have covered a lot of ground in this chapter, as usual, moving on several fronts. In our more theoretical moments, we've learned the basics of CGI, and quite a few database concepts. Here are some of the terms you should now be familiar with: table, record, field; join, query, virtual table; recordset.

An important part of working with databases is search and sort. We have implemented both, including two versions of user interface for search.

We have designed and implemented a database class and used it to develop a database application. The application can be used in three modes: browsing, editing, and data definition. The data definition mode is not specific for any given application; it gives you the ability to create applications of your own. So, in addition to a specific application, we have also provided you with an authoring tool.

In order to make our database class into an authoring tool, we have adopted several naming conventions. Naming conventions are an important part of programming in JavaScript; a few well-chosen ones can greatly simplify your code, and make complex tasks available to users with only HTML skills.

We have provided several server-side arrangements for saving and loading files. One of them is a CGI program written in C whose source code can be found in the code files. The rest use Java and are discussed in Chapter 9.

The application we've developed in this chapter is sparse, with very limited functionality. (We had enough trouble fitting it all in one chapter as it is.) In the next chapter, we will not bring in any new theory, but develop our application into a more realistically useful one. In particular, we'll combine a database application with a tree controller, providing a more informative user interface to a database.

7

Databases with Tree Controllers

Introduction

In this chapter, we will further develop our database application, so it becomes more active and Dynamic (as in Dynamic HTML). The material of the chapter came into being in response to a set of specifications, and we recommend that you approach it that way, as an example of software development in response to user specifications. This is what we set out to do:

- ❑ Our database contains tree structured data (for instance, a college consists of divisions, divisions consist of departments, and departments consist of faculty members). We'd like to show the database not only in the table-form view, but also in a tree view, as a tree controller.
- ❑ Currently, we can associate one data item (a Web page) with a record. We'd like to be able to associate a data item with every tree node (i.e., with individual fields of a record), and access that item from the node label.
- ❑ We'd like to be able to search the database both in the table-form view and in the tree view, where a successful search would show a tree path leading to the found item.

These specifications determine the code content of the chapter. We will approach this code in the same way as we did in Chapter 6. First, we'll go through a tutorial that shows how to build a database application with a searchable tree controller. This part does not require significant programming background: it is addressed to those readers who will use our classes as an authoring system for their applications. Second, we'll investigate the code, and see what new interesting facts and techniques we can learn from it. In outline, the chapter will proceed as follows:

- ❏ New HTML data elements to support database trees
- ❏ New HTML control elements to support database trees
- ❏ Additional features for database trees
- ❏ Searching the database in the tree view
- ❏ Minimal implementation of the database tree and tree view
- ❏ Additional functionality for the database tree

Try It Out

Point your browser at `http://webdev.wrox.co.uk/books/1894/Chapter07/facDB.htm`. The initial screen will be very similar to `tmp1DB.htm` (from Chapter 6). The only difference is that the select element on top now has an additional Tree View option. If you select it, you will see two tree controllers, one for the Administrative tree of Divisions and Departments, the other for the Physical tree of Buildings, Floors, and Offices. They behave the way tree controllers usually do. Clicking on a node icon toggles the node between open and closed, while clicking on the node's label loads a Web page into the rightmost frame. You can also use search and lookup buttons to look for specific database records; as before, clicking on the button cycles through the recordset.

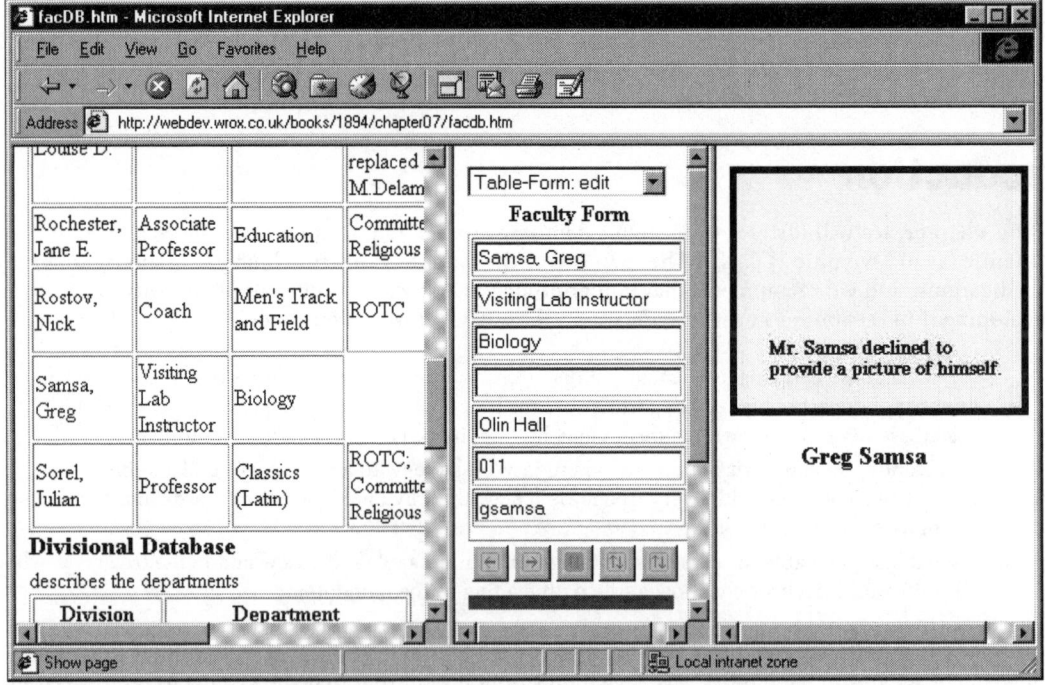

As you browse through the data, you will notice that the faculty pages are the same, but in addition we now have pages for Buildings, Divisions and other internal nodes of the tree. It is important to understand that it would make no sense to attempt to provide an image for every cell in a database table (that is, for every field of every record) because a record field doesn't have an identity outside the entire record. A node in the tree does have an identity, because it is completely specified by its tree address.

How It Works

Just as with the template application, there are two levels of understanding how this program works. At one level, we take the database class for granted, and expose the workings of the HTML files. The purpose is to understand how to develop your own application of similar functionality; only a minimal reading knowledge of JavaScript is assumed. At another level, those who want to write a better database class will also have to work through our implementation of it.

Components of a Database Tree Application

There are three HTML files: the main frameset page, and the source pages for the data and control frames. Following the same naming conventions as in Chapter 6, we called them facDB.htm, facData.htm and facCtrl.htm. Much in them will be familiar from the template application, discussed in the previous chapter.

The Main Page

Here's the code for the main page, with new code highlighted:

```
<HTML> <HEAD> <TITLE>facDB.htm</TITLE>
<SCRIPT SRC='../class7/dbob.js'> /* Database class */ </SCRIPT>
<SCRIPT SRC='../class6/treecon.js'> /* tree controller */ </SCRIPT>
<SCRIPT SRC='../class6/simptree.js'> /* tree */ </SCRIPT>
<SCRIPT SRC='../class8/dbtree.js'> /* database-tree */ </SCRIPT>
<SCRIPT SRC='../utils/arrutils.js'> /* controllers */ </SCRIPT>
<SCRIPT SRC='../utils/strutils.js'> /* controllers */ </SCRIPT>

<SCRIPT>
function setupDatabase(view)
{
 var D=new Database();
 D.join("Faculty","Divisions","Department","FullFaculty"); // create join
 D.makeTree('FullFaculty',
   dbControl.tr1Faculty.treeOrder.value,       // create tree and tree controller
   dbControl.PhysTree); D.makeTree('FullFaculty',
   dbControl.tr2Faculty.treeOrder.value,       // another one
   dbControl.AdmTree);
 D.hasBeenChanged=false;
 dbControl.selectView.value='tfe';
 setupView(view);
}
function setupView(view)
{
 if(view=="tree"){                              // tree view
    document.body.cols = "0%,60%,40%";
    dbControl.frmFaculty.className = "hidden";
    dbControl.treeTable.className = "";
 }
 else
   if(view=="tfe"){                             // table-form edit view
    document.body.cols="40%,30%,30%";
    dbControl.treeTable.className = "hidden";
    dbControl.frmFaculty.className = "";
```

```
        dbControl.editBtns.className = "";
        dbData.dbInfo.className = "hidden";        // hide dbInfo form
      }
      else
      if(view=="tfb")        // table-form browse view, hide everything
      {
        document.body.cols = "40%,30%,30%";
        dbControl.treeTable.className = "hidden";
        dbControl.frmFaculty.className = "";
        dbControl.editBtns.className = "hidden";
        dbData.dbInfo.className = "hidden";
      } else                 // unhide everything in data-definition view
      {
        document.body.cols = "40%,30%,30%";
        dbControl.treeTable.className = "hidden";
        dbControl.frmFaculty.className = "";
        dbControl.editBtns.className = "";
        dbData.dbInfo.className = "";
      }
    }
    </SCRIPT> </HEAD>

    <FRAMESET onload="setupDatabase('tfe')" >
      <FRAME NAME=dbData    SRC="facData.htm">
      <FRAME NAME=dbControl SRC="facCntrl.htm">
      <FRAME NAME=dbMsg     SRC="pages/initDoc.htm">
    </FRAMESET> </HTML>
```

New Code

Apart from including the code files for tree controllers, the new elements of the code do the following:

- ❑ join two base tables into a new table from which trees are created
- ❑ make two tree controllers
- ❑ provide the tree view
- ❑ hide and unhide new data and control elements

The first step is only needed in databases with two or more base tables that need to be joined to obtain tree-structured data in one table. Why do we need it here? Take a look at the screen shot: one of the trees shows the administrative structure of Divisions, Departments and individual instructors. In our base tables, Divisions and Departments are in one table and instructors, together with their departmental affiliation, are in the other one.

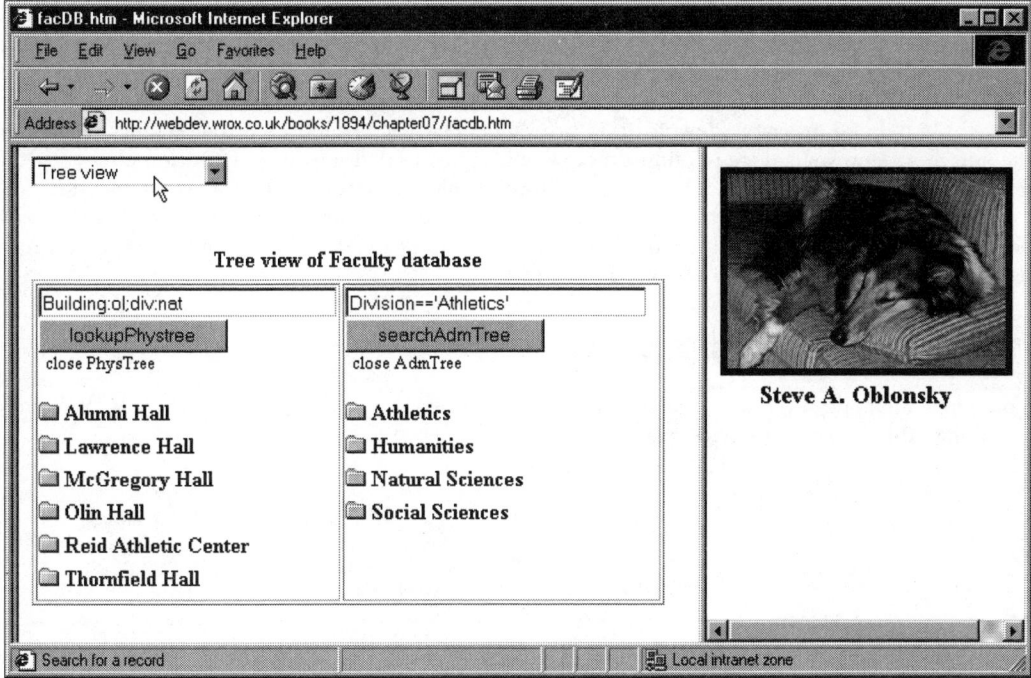

To get the tree we have to join the tables. Since you already know how join() works, you can see from the corresponding line of code that we join the Faculty and Divisions tables, using the Department field, and store the result as the outerHTML of the page element called FullFaculty.

(We could also use the query mechanism to produce a virtual table for each tree we want. It would make a good medium-size exercise to rework our entire program using query instead of join.)

The next step is to build two tree controllers from a database table, using the makeTree() method. The method needs to know three things: the table that provides the data; the tree categories, from the most general to the most specific (e.g., 'Division,Department,Name'); and the place to put the resulting tree controller. The name of the table and the place to put the controller are given to makeTree() as the first and the third argument, respectively. The list of categories comes from a text input box in a form.

Instead of giving makeTree() three arguments, one for each item it needs, we could give it just a form whose fields contain all three items. The first action of makeTree() would then be to extract the items from the form. You will see many examples of this style of programming in the rest of the book, and in fact our source code uses it here. For the first time around, we submit three arguments to makeTree() separately. So, in the page above, the first call on makeTree() is told to build a controller for the FullFaculty table, find the order of categories in the treeOrder element of the tr1Faculty form, and place the result into PhysTree. Both tr1Faculty and PhysTree are in the control frame. The form for the other tree and the DIV for its controller are also in the control frame, as tr2Faculty and AdminTree. We're going to see them all in a moment.

You can stop here if you don't mind having both the control form and the tree view visible at the same time. We found that arrangement too crowded and made the tree view an additional option in view selection. The selection function `setupView()` now has another complete view to worry about: it has to make sure the trees are not visible in all the table-form views.

We have only defined one new view, for tree browsing. There's no record-editing activity in the tree mode, and there's no special tree-definition view; we've just added new tree-definition elements to the general database definition view. The view-switching mechanism itself is the same. To change a view, you make some frames, or some elements within frames, visible or invisible. To make a frame invisible, you give it 0% space allocation. To make an element within a frame invisible, you set its "class" (in the style sheet sense of the word) to "hidden".

The Data and Control Frames

The only new element of the data frame is a `<DIV>` that gets replaced by the joined table. We made the resulting table invisible to avoid clutter.

```
<DIV style="display:none">
<H2> Complete Faculty Database </H2> Produced automatically during onload.
<DIV id=FullFaculty>
This space will be filled by a full faculty dbase, produced by join.
</DIV> </DIV>
```

Most of the new elements, by far, are in the control frame. Let's summarize them before looking at the code:

- ❑ a revised select element to switch views
- ❑ two forms, each with a `treeOrder` element whose value specifies a tree
- ❑ two dummy elements to be replaced by tree controllers

The select element, as before, is at the very top of the page. All the other new elements are in one big table, so the page, in outline, looks as follows:

```
<HTML> <HEAD> title, links to style sheets </HEAD>
<BODY>
<select id="selectView" size=1 ...> /* options...*/ </select>
<form name="frmFaculty"> /* unchanged from tmplCtrl.htm */ </form>
<div id="treeTable"> /* new material, placed in a DIV for ease of hiding */ </DIV>
<form id="queryEntry"> /* unchanged, hidden */ </form>
</BODY> </HTML>
```

Tree Definition Elements

The `treeTable` `<DIV>` element consists of a one-row table with two identically structured cells, one for Physical tree, the other for Admin tree. Let's look at the Admin tree first:

```
<TD size=50% valign=top>
<form id=tr2Faculty
 ACTION='javascript:parent.Database.dbData.searchTree(tr2Faculty)'>
<!-- the search section -->
 <input type=button value="searchAdmTree"
  onclick='parent.Database.dbData.searchTree(this.form)'>
```

```
  <div onclick='parent.TreeController.AdmTree.closeTree()'>
     close AdmTree </div>
 <!-- the tree definition section -->
  <input type=hidden name=treeOrder value="Division,Department,Name,Page">
  <input type=text size=30 name=SearchExpr value="Division=='Athletics'">
  <input type=hidden name=tableName value="FullFaculty">
  <input type=hidden name=treeConName value="AdmTree">
 </form>
 <DIV id=AdmTree > Administrative-tree Tree Controller goes here </DIV>
 </TD>
```

The material inside the TD consists of a form that defines the tree and its search facility, and a <DIV> that gets replaced by the tree controller. Within the form, there are two major parts: the search part and the tree-definition part. The search part has a text box to enter the search expression and a command button. In case the user types an expression and presses Return, which is equivalent to pressing the Submit button, the action of the entire form is also a call on searchTree(). That function doesn't do anything original; it simply passes on the search expression to the Search() method, and uses the result to show the right node.

The crucial lines are those that specify the treeOrder values. These values define the tree, from the root down. If you wanted to add another level to the administrative tree and group department members by rank, then you would insert the field name 'Position' between Department and Name. The last item in the treeOrder list is the name of the HTML page associated with the leaf node. In our application here, the node whose label comes from the Name field gets its data item from the Page field.

Can we associate data items (HTML page names) with **internal nodes**, e.g., provide a page that shows Thornfield Hall and describes its proud history? This will require some additional machinery, both in the control frame and in the data frame. Let's do all the additional features later, after we summarize the basics.

Creating Your Own Database With a Tree Controller

Recall the course picturebook application that we described in Chapter 6. It had to do with an imaginary professor who received a small grant to develop a 'picture book' for a literature course: a body of visual materials to supplement the textbook. If you remember from our discussion in Chapter 6, the course consists of several topics, each topic covers several authors, for each author there are several texts, and each text can be appropriately illustrated by a photograph and some commentary.

You can see that this is a perfect little exercise for a tree-structured database. It is easier than the faculty database because it uses only one table, builds only one tree controller, and shows one page per record rather than a record field. You can follow these steps in creating your own application:

1.   Make a copy of our facDB.htm, facData.htm and facCtrl.htm files. Rename them appropriately, e.g., Fr345.htm, Fr345Data.htm and Fr345Ctrl.htm. Make the changes in the frameset document so that, for instance, the source file for the dbData frame is Fr345Data.htm.

2.   In the data frame, replace our tables with your one table, and make the necessary renamings in the dbInfo form. As before, use your favorite Web page editor (which may or may not be Notepad).

3.   Make all the necessary changes in the control frame, such as renaming the form and its text input elements in accordance with the names in the data frame. If your table's name is Fr345 then the control frame must have a form whose name is frmFr345. If one of your table headers is "Author", that form must have an hhAuthor text input element. So far, it's been a repetition of what you learned in Chapter 7 when you created a database without a tree controller.

4.   Now comes the new part. Go into the control frame and specify the tree order for your tree controller. A possible text to type into your treeOrder text box is 'Topic,Author,Text,Page'. Make sure that the last item is the name of the field that contains HTML pages for the leaf node.

5.   Finally, make all the necessary HTML changes the names of the buttons and in the structure of the table that receives the controller. Get rid of the table altogether if you'd rather use another structure.

That's it, you're done.

Beefing it up With "Features"

It's time to consider a couple of additions that will make our application even better. One has to do with search and lookup, another with labels, and the third and last one with providing data items for internal nodes.

The Physical Tree

The code for the Physical tree is very similar to the code for the Admin tree, except we put a lookup facility here, to show that it also works. In your own application, you can provide both search and lookup, or neither, for all or some of your trees.

```
<TD size=50% valign=top>
<form id=tr1Faculty
 ACTION='javascript:parent.Database.dbData.lookupTree(tr1Faculty)'>
<!-- the lookup section -->
 <input type=text size=30 name=LookupFld value="Building:ol;div:nat"> <BR>
 <input type=button value="lookupPhystree"
  onclick='parent.Database.dbData.lookupTree(this.form)'>
<!-- the tree definition section -->
 <input type=hidden name=treeOrder
  value="Building,Department,Office,Name,Page">
 <input type=hidden name=tableName value="FullFaculty">
 <input type=hidden name=treeConName value="PhysTree">
</form>
<DIV id=PhysTree> Physical-tree Tree Controller goes here </DIV>
</TD>
```

Search and Lookup together

Do you notice a problem here? The form has an Action attribute in case the user presses the Enter key, which is equivalent to pressing the Submit button. If you provide both the Search and the Lookup facilities, which of them should be the default action of the entire form? The answer is: either Search or Lookup, depending on where (in which text box) the user pressed the Enter key. How do we find out? Here's one possible way. We can keep track of which of the two text inputs has the focus when the Enter key is pressed by giving both an onfocus event handler. The handler will put the name of the function to call (lookupTree() or searchTree()) into a property of the form added specifically for that purpose. The handler of the LookupFld element would be like so:

```
onfocus='this.form.srchFntoCall="lookupTree"';
```

The rest is a good exercise for you. Check with our suggested solution from the website.

Flexible Labels

As long as we're in the problem-solving mood, let's attack another one. All our tree labels have so far come directly from field values: whatever is in the table cell ends up, unprocessed, as a label in the tree. This may be too restrictive. The records of the data base may contain all sorts of in-house abbreviations or special symbols, while the tree labels are descriptive elements of the user interface.

Another reason for flexible labels is that you may want to create a tree category that is not in the database at all but can be computed from it. Suppose our imaginary college follows the practice (common in North America but rather exotic in other parts of the world) of numbering the offices so that the first digit indicates the floor. We may use this information to create a Physical tree that has a Floor level: Building -- Floor -- Department -- Name. This will not require any programming on your part (we've done it), only familiarity with another convention. This is what you have to enter in the treeOrder text box:

```
Building,Floor:Office.charAt(0),Department,Name,Page
```

A tree label, it turns out, doesn't have to be a field name. It can be any text you wish, followed by a colon and a JavaScript expression. In this case, the expression extracts the first character of the office number. If the office number is 1xx, the label in the tree will come out as 'Floor 1' (i.e., the prefix that comes before the colon, followed by a space, followed by the value of the expression that comes after the colon). If you'd like to combine the prefix and the value in some other way, you'll have to dig, we're sorry to say, into the code of the labelPairsFn() function and edit a couple of lines of code. We discuss that function in great detail in the Implementation section.

Data for Internal Nodes

We would like to associate some data items with internal nodes of the tree. In order to do that, we need some way to establish a one-to-one correspondence between tree paths (or tree addresses) and some data items (file name, in our case). There are two ways to establish a one-to-one correspondence, by a complete listing of all path-data pairs in a two column table, or by some sort of a formula that, given a tree path, computes the corresponding file name. What kind of formula would that be? It would be another naming convention, something like: take the first two characters from each component of the path, and prepend them to the beginning of the last component. If the path is "Lawrence Hall, Floor 3, English" then the file name would be LaFlEnglish.htm.

As you might have noticed, we like naming conventions; they're frequently very helpful in JavaScript programming. However, this time around we decided in favor of the table, partly to break the mold, partly to reuse all the brand-new wonderful gleaming machinery we have for working with tables. A naming convention would be easy to institute, and you're welcome to try (another exercise!), but even with the convention, you'd probably want to run the computation once and save the results in a table, for reasons of efficiency. So, much of the material in this section would have to be written anyway.

Additions to the Frames and the Database Setup

Once we've decided on the table, the natural questions are: How is it created, where and when? How do other parts of the program learn about it? Pause to think how you would do it before reading about our solution. Chances are, your solution is very similar to ours because the choices are few and obvious. A good place to put a table is the data frame which already has tables, and a good place to advertise a table is the dbInfo form. Let's say the name of the new table is PhysTreeData. The new material in the data frame will look as follows:

```
<H2> Phys Tree Data Table for FullFaculty </H2>
<TABLE BORDER id="PhysTreeData">
<TH>TreePath</TH><TH>Data</TH>
<TR><TD>Alumni Hall</TD><TD>alumni.htm</TD></TR>
<TR><TD>Alumni Hall,Floor 3 </TD><TD>alumni3.htm</TD></TR>
...
</TABLE>
```

and in dbInfo:

```
<input type=TEXT name="Tables" value="Divisions,Faculty,PhysTreeData">
```

Another place that needs to know about this table is the form that defines the tree from which the path data will come. So, we insert a new line into the tr2Faculty form in the control frame, right after the lines that identify the names of the data table and the tree controller:

```
<input type=hidden name=tableName value="FullFaculty">
<input type=hidden name=treeConName value="PhysTree">
<input type=hidden name=TreeDataTableName value="PhysTreeData">
```

If you have write privileges on the server AND if you're willing to go ahead and type in all the paths and corresponding file names by hand, that's all you would need. Our program will retrieve the data items from the PhysTreeData table and place them into the appropriate nodes of the tree. However, typing all tree nodes by hand is back-breaking work because even a small tree has a lot of nodes. (The number of nodes is an exponential function of the depth of the tree.) So, we added a bit more stuff, to get the computer to do the boring part. Basically, we provide a function that enters all the paths from the tree in the left column of the table. The human operator is left with less than half the work. However, the procedure for creating the two-column table becomes more intricate; it's summarized in the subsection Procedure Summary below.

Now the human operator needs some way to enter the remaining data into the table. We could say, as we sometimes do: "Oh, just use your favorite Web editor", and you can, of course, do that. On the other hand, we already had this convenient function lying around that takes a table as argument and generates an appropriate data entry form. So, we decided to provide a form also, so that even those who don't have or use or like Web editors can enter the file names. (Note that you really enter just the file names in the table, not HTML links.)

What it boils down to is that we have another new line in the data frame, that creates a receptacle for that form:

```
<DIV id="willbefrmPhysTreeData"> form goes here </DIV>
```

Code to create the table and the form

OK, we have receptacles for the table and the form, and we've advertised the table in all the right places, but who will make the move and actually create the table and the form? Looks like we need a new function, getEditTreeData(). It consists of a single with statement that contains exactly two lines of code, corresponding to the two actions that the function performs:

```
function getEditTreeData()
{
  with(Database.dbData)
  {
    getTreeData(dbControl.tr1Faculty);
    makeForm("PhysTreeData",dbData.willbefrmPhysTreeData);
  }
}
```

Now we need a trigger that will set this function in motion. It's important to remember that we only want it to run once, in order to create a table of tree paths. After that, the database creator will fill in the table with URLs corresponding to those paths, and we don't want this table touched again, except to replace a URL.

Given these peculiar circumstances, we've come up with an idea of a "self-destructing" event handler. Remember that in the previous subsection we've created a DIV element that will house the input form for the table. One of the actions of getEditTreeData() is to replace the outerHTML of that DIV with a new input form. So, we'll give that DIV element an onclick handler that will call getEditTreeData() and thereby self-destruct. Nobody will be able to get an onclick action from that DIV ever again:

```
<DIV id="willbefrmPhysTreeData" style="color:green"
  onclick="parent.getEditTreeData()"> get and edit the tree data  </DIV>
```

As you can see, we have also colored it green so it's easy to find (and destroy).

The Procedure Summary

In summary, if you want to associate Web pages or other data items with internal nodes, proceed as follows:

❑ Make three additions in the data frame: a table, a receptacle for a form, and the new table's name in dbInfo.

❑ Add one line to the tree-defining form in the control frame.

❑ Open the main file of the application (equivalent to our facDB.htm) and click on the green DIV element in the data frame. This will create a table of tree paths and an entry form for it.

❑ Still in the application, fill in the right column of the table with the appropriate URLs and save the table using the database Save button.

❑   Quit the application and open your web page editor. Locate the saved database file; refer to
    JClasses/dbreadme.htm for the default location of saved database files. Copy the resulting
    table from the saved database file to the source file for the data frame (equivalent to our
    facData.htm). You may want to make the table invisible in the data frame.

Implementation of Database Tree

This section develops an implementation of a "database tree," i.e., a collection of methods and
functions that construct a tree based on tabular data and outfit it with a tree controller. We'll proceed
in the top-down fashion, starting with the makeTree() method (of the Database class) that constructs
the tree, then working through the functions that it calls upon. On the first pass, we'll cover the
minimal implementation, saving support for data items in internal tree nodes for the very end.

The makeTree() method

Thinking It Through

Let's think the problem through and work through an example before looking at any code. Our
makeTree() function (really a method of the database class) has to do two things: construct a tree
and make a tree controller for it. The second step is easy; once the tree is constructed, all you need is
a receptacle for the tree controller, which the data frame provides. How do we construct a tree?

A tree consists of paths, so if we know how to construct a path we'll go through a loop that constructs
all the paths and we're done. How do we construct a path? Remember that every complete path from
the root to a leaf corresponds to a database record. More precisely, it corresponds to a selection of
fields from that record as specified in the treeOrder text element.

Let's work through an example. Suppose we have the record shown below in the FullFaculty table,
and the treeOrder is "Building,Department,Office,Name,Page", which means that we want a tree
view containing Building, Department, Office, and Name, and clicking on a name would show the
Web page specified in the Page column.

Name	Posi-tion	Depart-ment	Admin	Building	Of-fice	Email	Page
Roch ester, Jane E.	Associate Professor	Edu-cation	Com-mittee on Religious Life	Thornfield Hall	411	Jero chester	jeroches. htm

It's clear what we need to do. Starting from the root, select the Thornfield Hall child. If no such child
exists, create it and continue. Next find the Education child of Thornfield Hall; if no such exists,
create it and continue. It looks like a loop, but when does it stop? It stops with the node before the
last field (page) on our list (Name: Rochester, Jane E), which becomes the leaf node. The last field
contains the data item for that leaf node.

Does all this discussion ring any bells with you? It should, because the procedure is very similar to
what we did in Chapter 5 with our SiteTree application. If no bells are ringing, it would certainly
be useful to look over that section, especially the part where the tree is built by the insLabel()
function. We will not be able to reuse that function, but we'll follow a very similar approach.

The arguments to makeTree()

We can now look at the code of the makeTree() method. You've already seen it used in the setupDatabase function, as follows:

```
D.makeTree(dbControl.tr1Faculty);
```

Looks like it takes only one argument, but we know that it needs three pieces of information: the table that has the data, a list of fields to use in constructing the tree, and a receptacle for the tree controller. Well, as often in JavaScript, it takes three arguments, but will be equally happy with one, provided it has all three pieces packaged in it. By now you should know enough about JavaScript and our programming approach not to be surprised. You may also remember that a tree-definition form like tr1Faculty has the treeOrder text input and two hidden input elements that together contain all the required information:

```
<input type=hidden name=tableName value="FullFaculty">
<input type=hidden name=treeConName value="PhysTree">
```

So, makeTree() starts, naturally enough, by asking: "How many arguments do I have?" If it has three, it gets to work right away. If it only has one, it says "It must be a form with three input elements I'm interested in. Or, if those input elements were placed in the control form of the table, rather than in a separate form somewhere, then the argument can be the name of that table." Here's the code:

```
function db_makeTree(tblName,fieldsStr,treeConObj)
{
 var form=null;
 if(db_makeTree.arguments.length==1)
  {
  if(typeof tblName=="string")          // argument is the name of table
   form=this.Tables[tblName].form;
  else
   {                          // the argument is not a name but the actual form
   form=tblName; tblName=form.tableName.value;
   }
  fieldsStr=form.treeOrder.value;
  treeConObj=form.document.parentWindow[form.treeConName.value];
 }               // the three arguments are now set up; form is NULL or a form
 var table=this.Tables[tblName];        // get the table by its name
```

The effect of this code is that makeTree() can be used with three different sets of arguments, each specified quite precisely in terms of the number of arguments and their data types. Many of our functions and methods will use this technique.

The rest of makeTree()

Now the real work begins; we construct a tree, sort it, and give it a tree controller:

```
var theTree=new Tree(new dataNode("top","data"));
var insFn=labelPairsFn1(fieldsStr);
for(var i=0;i<table.length;i++)        // loop constructing a path for each record
 if(!(theTree.insLabelN(insFn(table[i]),newNodeFn))) return;
theTree.sort(cmpNode);
new TreeController(treeConObj,theTree,clickPicDataTree,1,0);
}
```

The first line of this piece of code constructs a dummy root for a "database tree," using the dataNode constructor. Lines 2 through 4 extract a tree structure from a database table. Line 5 sorts using a comparison function. Line 6 creates a tree controller, passing it a click function as a parameter. Notice that the last two lines of `makeTree()` come straight from chapter 6; there's nothing database-related in them.

We're going to proceed as follows. The remainder of this section will present the dataNode constructor, the comparison function for data nodes, and the click function. After that, we'll spend several sections on lines 2 through 4. That piece of code is tricky, but in instructive ways.

The Node Object and the Comparison Function

Referring back to Chapter 5, a tree node in the site tree application consisted of two elements, a label to display with the node in the tree controller, and the tree node's data. The node structure of a database tree is exactly the same except that we now allow the displayed node label to contain HTML tags:

```
function dataNode(innerT,data)          // a node of the tree of data refs;
  // the innerHTML is the standard string to display, data is for clickFn
{
this.innerHTML=innerT; this.data=data;
}
```

In addition to the constructor, we'll need a function that constructs a node and returns it. The function will be passed as an argument to the path-constructing function:

```
function newNodeFn(a,b){ return new dataNode(a,b);}
```

As long as we're looking at the node's internals, let's mention a function to compare tree nodes for sorting. This is very much a variation on familiar themes.

```
function cmpNode(A,B)                     // for sorting trees of data nodes
{
 var at=A.label.innerHTML; var bt=B.label.innerHTML;
 return at<bt?-1:at==bt?0:1;
}
```

The click function is also a recapitulation of familiar themes, going back all the way to Chapter 5.

The Click Function

The job of the click function, remember, is to decide what to do with the node's data when the node's label is clicked upon. For now, we make the assumption that only leaf nodes, corresponding to individual faculty members, have interesting data associated with them. We take this data to be the URL of a personal Web page, located in a subdirectory called `pages`. This allows for the possibility to decide whether all those pages should follow a specified format or the individual's fancy. Clicking on a leaf node will load the page into the vacant `dbMsg` frame. Clicking on an internal node will simply show its node label in an alert box:

```
function clickPicDataTree(h)
{
 var tAddr=h.name.substring(2);
 var T=this.theTree.getSubTree(tAddr);
```

```
  if(T.numChildren()==0)
  {
    top.dbMsg.location="pages/"+T.label.data;        // load page into dbMsg frame
  }
  else alert(T.label.innerHTML);
}
```

Only the last line of this function will need to be revised to show Web pages associated with internal nodes.

We're ready to dive into the internals of the tree construction process. These are found in three lines of `makeTree()`, which we repeat here for convenience:

```
  var insFn=labelPairsFn1(fieldsStr);
  for(var i=0;i<table.length;i++)        // loop constructing a path for each record
    if(!(theTree.insLabelN(insFn(table[i]),newNodeFn))) return;
```

We're going to spend so much time on these three lines that we'll have to "repeat them for convenience" another couple of times before we're fully done with them.

Tree construction, path by path

The process of constructing a tree is a loop that iterates through the records of a table, constructs a tree path for each record, and inserts the path into the emerging tree. The body of the loop is a call on the path insertion function, `insLabelN()`.

The Path Insertion Function

In our `SiteMap` application, all the hard work of path insertion was done by the `insLabel()` method. Here's its first line and a brief comment, repeated from Chapter 5:

```
function t_insLabel(x,A,f){
  // traverse tree, looking for labels A[0],A[1]...;
  // add node (f(x,A[i])) if missing
```

In the tree of `docNodes` constructed by `SiteMap`, the data stored in a node, the label of the node, and the path leading to that node were closely related. As you recall, each `docNode` contains its complete URL as its data, and the last component of that URL—a file or folder name—is that node's label. The array argument to `insLabel()` was just an array of strings resulting from splitting the URL at the "/" character (after cutting off the prefix). The elements of that array form the path to the node. The last element of the array is the label.

In the data tree, there is no simple relationship between a node's label and its data. That relationship is not defined by any formula, but stored in a table. Our path insertion method needs an array of label-data pairs. The easiest way to package a pair is in an array of two elements. So, our method, `insLabelN()`,expects an array of two-element arrays. It takes two arguments, an array of pairs and our `newNodeFn()`. Its operation is straighforward: it marches down the tree using the label component of each pair to find the next child to move to, and it constructs the child using `newNodeFn()` if the child is not there.

JavaScript Objects

The array of pairs is constructed by a separate function, `insFn()`. That array's only purpose in life is to be consumed by `insLabelN()` and become a tree path. It can just as well do it anonymously, without any intermediate stops to get a name for itself. So, we include a call on `insFn()` inside the call on `insLabelN()`. You can now untangle the loop in `makeTree()` that does all the work:

```
for(var i=0;i<table.length;i++)     // loop constructing a path for each record
   if(!(theTree.insLabelN(insFn(table[i]),newNodeFn))) return;
```

Constructing the Array of Pairs

You may notice that there's something quite strange about the `insFn()` function. In order to do its work, it needs two items, the current record of the table, and names of its fields that come from the `treeOrder` text in the HTML form. An example will make it clear: if the string of fields is "Division,Department,Name,Page" and the record we're working on has:
Division:Humanities,Department:History,Name:J.Jay,Page=JJay.htm
then we need to call

```
insLabelN([["Division Humanities"," JJay.htm"],
    ["Department History"," JJay.htm"]
    ["Name Jay,John"," JJay.htm"]],newNodefn);
```

However, if you look at the code right above, `insFn()` receives only one argument, the current record. Somehow, the knowledge of field names has been imprinted on `insFn()` at its creation. This is the major tricky point that we referred to earlier: `insFn()` is not defined directly but created by another function, `labelPairsFn()`. It's in this function that the user input in `treeOrder` is transformed into precise instructions on how to construct the tree. So we'll spend a section on `labelPairsFn()` and its variants. It's self-contained and can be skipped on first reading.

From treeOrder to Tree Specification

The contents of `treeOrder` are passed to `makeTree()` as the `fieldsStr` argument that contains a comma-separated list of items. It is those items that determine the composition of the tree nodes, so we call them "node determiners." There are three aspects to node construction, or three questions to be answered:

❑ What is the relationship between node determiners and the names of the record fields that are used in constructing the node?
❑ How do the names and values in those fields determine the labels with which the tree controller will decorate the nodes?
❑ What are the data items that will hang from those nodes?

In the simplest case that we have discussed so far, the answers are as follows:

❑ each node determiner is just a field name
❑ the node determiner determines the node label in the most direct manner: just use the field name itself followed by the field value retrieved from the database table
❑ the data item to hang from the node is the same for all nodes in a path (i.e., all nodes for the same record); it also obtained from the database table using the field name in the last node determiner.

To repeat a recent example, if the `fieldsStr` is a string of field names

```
"Division,Department,Name,Page"
```

and the record we're working on has

```
Division:Humanities,Department:History,Name:J.Jay,Page=JJay.htm
```

then the array of pairs that is passed to `insLabelN()` is

```
[["Division Humanities","JJay.htm"],
 ["Department History","JJay.htm"]
 ["Name Jay,John","JJay.htm"] ]
```

The Simplest Implementation

In this simplest case, the code could be very straightforward, with no higher-order functions (i.e., functions that take other functions as arguments or return a function):

```
function makeTree(table,fieldsStr)
{
 var fieldsArr=fieldStr.split(","); var N=fieldsArr.length-1;
 var datumFld=fieldsArr[N]; // store the data item in a separate variable
 fieldsArr.length=fieldsArr.length-1;
 var theTree=new Tree(new nodeFn("dummy HTML","dummy data"));
 for(var i=0;i<table.length;i++)
   theTree=theTree.insTreePath(makeTreePath(table[i],fieldsArr,datumFld));
 return theTree;
}
function makeTreePath(row,fieldsArr,datumFld)
{
 var R=new Array();
 for(var i=0;i<fieldsArr.length;i++)
  R[i]=new Array(fieldsArr[i]+" "+row[fieldsArr[i]],row[datumFld]);
 return R;
}
```

Here we give each two-element array the name and value of a field as its first item, and the value of `datumFld` (in our case, the value of the `Page` field) as the second. The two items become the label and the data of the resulting node.

In our actual code we remove the restrictions on all three items within the `new Array(...)` expression:

❑ instead of the field name `fieldsArr[i]` we allow an arbitrary prefix
❑ instead of the field value `row[fieldsArr[i]]` we allow an arbitrary JavaScript expression
❑ instead of the same data item `row[datumFld]` for all nodes in a path, we allow individual data items for internal nodes

In the next section, we concentrate on the second of those changes and show why, once it is introduced, the simple implementation sketched above becomes inefficient.

More Flexibility, at a Price in performance

To bring out the inefficiency, let's try to rewrite the body of the loop as a `with` statement. Our first obvious rewrite is wrong:

```
with(row){R[i]=new Array(fieldsArr[i]+" "+fieldsArr[i],datumFld)};
```

This is wrong; if `fieldsArr[i]` is 'Department' and the department is 'Computer Science' we'll get:

```
["Department Department","compsci.gif"]
```

rather than:

```
["Department Computer Science", "compsci.gif"];
```

The second mention of `fieldsArr[i]` has to be evaluated while the first remains quoted. The way to do it is to construct the `with` expression with the right parts quoted, then evaluate:

```
S="with(row)R[i]=new Array('Department '+Department,datumFld)";
eval(S);
```

In the general case, building it piece by piece, we get:

```
var S="with(row)R[i]=new Array("+quote(fieldsArr[i]+" ");
S+="+";
S+=fieldsArr[i];
S+=",datumFld)";
eval(S);
```

(The function `quote()` is a string utility that wraps its arguments in matching quotes, adjusting internal quotes if necessary. It can be found in `strUtils.js` in the `utils` directory.)

The version above shows the way the string is constructed, but its functioning is brought out more clearly if we use `replace()`, with a regular expression pattern. Recall that the "g" after the pattern means "replace them all":

```
var S="with(row)R[i]=new Array('fldARRi '+fldARRi,datumFld)";
S.replace(/fldARRi/g,fieldsArr[i]);
eval(S);
```

At this point we see that `fieldsArr[i]` could be any JavaScript expression which would become evaluated and placed into the label. For instance, if we put "2+2" there, we'd get "2+2 4" as the innerHTML of a tree label.

Where's the inefficiency?

We've achieved the desired generality but at a cost in performance. Think of what `eval()` has to do. It receives a string, parses it to make sense of what it says, then does the actual work. Much more time is spent in parsing the string than in carrying out the task specified by it. (The string supplies the information on the current record.) That's sheer waste because **every time the expression is parsed you get the same answer.**

We can separate the parsing stage from the action stage by saying

```
var S="with(row) return new Array('fldARRi '+fldARRi,datumFld)";
S.replace(/fldARRi/g,fieldsArr[i]);
var F=new Function("row",S); // S is evaluated right here, when F is constructed!
R[i]=F(table[i]);
```

Here the work of figuring out what S says is done within "new Function"; doing what it says is done within F(table[i]). But, as we said, every time we run "F=new Function", it produces **the same new function**. So, we can move it out of the loop! Let's have a function which produces that function for us.

Constructing insFn()

Let's look at that labelPairsFn1(). In the first half it takes apart the fieldsStr and packages its contents in a convenient way. (It assumes, in the process, that the last field of the record will contain the data item, and so the name of that field becomes datumFld.) In the second half, it constructs the body of the function that it returns. The body of the function is the with expression that we want.

```
function labelPairsFn1(fieldsStr){
 var fieldsArr=fieldsStr.split(",");
 var N=fieldsArr.length-1;
 var datumFld=fieldsArr[N];          // last component of fieldsStr is datumFld
 fieldsArr.length=N;                 // shorten the array of field names by one
 var pairsStrsArr=new Array();
 for (var i=0;i<N;i++){ // construct a string that, for each i,
                        // will construct a two-element array
  var S=fieldsArr[i];
  pairsStrsArr[i]="new Array("+quote(S+" ")+"+"+S+","+datumFld+")";
 }
 var Res="with(row)return new Array("+pairsStrsArr.join(",")+");";
 return new Function("row",Res);
}
```

This computation takes place only once, outside the loop that iterates over the records of the table.

Support for Arbitrary Prefixes

In our actual code we allow node determiners that have an optional prefix (arbitrary text), followed by a colon, followed by arbitrary JavaScript expressions. Only the for-loop inside labelPairsFn1() needs to be changed: instead of two lines it will have six.

```
for (var i=0;i<N;i++)
  {
  var preStr;
  var S=fieldsArr[i]; var pair=S.split(":");
  if(pair.length==1)preStr=""; else preStr=pair[0];
  var fldStr=pair[pair.length-1];
  pairsStrsArr[i]="new Array("+
        quote(preStr+" ")+"+"+fldStr+","+datumFld+")";
  }
```

Instead of pasting S=fieldsArr[i] directly into the pairsStrsArr, we now take it apart, separating preStr (if any) from fldStr, which are pasted into pairsStrsArr separated by a space. The rest works exactly the same way. The function containing the revised loop changes its name to labelPairsFn(), and becomes the value of insFn() inside insLabelN(). No other changes in the code are needed.

Data items for internal nodes

To accommodate individual data items, yet another minor change is needed: instead of adding `datumFld` as the second item to every two-element array, it's added only to the last one. The rest get an empty string instead, which is replaced by the code with items from the node data table. For details, consult the code.

Search and Lookup in a Database Tree

`Search` and `lookup` in the tree are done by two new methods of the database class, called, rather unimaginatively, `searchTree()` and `lookupTree ()`. The two functions have a lot in common: they take the same arguments, and both in the end call on the `openTree()` method. We'll discuss their common parts first.

Arguments to the New Methods

The new methods need a table, a form, and a tree controller to work on. The table provides the data, the form provides the search/lookup expression, and the tree controller opens the path to the result of the search. The question is: how do they find each other?

We want maximum flexibility here. In particular, we don't want to assume that the form is the control form of the table, but we don't want to exclude this possibility either. In either case, the form must know how to find the table and the tree controller. Finally, if the form is, indeed, the control form of the table then just passing the table name to our methods should be enough because we can find the table by its name, the table knows how to find its form, and the form will know how to find the tree controller.

What it boils down to is another case of overloading, JavaScript-style, in which the first few lines of the function figure out what its arguments are, and retrieve the missing values, if any. These lines repeat verbatim in `searchTree()` and `lookupTree()`, and with small variations in `openTree()`. As you read through them, keep in mind that we overload for these three possible sets of arguments:

- ❑   `tblName`, `form`, `tConName`
- ❑   `tblName` (a string which is a table name; assume that the form is that table's form)
- ❑   `form` (either the table's form or any form that knows which table and tree controller to use)

```
if(db_searchTree.arguments.length==1)
{
 if(typeof tblName=="string")// really a table name
   form=this.Tables[tblName].form;
 else { // actually, tblName is a form object!
   form=tblName;tblName=form.tableName.value;}
 tConName=form.treeConName.value;
}
```

As you can see, the functions assume that if there's only one argument and it's not a string, then it's a form somewhere that has `tblName` and `treeConName` input elements.

With the `openTree()` method the situation is a little different. The other two methods only needed a `treeConName` which they passed as an argument to `openTree()`, but `openTree()` needs the actual tree control object, `treeConObj`. In order to find it by its name stored in the `treeConName` element of the form, it has to go to the window that contains the form.

```
if(db_openTree.arguments.length==1){var form;
  if(typeof tblName=="string")// really a table name
   form=this.Tables[tblName].form;
  else{ // actually a form
   form=tblName;tblName=form.tableName.value;}
   fieldsStr=form.treeOrder.value;
   treeConObj=form.document.parentWindow[form.treeConName.value];
  } // the three arguments are now set up.
```

The Rest of the Code

The remaining code of `searchTree()` and `lookupTree()` is simple: it calls on `Search()` or `Lookup()` as appropriate, and if anything is found, calls on `openTree()` to show it.

```
if(this.Search(tblName,form))
{
 TreeController[tConName].closeTree();
 this.openTree(form);
}
```

Notice that the `TreeController` class has acquired a new little method to close itself. We felt that each new search should close the results of the preceding one, so at any given moment the results of only one search are shown.

The `openTree()` method has a bit more work to do. It has to bridge a gap between the database world of tables and field name and the tree world of paths and tree addresses. Ultimately, it will call on a new method of the tree control class, also called `openTree()`, to open a given path represented by a tree address. We'll look at that other `openTree()` method in the next section; until then, whenever we say `openTree()` we mean a method of the `Database` class.

The openTree() method of Database

For starters, `openTree()` has a table to work on, and it knows that its job is to show the current record of that table. It also has the `fieldsStr`. Out of these two things, it has to construct a tree path, and for this, of course, we can simply reuse the `labelPairsFn()` function:

```
var table=this.Tables[tblName]; var row=table[table.currentRow];
if(!row)return;
var pairsArr=labelPairsFn(fieldsStr)(row);
```

A call on `labelPairsFn()` produces, as you remember, another function which in `makeTree()` had a local name, `insFn()`. Here we leave it unnamed and immediately give it the current row as an argument. We get back an array of two-element arrays, but we only need their first elements, which are the tree labels, not the second elements, which are data items hanging from the nodes. So, we construct a "one-dimensional" array of labels:

```
var labelsArr=new Array();
for(var i=0;i<pairsArr.length;i++) labelsArr[i]=pairsArr[i][0];
```

Do you see an exercise here? Rewrite using map(), of course! (Map, you recall, is an array utility from Chapter 2, and as always, a suggested solution is available for download from our website.) But we have to move on. We don't need anything else from the database, so the rest of the work is done in the tree and the tree controller. First we go to the tree and say: here's a sequence of labels, give us the tree address of the node that it leads to. With tree address in hand, we go to the tree controller and say: here's a tree address, open all the nodes leading to it. As a final touch, for this application only, we show the page associated with that tree address:

```
var treeCon=TreeController[treeConObj.id];
var addr=treeCon.theTree.addrOf(labelsArr);
treeCon.openTree(addr);
dbMsg.location="pages/"+row['Page'];
```

New Methods of the Tree and Tree Control Classes

You can skip this section on first reading if you wish and return to it later, but it's here to explain the additions we make to the Tree Class we developed in Chapter 5. As you have seen, implementing a table-based tree required some new methods in the tree and the tree control class. Here they are, first the tree methods, then the tree controller methods.

New Tree Methods

The new tree methods are insLabelN() and addrOf(). The first of them is a minor variation on insLabel() in Chapter 5. (Refer back to the section on the Path Insertion Function in this chapter where the two methods are compared and the differences discussed.)

```
function t_insLabelN(A,f) // f is the function to make a new node
{
// traverse tree, looking for labels A[0][0],A[1][0] &c;
// addChild(f(A[i][0],A[i][1])) if missing
var t=this;
var P=new Function("t,s","return t.label.innerHTML==s")
for(var i=0;i<A.length;i++){
 var k=t.indexOf(A[i][0], P);
 if(k<0)
   {
   k=t.numChildren();
   t.addChild(new Tree(f(A[i][0],A[i][1])));
          // new subtree with new node as root
   }
 t=t.getNth(k);
 }
return this;  // for convenience, return at root of insertion
}
```

The other one is a genuinely new and useful method; it finds a tree address from a sequence of labels. Just as insLabel() and insLabelN(), it uses the indexOf method of the Tree class to find the index of a child with a given label. The procedure is to throw all those indices into an array and in the end join that array into a string with "." as the joining character. A little slippery banana peel to remember is that arrays of children are zero-based but tree-addresses start at one, so you have to add 1 to the index.

```
function t_addrOf(A) // traverse tree,
{
// looking for labels A[0],A[1] &c; return treeaddress.
var t=this; var X=new Array();
for(var i=0;i<A.length;i++)
  {
  var k=t.indexOf(A[i],
    new Function("t,s","return t.label.innerHTML==s"));
  if(k<0)return "";
  X[X.length]=k+1;
  t=t.getNth(k);
  }
return X.join(".");              // for convenience, return at root of insertion
}
```

New TreeController Methods

The new methods of the tree control class are openTree() and closeTree(), used by the tree search methods. They are completely transparent as long you remember that to open a tree node means to do two things: set the style-sheet class of its UL element to "open" and set the source of the image to open.gif. To close, you toggle both of these to the closed state.

```
function tc_openTree(addr)
{
 if(!addr)return; var T=this.theTree;
 addr=addr.split(".");
 for(var i=0;i<addr.length;i++)
   {
   var N=parseInt(addr[i],10)-1;
   var img=T.ul.children[2*N].children[0]; if(!img)return;
   img.src="open.gif";
   T=T.getNth(N);
   T.ul.className="open";
   }
}
function tc_closeTree()                     // closes at and below top
   {
   var A=new Array(); A[0]=this.theTree;
   while (A.length>0)
     {
     var T=A[A.length-1]; A.length-=1;
     if(T.ul) T.ul.className="closed";
     for(var i=0;i<T.numChildren();i++)
       {
       A[A.length]=T.getNth(i);
       var img=T.ul.children[2*i].children[0];
       if(img) img.src="close.gif";
       }
     }
   }
```

This concludes the code for a database tree, as long as you're satisfied to have one data item per record. If you want to have a data item per tree node, then you'll have to work through another section's worth of code.

Data for Internal Nodes

Let's remind ourselves of the HTML setup, as presented in an earlier section with the same title. Data items for internal nodes are stored in a two column table that sits in the data frame. The name of that table is stored in the `TreeDataTableName` element of the tree-defining form in the control frame. When a database tree is created, data items from that table should be added to the internal nodes of the tree. This obviously has to be implemented by a function call in the `makeTree()` method.

How does the data get into that `TreeDataTable` in the first place? This is done, you recall, by the database creator, the same person who created the database tables in the first place. The new table can be created by hand, listing all the tree paths and corresponding data items in a two column table in the data frame. Alternatively, this process can be automated, using the `getEditTreeData()` function that copies tree paths from the newly-created tree to that table, and provides a control form for it, complete with editing buttons. The procedure for using `getEditTreeData()` is presented in the subsection called "Procedure Summary," in the first half of this chapter.

In terms of code, we need two new methods, one to copy data items from a two-column table to the tree every time the tree is created, the other to copy all tree paths from the tree to the table on that single occasion when `getEditTreeData()` is called. Not too bad.

The setTreeData() Method

This is the method that's called from `makeTree()` to copy data from the table:

```
function db_makeTree(tblName,fieldsStr,treeConObj)
{
var form=null;
 var table=this.Tables[tblName];
 var theTree=new Tree(new dataNode("top","data"));
 var insFn=labelPairsFn(fieldsStr);
 for(var i=0;i<table.length;i++)
  if(!(theTree.insLabelN(insFn(table[i]),newNodeFn)))return;
 theTree.sort(cmpNode);
 if(form && form.TreeDataTableName)
  {
  this.setTreeData(form.TreeDataTableName.value,theTree);
  }
 new TreeController(treeConObj,theTree,clickPicDataTree,1,0);
}
```

As you can see, `setTreeData()` gets called, reasonably enough, with a table name and a tree. Except, as usual, we overload so the table name can actually be a form, and we spend the first few lines analyzing the arguments:

```
function db_setTreeData(tblName,tree)      // reads tree data from table
{
 var form;
 if(db_setTreeData.arguments.length==1)
  {
  if(typeof tblName=="string")       // it's the name of a dbase table
   form=this.Tables[tblName].form;   // the only form is the default...
  else form=tblName;                 // "tblName" was actually a form, not a name
   if(form.TreeDataTableName)tblName=form.TreeDataTableName.value;
   tree=TreeController[form.treeConName.value].theTree;
  }
 }                                    // the arguments are now set up;
```

Each row of the table has two cells, one containing a path, the other a data item. Before we can work with them, we have to get them out of the HTML table into a usable data structure. What's a good data structure for this kind of situation when you have key-data pairs? A dictionary, of course, like the one we had in Chapter 5 with words and definitions. We create an object called `dict`, and for each path-data pair we say: `dict[path]=data`. Or something to that effect:

```
function db_setTreeData(tblName,tree)      // reads tree data from table
{
 var table=this.Tables[tblName];
 if(!table || !tree) return;
 var dict=new Object();
 for(var i=0;i<table.length;i++){
  var ti=table[i];dict[ti.TreePath]=ti.Data;
 }
}
```

OK, we now have the table info in a usable form, now what? We have to go through the tree and, recursively, add the data items to the nodes. We parcel this out to another function, `setTreeDataRec()`:

```
for(var i=0;i<tree.numChildren();i++)
{
 var subtree=tree.getNth(i);
 setTreeDataRec(dict,subtree,subtree.label.innerHTML);
}
```

The "Rec" in `setTreeDataRec()` stands for "recursive," not "record." (We're in the tree world, not database world.) It is called with a dictionary of path-data pairs, a subtree, and a label-path to that subtree. It retrieves the data item from the dictionary using the label-path and sets the data property of the tree's label to that data item. Then it recursively calls itself on the subtree's children, giving them the same dictionary and the label-path extended by their own label. It's easier to do than to say:

```
function setTreeDataRec(dict,tree,str)
{
 var val=dict[str]; if(val) tree.label.data=val;
 for(var i=0;i<tree.numChildren();i++)
 {
  var subtree=tree.getNth(i);
  setTreeDataRec(dict,subtree,str+","+subtree.label.innerHTML);
 }
}
```

The getTreeData() and getTreeDataRec()

These couple of methods works in very much the same fashion as the one we've just described. You've seen enough overloaded methods, databases and trees by now to figure them out by yourself or with a friend.

```
function db_getTreeData(tblName,tree       // get tree data from tree to table
{
 if(db_getTreeData.arguments.length==1){
  if(typeof tblName=="string")             // it's the name of a dbase table
   form=this.Tables[tblName].form;         // the only form is the default...
```

```
      else form=tblName;                    // "tblName" was actually a form, not a name
      if(form.TreeDataTableName)tblName=form.TreeDataTableName.value;
      tree=TreeController[form.treeConName.value].theTree;
      }                                      // the arguments are now set up;
   var table=this.Tables[tblName];
   if(!table || !tree) return;              // tableheaders = TreePath,Data
   for(var i=0;i<tree.numChildren();i++){
      var subtree=tree.getNth(i);
      getTreeDataRec(table,subtree,subtree.label.innerHTML);
   }
   this.update(tblName); this.setCurRow(table,0);
}
```

Apart for the new methods and functions described in this section, minor edits are needed in the click function and `labelPairsFn()`. They're self-explanatory, and can be found in the code.

A Few Programming Techniques

Perhaps the most important thing to learn from this chapter is a set of programming techniques which we summarize here.

Use the Same Object as an Array and an Associative Array

The same object can be used as an Array and an associative array. The `Tables` property of a database is used that way. As an ordinary array, `Tables` has the names of the tables. Each name is also the name of a property that refers to the table by that name, so, to go through all the tables in a method, you can say:

```
for(var i=0;i<this.Tables.length;++i)
{
  // do somethingto this.Tables[this.Tables[i]]
}
```

At the same time, we can always get to a specific table simply by its name, by saying:

```
this.Tables[tblName]
```

Of course you could use

```
for (tblName in Tables)
{
  do something to Tables[tblName];
}
```

but that usage would require `Tables` to be only an associative array, without the "length" property. It would also make impossible such simple statements as `alert(Tables)`, which are very useful for debugging. Our approach is simply more flexible.

Overload Your Functions and Methods

This chapter provided several examples of function or method overloading. We're abusing the term ever so slightly because, technically, overloading is when you write several versions of a function, each with its own signature, and let a compiler figure out which one to use in any particular call. (The notion of a function's **signature** - the data type of returned value and the number and data types of the function's arguments - does not quite apply to JavaScript either, because variables are not typed, and any function can take any number of arguments.) In JavaScript, you have to write your own code to analyze the arguments array and take appropriate action. However, the results to the user of your function or method are the same: the function or method can be used with several well-specified sets of arguments of specific data types.

This is especially helpful if you're going to follow our next tip:

Package Your Arguments Into a Form

If your arguments come from the user, provide a form in which they can be entered. If, in addition, you need some internal arguments, put them in the hidden elements of the same form.

This isn't just a way to simplify JavaScript calling statements: this way the HTML controls the JavaScript, as it should be. We have written several functions and methods that support the following options:

❑ If no arguments are given, use the defaults coded into the function.
❑ If two or more arguments are given, use them to override the defaults.
❑ If only one argument is given, check to see if it's a string. If not, it's a form with specific fields that contain the required arguments. The fields can be hidden and thus accessible only to users with HTML skills, or they can be text fields, accessible to anybody who can fill out a form.
❑ Finally, if the argument is a string then it's the name of a table that has a supporting form. Use that form as described in the preceding option.

This multiplicity of options is only possible because of JavaScript's free-wheeling attitude to function arguments and data types. What we're doing here follows our general strategy of imposing some coding patterns on JavaScript's total freedom.

Construct Your Functions

Whenever your function has to work on several properties of an object (e.g., several fields of a database record) consider constructing that function using the `Function` constructor, as follows:

```
var strFnBody="with(obj){ do what you need with the properties of obj }";
var fnToApplyToObj=new Function("row",fnBody);
```

This may involve meticulous counting or two different kinds of quotes, but your code can get simpler and, if your object manipulation is inside a loop, more efficient.

If you have trouble counting pairs of quotes, don't try to generate long strings in one complex statement. Break the job into small steps and use alert boxes to show the gradual construction of the string. Suppose you want to generate `Division Humanities` from

```
new Array('Division '+Division,'')    // inside with(row) statement
```

Instead of saying

```
var S="new Array('"+fieldStr[i]+delimStr+"'"+fieldStr[i]+",'')";
```

say something like

```
var S="new Array(";
S+=quote(fieldStr[i]+delimStr);  //new Array('Division '
S+="+";                          //new Array('Division '+
S+=fieldStr[i];                  //new Array('Division '+Division
S+=",";                          //new Array('Division '+Division,
S+=quote("");                    //new Array('Division '+Division,''
S+=")";                          //new Array('Division '+Division,'')
```

Note the use of the `quote()` string utility to add quotation marks explicitly to the result. They are guaranteed to arrive in matched pairs this way. Even with the help of `quote()`, writing this sort of code is somewhat error-prone and difficult to debug. Consider this:

```
var S="new Array("+quote(fieldStr[i]+delimStr)+fieldStr[i]+",'')";
```

How long will it take you to find what's missing from this line?

Conclusions

In addition to new coding techniques, this chapter has shown an extended example of code reuse. Most of the functionality of database trees has come from combining the database class, unchanged from Chapter 6, with the tree and tree controller classes, unchanged from Chapter 5. Application-specific `dbtree.js` code occupies less than a page, much of it to support data items for internal nodes.

In the next chapter, we will reuse the database class again, this time in working with the text of a document.

8

Texts and Commentaries

Introduction

A very common human activity is to comment on other people's texts. The text can be by a great writer or a friend of yours, and the purpose may be literary study or a joint report, but the elements of the activity are the same. Apart from general comments that have to do with the entire document, most of the time you select a stretch of text that you want to comment on and attach a comment to it. Comments can come in a great variety of formats, from a paragraph of text to a photograph to a special background color to indicate the position of a caesura (pause) in a line of poetry. If it's a technical text or a text in a foreign language, you may want to give definitions to words and phrases.

In this chapter and the next, we'll build a tool for doing this sort of activity in the web page. We'll proceed from two sets of specifications. One will help us determine the overall structure of the application. The other will describe several specific commentary formats.

A Need For Design

This is going to be a larger project consisting of several substantial modules. A large-scale software project requires a separate analysis-and-design stage. Before you start writing code, you have to sit down and produce some sort of an overall plan. As you can imagine, a lot of very smart people have spent a great deal of time figuring out how to produce such overall plans for a large software project, and how to write them down in a concise and precise way. This whole effort is called Object-Oriented Analysis and Design. It will be the first new topic of the chapter. Towards the end of that section, we should have detailed specifications for the project, but may revise them in response to unanticipated difficulties that usually arise in the process of writing and testing code.

The other big new topic of the chapter is working with text. In all the preceding chapters, we thought of the document as consisting of HTML elements. In this chapter, we also think of it as consisting of characters, words, lines (of poetry), and sentences. This will require new tools and a change of attitude: we can no longer ignore whitespace, because a line is a meaningful unit in poetry, and a paragraph or stanza may no longer be defined by an HTML tag but by a blank line before and after it.

In outline, the chapter will proceed as follows:

- ❏ analysis-and-design methodologies for a software project
- ❏ commentary formats
- ❏ use cases and further analysis
- ❏ the role of the database class
- ❏ the session object and its variants
- ❏ simple formats
- ❏ the selection and the `TextRange` object
- ❏ more involved formats
- ❏ hypertext comments

Try It Out

Point your browser at `http://webdev.wrox.co.uk/books/1894/chapter08/index.htm`. Login as `'Guest'`, the password may be left blank.

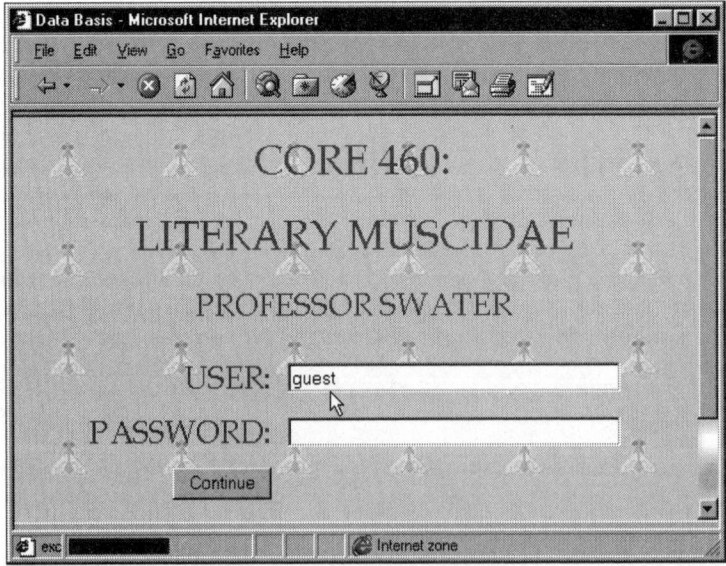

On the second screen, select a text to work on, and a commentary format. We recommend that at this early stage you use one of the simple formats, such as Commentaire (associate a comment with a selected word or phrase). Review the work of previous guests. Select text, attach commentaries, add, delete and edit text-commentary pairs. Currently, you cannot save your work to our server, but if you wish to download the samples and set it up on your own machine, feel free to do so.

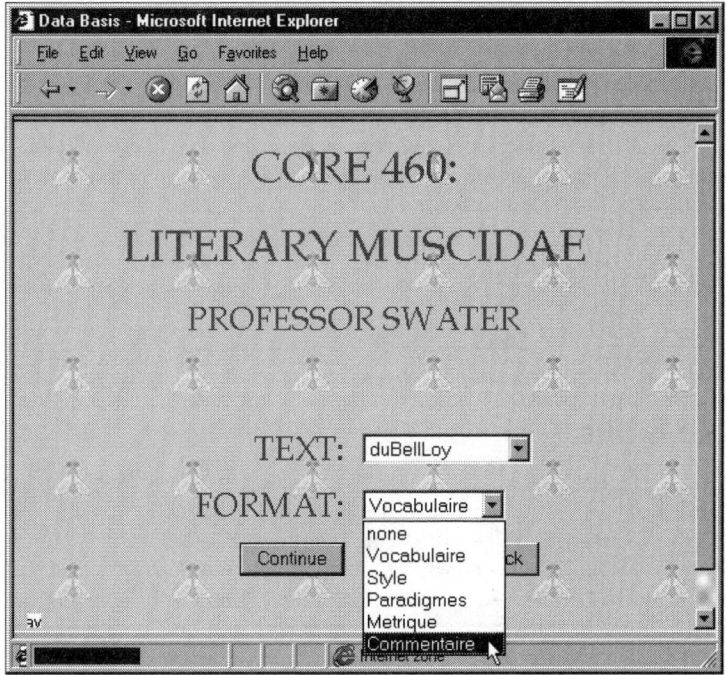

Analysis and Design

Let's try to understand what we want to achieve in the analysis and design stage. In the end, we'd like to have a list of classes that we need to program, and for each class, a list of its properties and methods, with a clear division between the interface and the implementation. We would also like to know how our classes relate to each other, and how the objects—the instantiations of each class—interact at runtime. As we tease out all this information, we'd like to write it down. So, we need two things: a methodology for designing classes and a notation for writing down the resulting design. These are two different things and shouldn't be confused with each other.

For a while, there were many competing methodologies and a great many competing notations. Within the last couple of years, three major players in the field, Booch, Jakobson and Rumbaugh, got together to integrate their methodologies and unify their notations. The result is called UML, short for Unified Modeling Language. We will not be using that language, but we will use the basics of the methodology behind it.

Commentary Formats

This whole project started life as a letter from a colleague, a professor of French literature, telling us about the kinds of assignments he'd like his students to do. The assignments all have to do with analysing or "explicating" a French literary text. The texts are usually short and highly structured: a poem, perhaps, or a passage from Pascal. We list four assignment "formats" whose implementation constitutes the main thread of this chapter. (There are more, some of them too specific to French versification to be of interest to the general reader. We mention them in the *Conclusions*.)

- ❏ **Format 1**. Given a text, identify those words and phrases in it that express its most important themes and provide English translations for them. (From now on, we'll say "word" meaning "word or phrase".) Display words and definitions in a table in a separate window.
- ❏ **Format 2**. Instead of translations, or in addition to them, provide a brief comment explaining why you think the word is related to a major theme of the text.
- ❏ **Format 3**. Identify a group of abstract notions that the text tries to convey, such as danger, peace, consolation or pain. Find words that express those notions and mark them in some way, perhaps by associating each notion with a color.
- ❏ **Format 4**. Same as Format 2, but each comment is given a unique id so that it can be found and displayed in response to a mouse click.

An important part of the specifications is that students ought to be able to view each other's work and comment on it. Also, several students ought to be able to merge their work into a single joint project.

From Goals to Specs

We were quite attracted to the problem because it seemed a better approach to computer-aided instruction than most we've seen. Instead of multiple-choice questions with branching paths through the material, students are given, in effect, research assignments in several specific formats. The student's activity here is not dissimilar to what many scholars would do themselves when first approaching a text to study. (Present-day scholars are more likely to use a book and 3x5 cards than a computer and our program, but this may change soon.) Our first task is to make the formats more specific, and incorporate them into the overall design.

Use Cases

For all their disagreements, all designers seem to agree that the best starting point for designing a large software application is a text in English (or whatever language you express yourself most commonly) that describes the application. Once you say "a text that describes the application", the natural impulse is to think of a descriptive, expository text that tells us what the application is like. In our case, we could start with:

The commentary application provides support for attaching various annotations to a text. The text itself remains unchanged except for possibly new HTML markup. The user indicates which portion of the text is the subject of the current commentary by selecting it. (No retyping!) The accumulated comments should be saved and reloaded. In the context of the course, we should have an authentication system so that only students in the course have access to their work. Some work is done jointly; students can view their teammates' work and merge it with their own.

It was an important insight (by Ivar Jacobson) that you'll get a much better coverage of the requirements if you think in terms of stories rather than descriptions: in terms of roles and scenarios rather than properties of the application. He called such scenarios "use cases".

Actors and Scenarios

We begin by separating the system to be designed from the "actors" who are going to use it. We pose the question: "who are the different actors who will use the system in different capacities?" Once the actors are identified, we ask: "what are the main uses that each actor will put the system to?" Finally, for each use, we're trying to come up with as many different scenarios as possible. We end up with a lot of scenarios for each of the main uses of the system by all its possible users.

Why is this better than writing descriptive specifications? Because different uses of the system is what actually happens. Deep down inside, a descriptive specification has got to be an analysis of possible uses; if you start with such a specification, you're just hiding from others and from yourself an important stage of the process. And there seems to be something congenial to our thinking in having to follow the logic of a story. (It is well known, for example, that when asked to describe an apartment, most people tell a story of what happens if you come in and turn left or right.) Try asking your informants: "Describe the kind of system you'd like," and many of them will clutch. But if you ask: "What is the first thing you do when you start working on an assignment?" you'd better have your tape recorder ready to run.

Who are Our Actors?

So, who would be the actors in our situation? Teacher is one, and student is another, of course. Is there anybody else? Well, yes and no. No, because most commonly there will be just those two characters in the play. However, if you think of everything the teacher and the student have to do, you'll see that they perform several roles, and indeed, in some situations, those roles will be performed by different people.

The Teacher Roles

One distinction that's important to make is between a teacher who creates a commentary format and a teacher who uses it in teaching. Frequently, it's the same person but not necessarily: imagine a course with multiple sections in which only one teacher creates the materials. Sometimes, in order to create a new format, the teacher will need a programmer's help, but for some formats, our application should act as an authoring tool.

A second distinction is between a teacher who teaches, or helps students learn some material, and a teacher who evaluates the students' performance, and otherwise administers the course. Again, it's frequently the same person but not necessarily, and in our model, they're best considered different actors. So we have accumulated three of them: teacher-creator, teacher-instructor, and teacher-administrator.

Since our application helps in creating materials that are saved in files on the server, at some point a technical person will have to become involved: a webmaster or a lab technician. We're not going to introduce another actor but rather roll the activities of that person into what the teacher-administrator has to do. It's up to individual instructors to work out the interface between them and technical support.

The Student Roles

In individual assignment, there's just one student role (but several scenarios). In group assignments, there may be a team leader whose role is different from the rest of the team. If there is no designated team leader, the role of each student as a team member is different from the role the same student plays in individual assignments.

What do our actors do? There's no room in this chapter or the rest of the book for a complete analysis. We'll present two simple student scenarios, to get an idea of what the process is like. Since the student is the ultimate end-user, we should end up with a reasonably informative general picture of the application.

JavaScript Objects

Student Scenario 1: Work on an Assignment from Beginning to End

The student starts a working session by going through an authentication process, most likely by entering a username and password. Once logged in, the student specifies the assignment: the text to work on and the commentary format. The student adds, deletes and edits comments until done. In the end, the student can switch to another assignment or quit the session altogether.

Student Scenario 2: Resume Work on an Assignment

What if our student has to quit the working session before finishing the assignment? Next time the student logs in, he's given a choice of resuming earlier work or starting from scratch. This little vignette illustrates the principle: start with an obvious scenario, then try to think what can go wrong with it.

Analyzing Nouns and Verbs

The next step may seem simplistic but it works remarkably well for the first approximation. Look at the nouns in your use cases (and other descriptions) and think of them as candidates for classes. Look at verbs, and think of them as candidates for methods of those classes. As you do that, make sure you don't confuse entities that are outside the system (such as actors who work it) with the components of the system itself.

In our two brief stories, we have the following nouns and noun phrases:

student, working session, session, authentication process, username, password, assignment, text, commentary format, comment, earlier work.

We can immediately leave out "student" as being outside the system, and "authentication process" as being too abstract. We can collapse "working session" and "session" together, and we can abbreviate "commentary format" to simply "format". We're left with:

session, username, password, assignment, text, format, comment, earlier work.

Further Analysis

What can we make of this? Cutting the discussion short, we propose that session is clearly a class of objects. Username and password are just strings (a primitive data type), so they can be made properties of session. (This is a good working principle.) We're left with assignment, text, format, comment, earlier work.

Since assignment is just an abbreviation for a text-format pair, we can cross it off our list because after we've dealt with texts and formats, the assignments will have been dealt with (see below). The text is just an HTML document that will sit passively in a frame waiting to be commented upon; we don't need to make it into an object of any sort. (It's an HTML object already.) We may want to save it as a property of something, in case it gets messed up. Would it be a property of session? It might be, or maybe it should be a property of format. Suppose (which is indeed the case) some formats leave text completely alone while others insert all sorts of HTML into it. For the latter kind, we'll want to save the initial clean text as a property of whatever defines format.

So we have to think of format, comment and earlier work. But notice that earlier work consists of comments, so if we figure out what an individual comment is, earlier work will be just a collection of those. When we decide how we're going to implement comments, we'll also see how to implement a collection of them.

Time to look at the verbs: what does the student do with comments? She adds, deletes and edits them; saves them to a file and reloads them at a later date. Does this ring a bell? A comment looks very much like a record in a database table, and that's what earlier work is, a database table.

Once we've made this decision, a lot of our application begins to take shape. We'll have a database table and an associated form; the student will enter comments into a text area in the form, and the standard database buttons—Add, Delete and Replace—will carry out the right operations. For simple formats, the database will consist of just one table, but for more complex ones, additional tables or other structures may be required. A format, then, is just an empty database whose tables and fields are specified in the dbInfo form and HTML tables. Or perhaps not quite empty: it can contain sample records and other initial information from the instructor.

We've identified two major classes in our application, a `session` class and a `format` class, which is the same as, or derived from, the Database class. What is the relationship between them? Remember that a `session` object is probably going to be created after the student specifies the text and the format. A `format` object can be stored as a property of `session`.

Design Conclusions

This discussion has been necessarily sketchy, trying to compress a lot of material into a brief section. Our goal was to provide you with a glimpse of the kind of thinking that goes into the design process, and of a possible methodology to follow. If you're in the business of programming, you have to develop a design methodology that suits you, and use it in your projects. As for us, we proceed to the conclusions.

The States of the Application

We present our conclusions as a series of steps that the user follows in working with the application. At every step, we describe what the user has done, and the corresponding changes in the application itself. We illustrate the steps of the user with a **state transition diagram**. These are commonly used to describe the states of a computational process; we're just using the format because it's quite intuitive and will be familiar to some readers:

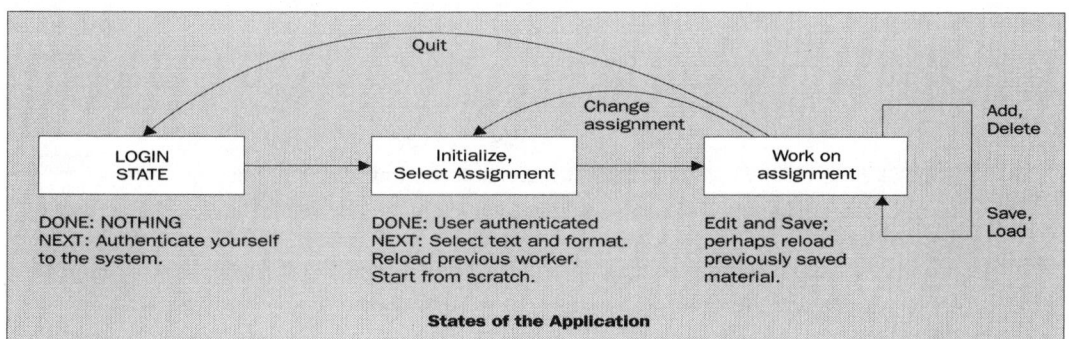

States of the Application

JavaScript Objects

Login State

User enters username and password; the program authenticates the user.

Initialization State

User selects a text to work on and the format of the commentary. The program creates a Session object, loads the files, and initializes the format. The user is given a choice between resuming previous work or starting from scratch.

Working State

Within a given format, add, delete and modify commentaries. At any time, the user can save the current content, revert to previously saved content, or start from scratch with the initial content. The user can also switch to another format without quitting the application.

Files and Screens

Arrangement of Files

We have many students working on the same assignment; how will their work be kept separate? The simplest approach is to put each student's work in a separate file. The file would be uniquely determined by three items: the assigned text, the format of the assignment, and the student's username on the system. This can be achieved by grouping files into directories: all materials for a given course are contained in a single directory; within that directory, there's a subdirectory for each text studied in the course; within the subdirectory for a given text there are further subdirectories for each assignment format.

Progression of Screens

In the beginning of a working session the student will be asked for the username and password, the text to work on and the format of the assignment. The password will be used for authentication and establishing the level of access. The text and format will determine the path to the working directory, and the username will determine the name of the file. We'll probably want an initial "splash screen" that will identify the course and collect four pieces of information from the student (username, password, text and format). We have used two screens: one for identification purposes, the other for determining work content. Since the student may want to work on two different assignments during one login session, it ought to be possible to change the text or format without seeing the login page.

The Working Screen

Once the user passes through the login screens and the main parameters of the session are set, the user is presented with the working screen. The contents of the working screen or screens have to include:

❑ The text itself, probably in a separate frame. Given its central role, we'll put it top left.
❑ A form for student input. Depending on the format, there may be one (definition *or* commentary) or two (definition *and* commentary) or more text input elements in it. A text area may be more appropriate for commentary, while a single-line text box is probably adequate for definitions.
❑ Another text input in the same form, to hold the word or phrase that is the subject of comment or definition.
❑ A number of buttons: to add, delete or replace a comment; to sort them; to save the work and reload it.

Some formats may require additional control elements.

Main Code Modules and Code Files

What are the main code components of the application? First, we need the code for the introductory screens: collect the information from the user and send to the server for authentication. This code is trivial and can go into the HTML file for the introductory screens. We call this file `page0.htm`. Second, we need to create and initialize a session object, including its format. This involves loading all the files into appropriate frames, always a tricky proposition. We put this code into `session.js`. Finally, we present the working screen to the user, and let him drive the application.

Code for the Work Screen

Behind the work screen, we need two code modules. One is to establish the connection between the text and the form in which the current comment is created or edited. In the simplest case, the task is to move the text selected by the user into a text box in the form. In more complex cases, a substantial amount of text-processing code will be required. We put this code into `txtrange.js`.

The other module for the working screen associates the selected text with a comment created by the user, saves and reloads text-comment pairs, and makes them available for further editing. All we need to do here is to include the database class, `dbob.js`.

Format Definition Files

Each format is defined by two files. One contains the control elements for working with the format, the other contains the data definition form, the table or tables for the format, and whatever initial materials the instructor may wish to put there. We've adopted a naming convention for format definition files, illustrated by this example. Suppose we're creating the simplest word-remark format, `wr` for short. The control elements file will be called `wr.htm`, and the data definition file will be called `wrDB.htm`. Similarly we have a pair of `wdr.htm` and `wdrDB.htm` (for "word-definition-remark"), `wc.htm` and `wcDB.htm` (for "word-category"), and so on.

Code for a Simple Format

Our minimal application is a word-commentary assignment. Its introductory screens are the same as in the full-featured application, but its text processing capabilities are minimal.

Since we're approaching the end of the book, the more familiar parts of the code are given very light treatment, if any. We concentrate on the overall structure and new elements.

The Main Frameset File

The main file includes all the appropriate code files, defines the frames, and displays the initial screen:

```
<HTML><HEAD><TITLE> Data Basis </TITLE>
<SCRIPT SRC="sessinit.js"> </SCRIPT>
<SCRIPT SRC="txtrange.js"> </SCRIPT>
<SCRIPT SRC="../class7/dbob.js"> </SCRIPT>
<SCRIPT>
```

```
function doOnLoad(){
 topControl.showFirstPart();        // defined in page0.htm
}
</SCRIPT></HEAD>
<frameset name="theFrameSet" onload="doOnLoad()" rows="0%,100%,0%,0%">
  <frameset name="dataPair" cols="55%,45%">
   <FRAME name=dbDoc src=poem1.htm >
   <FRAME name=dbData src=initDB.htm >
  </frameset>
  <FRAME name=topControl src=page0.htm >
  <FRAME name=dbControl src=wr.htm >
  <FRAME name=dbMsg src=poem1.htm >
</frameset></HTML>
```

The code files included in the page are as we described a moment ago. There are five frames. The "db" frames—dbData, dbControl and dbMsg—are exactly as in previous database applications. The dbDoc frame is for the document, and topControl frame is for the two initial screens. It is this frame that is shown in the beginning; the rest are given 0%. The function doOnLoad(), in page0.htm, presents the first initial screen.

Collecting the Information: page0.htm

The file page0.htm is mostly occupied by a big form arranged in a table whose id is p0Tab. The code mostly hides and unhides the rows of that table.

JavaScript Code in page0

```
<html><head><title>WELCOME TO MY WEB PAGE</title>
<style> TR.hidden {display:none;} </style>
<SCRIPT>
function hideRows()
{
 var A=hideRows.arguments;
 for(var i=0;i<A.length;i++) p0Tab.rows[A[i]].className='hidden';
}
function showRows()
{
 var A=showRows.arguments;
 for(var i=0;i<A.length;i++) p0Tab.rows[A[i]].className='';
}
function showFirstPart()
{
 hideRows(3,4,5);showRows(0,1,2); page0Form.username.focus();
}
function showSecondPart()
{
 hideRows(0,1,2);showRows(3,4,5); page0Form.Text.focus();
}
function inFirstPart(){return "hidden"==p0Tab.rows[3].className;}
</SCRIPT></head>
```

The functions hideRows() and showRows() illustrate the use of the arguments property of the Function object. The two functions are used to switch between the first part of page0, where the login information is collected, and the second part, where the user specifies the text and format. The predicate inFirstPart() is used to differentiate the program's response to the Enter key: if the user is in the first part, we proceed to the second part; if the user is in the second part, we check his input for completeness. This is done in the Session() constructor, itself called from doPage0(), which is the action of the page0 form.

Elements of page0Form

The big form in page0.htm has, in its first part, text input elements for entering username and password, and in its second part select and option elements for selecting the text and format. There are also navigation buttons to move between the first part, the second part, and the larger application beyond. The Text select element returns the name of the file (without the .htm extension) that contains the text. The Format select element returns the abbreviation for the format; on the basis of this abbreviation we can identify the data and control files for the format. The navigation buttons (Continue and Go back) have onclick methods that call showFirstPart() or showSecondPart(). The Reset button returns the form input elements to their initial values. The Submit button calls doPage0(), which calls the Session constructor:

```
<form NAME="page0Form" ACTION="javascript:parent.doPage0()">
```

The Session Constructor

The Session constructor is a very busy function that performs a number of tasks and may take a good deal of time performing them, during which period nothing visible is happening. Some users may get worried and start clicking on the Submit button again and again, creating multiple session objects each of which will try to load the documents into frames. The first task of the Session constructor is to anticipate this behavior (which we actually observed).

Protect From the User

Several approaches are possible here, and you're welcome to try them out. We could disable the Submit button by setting its disabled attribute (new in HTML 4.0) to true. We could put a modal dialog on screen saying "Setup in progress, please wait." Or we could (and did) add a Boolean property to the Session object, setupInProgress, which is set to true by the constructor, and eventually reset to false by the initFormat() method which the constructor calls when it's done with all its chores.

```
function Session(){// args: topFrame,dataFrame,ctlFrame,msgFrame,docFrame){
{
  if(Session.setupInProgress)
   return alert("session setup in progress; please wait (or reload page)");
  Session.setupInProgress=true;
```

Thus protected, the constructor proceeds to set up all its bookkeeping machinery.

Set up Names

Each frame in this application has two names. One of them comes from the frame's HTML id attribute. We provide defaults for them, but the user can override those defaults in the HTML page. The other name is a private nickname that the program uses to refer to the frame. We wanted to keep references in the code isolated from user-introduced changes, and so we gave each frame a private nickname and set up a little dictionary that holds correspondences between actual names and nicknames used in the code. Another dictionary holds correspondences between actual names and the frame objects:

Name	Data type	Content
`FrameTags`	Array	nicknames for frames, same for all Session objects, independent of actual frame names
`FrameNameArr`	Array	actual frame names; defaults can be overriden by arguments to the constructor
`FrameNames`	Object: nickname->name	associative array for getting from nickname to name
`Sframes`	Object: name->frame	associative array for getting from name to frame itself

In addition, the constructor gives the newly created object a name, the same as the name of the page0 frame. (The nickname for that frame is page0; its default name is topControl.) The object is stored in the constructor under that name. The page0 frame is also accessible as this.theFrame.

```
var frameTags="page0,db,ctl,msg,doc".split(",");  // nicknames for frames
var frameNameArr=        //default frame names
  "topControl,dbData,dbControl,dbMsg,dbDoc".split(",");
with(Session)
  for(var i=0; i<frameTags.length; i++)
    if(arguments[i])        // user supplied a frame name to override default
      frameNameArr[i]=arguments[i];
this.frameNames=new Object();  // from frameTags to frameNames
for(var i=0; i<frameTags.length; i++)
  this.frameNames[frameTags[i]]=frameNameArr[i];
this.sframes=new Object();    // from frameNames to frame objects
for(f in this.frameNames)
  this.sframes[f]=document.frames[this.frameNames[f]];
this.name=this.frameNames.page0;
Session[this.name]=this;
this.theFrame=this.sframes.page0;
```

Collect Data from page0 and Check for Completeness

With naming machinery in place, we can collect the session information from page0. This is done in a sequence of assignment statements that have the Session object properties on the left hand side and the page0Form's input fields on the right hand side:

```
with(this.theFrame.page0Form)
  {
  this.userName=username.value;
```

```
this.password=password.value;
this.text=Text.value;
this.format=Format.value;
this.projectPrefix=projPrefix.value;
this.project=this.projectPrefix+this.text+"/"+this.format;
}
if(!this.userName){this.theFrame.showFirstPart(); return false;}
if(!this.text || !this.format){this.theFrame.showSecondPart();return false;}
```

Load the Frames

The stage is set for loading all the frames with data. As we discovered in working on this application, when the number of frames is greater than three, you can no longer rely on the value of `document.readyState` to check whether or not the document has loaded. What happens is that the value of `readyState` is not yet set to `interactive` when the checking takes place. So we resort to the brute-force method of putting a mark on each frame, and removing the marks when loading is complete. The whole loading process unfolds in three methods of the `Session` object: `prevDBLoad()`, `afterLoads()`, and `continueLoading()`. We're not going to look at that code in any great detail; suffice it to say that it reliably loads previously saved work into the `msg` frame, the format's controls into the `ctl` frame, the format's data into the `db` frame, and the text into the `doc` frame. (We're using nicknames to refer to frames.) Note that all text files are assumed to have been placed into the `Text/` subdirectory:

```
for(x in this.sframes) this.sframes[x].document.body.marked=true;
this.prevDBLoad();  //try to preload earlier work by this user into msgFrame
with(this.sframes)
  {
  ctl.location.href=this.format+".htm";
  db.location.href=this.format+"DB.htm";
  doc.location.href="Text/"+this.text+".htm";
  }
this.afterLoads.count=0;
this.afterLoads();
}
```

Previous Work and Joint Work

The function `prevDBLoad()` submits a copy of `loadDBForm` that is found in `page0`. The target of that form is the `msg` frame, reused as a temporary storage place for previously created content. Later on, in `afterLoads()`, the innerHTML of the document in that frame is copied to the `db` frame.

Apart from giving the user a choice between reloading earlier work or starting from scratch, we also have here all that is needed for merging several students' work into a single joint commentary. Recall that our Database class has the methods for copying rows from one table to another identically structured one, and for removing duplicates. To merge commentaries, the user would load each one of them in turn and copy its tables into the result of the merge. In order for this to work, the content-creation process should leave the text unaffected, for otherwise, merging would also involve the impossible task of undoing all the traces left by individual users in the text.

Format Initialization and Use

The `Session` object has been constructed, and all the content has been loaded into the frames of the application, but something essential is still missing: the `format` object, to which we now turn. The sequence of events is as follows:

- ❑ `afterLoads()` calls `initFormat()`
- ❑ `initFormat()` creates a new Database object (which is the `format` object) using the `db`, `ctl` and `msg` frames
- ❑ `initFormat()` calls `onInitFormat()` function found in the format's control file (one such function for each format)
- ❑ `initFormat()` initializes help messages for the format displayed in the status bar

Here is the code for `afterLoads()` and `initFormat()`. By the time `initFormat()` is finished, the user is presented with the work screen, ready to receive new content:

```
function s_afterLoads()
 {
 if(this.continueLoading())
  return setTimeout("Session."+this.name+".afterLoads()",200);
 if(this.sframes.msg.dbInfo && confirm("reload previous work?"))
  this.sframes.db.document.body.innerHTML =     //overwrite default db
   this.sframes.msg.document.body.innerHTML;   // with previous db
 setTimeout("Session."+this.name+".initFormat()",200);
 }
function s_initFormat(){
 if(this.sframes.db.document.readyState!="complete")
  // still parsing work copied from the msg frame
  return setTimeout("Session."+this.name+".initFormat()",200);
 with (this.frameNames)
  this.database=new Database(db,ctl,msg);      // create a format object
 with(this.sframes.db.dbInfo)
  {
  Project.value=this.project;
  User.value=this.userName;
  Password.value=this.password;
  }
 with(this.sframes.ctl)
  this.onInitFormat=onInitFormat;   // the format's code for attaching itself
 if(this.onInitFormat)this.onInitFormat();
 this.database.initClickBHelp();
 Session.setupInProgress=false;
 self.document.body.rows="55%,0%,45%"; // on to the work screen
 }
```

What's in the Format?

In order to understand a format, you have to look at its `onInitFormat()` function. It is found in the control file for the format, (which is `wr.htm` for the word-remark format). Since this is our first format, we'll look at the entire file. Much of its content will be familiar to you from an earlier database application; even more of its content repeats from one format to another. The structure of the file is as follows:

```
<HTML> <HEAD> generic format code and format-specific code </HEAD>
<BODY> <FORM>
<DIV id="texts" class="txtFields">
text fields for working with and looking up comments
</DIV>
<DIV>one or more DIVs with database control buttons and possibly other buttons
</DIV>
</FORM> </BODY> </HTML>
```

We'll look at the main components of the file in turn.

Generic Format Code

Every format has a link to the stylesheet, an `onInitFormat()` function, and local abbreviations for `clickb()` and `clickBHelp()` methods of the Database class. (`clickb()` should be familiar from Chapter 6, `clickBHelp()` is an addition in `dbobx.htm`.)

```
<link rel="stylesheet" type="text/css" href="controls.css"></link>
<SCRIPT>
function onInitFormat(){
  // one such function for each format: wdr, mdr, wr, or wc
  this.sframes.doc.document.body.onselect=parent.setSelection;
}
function clickb(btn,ev){parent.Session.topControl.database.clickb(btn,ev);}
function clickBHelp(btn){parent.Session.topControl.database.clickBHelp(btn);}
</SCRIPT>
```

In simple formats, the only action in `onInitFormat` is to set the onselect event handler. The local names for `clickb ()` and `clickBHelp()` are created for convenience: the two functions are used many time in creating command buttons.

The Form and its Elements

The form that constitutes the entire body of `wr.htm` is a straight database control form with all the naming conventions for itself and its elements as defined in Chapter 6. The name of the form is `frmGlossary` because it's the companion form for the Glossary table. The names of the text elements are `hhWord` and `hhRemarks`, corresponding to the `Word` and `Remarks` columns of the table. The buttons are all the familiar database buttons (**Prev** and **Next**, **Add**, **Del** and **Replace**, **Save** and **Load**) with a couple of additions (**Assignment** and **Quit**). The `sort` and `lookup` facilities work exactly as before. The buttons are created in the same fashion as in Chapter 6:

```
<input type="BUTTON" name="Prev" value="Previous" onclick='clickb(this,event)'
  onmouseover="clickBHelp(this)">
```

Each button has a `mouseover` event handler which shows a help message in the status bar. In the next version we'll probably replace `<INPUT TYPE=BUTTON ...>` elements with the new (HTML4.0) `BUTTON` elements that provide a title attribute; the titles specified in the attribute appear as a popup when the mouse goes over the button.

The two non-database buttons, **Assignment** and **Quit**, are defined as follows:

```
<input type="BUTTON" value="Assignment" onclick='parent.toPage0()'><BR>
<input type="BUTTON" value="Quit"
  onclick='parent.Session.topControl.quitSession()'>
```

Their event handlers do the expected things. The `quitSession()` method, for example, cleans up the form in page0, returns to that page, and removes the name of the `Session` object from the constructor's properties:

```
function s_quitSession()
{
 with(this.theFrame)
  {
  with(page0Form){ // reset the fields of the form
  Text.selectedIndex=1; Format.selectedIndex=1;
  username.value="";password.value="";}
  showFirstPart(); // prepare page0 ...
  }
 toPage0(); // and show it
 Session[this.name]=null; //the suicide line;
}
```

Working with Text

We're finally done with all the preliminaries and ready to look at the work screen. The student's actions in that screen are the usual database actions, with one big addition: the onselect handler in the doc frame. It is triggered when the student selects a word or phrase, either by dragging or double-clicking, and releases the button. The selected text appears in the text box labeled "Selected text." What's the mechanism for doing that?

Meet the TextRange Object

This is where the world's divisions into different browsers and platforms is particularly sharp. Without going into details, let's simply say that only IE4 on Win95/98/NT has the tools to associate a stretch of selected text with an object that becomes part of the document's object tree. (These tools were also at work in the application of Chapter 4 which determined from a mouse click the minimal page element that contained it.) It is possible to get the selected text itself in NC4 also, but the place of the selection within the document is irretrievable.

A document in IE4 has a `selection` property. There's nothing much you can do to that property directly: you can't assign to it, and it doesn't have any properties itself. It does have a method, `createRange()`, which creates a `TextRange` object. This is the tool for working with selected text. For instance, to change the selection programmatically, you would use the `select()` method of `TextRange`.

A `TextRange` object has a `text` property and an `htmlText` property. Both properties are read-write. The object doesn't contain any text within itself but only references to it. You can think of it as two pegs and a rubber band. The pegs are called "endpoints." You can get a fresh new pair of pegs only around the entire document body or around the current selection, but once they're created, it's easy to move them around. For instance, you can move the pegs so the rubber band stretches over any given HTML object in the page.

We will introduce the many methods of the `TextRange` object as we need them. In this section, we only need to know how to create a `TextRange` object so that its endpoints are those of the current selection. If the document we're working on is the dbDoc frame, then you say:

```
var tr=dbDoc.document.selection.createRange();
```

Suppose the name of the entry form is `frm` and the name of the field for the selected text is `fld`. To complete the task, all we have to say is:

```
dbDoc.frm.fld.value=tr.text;
```

We can now look at the code for `setSelection()` in detail.

The setSelection Function

The complete text of `setSelection()` elaborates on the two actions we've just presented: get the selection into a `TextRange` object and assign its `htmlText` to the appropriate field of the form. Much of the rest is just checking that everything's in order, but there's one important additional wrinkle. When a text is selected, especially by double-clicking, there may be whitespace on either end of it included in the selection. For many reasons, some of them more obvious than others, we want to get rid of that whitespace. This is done by a call on our `skipBlanks()` function:

```
function setSelection() // used in several formats, as eventhandler for doc
{
with(Session.topControl)
{
if(sframes.doc.document.selection.type=="Text"){
 var tr=sframes.doc.document.selection.createRange();
 skipBlanks(tr);     // trim blanks on both ends of textRange object
```

Now the text in the `TextRange` object may be different from the selection, and we want to change the selection to conform to the object. The `select()` method of `TextRange` does exactly that:

```
tr.select(); // set selection to the trimmed text
```

The rest of the code finds the form and the field to which the selection should be copied, and copies it:

```
with(format){
  var T=Tables[Tables[0]];
  var frm=Tables[Tables[0]].form; var fld;
  if(!frm || !(fld=frm["hh"+T.Headers[0]]))
    return alert("no form-field for insertion of "+tr.text);
  fld.value=tr.htmlText;
  }   // close with(format)
 }   // close if(sframes.doc.document.selection.type=="Text")
}}   // close with(Session.topControl), end of function
```

Skip Blanks

The `skipBlanks()` function introduces two new methods of `TextRange`, `moveStart()` and `moveEnd()`. They take two arguments. The first argument is the name of a text unit, which can be "character", "word" or "sentence". The second argument is a number indicating how many units to move; it defaults to 1. The `moveStart()` method moves the endpoint left (or whatever the direction of text in the current locale), and `moveEnd()` moves the endpoint right, unless the second argument is negative, which reverses the direction.

The function itself takes two arguments, the second of them optional. If it is not supplied, the function trims blanks on both ends, otherwise it trims blanks only at the end specified by the optional argument:

```
function skipBlanks(tr,endp)  // skips blanks at front or end or both
{
  if(!endp||endp!="RightOnly")
  while(tr.text.length>0 && tr.text.charAt(0)<=" ")
   tr.moveStart("character");
 var N;
 if(!endp||endp!="LeftOnly")
  while((N=tr.text.length)>0 && tr.text.charAt(N-1)<=" ")
   tr.moveEnd("character",-1);
 return tr;
}
```

Summary of the Initial TextRange Experience

So far, working with the TextRange class has been pure pleasure. You create a TextRange either around the entire document or around the current selection, move it where you want it, and you have an HTML object whose innerText is exactly what you want. As we move (in the next section) to applications with more complex behavior and more sensitive to whitespace, we'll start bumping against the limits of what TextRange can do. Some of those limits are the result of a specific implementation, others are the matter of principle: in a document that is structured by HTML tags into a tree, it is difficult to work with stretches of text that start in the middle of one element and end in the middle of another one.

Creating Another Simple Format

Before we move on to more complex formats, let's recapitulate how you would create another simple one. Since a format is just a database of a specific, well, format, we have inherited, for free, the "authoring system" quality of the Database class. From the beginning, we set ourselves the goal of making not only the contents of assignment formats, but the formats themselves, easily editable by somebody with only HTML skills. If one day, an instructor wants the students to provide three different commentaries (on grammar, style, and cultural background, for instance), it should be easy to accomplish.

The database, as you recall, is fully determined by its tables, and a table is determined by an HTML table from which it is created. To create a new format, you have to do two minor edits in the data file, and the corresponding edits in the control file. In the data file, rename the table in the dbInfo form and edit the table itself so it has the right number of appropriately named columns. In the control frame, change the form so it's name is according to our naming conventions ("frm" + the name of the table), add text fields as needed, and name them according to our naming conventions ("hh" + the name of the column in the table). That's all the authoring tools you need for creating simple formats.

Formats With more Elaborate Behavior

In this section, we present two formats that do more elaborate things with texts and text ranges. The first of them, the category format, was described in the beginning of the chapter:

❑ **Format 3.** Identify a group of abstract notions that the text tries to convey, such as danger, peace, consolation or pain. Find words that express those notions and mark them in some way, perhaps by associating each notion with a color.

The second format changes the way in which words or phrases are associated with the commentary. In the simple formats, a commentary is attached to a certain sequence of words. Both are stored in the database table, without any information about where in the document that sequence of words appears. The format in this section associates a comment with a sequence of words and their location in the document. This makes it possible to create a hyper-text link between the text and the comment.

The Category Format

The first thing to do is to spell out the specifications in more detail. After going back and forth for quite a while with our client, the conclusions arrived at were:

❑ The instructor must be able to create a list of categories and associate each with a color. This can be done via a database table.

❑ The content creation phase should proceed as follows: select a word or phrase; select its category from a drop-down list; click a button.

❑ The viewing phase should provide for these options: color all occurrences of a particular category; color all categories; remove all colors.

Try It Out

Point your browser at http://webdev.wrox.co.uk/books/1894/chapter08/index.htm and login as 'Guest'. Select the text 'Crusoe' and the category 'Paradigmes', then click on Continue to arrive at the following page:

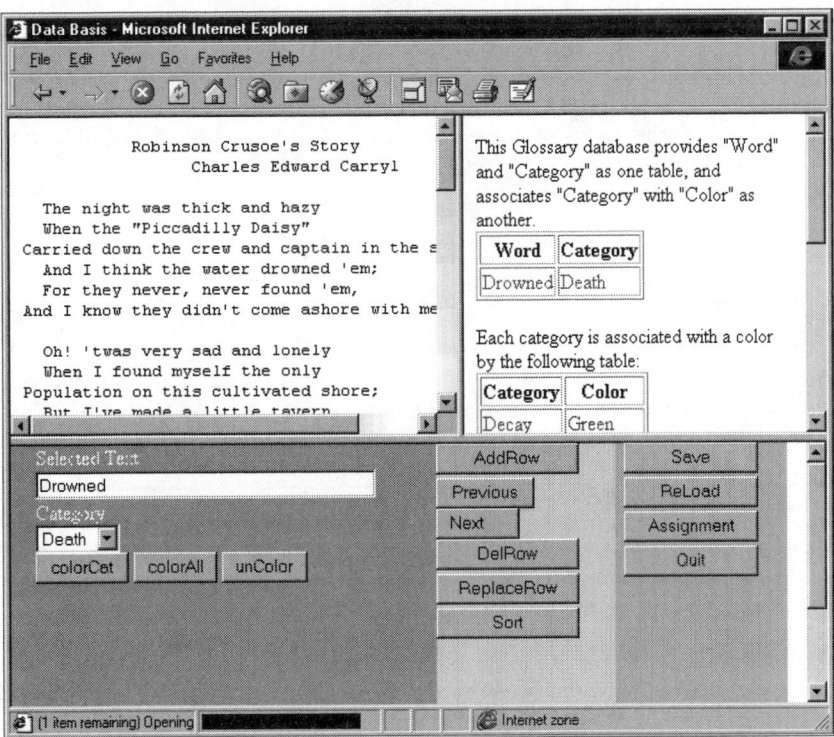

A word or phrase can be selected from the top left frame, and associated with a category. The page has already selected 'Drowned' and put it in the category 'Death'. Each category is also associated with a color, and a list of categories and colors is provided in the top right frame, which is wcDB.htm. Clicking the colorCat button will color all occurrences of 'Drowned' yellow. To add a new phrase to the Word-Category table, select the phrase and its category, then click the AddRow button in the light purple area of the lower frame.

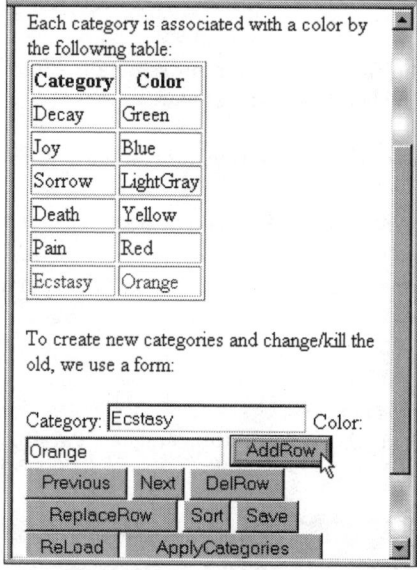

To modify the categories or color associations, open wcDB.htm in the text editor and change the Categories table, or use the control form for that table, also in wcDB.htm, as illustrated above.

How It Works

The rest of this section goes through the code for the category format.

Changes in the Data File

The first addition here is another table that associates an abstract notion or category with a color (pain is red, joy is blue). This results in straightforward changes in the dbInfo form. We also add a form to control the category table right there in the data file. Most of the time, the category table and its control form are invisible.

Changes in the Control File

The form in the control file needs a new select element showing the categories. Since categories are subject to change by the user, we felt that the element should be automatically generated to reflect the changes (rather than rely on the user to make matching changes in two places). So we need a function, makeSelect() that creates the HTML, including all the options, for a select element. We'll give it three arguments: the name by which the element will be known, a list of values for options, and the object in the page that will become the select element. The function hardly needs comment:

```
function makeSelect(name,vList,ob)
{
 var S="<select name='"+name+"' size='1'>\n";
 if(vList.length>0)
   {
   S+="<option value='"+vList[0]+"' selected>"+vList[0]+"<\/option>\n";
   for(var i=1;i<vList.length;i++)
     S+="<option value='"+vList[i]+"'>"+vList[i]+"<\/option>\n";
   }
 S+="<\/select>\n"; ob.outerHTML=S;
}
```

That function will be called from `applyCategories()` which gets the list of categories from the table and constructs the SELECT element:

```
function applyCategories()    // runs within wc format control page
{
 with(parent.Session.topControl)
   {
   var L=format.getList("Categories","Category");
   makeSelect("hhCategory",L,sframes.ctl.frmGlossary.hhCategory);
   }
}
```

The `getList()` method is a fairly obvious addition to the Database class, found in `dbob.js`. It takes the name of a table and the name of a column in that table, and returns an array of strings.

Initializing the Category Format

The function `applyCategories()` itself is called from `onInitFormat()`:

```
function onInitFormat() // wc: one such function for each format
{
  this.sframes.doc.document.body.onselect=parent.setSelection;
  onInitFormat.initHTML=this.sframes.doc.document.body.innerHTML;
  applyCategories(); // category list -> <SELECT option list ..> in form
  this.format.loadRow("Glossary"); // sets category item value within list;
     // was set by new Database, but overwritten by applyCategories
  this.format.Tables.Categories.onUpdate=applyCategories;
     // update SELECT element whenever the Categories table is changed
}
```

You can think of this code as, in effect, deriving a more specialized category format from the more general simple formats of the preceding section.

Viewing Options

For viewing categories in color, we have the `colorCat()` function. If given a category name as an argument, it colors all the words and phrases in that category. If given no argument, it colors them all. Or rather, it asks the `colorWord()` function to color them all, because `colorCat()` only retrieves information from the two tables of the format.

```
function colorCat(catName) //colors all words of category or all categories
{
 with(parent.Session.topControl) with(format)
```

```
      {
      var TW=Tables.Glossary; var TC=Tables.Categories;
      if(!TC || !TW)return alert("missing Glossary or Categories tables");
      for(var i=0;i<TW.length;i++)
        {
        var row=TW[i]; rowCat=row.Category;
        if(!catName || catName==rowCat)
          {
          var color=lookup1(TC,"Category",rowCat,"Color"); // get color
          colorWord(sframes.doc,row.Word,rowCat,color);  // color the word
}}}} // close if, for, with; end function
```

colorWord(), with Regular Expressions

The actual hard work of coloring is done by `colorWord()`. It uses the `replace()` method of the String class to find all the occurrences of the word in the document and make them into a `span` element with a style attribute.

```
function colorWord(aFrame,aWord,aCat,aColor)
{
var S=aFrame.document.body.innerHTML;
var P="\\b("+parent.trimSpace(aWord)+")\\b";
S=S.replace(new RegExp(P,"gi"),
  "<SPAN onclick='parent.Session.topControl.ctl.showCatClick(this)' cat='"
  +aCat+"'"+" style='color:"+aColor+"'>$1<\/SPAN>");
aFrame.document.body.innerHTML=S;
}
```

The pattern that the function uses to find the word's occurrences says: "trim whitespace around the `aWord` argument, and match the resulting string surrounded by whitespace". (Note that the backslash in \b has to be escaped.) Since the trimmed word is in parentheses, it can be referred to as `$1`.

showCatClick() and unColor()

You notice that the `<SPAN>` element has not only a style attribute, but also an onclick handler, so the user can click on the colored word and see its category. The category itself is stashed away as the `cat` property of the `<SPAN>`. The `showCatClick()` function does it:

```
function showCatClick(aSpan)
{
parent.Session.topControl.sframes.doc.event.cancelBubble=true;
alert("category "+aSpan.cat+" for "+aSpan.innerText);
}
```

Finally, to remove color from the document, we restore its initial condition, saved as the `initHTML` property of `onInitFormat()`:

```
function unColor()
{
with(parent.Session.topControl)
  sframes.doc.document.body.innerHTML=onInitFormat.initHTML;
}
```

Buttons for Viewing Options

We have provided all the functionality required by our specifications. All that's left to do is add three new buttons in the control frame: to color a specific category, to color all categories, and to reset to no colors. You'll find the three buttons already installed in the control frame.

The Hypertext Commentary Format

While the category format required some ingenuity to implement (if we may say so), it did not put any additional pressure on the `TextRange` class. The `com` ("Commentary" or "Commentaire") format will, however. Our task now is to retrieve not only the text of the selection, but also its position in the document: the byte offset from the beginning and the length. Since the selection can cross line boundaries, we'll have to deal with whitespace and other difficult issues.

As before, we'll start with more precise specifications. They will entail some restructuring of the format's data table which will acquire three additional columns. Once the static picture is in place, we'll trace the dynamic functioning of the format, both in the content-creation mode, and in viewing mode. In the end, we'll review the new functionality that has been added to `TextRange`.

More Precise Specifications

In content creation mode, this format will look and feel exactly the same as the simple commentary format: the user selects some text, enters a comment and clicks the **Add** button. However, the resulting record will give the text-comment pair a unique id, and register the text's position in the document. (We register the text position by recording its starting point and length.) The commented-upon text will become highlighted, and clicking on it will bring up the associated comment, in another window.

An essential requirement is that the changes to the text are not saved, only the commentary database. When the document is loaded, the commentary records are "applied" to the document, and the HTML markup is restored. The requirement is important because we want different users to work on the same text without messing up each other's work. If all the information is kept in a database table, different users' work can be merged, using the database facilities we already have: the `copyRows()` and `remDups()` method, provided in the code for Chapter 6 as part of the Database class. We will thus have everything set up for joint projects, a very useful educational tool and an absolute must for our customer.

The reason we need both the byte counts (offset and length) for a commented block of text and a unique id for it, is because we treat the same document both as a stream of bytes into which we insert HTML markup, and as an HTML document that responds to clicks with hypertext jumps. The HTML markup we use to identify a comment is a `span` element that has a style attribute, an onclick event handler, and our own `xsym` property which holds the comment's unique id.

Main Actions of the Format

The code for the `com` format is organized around three main actions it performs. The actions are:

- ❑ in the comment-creation stage, create a new text-comment pair and place it in the data table
- ❑ on initialization or editing, apply all comment information to a clean document
- ❑ in the comment-use stage, respond to a click in the document window by a hypertext jump to the corresponding comment

We will review the code in this order after commenting upon a few technical issues.

Some Technical Issues

Changes to the Data Table and Its Form

As our specifications indicate, the data table will have five columns: a block of text, the comment attached to it, the byte offset and length of the selection, and its unique id which we call SymNum, for "Symbol Number". The form, accordingly, has new text fields called hhLoc, hhLen, and hhSymNum.

Unique id's

We generate unique id's in the form "CommentSymN", where N is some number. The number is kept as a property of onInitFormat() and incremented every time we need a new one. The function that places the selection's data into the form (before the user transfers it into the table), has this line:

```
hhSymNum.value=onInitFormat.symNum++;
```

Multi-line Selection

The selected text moves from the document window to the data table through these intermediate stages:

- surround it by a TextRange
- copy the "contents" of the TextRange into the form field
- move it from the form into the table

As long as we were only interested in the textual content of the selection, it didn't matter to us what the TextRange object did to the whitespace within the selection. Now that we want to preserve line breaks (within the <PRE> tag) multi-line selections require special treatment. (IE4, and HTML in general, replace end-of-lines with a blank character.) We deal with the problem by breaking multi-line selections into an array of single-line TextRanges and re-assembling them when needed.

Initializing the Format

The code in onInitFormat() is a good starting point for tracing the functioning of com:

```
function onInitFormat(){  // com: one such function for each format
 onInitFormat.initHTML=  // save the initial condition of the document
   this.sframes.doc.document.body.innerHTML;
  this.sframes.doc.document.body.onmouseup=setCommentRange;
  this.format.Tables.Comments.onUpdate=refreshDoc;
  applyAllCommentRows();
}
```

The first new line of code gives the document an onmouseup event handler. The second new line simply says that whenever the data table of the format is changed, the document's appearance should be refreshed. (The onUpdate method of a table, if defined, is run by the update() method of the Database, defined in dbob.js.) Refreshing the document's appearance involves two steps: restore the document to its initial condition and apply all comments to it. The second step is performed by applyAllCommentRows(), which is also the last action of onInitFormat().

We're ready to delve more deeply into the code, beginning with comment creation.

Creating the Comments

Creating a comment starts with selecting a stretch of text to comment upon. In our simple formats, that action is captured by an `onselect` event handler, but not here, because `onselect` is fired every time selection changes as the user is dragging the mouse over the text. If we used `onselect`, we'd end up with a huge number of nested <SPAN>s where we want only one. So, we have to use `onmouseup` instead. Fortuitously, since a `onmouseup` event is part of a mouse click, the same handler can process mouse clicks as well, as selections of zero length. The first half of the `onmouseup` event handler deals with this possibility:

```
function setCommentRange(){with(parent.Session.topControl){
 var tr=sframes.doc.document.selection.createRange();
 if(tr.text==""){
  var p=tr.parentElement();
  if(p.tagName=="SPAN" && p.xsym) // check if it's a SPAN for a comment
   return commentClick(p);    // respond to click with a hypertext jump
  else return;
 }
```

(The comments in this piece of code indicate how it *should* work. What actually happens is a cludge, triggered by an incomplete implementation of `TextRange`. Its `parentElement()` method does not, in fact, recognize span as the parent element, so the `else` branch is executed. However, the event then bubbles up to the span and is captured by the onclick there, which cancels further bubble.)

The second half of the handler creates a comment record. To calculate byte offsets, it calls on `rangeLocLen()` which calculates the location and length of the selection. Otherwise, it just stores the information in the control form:

```
 var locLen=parent.rangeLocLen(sframes.doc,tr);
 with(sframes.ctl.frmComments)
 {
  hhLoc.value=locLen.loc; // starting point of selection, in bytes
  hhLen.value=locLen.len; // length of selection, in bytes
  hhSymNum.value=onInitFormat.symNum++; // generate a new symNum
  hhBlock.value=tr.text; // the text of the selection
 }
}}
```

The standard `addRow` database operation transfers the data from the control form to the data table named `Comments`. Since the table is updated, its `onUpdate()` event handler is called, which in turn calls on `refreshDoc()`, which you saw mentioned in `onInitFormat()`:

```
function refreshDoc(){
 parent.Session.topControl.sframes.doc.document.body.innerHTML=
  onInitFormat.initHTML; // put clean document back into the doc frame
 applyAllCommentRows();  // re-run the table data
}
```

What this means is that every time we add, delete or replace a comment, the entire table of comments is re-applied to a clean document. There may be performance penalties in this if the table gets large enough (hundreds of multi-line text blocks with comments), but we haven't encountered them yet. A document of that size is likely to be broken into smaller documents, anyway.

Applying Comment Information to the Document

This is done by `applyAllCommentRows()`, which is a loop that calls `applyCommentRow()` on each iteration. We start with the single-row function, which basically passes the buck to yet another function, `applyLineRanges()`, which does all the work:

```
function applyCommentRow(commentRow)
{ // returns symNum or -1;
 with(commentRow)
 {
  var N=parseInt(SymNum,10);
  var tr=parent.makeTextRange(parseInt(Loc,10),parseInt(Len,10));
  applyLineRanges(tr,SymNum);
  return N;
 }
}
```

Each row of the Comments table, as you recall, has `Loc`, `Len` and `SymNum` fields. We give the `Loc` and `Len` fields to `makeTextRange()` which goes to the document and retrieves the range on the basis of its location and length. We then pass the `TextRange` object and the `SymNum`, to `applyLineRanges()`:

```
function applyLineRanges(tr,sym)
{
 var trArr=parent.lineRanges(tr);
 for(var i=0;i<trArr.length;i++)
 {
  var S="<SPAN class=commentStyle "+
   "onclick='parent.Session.topControl.sframes.ctl.commentClick(this)'"+
   "xsym='CommentSym"+sym+"'>"+
   trArr[i].htmlText+'</SPAN>';
  trArr[i].pasteHTML(S); // replace htmlText with new SPAN
 }
 // create an empty textrange and select it, to deselect current selection
 var t=tr.duplicate(); t.collapse(false); t.select();
}
```

As we explained, in order to preserve line breaks, a multi-line `TextRange` has to be broken into single-line text ranges, each of which is made into a separate `span`. This happens in `applyLineRanges()`. It calls on the `lineRanges()` utility to break its argument `TextRange` into an array of ranges. A `SPAN` is then constructed for each element of the array. The `span`'s attributes consist of a style sheet, an onclick, and an `xsym` attribute that holds the unique id. The innerHTML of the `span` comes from the `htmlText` property of `trArr[i]`, which gets replaced by the newly created `span`. This is done by the `pasteHTML()` method of the `TextRange` class which pastes the HTML content of its argument into the text range object. See commented code above.)

The last line deselects the current selection by creating an text range, collapsing it into an empty range, and selecting it.

TextRange Utilities for Creating and Applying Comments

In the process of creating comment records and applying them to the document, several `TextRange` utilities are called upon. We bring them together in this subsection. (They can all be found in `textrange.js`, available as part of the download from our site.)

From TextRanges to Offsets and Back

The pair `rangeLocLen()` and `makeTextRange()` are a converse of each other and use the same technique. The length of a `TextRange` is given by its `text.length`. To find its offset, we create another `TextRange` and stretch it from the beginning of the document to the beginning of our range. `makeTextRange()` retraces the steps in the opposite direction:

```
function rangeLocLen(theFrame,tr){
 var br=theFrame.document.body.createTextRange();
 br.setEndPoint("EndToStart",tr);  // move end of br to start of tr
 var Ob=new Object();
 Ob.loc=br.text.length; Ob.len=tr.text.length;
 return Ob;
}
function makeTextRange(loc,len){  //92,5 = "thick"
 var tr=Session.topControl.sframes.doc.document.body.createTextRange();
 tr.collapse();           // collapse to start point
 while(tr.text.length<loc)tr.moveEnd("character");
 tr.collapse(false);         // collapse to end point
 while(tr.text.length<len)tr.moveEnd("character");
 return tr;
}
```

Processing Multi-line Ranges

The first thing to do is determine whether the range we're dealing with is multi-line or not. Fortunately, the `TextRange` object has an `offsetTop` property which returns the number of lines from the top of the document to the text range. We create an empty text range and place it at the end of our range. If its `offsetTop` is different, our range is multi-line:

```
function isMultiLine(tr)
{
 var tr2=tr.duplicate();
 tr2.collapse(false);
 return tr.offsetTop!=tr2.offsetTop;
}
```

The predicate just defined is used in `lineRanges()`, the main workhorse of this batch. It also uses the already familiar `skipBlanks()` and `addCurrRange()`, to add a single-line range to the resulting array:

```
function lineRanges(tr)  // turn tr into an array of oneline line ranges
{ var t=tr.duplicate();
 if(!isMultiLine(t))     // trim blanks and return one-element array
  return new Array(skipBlanks(t));
 var mama=tr.parentElement();
 while(mama && mama.tagName!="BODY") mama=mama.parentElement;
 var fullRange=mama.createTextRange();
 var R=new Array();
 t.collapse(); var currT=t.duplicate();
```

At this point, `t` and `currT` are empty ranges at the beginning of `tr`. We start a loop that runs `t` forward until one of three things happens: `t` reaches the end of `tr`, or `t` reaches the end of the document, or `t` finds itself on the next line but still within `tr`. We respond appropriately:

287

```
    while(true)
    {
    t.move("character");
    if(!tr.inRange(t))                    // t has passed beyond tr
     return addCurrRange(R,currT,t,-1);
    else if(0==fullRange.compareEndPoints("EndToEnd",t)) // t at end of doc
     return addCurrRange(R,currT,t);
    else if(currT.offsetTop!=t.offsetTop)  // t on next line
     {
     addCurrRange(R,currT,t,-1);
     currT=t.duplicate();
     }
    }
  }
```

Now you're probably curious about what addCurrRange() does. It stretches currT to catch up with t, adjusts by one character if necessary, trims blanks, and adds currT to the array:

```
function addCurrRange(R,currT,t,offset)
{
 currT.setEndPoint("EndToEnd",t);
 if(offset) currT.moveEnd("character",offset);
 skipBlanks(currT);
 R[R.length]=currT; return R;
}
```

Aren't text ranges wonderful?

Processing the Click

The last remaining task is to show a comment in response to a click on a commented block of text. We pop up a special comment window for the purpose, just to make sure that we can do it. Other options are of course available. We could scroll the data table to the appropriate row. We could pop up an alert box. Perhaps the best option would be to collect all comments into a separate document with named anchors at the beginning of each comment, and replace our <span>s with <A>s and appropriate HREFs. We leave this and other possibilities as an exercise for the reader.

The commentClick() falls into two parts. The first part processes the function's span argument to find the comment's SymNum, and uses it to retrieve the comment from the table. This part would probably remain the same in any implementation. The second half opens a window and places the comment in it. There's nothing remarkable about it. It ends with the usual little continuation, to make sure that the window is loaded:

```
function commentClick(comSpan){with(parent.Session.topControl)
 {
 sframes.doc.window.event.cancelBubble=true;
 var T=format.Tables.Comments;
 var Sym=comSpan.xsym;
 if(!Sym || Sym.indexOf("CommentSym")!=0) return;
 var SymNum=Sym.substring(10);
 var theComments=format.lookup1(T,"SymNum",SymNum,"Comments");
 if(!theComments) return;
```

End of the first part. Proceed to opening the window and displaying the comment.

```
  if(!commentWindow || commentWindow.closed)
  {
    commentWindow=window.open("comwin.htm","commentWindow",
             "height=300,width=300,resizable");
    if(!commentWindow.opener)commentWindow.opener=self;
    else commentWindow.focus();
    setCommentWindow.theComments="<P> "+theComments; setCommentWindow();
  }
}
function setCommentWindow()
{
  if(commentWindow.document.readyState!="complete")
    return setTimeout("setCommentWindow()",100);
  commentWindow.document.body.innerHTML=setCommentWindow.theComments;
}
```

This concludes our discussion of the com format. As you can see, it makes a substantial use of TextRange in order to preserve the whitespace layout of the original text. Our next format goes even further and really pushes the envelope on TextRange.

Think of comDB.htm as a sequence of edits: to apply comment1 to characters 183..314, then comment2 to characters 96..130, and so on is to replace each character sequence with a new one. We will generalize in three ways. First, we will allow more general replacements, defined by an HTML table of rules based on regular expressions. The rules can be created or changed by a Web page author who is not a programmer. Second, we'll create the edit database in such a way as to support an "undo" button. Finally, we'll record which rule did each task, so that highlighting or other effects can be applied to all the edits created by a given rule.

The metrique Format

The format's fancy name has to do with French poetry: it was created to help students mark up poetic lines in various ways and with different colors to indicate important elements of rhythm and meter. However, it can be used for more prosaic purposes as well.

To use a tool, it needs to be associated with a button. Clicking on a tool's button activates the tool. Once a tool is active, you use it by clicking in the document window. If the text at the click position matches the regular expression pattern of the tool, the match gets replaced with the tool's replacement pattern. To change tools, simply click on another tool-button.

Adding a new tool does require adding a new button: just copy one of the old buttons, then change the button name to the ToolName in the database. Its pattern will be looked up when this button is clicked on, and applied to the document clickpoint from then until the next tool-choice.

To give one example, one of the tools in metrique looks for the letter e at the end of the word (the French call them "mute e") and colors it blue. We don't have room in the book to explain the workings of metrique, but the code is included for your enjoyment.

Conclusions

In this chapter, we have covered two major new topics: the basics of object-oriented design, and the tools for working with text in JavaScript. We have also traced the design and implementation of a substantial text-annotating application with elements of an authoring system. The application can be used for educational and professional purposes. As far as we know, this is the first application that supports online web page document review by a group of people.

In more detail, the main points of the chapter are:

- ❑ Object-oriented analysis and design starts with an English-language description of the system. The description can take several forms. A very good format for describing the system is use-cases and scenarios. On the basis of such descriptions and further analysis, the classes and their relationships can be established.

- ❑ The commentary program started out as several use cases and a set of specifications for commentary formats. Subsequent analysis showed that it consists of two major classes, `Session` and `Format`, with `Format`, in effect, derived from the Database class.

- ❑ The tool for working with text in JavaScript is the `TextRange` class. It is available only in IE4 on Win95 machines. The simple formats required only limited programming with the `TextRange` class. In more complex formats, the `TextRange` class can be used to work with the HTML structure of the document while preserving its whitespace layout.

- ❑ The `TextRange` class, when combined with regular expressions, can provide powerful tools for text transformation and markup.

- ❑ `TextRange` should be used with caution because there may be no legal HTML corresponding perfectly to a given textrange. (Think of a textrange that goes from the middle of one `span` into the middle of the next.) It is tempting to think that `tr.pasteHTML(tr.htmlText)` is an identity operation, but it may actually give illegal results. Our general advice is: check what you're pasting, and allow both undo and refresh.

- ❑ Straightforward undo of replacements is difficult to implement well in HTML documents because, as we indicated, HTML cut and paste doesn't work as simply as string cut and paste, and what you paste may turn out to be different from what you cut a moment ago. However, if you are saving edit-chains, which is feasible in a significant range of applications including ours, then to undo operation N cleanly we can go back to the start, then redo operations up to N-1 inclusive.

9

Beyond JavaScript

Introduction

In this chapter, we'll use JavaScript as a driver for code modules written in other languages, primarily Java. A Java code module embedded in a Web page is called an applet, so, in more precise terms, we'll learn how to use JavaScript to control a Java applet. In effect, we will be extending the vocabulary of JavaScript with the methods of Java classes.

DOCUMENT ATTRIBUTE:	APPEARANCE	STRUCTURE	BEHAVIOR
CONTROLLED BY:	STYLE SHEET	HTML 4.0	JAVASCRIPT CLIENT-SIDE JS CORE JS
		ELEMENTS ◄► OBJECTS ATTRIBUTES◄► PROPERTIES METHODS	

JAVA
APPLETS

Native Code
(C, C++)

The reason this is a good thing to learn is because Java has a number of capabilities that JavaScript doesn't. One such capability is graphics. JavaScript has no graphics primitives whatsoever: it's a language to manipulate text strings, because that's what HTML is. Java does have extensive graphics facilities, making it possible to draw and to paint on its surface. If we connect the two, we can define a function in JavaScript and graph it in Java. Put differently, we can add graphics primitives, such as `drawLine()` to JavaScript, and we will.

Another capability that Java has is reading and writing files. This capability is, of course, hobbled in an applet, for security reasons, but it is in the language, and it is possible to declare an applet "trusted" and thus enable file reading and writing from JavaScript. There are several twists, as you will see, but ultimately, we will have a setup in which a JavaScript program can read and write files on the local machine and the local network (an intranet).

Java also has excellent support for **sockets**. Sockets are the basic network connectors; every computer connected to a TCP/IP network does it through a software socket. There are client sockets and server sockets, and both are quite easy to implement in Java. Once we have them running, we can control the client socket from JavaScript, and thus obtain another way of reading and writing files on the local network, or anywhere on the Internet (although this would raise security issues that we're not trying to deal with). At this point, we'll be able to get rid of CGI and re-implement our text annotator from Chapter 8 on a local network using **sockets.** This will let the user save database files locally or anywhere on the internet, without using a web server as an intermediary.

Finally, JavaScript can only control software modules embedded in the web page (Java applets, ActiveX components) or in the browser itself (plugins). Java can call compiled software modules written in other languages, especially C and C++. (They are called "native methods" because they are specific to a particular operating system and CPU.) Since Java can run C functions, and JavaScript can run Java methods, we can establish JavaScript control over native software. If you have a large program written in C, you can arrange a browser interface for it, and run it from JavaScript.

In outline, the chapter will proceed as follows:

- ❏ Java setup
- ❏ reading Java
- ❏ calling Java methods from JavaScript
- ❏ graphics in Java, controlled from JavaScript
- ❏ trusted applets: a problem and a workaround
- ❏ file reading and writing
- ❏ sockets and networking
- ❏ from Java to compiled native code

The Java world

Java programs come in two flavors: applications and applets. We'll mostly be looking at applets, Java programs embedded in Web pages. In the last section, you'll see an application as well.

Java is a compiled language. This means that you can't use the text of an applet directly, the way you use JavaScript programs; you have to put it through a Java compiler to translate it into **bytecodes**. Bytecodes are then interpreted by a **Java Virtual Machine** (JVM) that was installed on your computer as part of the Web browser installation (if it hadn't been installed already). They may even be compiled, behind the scenes, to the native machine code of the machine you're running on, with a **Just-In-Time** (JIT) compiler. This makes things run faster, but otherwise makes absolutely no difference to anything you have to do.

Java bytecodes come in files that have the extension `.class`, or, if compressed, in files that have the extension `.jar`, for Java archive. The text of a Java program is in a file with extension `.java`.

Java Reading Skills

We're going to dive right in and read an applet. Hold on to your seats (or yawn and skip this section).

```
import java.applet.*;
import java.awt.*;
public class Applet0 extends Applet {
  public String msg = "Hello";
  public String addToMsg(String str) {return msg+=", "+str);
  msg = addToMsg("JavaScript");         // msg=="Hello, JavaScript"
  int xPos=10, yPos=20;
  public void paint(Graphics g){        // what does this applet look like?
    g.drawString(msg,xPos,yPos);        // it prints "Hello, JavaScript"
  }
}
```

Going line by line, let's take a look at line 3 first, lines 1 and 2 second, then the rest of them. As we're going through the code and the basics of Java, we will encounter many of the concepts of Object-Oriented Programming that were introduced in Chapter 4.

Everything is a Class

All Java code, except for the initial `import` statements, is inside some class or another. Classes can be public or private. You're not going to see private classes in this book. Public classes can be used by other classes.

Functions defined inside a class are called methods. Variables declared inside a class are called class fields. Class fields and methods are jointly known as class members. (Variables declared inside methods, or member functions, are local variables and behave just as you would expect.)

Inheritance

A class rarely comes out of nowhere. It usually extends, or is derived from, another class. In our example, class `Applet0` extends the class `Applet`. This means that `Applet0` inherits all the methods and fields of the `Applet` class. The `Applet` class, incidentally, extends the `Panel` class, which extends the `Container` class, which extends the `Component` class, which extends the `Object` class, the mother of all classes.

Class members can be **public**, **protected** or **private**. You're not going to see private class members in this book. Public class members, both methods and fields, are accessible from other classes. Protected class members of a class are accessible from classes derived from that class.

Packages and Imports

Where are all those classes? They come in packages that are installed together with the Java Virtual Machine. Each package contains many `.class` or `.jar` files. You don't have to "import" a class in order to use its methods, but you would have to give their complete names, going all the way back to the class in which they're defined. For instance, instead of `Graphics g` you'd have to say `java.awt.Graphics g`. Here, `awt` is the name of a package (**Abstract Windowing Toolkit**) that contains all the graphics and GUI utilities of Java, and `Graphics` is the name of a class that is defined in `Graphics.java` file within the `awt` package. You can import individual files by giving their full name, or you can import all the files in a package by saying, as we did, `import java.awt`.

Java Declarations

When you declare a variable in Java, you specify the data type of its values. You can't simply say `var`, as in JavaScript. Otherwise, the syntax is the same:

```
public String msg="Hello, JavaScript";
```

This declares a public data member of type String (an object of the class `java.lang.String`, to be precise) and initializes it. Similarly, in the following line:

```
public void paint(Graphics g){    // what does this applet look like?
```

`Graphics g` specifies that the `paint()` method takes one argument, an object of the `java.awt.Graphics` class. We can now look at an entire method definition:

```
public String addToMsg(String str) {return msg+=", "+str);
```

This declares a public method that takes one argument, a String, and returns a String.

Class and Instance Members

Anticipating code that you'll see later in the chapter, we should mention methods and data fields that are declared `static`, as in:

```
static int sgClear=0;
```

The keyword static means that `sgClear` is created before any objects of its class are created. Static class members are not part of any individual object. There's only one copy of a static data field or static method, and it is created, as we said, before any objects are created. Since objects are also called "instances of" their class, static methods and fields are sometimes called **class methods and fields**, as opposed to **instance methods and fields**, which are created as part of an individual object.

Painting in an Applet

The main action of our applet is in the inherited `paint()` method. It calls on the `drawString()` method of the `Graphics` class to put out our message so that it starts 10 pixels down and 10 pixels to the right from the top right corner of the applet window:

```
public void paint(Graphics g){ // what does this applet look like?
    g.drawString(msg,10,10);    // it prints "Hello, JavaScript"
}
```

Applets in the Web Page

To include an applet in a Web page, you use the `<APPLET>` tag:

```
<APPLET id=theApplet code="Applet0.class" codebase="jclasses/"
    width=300 height=100>
</APPLET>
```

This says that the code for the applet is in file `Applet0.class`, to be found in the subdirectory called `jclasses`. (All our `.java` and `.class` files are in that subdirectory.) The rest of the attributes are self-explanatory. The width and height are in pixels.

Controlling an Applet from JavaScript

JavaScript is very well set up to work with a Java applet. The rules of engagement are very easy:

If the applet's id is `"theApplet"` and it has a public method called `getMsg()` that returns a (Java) String, then the following is good JavaScript:

```
var jsString=document.applets.theApplet.getMsg();
```

Similarly, if the applet has a public data member `javaStr` of class String, you can assign its value to a JavaScript variable:

```
var anotherJSString=document.applets.theApplet.javaStr;
```

Complexities arise when you try to move data items that are not strings or integers across the language barrier, but we'll stay away from them. Integers are easy because they're automatically converted to and from strings as needed.

We illustrate with `appletJS.java`, embedded in `appletJS.htm`.

Try It Out

Before you try this page, make sure that Java Console is enabled in your browser. If it is, you will see a Java Console item on the browser's View menu. If the item is not there, go into View | Internet Options and click on the Advanced tab. Scrolling all the way down, you'll see an Enable Java Console checkbox. Click on it and restart the computer in order for the new setting to take effect.

Point your browser at `http://webdev.wrox.co.uk/books/1894/chapter09/ appletJS.htm`. View the applet. Set the values of its variables in the JavaScript form. Change the String and click on the **setMsg** button–nothing happens. Click on **getMsg** and see that the message has changed; it just hasn't been redrawn. Click on **showIt** and it will be redrawn. Instead of clicking on **showIt**, you can just scroll the message out of sight, resizing the window if necessary. When you bring the window back, you'll see that the change has taken place.

How It Works

This page is very much like `Applet0.htm`, with a couple of new elements. First, we've made some changes in the Web page, to show how you can initialize an applet's parameters:

```
<APPLET id=theApplet code="Applet1JS.class" codebase="jclasses/"
    width=300 height=100>
<PARAM name="msg" value="goodbye world">
<PARAM name="xPos" value=20>
<PARAM name="yPos" value=10>
<PARAM name="xMax" value=300>
<PARAM name="yMax" value=100>
</APPLET>
```

As you can see, you can use <PARAM> tags to specify initial values of Java variables. These values are read in by the getParameter() method which every applet inherits from the Applet class. Parameters are usually read in within the init() method, as in our code below. Here's the applet's beginning:

```
import java.applet.*;
import java.awt.*;
public class AppletJS extends Applet
{
    // This applet shows a message at an xPos:yPos position
    // within 0:0..xMax:yMax range
    // The message content and position can be set by JavaScript
    String msg="Hello Again";
    int xPos, yPos, xMax, yMax;
    Color bgColor=Color.yellow;        // background color
    Color textColor=Color.blue;        // color of text

    public void init()
    {
        setBackground(bgColor); setForeground(textColor);
        msg = getParameter("msg");
        xPos = Integer.parseInt(getParameter("xPos"));
        yPos = Integer.parseInt(getParameter("yPos"));
        xMax = Integer.parseInt(getParameter("xMax"));
        yMax = Integer.parseInt(getParameter("yMax"));
    }
```

More Applet Methods

In addition to init(), paint() and getParameter(), the Applet class has start(), stop() and destroy() methods. Usually, we don't have to override them, but since we initialize variables from parameters in the Web page, we have to repaint() (another method!) for the new values to take effect. We do it in the start() method:

```
public void start(){repaint();}
```

The paint() method is exactly the same as before:

```
public void paint(Graphics g)
{                                    // what does this applet look like?
    g.drawString(msg,xPos,yPos);
}
```

JavaScript Connections

Now we define methods that provide JavaScript access to the variables.

```
public String getMsg(){return msg;}
public void setMsg(String S){msg = S;}
public void setXPos(String S){xPos = Integer.parseInt(S);}
public void setYPos(String S){yPos = Integer.parseInt(S);}
```

We could activate these methods by putting a `"repaint()"` at the end of each, but for a tutorial piece of code it makes more sense to split that off into another function, fired from another button:

```
public void showIt()
{
  repaint();
  showStatus("showIt..." + msg + " " + xPos + ":" + yPos);
}
```

Finally, we add a `showAppletStatus()` method, useful in debugging:

```
public String showAppletStatus(){
  String S = "msg=" + msg + "\n";
         S += "xPos=" + xPos + "\n";
         S += "yPos=" + yPos + "\n";
         S += "xMax=" + xMax + "\n";
         S += "yMax=" + yMax + "\n";
  return S;
}
```

Now we provide control elements in the Web page to activate the behavior of the applet.

HTML Controls for a Java Applet

```
<FORM id=theForm ACTION="javascript:''">
the String: <INPUT TYPE=TEXT NAME=theString VALUE="Hello world">
 theXPos: <INPUT TYPE=TEXT NAME=theXPos VALUE=10 SIZE=10>
 theYPos: <INPUT TYPE=TEXT NAME=theYPos VALUE=10 SIZE=10><BR>
<INPUT TYPE=BUTTON value=setMsg
   onclick='document.all.theApplet.setMsg(this.form.theString.value)'>
<INPUT TYPE=BUTTON value=getMsg
   onclick='alert("the String is: "+document.all.theApplet.getMsg())'>
<INPUT TYPE=BUTTON value=setXPos
   onclick='document.all.theApplet.setXPos(this.form.theXPos.value)'>
<INPUT TYPE=BUTTON value=setYPos
   onclick='document.all.theApplet.setYPos(this.form.theYPos.value)'>
<INPUT TYPE=BUTTON value=showIt
   onclick='document.all.theApplet.showIt();'>
<INPUT TYPE=BUTTON value=showAppletStatus
   onclick='alert(document.all.theApplet.showAppletStatus());'>
</FORM>
```

You can use this form to experiment with the applet in several instructive ways, as suggested in the *Try It Out* section.

Applets for Graphics

In this section, we develop an applet to graph an array of numerical values. The array may evolve over time, leading to dynamically evolving graphs.

Graphics Methods and Their Arguments

The `Graphics` class, which you've seen drawing a string, has many other methods for drawing and filling simple shapes. Most methods of the class begin with `draw`, `fill`, `set` or `get`, as in `drawOval()` or `setColor()`. A graphical shape like an oval is defined by the rectangle that contains it, and a rectangle is defined by four integers (two pairs of coordinates), so `drawOval()` takes four arguments, which it can receive from JavaScript. All other `Graphics` methods that we need can also be controlled by string arguments received from JavaScript and converted to integers as needed.

Drawing a graph (or anything else) is a sequence of `Graphics` operations. For instance, drawing a bar graph is a sequence of `fillRect()` operations. For a general purpose graphing program, we need to organize computation so that the required sequence of computations can be constructed in a data structure and read off it in a systematic manner. That sequence of computations has to be redone whenever we repaint the screen, so it's not enough for Java to draw the lines and rectangles on command: it has to remember those commands as if they were a program, so that the commands can be replayed at need. How can Java remember a program?

Array of Operation Codes and Arguments

Imitating a standard approach to interpreters, we'll assign a code to each operation, and describe an operation by its numerical code followed by the requisite number of arguments. A sequence of operations will be an array that holds a sequence of such operation descriptions. In order to interpret such an array, we need to know how many arguments each operation requires, which calls for another array.

```
    int sgMaxOps = 100,        // array size, doubled as needed (sg stands for
howGraph)
        sgNextOp = 0;          // current operation to perform
    int[] sgOps = new int[sgMaxOps];    // instructions for drawing graph
    // numerical codes for operations:
    static final int
        sgClear = 0,           // clears the region
        sgSetFillColor = 1,    // set color to value of next item in sgOps
        sgSetDrawColor = 2,
        sgDrawLine = 3,        // use next four items in sgOps as x0,y0,x1,y1
        sgFillRect = 4;
    int[] sgOpCount = {1,2,2,5,5}; // sgOpCount[sgDrawLine] is #items used
```

The keyword `final` means that the value of `sgClear` (and the other operation codes) cannot be changed at run time; `sgClear` is a constant. The keyword `static`, as you recall, means that `sgClear` and the other operation codes are **class** data members, not **instance** data members. They're created before any individual objects of the `ShowGraph` class are created.

To add an operation, we store its code in the array at the `sgNextOp` position. If the array is full, we double its size. Unlike JavaScript arrays, Java arrays do not resize automatically:

```
   public void addOp(int x)
   {                                  // add an operation; double array size if needed
     if(sgNextOp>=sgMaxOps)
     { int[] A = new int[2*sgMaxOps];
       for(int i=0; i<sgMaxOps; i++) A[i] = sgOps[i];
       sgOps = A;
       sgMaxOps *= 2;
     }
     sgOps[sgNextOp++] = x;
   }
```

Other Constants and Supporting Methods

All the above code is, of course, inside a class, called ShowGraph. It has integer data members to hold the color codes and the size of the graph area. We also provide a method to show the status of the graph: its colors, the area size, the operations in the array, and everything else:

```
import java.applet.*;
import java.awt.*;
import java.io.*;

public class ShowGraph extends Applet{
   int fillColor = ((255<<8)+0<<8)+255,     // red==max; green==0; blue==max
       drawColor = 255<<8,                  // draw color is green
       maxX=350, maxY=300;                  // graphing area size
   public Color intColor(int C){ return color object from integer
       return new Color(C>>16,(C>>8)&255,C&255);}

   public void init(){
     setBackground(intColor(fillColor)); setForeground(intColor(drawColor));}
   String[] sgOpNames= // operation names, for ShowGraphStatus()
     {"Clear","SetFillColor","SetDrawColor","DrawLine","FillRect"};

// all the preceding code for operations goes here

   public String ShowGraphStatus(){
     String S="maxX="+maxX+"; maxY="+maxY+
         "; fillColor="+fillColor+";drawColor="+drawColor+"\n";
     int i=0;
     while(i<sgNextOp){ // show sgOps array
       int op=sgOps[i]; S+=sgOpNames[op]+ " ";
       for(int j=1;j<sgOpCount[op];j++)S+=sgOps[i+j]+" ";
       S+="\n"; i+=sgOpCount[op];
     }
     return S;
   }
```

A Note on RGB Color Codes

A common way of representing colors is by three integers, each in the range 0-255, showing the red, green and blue (RGB) components of the color. (For instance, the color purple corresponds to 153,0,204.) Instead of three integers, each a byte size, it is frequently more convenient to have a single 3-byte (24-bit) integer in which the original three bytes are placed side-by-side, in the RGB order. To convert from three bytes to a single integer, shift the red byte left by 16 and the green byte left by 8, then add the three bytes together. So, the color purple would become:

```
var clrPurple=153<<16+0<<8+204;
```

You can go all the way back to Chapter 1, open `evalExp.htm,` type this expression into the text box and click Eval to get the answer. As long as you're in Chapter 1, you may also review the table of JavaScript operators, if necessary.

To take a 24-bit representation apart, shift the other way and do bitwise AND with 255, which will set to 0 everything to the left of the first byte. To get the red byte (153) out of `clrPurple`, do this:

```
var greenByte=clrPurple>>16 & 255
```

The reason we need the `intColor()` function is because we want to set colors from JavaScript by sending a single integer over to Java; `intColor()` takes it apart and constructs a `Color` object. In HTML, we would describe a color as a series of six hexadecimal (base-16) digits, such as 00FF00 for green. That's precisely what we're doing here, because each hexadecimal occupies four bits, so six of them occupy three bytes, and the HTML notation is just another way of expressing the 3-byte integer we need. We could get the same three-byte integer in JavaScript by saying `parseInt("0x00FF00")`. (Note that we're talking about JavaScript's `parseInt()` here, not Java's.) So, you have two ways to express color numbers; choose the one you like better.

The Method to do Ops

The method that does the actual work of drawing the graph is `doOps()`. It takes one argument, a `Graphics` object. Its structure is a `while` loop with a `switch` statement inside. The loop retrieves the next operation code, determines how many arguments the operation requires, retrieves those, and calls on the appropriate method of the `Graphics` class:

```
    public void doOps(Graphics g)
  {
     int i=0;
     while(i<sgNextOp)
       {
       int op=sgOps[i];
       if(op<sgClear || op>sgFillRect) return; // no such operation
       int opCount=sgOpCount[op]; // how many arguments?
       int nextOp=i+opCount;  // advance i
       if(nextOp>sgNextOp) return; // could be ==, not >
       switch(op)
         {
         case sgClear:
           g.setColor(intColor(fillColor)); g.fillRect(0,0,maxX,maxY); break;
         case sgSetFillColor: fillColor=sgOps[i+1]; break;
         case sgSetDrawColor: drawColor=sgOps[i+1]; break;
         case sgDrawLine: g.setColor(intColor(drawColor));
           g.drawLine(sgOps[i+1],sgOps[i+2],sgOps[i+3],sgOps[i+4]); break;
         case sgFillRect: g.setColor(intColor(fillColor));
           g.fillRect(sgOps[i+1],sgOps[i+2],sgOps[i+3],sgOps[i+4]);
           g.setColor(intColor(drawColor));
           g.drawRect(sgOps[i+1],sgOps[i+2],sgOps[i+3],sgOps[i+4]);
           break;
         }
       i=nextOp;
       }
     }
    public void paint(Graphics g){doOps (g);}
```

Methods for JavaScript to Call

In order to give JavaScript control over the applet, we need to provide methods for JavaScript to refer to. We're going to give them the same names as the corresponding methods of the `Graphics` class. They all start by converting the String arguments received from JavaScript into integers, then carry out the operation and/or put the appropriate operation code and the argument(s) on the `sgOps` array, as appropriate:

```java
public void setFillColor(String nS)
    {
    fillColor=Integer.parseInt(nS);
    addOp(sgSetFillColor); addOp(fillColor);
    }

public void setBGColor(String nS)
    {
    setBackground(intColor(Integer.parseInt(nS)));
     repaint();
    }

public void setDrawColor(String nS)
    {
    addOp(sgSetDrawColor); addOp(Integer.parseInt(nS));
    }

public void clear(){addOp(sgClear); repaint();}

public void drawLine(String aS,String bS,String cS,String dS)
    {
    int aN=Integer.parseInt(aS),bN=Integer.parseInt(bS),
        cN=Integer.parseInt(cS),dN=Integer.parseInt(dS);
    addOp(sgDrawLine); addOp(aN); addOp(bN); addOp(cN); addOp(dN);
    repaint();
    }
public void fillRect(String aS,String bS,String cS,String dS)
    {
    int aN=Integer.parseInt(aS),bN=Integer.parseInt(bS),
        cN=Integer.parseInt(cS),dN=Integer.parseInt(dS);
    addOp(sgFillRect); addOp(aN); addOp(bN); addOp(cN); addOp(dN);
    repaint();
    }
public void setSize(String aS,String bS)
    {
    int aN=Integer.parseInt(aS),bN=Integer.parseInt(bS);
    maxX=aN; maxY=bN;
    repaint();
    }
```

There is a seemingly unnecessary step in this code: if we declared our arguments to be of type `int` then Java would automatically convert the strings it receives from JavaScript into integers, and we wouldn't have to call `parseInt()` ourselves. For example, we could have defined the last function as:

```java
public void setSize(int aN, int bN){
    maxX=aN; maxY=bN; repaint();
}
```

In `ShowGraph2.java`, used within `Bifur2.html`, we use the more concise version. However, it's worth remembering that if you pass a string argument then Java can inspect it for error before converting to integer, and intelligently handle possible errors.

The JavaScript Side

The simplest arrangement on the JavaScript side is to provide a couple of arrays of numbers to display as a graph, and the functions to graph them. The functions will call on the Java methods we've just introduced. The arrays are specified as comma-delimited lists in text boxes. The graphing functions are fired from buttons in the same form. We will provide for bar graphs, stacked bar graphs and line graphs.

```
<FORM id=theForm ACTION="javascript:formAction()">
ArrayVals:
  <INPUT TYPE=TEXT NAME=arr1 VALUE="10,20,30,40,50,60" SIZE=30
    DrawColor=255 FillColor=60000>
  <INPUT TYPE=TEXT NAME=arr2 VALUE="1,2,4,8,16,32" SIZE=30
    DrawColor=64000 FillColor=15000000><BR>
<INPUT TYPE=BUTTON VALUE=barGraph
    onclick="StackedBarGraph(this.form.arr1)">
<INPUT TYPE=BUTTON VALUE=doubleBar
    onclick="StackedBarGraph(this.form.arr2,this.form.arr1)">
<INPUT TYPE=BUTTON VALUE=multiBar
    onclick="multiBarGraph(this.form.arr2,this.form.arr1)">
<INPUT TYPE=BUTTON VALUE=lineGraph
    onclick="lineGraph(this.form.arr2,this.form.arr1)">
<INPUT TYPE=BUTTON VALUE=clearGraph
    onclick="document.applets.theApplet.clearGraph()"><BR>
```

In addition to graphing, we provide input boxes and buttons to set colors for drawing, filling or background. You specify a color by giving three numbers for its RGB components; a JavaScript function, `colorCode()`, combines them into a single number and sends it over to Java, where that single number is taken apart again:

```
Color:
  <INPUT TYPE=TEXT NAME=R VALUE=50 SIZE=5>
  <INPUT TYPE=TEXT NAME=G VALUE=150 SIZE=5>
  <INPUT TYPE=TEXT NAME=B VALUE=250 SIZE=5><BR>
<INPUT TYPE=BUTTON VALUE=fillColor
    onclick="document.applets.theApplet.setFillColor(''+colorCode(this.form))">
<INPUT TYPE=BUTTON VALUE=drawColor
    onclick="document.applets.theApplet.setDrawColor(''+colorCode(this.form))">
<INPUT TYPE=BUTTON VALUE=bgColor
    onclick="document.applets.theApplet.setBGColor(''+colorCode(this.form))"> <BR>
```

Finally, we provide input boxes to provide arguments for `drawLine()` and `fillRect()`, and buttons to test them:

```
Args for drawLine, fillRect:<BR>
  X0: <INPUT TYPE=TEXT NAME=X0 VALUE=10 SIZE=5>
  Y0: <INPUT TYPE=TEXT NAME=Y0 VALUE=20 SIZE=5>
  X1: <INPUT TYPE=TEXT NAME=X1 VALUE=100 SIZE=5>
  Y1: <INPUT TYPE=TEXT NAME=Y1 VALUE=200 SIZE=5> <BR>
<INPUT TYPE=BUTTON VALUE=drawLine
    onclick="app4(this.form,'document.applets.theApplet.drawLine')">
<INPUT TYPE=BUTTON VALUE=fillRect
```

```
    onclick="app4(this.form,'document.applets.theApplet.fillRect')">
<INPUT TYPE=BUTTON VALUE=showStatus
    onclick="alert(document.applets.theApplet.ShowGraphStatus())"><BR>
</FORM>
```

JavaScript Code

The code for graphing functions is somewhat repetitive, so we'll show just one of them here, and you can read the rest in `ShowGraph.html`. As you read the code, keep in mind that the input elements that specify sequences of numbers can have the `DrawColor`, `FillColor` and `ItemWidth` attributes:

```
function StackedBarGraph()
{
  var S=new Array(); // S[i] records total height for pos i;
  for(var i=0;i<StackedBarGraph.arguments.length;i++)
    {                                 // for each sequence of numbers
    var e=StackedBarGraph.arguments[i];
    var A=e.value.split(",");  if(A.length==0)return; // nothing to graph
    for(var j=0;j<A.length;j++)A[j]=parseInt(A[j],10);
    var dc=e.DrawColor?parseInt(e.DrawColor,10):0;
    var fc=e.FillColor?parseInt(e.FillColor,10):dc;
    var iw=e.ItemWidth?parseInt(e.ItemWidth,10):10;
    with(document.applets.theApplet)
      {                               /     / call the applet methods
      setFillColor(fc); setDrawColor(dc);
      for(var j=0;j<A.length;j++){
        S[j]=S[j]?S[j]+A[j]+1:A[j]+1; // stack it or just add 1
        fillRect(j*iw,height-S[j],iw,A[j]);
      }
    }
}}
```

To test `drawLine()` and `fillRect()` separately, we use a higher-order function `app4()` which extracts four numbers from the form given it as the first argument and passes them on to its second argument, which is a function.

```
function app4(form,f)
{                            // applies "f" to the four coords
  eval(f+"("+form.X0.value+","+form.Y0.value+","+
          form.X1.value+","+form.Y1.value+")");
}
```

The function is called from onclick methods in the form above:

```
<INPUT TYPE=BUTTON VALUE=drawLine
    onclick="app4(this.form,'document.applets.theApplet.drawLine')">
```

Another Implementation

The file `Graph.html` shows a much more sophisticated JavaScript program for graphing. It defines a `Graph` class that can send over to the applet either explicitly defined arrays (as in `ShowGraph`) or columns of HTML tables. In fact, a series can be produced by any JavaScript expression, placed in a specific input element of the form that controls the graph. The `Graph` class also specifies default item width and colors for each series, and provides ways to override defaults by filling in a form input element or editing the form in HTML.

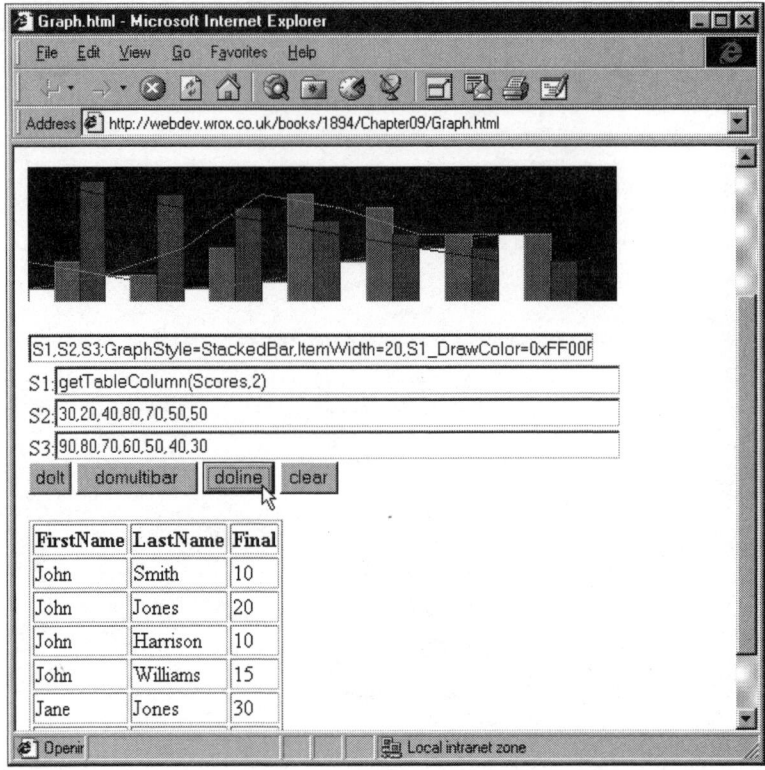

It is not an extensive graphing package, but it does follow our principles of class design, and illustrates the way that we try to create Java tools that are customizable from within an HTML page. Reading the code of the `Graph` class will have to be left as an exercise for the reader; we have to move on.

The Bifurcation Graph

As an example of the kind of things you can now do in your Web page, we have constructed a bifurcation graph based on the logistic equation. For the background information, consult many excellent books on non-linear systems (such as David Gleick's very readable *Chaos*). Our purpose in that exercise was to compare performance when the same computation is done in JavaScript and Java.

Try It Out

Point your browser at `bifur2.html` and click on **bifurJava**. You'll see a picture that may look familiar:

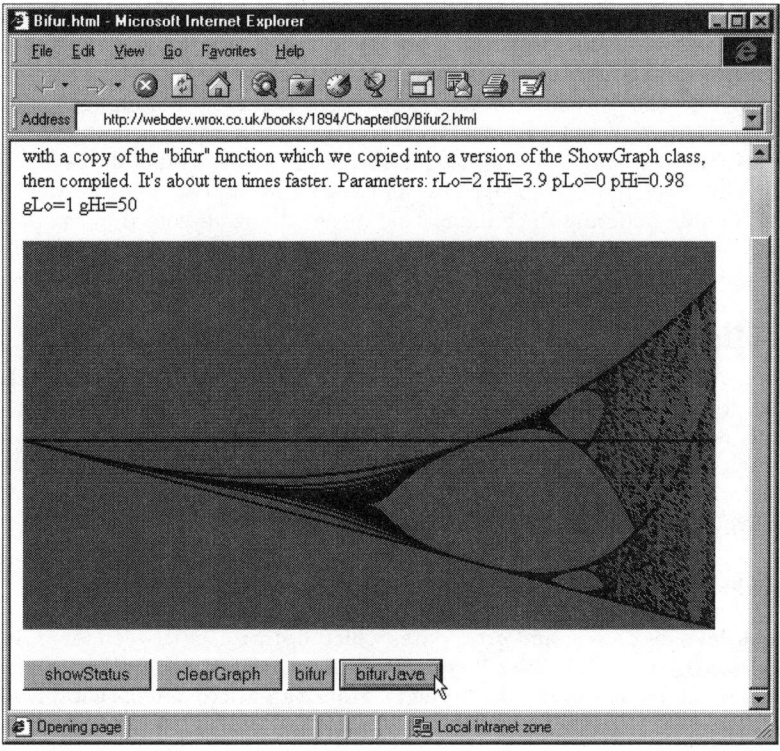

How It Works

The graph is produced by the following piece of Java code:

```
public void bifurJava(double rLo,double rHi,double pLo,double pHi,
    double pInit,int gLo,int gHi,int dColor){
    //displays bifur graph from 0:0 to width:height,
    // letting r vary from rLo to rHi on the 0..width x-axis,
         // so r=x*xScale+rLo, where xScale=(rHi-rLo)/width
    // letting p vary from pLo to pHi (0<=pLo<pHi<=1) on the 0..height y-axis
         // so y=(p-pLo)*yScale, where yScale=height/(pHi-pLo);
    // setting the starting population to pInit, with new p = p*r*(1-p)
    //  and displaying generations gLo..gHi
    setPaintPermission(0);
    setDrawColor(dColor);
    double yScale=maxY/(pHi-pLo); //(p-pLo)*yScale=y
    double xScale=(rHi-rLo)/maxX;   //x*xScale=(r-rLo)
    for(int x=0;x<maxX;x++){
        double p=pInit,g=0,r=x*xScale+rLo;
        while(++g<gLo){p=p*r*(1.0-p);}
        while(++g<gHi){int y=(int)Math.round((p-pLo)*yScale);
        drawLine(x,y,x+1,y+1);
        p=p*r*(1.0-p);
          }
      }
    setPaintPermission(1);
  }
```

As we said, our point in doing this was to compare the performance of two possible ways to produce that graph. An alternative to writing it in Java would be to do the computations and calls on drawLine() in JavaScript. Our conclusions are two. First, JavaScript code is virtually identical to Java code, once the declarations are re-written. (The only other change was to replace Math.round() with Math.floor().) Second, it takes about ten times longer to produce the graph, as you can ascertain by clicking on the bifur button. Part of the reason is that Java bytecodes are more efficient than JavaScript scripts. An even bigger part of the reason is that the JavaScript version repaints the screen many times. We leave it as an exercise for a Java-bound reader to rewrite the Java code using the "double-buffering" technique. That means doing all your drawing in an Image object in memory, without repainting the screen; when all the drawing is done, the Image object is copied to screen, in a single repainting.

Trusted Applets

Both JavaScript and Java applets are hobbled in various ways, for security reasons. For instance, they cannot read or write local files on the computers they visit. JavaScript is hobbled permanently: the language simply doesn't have any file I/O primitives. Java the language has a very elaborate collection of such primitives, but they're disabled in the browser. The precaution may sometimes seem excessive: what if this is an applet that you've written yourself, and it runs on your own computer, and you want to open your own file from it?

The security policy for local applets (i.e., those applets that come through the local file system rather than over the Internet) is not very well codified. It is basically up to an individual browser or applet viewer to establish levels of trust and procedures which distinguish between them. In the case of IE4, these procedures involve the Windows Registry, a difficult subject. We've found it much easier to establish trust through the use of the "Java plugin" from Sun Microsystems and the CLASSPATH environmental variable.

The Java Plugin

The Java plugin provides an alternative Java Virtual Machine which can run compiled Java code (the applets) bypassing the JVM that came with the browser. On Win32 machines, it is implemented as an ActiveX control. You can download it from:

`http://java.sun.com/products/plugin/1.1.1/`

or it will download automatically (after asking the user's permission) the first time that you use a page which needs it (such as the one below).

You include the Java plugin in your Web page using the standard ActiveX syntax:

```
<OBJECT classid="clsid:8AD9C840-044E-11D1-B3E9-00805F499D93" id=theApplet
   codebase="http://java.sun.com/products/plugin/1.1.1/jinstall-111
win32.cab#Version=1,1,0,0">
  No JDK 1.1 support for APPLET!!
</OBJECT>
```

The classid attribute gives the GUID (globally unique identifier) for the control. In case you have never seen one before, it's a very big (128 bits) random number, generated at some point on the basis of such arcane bits of information as the current time in hundreds of nanoseconds since 1562 and the ethernet card number of the machine that generated the number. There are so many 128-bit numbers, and the generator distributes them so evenly, that the probability of collision is extremely low. The id is stored in the Windows registry during the control's installation, and after that the system knows how to find it.

Note that Java plugin uses its own Java Virtual Machine (JVM), with its own console window. (The console window shows messages from its JVM.) This console window can be opened from the Java plugin control panel which you can reach from the Win95 Start menu.

Invoking an Applet Through the Java Plugin

In order to invoke an applet whose code is in `FileHandler.class` in the `jclasses/` subdirectory, you provide the information to the plugin through its `<PARAM>` elements:

```
<OBJECT classid="clsid:8AD9C840-044E-11D1-B3E9-00805F499D93" id=theApplet
    codebase="http://java.sun.com/products/plugin/1.1/jinstall-11
win32.cab#Version=1,1,0,0">
  width="10" height="10" align="baseline">
  <PARAM NAME="code" VALUE="FileHandler.class">
  <PARAM NAME="codebase" VALUE="jclasses/">
  <PARAM NAME="type" VALUE="application/x-java-applet;version=1.1">
      No JDK 1.1 support for APPLET!!
</OBJECT>
```

If your actual applet, whose code is in `FileHandler.class`, contains a function called `readTheFile()`, you refer to it in JavaScript as if it were defined in the plugin:

```
document.all.theApplet.readTheFile()
```

Note that we cannot use the `document.applets` array any more, and have to use the IE4-specific `document.all`. If we wanted to use this applet with the Java plugin within Netscape, we would have to use an `<EMBED>` tag rather than an `<OBJECT>` tag. The plugin documentation at

http://java.sun.com:81/products/plugin/1.1.1/docs/tags.html

explains this, as well as showing the more convoluted syntax required to have your applet functions work on both Netscape and IE4. Sun offers a free program to fix your `<APPLET>` tag appropriately.

The last remaining thing to do is to make sure that your applet's directory is in the classpath. (In case you haven't done a Java installation before, on Win95 machines, you specify the CLASSPATH environment variable in the `autoexec.bat` file.) After that, the Java plugin treats your local applet with total trust and lets it do anything it pleases. This includes access to local files and native code.

Reading and Writing Local Files from JavaScript

We can now look at the `FileHandler` applet in more detail. As always, we have an HTML file with JavaScript code in it and a Java file with the applet. Both are completely transparent; the biggest hurdle was to figure out how to overcome security restrictions.

JavaScript Code

We have two functions for file handling, and a dummy that pretends to be a form's action. The form has two fields, one to specify the file's name, the other to create some text content. The content can also come from the innerHTML of a document, or any other source:

```
function formAction()
{
function readTheFile(form)
  {
```

```
    var app=document.all.theApplet;
    with(form)
      {
      S=app.readFile(theName.value);
      if(S!="") theContent.value=S; // file contents assigned to a form field
      else
         {
         S=app.getErr();
         if(S!="") alert(S);
         else theContent.value="";
         }
      }
   }
 function writeTheFile(form){var app=document.all.theApplet;
    with(form)
      {
      var S=app.writeFile(theName.value,theContent.value);
      if(S!=""){alert(S); app.getErr();}
      }
   }
```

A reminder: the functions `readFile()`, `writeFile()` and `getErr()` are defined in `FileHandler.java`, but are treated as if they are methods of `theApplet`, which is the id we gave to the Java plugin.

Stream IO and Exception Handling

The Java code in `FileHandler.java` introduces two new features of the Java language, the stream IO and exception handling. Both are quite similar to the same features of C++, but a brief explanation is in order for those who have not seen them before.

Streams

In Java, as in C++, in order to do input and output, you create a **stream** object of the appropriate class. What's appropriate? It depends on whether you want to read or write, whether you want to do it by byte or by character or by some more specific data type; whether you're working with input devices or files, and whether your files are sequential or random access or, perhaps, compressed. Some people would argue that Java has too many different kinds of streams, while the proponents argue that extreme specialization of Java streams helps catch errors: if there is a mismatch between the stream type and the type of data it is asked to input or output, the error will be caught at compile time.

For our purposes, we only need to know that some streams only have methods for processing input a character at a time, while others, more oriented toward text files, can input or output an entire line of text in one operation. We'll show examples of both kinds in this section.

Exception Handling

An exception is usually a polite word for error: the program takes exception to what you're trying to do. Actually, the technical term is **throw an exception**. An `exception` is an object that carries information about the error. When an error occurs, an appropriate `exception` object is thrown up in the air and needs to be caught. The code that catches the exception takes an appropriate action. If the error is fatal, the catch code will clean up and quit. If the error is such that it's possible to recover, the catch code will try to do that.

You can define your own exception classes but many of them come pre-defined with the Java language. They're all derived from the `java.lang.Throwable` class. Predefined exceptions cover many common error conditions, such as trying to read from a non-existent file or access an array element out of bounds of the array.

Syntactically, the exception handling mechanism involves four key words: `throw`, `throws`, `try` and `catch`. The keyword `throws` is used in method declarations to indicate what kind of exceptions you can expect from the method, as in:

```
public String writeFile(String Name,String Content) throws IOException{
```

In the body of the method, when you come to the part where an error can take place (e.g., you're trying to open a file), you enclose that part in the `try` block:

```
Try
{
   // error-prone code; expect an IO exception
   ...
}catch(IOException e)
{
    errString="Error: "+e; return errString;
}
```

As you can see, a `try` block is followed by one or several `catch` statements. Each `catch` takes an `exception` object as argument. In this case, it's an object of the pre-defined `IOException` class. The class has a data field of type String that contains an error message, and automatically returns that message if placed in a String context, as in the example above.

You can declare your own `exception` classes to anticipate your own errors. You throw objects of those classes from inside a `try` block:

```
try
{
    // some code
    if(myExceptionCondition) throw new MyException("My error occurred!");
    // more code
}
{catch(MyException me)
```

In the code below, we throw only pre-defined exceptions, but quite a few of them.

The Java Code

The `FileHandler` class has an `errString` data field which is initialized to the empty string. Both `writeFile()` and `readFile()` put their file access code inside a `try` block, and catch a possible `IOException` object right after it. An IOException may be raised for a variety of reasons, many of them anticipated in the `IOException` class

To output data to a file, you can open a `FileOutputStream`, which takes a `File` object as an argument. It is important to close the stream after you're done. The `FileOutputStream` works character by character, without buffering:

```
import java.applet.*;
import java.awt.*;
import java.io.*;

public class FileHandler extends Applet {
  String errString;
  public void init(){errString="";}
  public String writeFile(String name,String content) {
    try
      {
      File outFile = new File(name);
      FileOutputStream os=new FileOutputStream(outFile);
    // if the file exists and is not writable, an IO Exception will occur
      for(int i=0;i<content.length();i++)
        os.write(content.charAt(i));
      os.close();
      } catch(IOException e)
        {
        errString="Error: "+e; return errString;
        }
    return "";
  }
```

To input data from a file, you could use the character-based unbuffered `FileInputStream`, but it's more convenient to create a `BufferedReader` object which has a `readLine()` method. That method returns the next line of input or null if the end of file is reached. Typically, you create a local variable (e.g., `nextLine`) and assign the value returned by `readLine()` to it.

Assignment in Java works exactly the same way as in JavaScript (or C and C++): it is both a statement and an expression that returns the assigned value. It is a common idiom to call `readline()`, assign the value it produces to a local variable, and compare the value returned by the assignment to null, all in one boolean expression that is also the condition of the loop that reads one line after another from the file:

```
public String readFile(String name)
{
 String content="";
  try
  {
    BufferedReader brin=new BufferedReader(new FileReader(name));
    String nextLine;
    while(null!=(nextLine=brin.readLine()))
      content+=nextLine+"\n";
    brin.close();
  }catch(IOException e){errString="Error: "+e; return "";}
 return content;
}
```

Finally, the `getErr()` method returns the error message (and resets `errString`):

```
public String getErr(){String S=errString; errString=""; return S;}
```

As we said, the code is quite simple but it provides an extremely useful capability to JavaScript: write and read files on the local machine. You can also read and write to machines on the local network, as long as you use the file system protocol. (We tested on a peer-to-peer Win95 network.) This makes it possible to implement our Database class within a local file system, without a Web server or any CGI programming at all. In the text-annotating system of Chapter 8, for example, we would simply place the `FileHandler` applet on `page0.htm,` and replace the `<ACTION>`s of the submit and load forms with JavaScript calls on the applet's `readFile()` and `writeFile()` functions.

Our next task is to provide the same capability over a TCP/IP network, so that our server can be anywhere on the Internet.

Do-it-Yourself Networking

Communication over TCP/IP networks goes through data structures called sockets (TCP sockets, to be precise; there are also datagram sockets about which we'll say nothing else). There are two kinds of sockets, server and client. Both are quite complex internally, but Java does a very good job hiding this complexity in the implementation of two well-designed classes, `Socket` and `ServerSocket`.

Recall that when you establish a connection over the Internet, you need to specify the remote host's URL (or IP address) and the port, unless it's a standard port for Web connections. Those are the two arguments to the `Socket` constructor: the IP number or URL, and the port number. For server sockets, you can leave the port number out if you're going to use the standard port number for the service: FTP usually goes on port 21, gopher (remember gopher?) goes on port 70, and HTTP goes on port 80. For client sockets, you pick a number yourself in a safe range. Never use a number that is less than 1024. In general, the ports between 49152 and 65535 are preferred for private, unauthorized use.

Once you've created a socket object, you think of it as just another data source or sink; in other words, as another stream. This is why networking and IO are frequently discussed together in Java books. You open a socket, establish a connection to a remote computer, and start using it as a stream.

A Client Socket

In outline, you proceed as follows:

- create a socket object
- create an appropriate stream object associated with the socket
- send the command: READ, WRITE, or QUIT
- if QUIT, you've just told the server to stop working: you're done.
- wait for the OK message from the server
- send the name of the file to be read or written
- wait for an OK message from the server
- send or receive data

Throughout your code, put everything that can go wrong inside a `try` block.

The NetFileHandler Class

You start very much as in `FileHandler` class, except you also import the `java.net` package:

```
import java.applet.*;
import java.awt.*;
import java.io.*;
import java.net.*;

public class NetFileHandler extends Applet // pass read/writes to SockServ
{
  String errString;
  public void init(){errString="";}
  public String getErr(){String S=errString; errString=""; return S;
}
```

Now we define `writeFile()`. The name is intentionally the same so that from JavaScript, `FileHandler` and `NetFileHandler` look exactly the same:

```
public String writeFile(String Name,String Content) throws IOException
{
  String results=""; Socket outS;
  DataInputStream is; DataOutputStream os;
  try{outS=new Socket(InetAddress.getLocalHost(),56789);
```

In the last line, we've created a `Socket` object. The arguments to the constructor are two: a specification of the host to connect to, and a port number. The specification of the host comes from a call on a static method of the `InetAddress` class. The `getLocalHost()` method used here returns a reference to the same machine on which the socket is created. (The IP number 127.0.0.1 and the `http://localhost` URL are reserved for the local host.) To connect to a remote machine, whether on the local network or on the Internet, we'd use `getByName()`.

```
    is=new DataInputStream(outS.getInputStream());
    os=new DataOutputStream(outS.getOutputStream());
  }catch(Exception e){errString="Failed on connection "+e;
                    return errString;}
```

As you can see, the `Socket` class has `getInputStream()` and `getOutputStream()` methods which return `InputStream` and `OutputStream` objects, respectively. You pass them as arguments to the constructors of `DataInputStream` and `DataOutputStream`. This pair's speciality is to do IO for the primitive data types of Java: they have methods like `writeBoolean()` or `readFloat()`. In our case, we want to read and write Unicode characters. For IO purposes, these are usually transformed into a different representation called UTF (Unicode Transformation Format). The Data input and output streams have the methods for reading and writing UTF data:

```
try{os.writeUTF("WRITE");
    String res=is.readUTF();
```

At this point, our socket is in a dialog with a remote socket that can be on the same local network or anywhere in the world. The dialog is simple. We check to see that the response is OK, and if so, proceed to write the file name and its content to the data output stream. If anything goes wrong, we close the two streams and the socket, and return the error string.

```
        if(!res.equals("OK"))
      {
         os.close(); is.close(); outS.close();
         errString= "failure on WRITE: "+res; return errString;}
      os.writeUTF(Name);
      res=is.readUTF();if(!res.equals("OK"))
      {
         os.close(); is.close(); outS.close();
         errString= "failure on WRITE("+Name+"): "+res; return errString;
      }
      os.writeUTF(Content);
      res=is.readUTF();if(!res.equals("OK"))
      {
         os.close(); is.close(); outS.close();
         errString="failure on Write("+Name+") of "+Content;
         return errString;
      }
   }catch(IOException e)
      {
         os.close(); is.close(); outS.close();
         errString="Failed in writing "+e; System.out.println(errString);
         return errString;
      }
   os.close(); is.close();outS.close();
   return "";
}
```

The `readFile()` method is very similar in its operation. It issues the READ command, and the socket on the other end adjusts its actions accordingly.

Quitting Gracefully

The remaining `killServer()` method tells the server socket on the other end to quit. Note that we don't have to do anything to close the dedicated client socket created for exchanging data with our client socket: it closes by itself once the transaction is complete.

```
public String killServer() throws IOException
{
   Socket outS=null; DataOutputStream os=null; DataInputStream is=null;
   Try
      {
      outS=new Socket(InetAddress.getLocalHost(),4444);
      os=new DataOutputStream(outS.getOutputStream());
      is=new DataInputStream(outS.getInputStream());
      }
      catch(Exception e)
        {
          errString="Failed on connection "+e; return errString;
        }
   os.writeUTF("QUIT");
   os.close(); is.close();outS.close();
   return "";
}
```

In summary, our socket knows three commands, WRITE, READ and QUIT. The socket on the other end will have to know how to respond to them.

In the Meantime, on the Server...

In outline, activities on the other end unfold as follows. There's a `ServerSocket` object running on the "other machine" (which is the same machine here). It listens to its port, whose number we've given to the client server constructor. If a request is detected, the `ServerSocket` creates a client socket partner for the socket that originated the request, and the two client sockets engage in a transaction. Once the transaction is complete, the newly-created client Socket goes away. If the originator sends the QUIT command, the `ServerSocket` closes down and has to be restarted from the command line.

The SocServ Class

This is our first example of a Java application rather than an applet. The `SocServ` class doesn't live in a Web page; it's a program on a server computer that listens to its port for incoming requests. In this case, the client and the server are the same computer, but the difference remains: the client socket lives in an applet in the browser page; the server socket talks directly to the server.

There are two big differences between an applet and an application. An application class is not derived from applet, and it must have a `main()` method. The signature for a `main()` method is the same for all classes:

```
public static void main(String[] args)
{
```

The method is `public` and `static`, returns void, and receives an array of Strings as its argument. It can analyze its arguments in much the same way that JavaScript functions can analyze theirs.

As with the client socket, the first crucial step is to create a socket object. This time, the only argument needed is a port number. It has to be the same as the number we gave to the client socket:

```
ServerSocket serverSocket=null;
try{serverSocket=new ServerSocket(4444);}
catch(IOException e)
{
   System.out.println("failed to listen on 4444, "+e);System.exit(1);
}
```

With a `ServerSocket` in place, we create a local partner for the client socket by calling on the `accept()` method. The idea is that the two client sockets on the two ends of the connection will be talking to each other, while the server socket will resume listening to the incoming port for other requests. In a real server that can handle multiple simultaneous requests, each connection would run in a separate thread, but in our case, with the client and the server on the same machine used by a single user, we can keep things simple:

```
Socket clientSocket=null;
try{while(true)
  {
  try{clientSocket=serverSocket.accept();
  }
  catch(IOException e)
    {
    System.out.println("Accept failed: 4444; "+e); System.exit(1);
```

```
            }
        DataInputStream in=new DataInputStream(clientSocket.getInputStream());
        DataOutputStream os=
            new DataOutputStream(clientSocket.getOutputStream());
        String commandLine,fileName,fileContent;
```

At this point, the client socket on our side is ready to receive commands and data. If you look in the `NetFileHandler` class, you'll see that its entire vocabulary is limited to three commands, WRITE, READ and QUIT. The remaining code of `SocServ` is an `if-else` statement with four branches, one for each command and one for anything else:

```
        commandLine=in.readUTF();
        if(commandLine.equals("WRITE"))
            {
            os.writeUTF("OK");   fileName=in.readUTF();
            os.writeUTF("OK");   fileContent=in.readUTF();
            String res=writeFile(fileName,fileContent);
            os.writeUTF("OK");
            System.out.println("wrote file "+fileName);
            }
        else if(commandLine.equals("READ"))
            {
            os.writeUTF("OK");   fileName=in.readUTF();
            os.writeUTF("OK");   fileContent=readFile(fileName);
            os.writeUTF(fileContent);
            System.out.println("read file "+fileName);
            }
        else if(commandLine.equals("QUIT"))
            {
            os.close();in.close();clientSocket.close();
            System.out.println("Received QUIT from client"); System.exit(1);
            }
        else os.writeUTF("I can READ and WRITE files, or QUIT; command is ["
                        +commandLine+"]");
        os.close();in.close();clientSocket.close();
        }
    }catch(IOException e){e.printStackTrace();}
}
```

The `writeFile()` and `readFile()` methods of `SocServ` are completely straightforward, and need no comment on our part.

The HTML Page

The only remarkable thing about the HTML page for `NetFileHandler` is that its JavaScript functions, `readTheFile()` and `writeTheFile()`, are identical to those of the `FileHandler` page. The body of the page is also the same:

```
<BODY><OBJECT classid="clsid:8AD9C840-044E-11D1-B3E9-00805F499D93"
    id=theApplet width="10" height="10" align="baseline"
    codebase="http://java.sun.com/products/plugin/1.1/jinstall-11
win32.cab#Version=1,1,0,0">
        <PARAM NAME="code" VALUE="NetFileHandler.class">
        <PARAM NAME="codebase" VALUE="jclasses/">
        <PARAM NAME="type" VALUE="application/x-java-applet;version=1.1">
```

```
         No JDK 1.1 support for APPLET!!
</OBJECT><FORM id=theForm ACTION="javascript:formAction()">
  the name: <INPUT TYPE=TEXT NAME=theName
    VALUE="file name goes here" SIZE=80>
  the content: <TEXTAREA NAME=theContent VALUE="" ROWS=10 COLS=80></TEXTAREA>
<INPUT TYPE=BUTTON VALUE=read    onclick="readTheFile(this.form);">
<INPUT TYPE=BUTTON VALUE=write   onclick="writeTheFile(this.form);">
</FORM></BODY>
```

A major new capability provided by `NetFileHandler` is that it is now possible to use shared data on a local machine *or over the Internet*, without any Web server or CGI at all. Instead, the server computer will be running the `NetFileServer` application in a DOS (or Unix shell) window. Files will be shared just as they are with a CGI implementation, but the HTML effect is like `FileHandler`'s. For the text-annotation program of Chapter 8, just as with `FileHandler`, we would place the applet on `page0.htm`, and replace the `<ACTION>`s of the submit and load forms with JavaScript calls on the applet's `readFile()` and `writeFile()` functions. The only HTML difference from `FileHandler` is in the applet's name, and the only administrative difference is that `NetFileServer` (`SockServ`) has to be running on the server computer.

Using Native Code

You can write anything in Java that you can write in C or C++, but what if you have already written it? There's a great deal of stable pre-Java code out there, and it would be wasteful to rewrite it all in Java. The code, once compiled, is native to a specific machine, but you may still want to be able to access it over the network, or put its output into a Web page. Or, in another scenario, you don't care for portability, but you do care for efficiency, and so you want to write your labor-intensive routines in C and compile. For reasons such as these, we want to be able to call "native code" from Java. If we learn how to do that, we can, of course, go one more (familiar) step, and call compiled native code from JavaScript.

The Overall Framework

In order to be useable from Java, our C code has to be compiled into a library. On Win32 systems, it would be a dynamically-linked library or **dll**. A dll has specific entry points that are exposed to the world outside. These require special attention.

Names and Data Types

Those functions in the library that send or receive data from the outside have to be re-written: their names have to correspond to the names of their Java "stubs," and the data types of their input and outputs have to correspond to Java data types. For instance, suppose our Java native methods are in the class `HelloNative`, and one of the methods is declared in Java as

```
public native static String strCat(String A,String B);
```

The corresponding C function in the dll will then be declared as:

```
JNIEXPORT jstring JNICALL Java_HelloNative_strCat
  (JNIEnv *, jclass, jstring, jstring);
```

As you can see, the name of the function includes the name of the Java class and the name of the method. You don't write such declarations yourself: they're produced automatically by the `javah` tool which outputs C header files. If your code has already been written, you have to rewrite it with the new data types. Remember, you only have to do that for the routines that communicate with the outside world.

On the Java Side

As you just saw, stubs for native methods are declared `native` and `static`. The class that contains those declarations, must also load the compiled C library, to link it with the Java code that calls on it. The loading is done by a call on a method of the System class. (In the line of code below, assume that the name of the dll is `HelloNative.dll`.) In order for the call to go through, the location of the dll has to be in the `PATH` variable.

```
static {System.loadLibrary("HelloNative");}
```

We're now going to work through a complete example beginning from the other end.

Try It Out

Point your browser at:

`http://webdev.wrox.co.uk/books/1849/Chapter09/helloNativeApplet.html`.

Enter two strings into the text boxes called **StrA** and **StrB** and click the **strCat** button. The result will appear in the **Result** box. The computation proceeded from the onclick handler to a JavaScript function to a Java method to a Java stub for a native function to compiled C code in a dll. You can also add two integers that way:

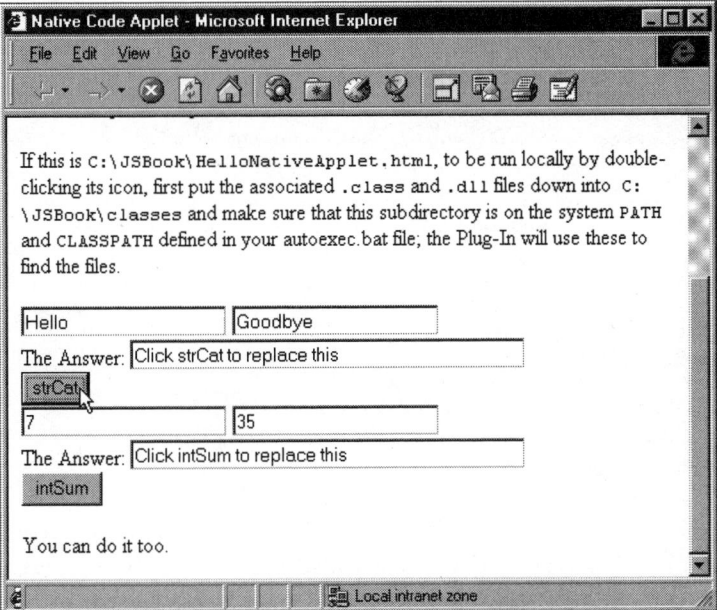

The HTML Page, the Applet, and Native Code Stubs

The HTML page is completely unremarkable. Its JavaScript functions call applet methods:

```
function formCat(A,B,C)
{
  var app=document.all.theApplet;
  C.value=app.concat(A.value,B.value);
}
function formAdd(A,B,C)
{
  var app=document.all.theApplet;
  C.value=app.intSum(A.value,B.value);
}
```

The applet is `HelloNativeApplet`. Its methods, in turn, call on native code stubs in the `HelloNative` class:

```
import java.applet.*;
import java.awt.*;
public class HelloNativeApplet extends Applet
{
  public void init(){showStatus("HelloNativeApplet running");
}
  public void paint(Graphics g)
    {
      g.drawString("I am HelloNativeApplet",20,20);
    }
  public  static void sayHello()
  {
    HelloNative.greeting();} // puts out a message
  public  String concat(String A,String B){
    showStatus("concatenating "+A+" and "+B);
    String C=HelloNative.strCat(A,B); // concatenates two strings
    return C;
    }
  public  int intSum(int A,int B){
    return HelloNative.intSum(A,B);} // adds two numbers
  }
```

The stubs should look familiar by now. Here's the entire `HelloNative` class:

```
public class HelloNative
{
  public native static void greeting();
  public native static String strCat(String A,String B);
  public native static int intSum(int A,int B);
  static {System.loadLibrary("HelloNative");} // load the dll
}
```

The C Code

The last line of `HelloNative` assumes that a DLL called `HelloNative.dll`, has already been created and placed in the PATH somewhere. This involves the following steps:

- ❑ run `HelloNative` through the `javah` utility to generate the header file
- ❑ write the C code using the declarations in `HelloNative.h`
- ❑ compile the C code into a dll

The Header File

The `javah` utility (which also has to be in the PATH) is invoked like this:

```
javah -jni HelloNative
```

The `-jni` option says that we're using the JNI (**Java Native Interface**) API of Java Development Kit 1.1, rather than the older jdk1.0 version. There are other options that you can see if you enter `javah -help`. You can specify more than one class name.

The result for our `HelloNative` class is shown below, broken into parts by brief comments:

```
/* DO NOT EDIT THIS FILE - it is machine generated */
#include <jni.h>
/* Header for class HelloNative */

#ifndef _Included_HelloNative
#define _Included_HelloNative
```

The three lines above are preprocessor directives to include header files with declarations. The code that follows is a standard preprocessor directive to avoid multiple inclusions.

```
#ifdef __cplusplus
extern "C" {
#endif
```

If the code was compiled on a C++ compiler, it has to be placed inside `extern "C" {...}`. The matching right curly bracket can be found at the bottom of the file:

```
/*
 * Class:     HelloNative
 * Method:    greeting
 * Signature: ()V
```

The signature above says: no arguments, returns void.

```
 */
JNIEXPORT void JNICALL Java_HelloNative_greeting
  (JNIEnv *, jclass);

/*
 * Class:     HelloNative
 * Method:    strCat
 * Signature: (Ljava/lang/String;Ljava/lang/String;)Ljava/lang/String;
```

This signature says: two Java String arguments, returns a Java String.

```
 */
JNIEXPORT jstring JNICALL Java_HelloNative_strCat
  (JNIEnv *, jclass, jstring, jstring);

/*
 * Class:     HelloNative
 * Method:    intSum
 * Signature: (II)I
```

You get the idea.

```
 */
JNIEXPORT jint JNICALL Java_HelloNative_intSum
  (JNIEnv *, jclass, jint, jint);

#ifdef __cplusplus
}
```

The closing curly bracket, as promised.

```
#endif
#endif
```

The C Code File

To create C code, copy the declarations from the header file and add function argument names and bodies. In the simplest case, they're just plain C code:

```
#include "HelloNative.h"
#include <stdio.h>
JNIEXPORT void JNICALL Java_HelloNative_greeting
  (JNIEnv * env, jclass cl)
  {printf("Hello from the natives!\n");}
JNIEXPORT jint JNICALL Java_HelloNative_intSum
  (JNIEnv * env, jclass cl, jint A, jint B){
     return A+B;}
```

Things get more complicated with strings (and even more so with structured objects but we won't get that far). Java Strings are sequences of Unicode characters, while C strings are null-terminated sequences of ASCII characters. Some sort of conversion has to take place. There's more than one way to do it, but the best way for Unicode to ASCII and back is via UTF. (You saw UTF earlier in the chapter.)

All data type conversions are done by JNI functions. All calls to JNI functions use the env pointer, which points to a table of JNI function pointers. So you de-reference env to get to the table, and de-reference again to get to the actual function. The functions in our case are `GetStringUTF()`, `NewStringUTF()` and `ReleaseStringUTF`. The code below illustrates:

```
JNIEXPORT jstring JNICALL Java_HelloNative_strCat
  (JNIEnv * env, jclass cl, jstring A, jstring B){
     jstring C;
     const char * cA = (*env)->GetStringUTFChars(env,A,NULL);
```

```
          const char * cB = (*env)->GetStringUTFChars(env,B,NULL);
          char * cC=(char *)malloc(1+strlen(cA)+strlen(cB));
          sprintf(cC,"%s%s",cA,cB);
          C=(*env)->NewStringUTF(env,cC);
          free(cC);
          (*env)->ReleaseStringUTFChars(env,A,cA);
          (*env)->ReleaseStringUTFChars(env,B,cB);
          return C;
      }
```

This concludes our brief foray into native code interface. Obviously, we've just scratched the surface. To do a real project, get yourself a Java book and a lot of native code.

Conclusions

We haven't written a large application in this chapter, but we've laid the groundwork for a greatly expanded functionality of JavaScript applications. It would take another book to explore all the possibilities of HTML, JavaScript and Java working together, especially in the area of multimedia applications on an intranet. Now, time for some conclusions.

Although a very fine language, JavaScript has limitations. For instance, it has no file IO, and no graphics primitives. In this chapter we have learned how to overcome those limitations. In particular, you've learned how to:

- ❑ write a simple Java applet
- ❑ add graphics capabilities to a JavaScript program
- ❑ make your applet trusted on the local system and local network
- ❑ read and write files locally from a JavaScript program
- ❑ read and write files over the Internet using a socket connection
- ❑ invoke native code from a Java applet (and therefore from a JavaScript program)

This concludes the chapter and the book. We hope you have a better grasp of the power of JavaScript, and a greater willingness to utilize that power. Above all, we hope we're leaving you with a feeling that there are large open vistas in front of you, for you to explore and make your own.

ECMAScript Core Language

The ECMAScript standard describes the central features of the JavaScript language. A vendor's particular implementation conforms to the standard if it implements all the features described in the standard. An implementation may add further features, particularly host objects and still conform.

❑   Host objects are described in later Appendices.
❑   Non-host object enhancements are described in Appendix B.

Comparison tables at the end of each section only show a value if there is a non-conformance to the standard.

Script Formatting and Comments

❑   **Unicode 2.0** characters may be used to write a script. Only ASCII characters can appear outside string literals and comment text.
❑   **Whitespace** separates language elements not otherwise separated by punctuation characters, improves readability and consists of one or more of these characters:

Character name	Unicode value	ASCII decimal code
Tab	\u0009	9
Vertical Tab	\u000B	11
Form Feed	\u000C	13
Space	\u0020	32

❑ **Line terminators** also separate language elements, but cannot appear directly inside a string literal:

Character name	Unicode value	ASCII decimal code
Line Feed	\u000A	10
Carriage Return	\u000D	14

❑ **Comments** are non-functional text. Single line comments can appear inside multi-line comments but no other combination is possible, e.g. multi-line comments cannot be nested.

```
// single line comment
```

```
/* multi-line
   comment */
```

❑ **Identifiers** consist of one or more alphabetic letters, decimal digits, underscores ('_') or dollar signs ('$'), and are case-sensitive. The first character must not be a decimal digit.

❑ **Automatic semicolon insertion**. Statements normally end with a semi-colon(';'). If left out, the interpreter will assume one, except within the parentheses of a `for` loop. If a `return` statement with an argument, or an expression with a post-increment ('++') or post-decrement ('--') operator, is split over two lines, an unexpected semicolon may be inserted.

Literals

Literals are data values embedded directly in a script.

❑ `void` is an operator, not a literal.

❑ There is no literal representation of the Undefined type's sole value, called `undefined`. Any variable that has not been assigned a value is of type Undefined.

❑ `null` is the Null type's sole literal value.

❑ `true` and `false` are the Boolean type's literal values.

Numeric literals for the Number type may be represented in several ways:

❑ **Signed integer**: an optional + or – leads at least one character instance from the set `0123456789`, but the first may not be `0` (zero) if there is more than one character instance.

❑ **Signed decimal**: either a signed integer, +, – or nothing, then a . (period) followed by at least one character instance from the set `0123456789`.

❑ **Signed scientific**: a signed decimal followed by one of `eE` followed by a signed integer.

❑ **Octal**: a `0` (zero) followed by at least one character instance from the set `01234567`.

❑ **Hexadecimal**: a `0x` (zero-x) or `0X` (zero-X) followed by at least one character instance from the set `0123456789abcdefABCDEF`. Therefore hexadecimal numbers are case-insensitive.

❑ **NaN and Infinity**: There are no literal representations–see the **global** object for properties with these values.

Numeric literals may not exactly match any computer-representable number. In that case, rounding will occur when interpreted - see *Data Types* section below.

String literals for the String type may be represented as follows:

A harmless item is any Unicode character except line terminators, \ (backslash), ' (single quote) and " (double quote).

- ❑ A String literal is a " followed by at least zero items from the set of harmless items plus ', and then a further ".
- ❑ A String literal is a ' followed by at least zero items from the set of harmless items plus ", and then a further '.

A String literal may also contain escape sequences. An escape sequence is a \ followed by special characters which together identify a single Unicode character. If a non-special character follows the \, the \ is ignored. The list of escape sequences is:

Escape Sequence	Name	Unicode value
\b	backspace	\u0008
\t	horizontal tab	\u0009
\n	line feed (new line)	\u000A
\f	form feed	\u000C
\r	carriage return	\u000D
\"	double quote: "	\u0022
\'	single quote: '	\u0027
\\	backslash: \	\u005C
\0DDD (see below)	octal sequence	\u0000 to \u00FF
\xDD (see below)	hexadecimal sequence	\u0000 to \u00FF
\uDDDD (see below)	Unicode sequence	\u0000 to \uFFFF

- ❑ An **octal escape sequence** is a backslash followed by 0 (zero), followed by an optional character from the set 0123, followed by one or two characters from the set 01234567. This is an octal value in the range 0 to 255 (decimal).
- ❑ A **hexadecimal escape sequence** is a backslash followed by one of x or X, followed by two character instances from the set 0123456789abcdefABCDEF. This is a case-insensitive hexadecimal number in the range 0 to 255 (decimal).
- ❑ A **Unicode escape sequence** is a backslash followed by a u, followed by four character instances from the set 0123456789abcdefABCDEF. This is a case-insensitive hexadecimal number in the range 0 to 65535 (decimal).

Data Types

Every data item in a script has a type. Variables can contain any type of data. The standard draws a distinction between the names of types and allowable values for those types - names of types start with an uppercase letter. The standard doesn't say how the values of various types should be output to the user, except for rounding of numbers. See also the *Native Objects* heading.

Undefined. The type of a variable that hasn't been assigned a value: e.g. 'var x;'. This type has one value: undefined, with no literal representation.

Null. The type for empty values. This type has one value: null, written `null` literally.

Boolean. The type for truth values. This type has two unique values: true and false, written `true` and `false` literally.

Number. The type for integral and floating point numbers. The Number type is a double precision 64-bit IEEE 754 value, with special values NaN (Not a Number) and positive and negative `infinity`. Numbers as big as 1×10^{300}, and as small as 1×10^{-300} are possible, as well as their negatives. Roughly 18 significant digits are possible.

Because computers are finite, real numbers such as π cannot always be exactly represented.

> **Special care must be taken to convert those numbers to a human readable format so that they appear as expected–this is a rounding problem.**

Mathematics introduces tiny errors when numbers with many digits are operated on. This usually only interests mathematicians and statisticians, and is a general problem with computers. Small integer operations, such as `234 * 12`, are usually unaffected.

> **Some numbers can be represented in more than one way. There are positive and negative zeros, and many different values of NaN. This is invisible to the scriptwriter.**

String. The type for sequences of Unicode characters. The minimum length is 0; the standard mandates no maximum length. Current implementations allow for strings of at least a Megabyte in size. According to the standard, the String type uses a Unicode 2.0 encoding which covers the whole world of characters. Browsers at version 4.0 or less only support smaller character sets such as ISO 8859-1 (Latin1), which is English ASCII plus Western European characters. So, no Chinese symbols are available without changing the browser's language. The subject of character sets versus character set encodings is a complex one; read the Unicode standard, or investigate on the Web.

Object. The underlying type of all ECMAScript/Javascript objects. It has no innate values exposed to the scriptwriter's control. Instead it supplies behavior that the scriptwriter can use and that other object types can inherit:

- ❏ properties may be attached to it.
- ❏ The `prototype` property may be exploited to support inheritance.
- ❏ The `typeof()` method returns `"Object"` for Object type values.

In addition there are Reference, List and Completion type, but these are invisible to the scriptwriter. The Reference type is of some conceptual use to scriptwriters in that it is used to track values of the Object type. `void` is not a type, it is an operator.

Read the standard for all the gory details regarding types. For more details on standards see Appendix F.

The `typeof()` strings are:

Type operated on	Resulting string
Undefined	`"undefined"`
Null	`"object"`
Boolean	`"boolean"`
Number	`"number"`
String	`"string"`
Object (native object that isn't a function)	`"object"`
Object (native object that is a function)	`"function"`
Object (host)	No standard. Depends on the specific object.

Type conversion

The full type conversion story is very complex. See Chapter 1 for a fuller discussion, or read the standard very carefully. Two specific unusual cases are bit operators and array indices.

- ❏ Bit operators temporarily convert their left argument to a 32-bit value, and their right argument to an unsigned 5-bit value.
- ❏ Any number value (not string) used as an array element index will be converted to an unsigned 32-bit value.

Operators and Expressions

The ECMAScript operators are:

Operator	Name	Operator	Name
Unary operators			
delete	deletes an object	+	unary plus
void	force the undefined value to be returned	-	unary minus
typeof	report a value's type	~	bitwise NOT

Operator	Name	Operator	Name
++	pre- and post-increment	!	logical NOT
--	pre- and post-decrement		
Binary operators			
*	multiplication	<<	left shift
/	division	>>	right shift
%	modulus or remainder	>>>	unsigned right shift
+	addition or concatenation	&	bitwise AND
-	subtraction	|	bitwise OR
<	less than	^	bitwise XOR
>	greater than		
<=	less than or equal	&&	logical AND
>=	greater than or equal	||	logical OR
==	equals		
!=	does not equals		
Special operators			
this	refers to the current scope's object	?:	ternary conditional operator; allows 'if' inside an expression
new	construct an object of given type	,	'comma': separates function arguments or sequences of expressions
=	assigns result of right hand expression to left hand variable	( )	delimits function arguments and groups operators in expressions
op= *= /= %= += -= <<= >>= >>>= &= ^= |=	assignment with binary operator applied to old value and new value before final assignment:	[ ]	Associates a property name with an object in an array-like manner.
		.	Associates a property name with an object

Operator Precedence

Does $1 + 2 * 3$ equal $1 + (2 * 3) = 7$ or does it equal $(1 + 2) * 3 = 9$?

The ECMAScript standard doesn't yet clearly document operator precedence. However, JavaScript closely follows Java, and Java closely follows C. The table shows operator precedence as implemented in IE4, with lowest at the top and like operators grouped together. The third column explains whether to read $1+2+3+4$ as $((1+2)+3)+4$ or $1+(2+(3+(4)))$.

Operator type	Operators	Evaluation order for like elements
multiple evaluation	`,`	
assignment	`= += -= *= /= %=` `<<= >>= >>>= &= ^= |=`	right to left
conditional	`? :`	right to left
logical OR	`||`	left to right
logical AND	`&&`	left to right
bitwise OR	`|`	left to right
bitwise XOR	`^`	left to right
bitwise AND	`&`	left to right
equality	`== != === !==`	left to right
relational	`< <= > >=`	left to right
bitwise shift	`<< >> >>>`	left to right
additive	`+ -`	left to right
multiplicative	`* / %`	left to right
unary operators	`! ~ - ++ -- delete` `new typeof void`	right to left
postfix operators	`() [] .`	left to right

Statements and Control Flow

Statements are the basic unit of work in the language. Statements are terminated with a semi-colon which can be left out if the line ends after the statement. A block is a collected sequence of statements. Blocks and statements are generally interchangeable.

```
statement-body;        // a statement
```

```
{
    statement;         // one or more statements plus braces equal a block
}
```

If ... else ...

```
if (condition)
    statement or block
```

or

```
if (condition)
    statement or block
else
    statement or block
```

While ...

```
while (condition)    statement or block
```

If a block is used it may contain instances of

```
break;
```

or

```
continue;
```

For ...

```
for (setup-expression; continue-condition; change-expression)
    statement or block
```

or

```
for (variable in object-variable)
    statement or block
```

Only properties without the DontEnum special ECMAScript property attribute are revealed by the second form.

If a block is used it may contain instances of

```
break;
```

or

```
continue;
```

With ...

```
with (object)
    statement or block
```

Scope, functions and methods

There is always a current object, accessible via the special variable/operator this.

Functions are sections of executable script associated with a property name, also called a function name. The name follows the rules for property/variable names. Functions are first declared, then invoked.

Declarations can occur as follows:

```
function example1()
{
  // zero or more statements
}
```

or

```
function example2(arg1,arg2)     // as many named variables as needed
{
  // zero or more statements possibly using arg1, arg2
}
```

or

```
new Function("a", "b", "c", "return a+b+c");      // a,b,c are arguments
```

or

```
new Function("a, b, c", "return a+b+c");      // a,b,c are arguments
```

or

```
new Function("a,b", "c", "return a+b+c");      // a,b,c are arguments
```

or

```
new Function("return arguments[0] + arguments[1] + arguments[2]");
                                              // no arguments
```

Functions may contain one or more instances of

```
return;
```

or

```
return expression;
```

Invocation of functions occurs as follows:

```
example1(var1, var2)                          // zero or more arguments
```

or

```
object_variable.method_property_name(var1, var2) // zero or more arguments
```

- ❑ Any number of arguments can be passed to a function, regardless of its declaration.
- ❑ All function arguments are passed by value, if they are primitive types, otherwise by reference.
- ❑ Functions can be called recursively, therefore care needs to be taken to avoid infinite loops.
- ❑ The standard does not require that functions be declarable inside other functions.

If a function's body (main statement block) uses the this operator, it is said to be a method and must be invoked as a property of an object. Also see the Function object below.

Native Objects

Native objects are part of the JavaScript interpreter and the ECMA standard. The only built in object is Math. The standard explains the gory details of 'prototype inheritance', which allows one object to take on properties of another.

JavaScript Objects

Objects and their properties commonly form a tree data structure, with the global object at the root of the tree. Because properties and variables can track any object, more general structures than trees are possible. The most general structure possible where objects are tracked with no apparent plan is called a **cyclic directed graph**.

There is a full listing of all the ECMAScript host objects below. Note that because all objects inherit their prototype's properties, objects can call methods and properties of their own using the syntax

```
obj.property()
```

rather than using the full prototype syntax:

```
obj.prototype.property()
```

To aid reference, therefore, only the root name is given here. Where the argument of the property is the current object itself, then we have used the keyword `this` to indicate it.

All the objects of ECMAScript have `toString()` and `valueOf()` methods. However, these return different results depending on the object from which they are called, and are so detailed for each object.

Internal Properties

These are the internal properties of all ECMAScript objects. Note that instantiations of particular objects can have these properties read, using the `Get` property, but they are internal properties, and not accessible to the language. However, see Appendix B for details of JScript mechanisms for doing so.

Property	Parameters	Description
`[[Prototype]]`	none	The prototype of this object.
`[[Class]]`	none	The kind of this object.
`[[Value]]`	none	Internal state information associated with this object.
`[[Get]]`	(PropertyName)	Returns the value of the property.
`[[Put]]`	(PropertyName, Value)	Sets the specified property to Value.
`[[CanPut]]`	(PropertyName)	Returns a boolean value indicating whether a [[Put]] operation with the specified PropertyName will succeed.
`[[HasProperty]]`	(PropertyName)	Returns a boolean value indicating whether the object already has a member with the given name.
`[[Delete]]`	(PropertyName)	Removes the specified property from the object.

Property	Parameters	Description
[[DefaultValue]]	(Hint)	Returns a default value for the object, which should be a primitive value (not an object or reference).
[[Construct]]	a list of argument values provided by the caller	Constructs an object. Invoked via the **new** operator. Objects that implement this internal method are called *constructors*.
[[Call]]	a list of argument values provided by the caller	Executes code associated with the object. Invoked via a function call expression. Objects that implement this internal method are called *functions*.

Global Object

In every case, a length property of a built-in function object described in this section has the attributes {ReadOnly, DontDelete, DontEnum} (and no others). Note that all objects inherit the methods from the Global object:

Property Name	Read/write?	Enumerable?	Description
NaN	Yes	No	Initial value is NaN
Infinity	Yes	No	Initial value is positive infinity

Method Name	Arguments	Return	Description
eval()	x	String object	Returns either x if not a String object, the result of x as a program, a runtime error if x does not execute as a program or the undefined value.
parseInt()	string, radix	integer value	The parseInt function produces an integer value by interpreting the contents of the *string* argument according to the specified *radix*. Default radix is 10.
parseFloat()	string	**NaN** or number value	Interprets the string value as a decimal literal to give a number.
escape()	string	string	Replaces characters in string with special URL meanings with their corresponding hexadecimal escape sequence.

Table Continued on Following Page

Method Name	Arguments	Return	Description
unescape()	string	string	Translates hexadecimal escape sequences in a string back into characters.
isNaN()	number	True|False	Returns True if the argument is **NaN**, otherwise False
isFinite()	number	True|False	False if the argument is **NaN, +∞,** or **−∞,** otherwise True.
Object(...)	Value or empty	Object object	If value, must be **null** or **undefined**. Creates a new Object object.
Function(...)	as required	Function object	Creates a new Function object, with the arguments providing formal parameters. The last argument is executable code.
Array(...)	Array items or length or empty	Array object	Instantiates an Array object with the arguments as members. Length creates an array of length equal to length, empty creates an empty array.
String(...)	value or empty	string value; empty string	Value returns a string value computed by ToString(value); empty returns " "
Boolean(...)	value or empty	boolean value; false	Calculates a boolean value using ToBoolean(value); or simply returns false.
Number(...)	value or empty	Number value; +0	Calculates a number value according to ToNumber(value), or returns 0.
Date(...)	see description	string value	Returns a string value representing the current time in UTC (GMT)
Math	No	No	It is not possible to call the Math object as a method.

Object

There are no special properties for the Object object, other than those which it inherits from the special built-in prototype object; it does not have an initial value:

Property Name	Read/write?	Enumerable?	Descriptiom
constructor	Yes	No	Holds the built-in Object constructor

Method Name	Arguments	Return	Description
toString()	this	String value	Returns a string for the object of the form " [object ", class, and "] "
valueOf()	this	Object	Returns the object.

Function

The Function object can be called instead of a function value.

Property Name	Read/Write?	Enumerable?	Description
length	No	No	Establishes expected number of arguments as an integer.
arguments	No	No	Value depends on

Method Name	Arguments	Return	Description
toString()	this	String value	Returns an string value representation of the function. Precise whitespacing, formatting etc are left to the implementation.

Array

The Array object is used to store collections of information in an easily accessible fashion.

Property Name	Read/Write?	Enumerable?	Description
Length	Yes	No	This is always numerically greater than the names of all members of the array.

Method	Arguments	Returns	Description
join(separator)	see description	string	The array elements are converted to strings, then concatenated with the separator. Default separator is **comma**.

Table Continued on Following Page

Method	Arguments	Returns	Description
`reverse()`	`this`	Array	Returns a new Array object with the elements reversed.
`sort(comparefn)`	Function	Array	Sorts the array according to function of a form that establishes (x>y as −ve; x=y as 0; x<y as +ve)

String

The String object can be thought of as a wrapper for a simple string value; the string value passed to the object when it is created becomes in essence an unnamed, implicit, property of the object itself.

Property Name	Read/ Write?	Enumerable?	Description
`fromCharCode (char0, char1…)`	yes	no	Returns a string value containing as many characters as the resulting string.
`length`	No	No	An integer equal to the number of characters in the string; once created, it is unchanging.

Method Name	Arguments	Return	Description
`toString()`	`this`	string value	Returns this String value. Note that the toString method is not generic.
`charAt(pos)`	number	string value	Returns character number pos in the string as a string value.
`charCodeAt (pos)`	number	Number	Returns a non negative number that represents, according to Unicode, the character at position pos, else NaN.
`indexOf (searchString, position)`	`string, number`	Index of rightmost character; -1	Searches string for the next substring, `searchstring` to the right of position pos. Returns index position, or −1 if string is not found. Default position is 0.
`lastIndexOf (searchString, position)`	`string, number`	Index of leftmost character; -1	Searches string for the nearest substring, `searchstring`, to the left of position pos. Returns index position, or −1 if string is not found. Default position is 0.

Method Name	Arguments	Return	Description
`split (separator)`	`string`	Array object containing substrings.	Splits a string, left to right, by each instance of the `separator`, which are not included in the resulting array. If separator = `'empty string'`, then returns array containing one character per array element, and of a `length` equal to the `length` of the string.
`substring (start)`	`number`	string value	Returns a string value beginning at character `start` and running to end of string. If start is NaN or negative, then begins at pos 0.
`substring (start, end)`	`number, number`	string value	Returns a string value of the characters between start and end positions. Will be reversed if `start>end`; treated as 0 if negative or NaN; as string length if larger than string.
`toLowerCase()`	`this`	string value	Converts entire string to lowercase string value
`toUpperCase()`	`this`	string value	Converts entire string to uppercase string value.
`valueOf()`	`this`	string value	Returns the string, else runtime error if not a String object.

Boolean

The Boolean object can be seen as a 'wrapper' for a simple Boolean value. When created, the value of the boolean becomes essentially an implicit, unnamed, property of the object

Property Name	Read/Write?	Enumerable?	Description
`Boolean (value)`	Yes	No	returns a boolean value computed by `toBoolean(value)`

Method Name	Arguments	Return	Description
`toString()`	`this`	"true" or "false"	Returns a string "true" if `true`, "false" if `false`.
`valueOf()`	`this`	`true` or `false`	Returns value of object; generates a runtime error if not a Boolean object

Number

Like the String and Boolean objects, the Number object is primarily a wrapper, although it has a number of in built properties that represent significant values for ECMAScript.

Property Name	Read/Write?	Enumerable?	Description
MAX_VALUE	No	No	The largest possible value, approx $1.7976931348623157e^{308}$
MIN_VALUE	No	No	The smallest positive non-zero value, approx $5e^{-324}$
NaN	No	No	Value is NaN
NEGATIVE _INFINITY	No	No	Value is $-\infty$
POSITIVE _INFINITY	No	No	Value is $+\infty$

Method Name	Arguments	Returns	Description
toString()	radix	See description	If radix is 10 or not supplied, then a toString opration is carried out; if another integer from 2 to 36, the result is an implementation dependent string.
valueOf()	this	Number object	Gives error if not a number.

Math

The Math object is unusual in that essentially it provides a number of useful mathematical operations that are accessible through the Math object.

Property Name	Read/Write?	Enumerable?	Description
E	No	No	The number value for e, base of the natural logarithms. Approx 2.7182818284590452354
LN10	No	No	Number value of the natural log of 10, approx. 2.302585092994046.
LN2	No	No	Number value of the natural log of 2, approx 0.6931471805599453
LOG2E	No	No	Number value of the base-2 logarithm of 2, which is approx 1.4426950408889634

Property Name	Read/Write?	Enumerable?	Description
LOG10E	No	No	Number value of the base-10 logarithm, which is approx `0.4342944819032518`
PI	No	No	The number value for π (ratio of a circle's circumference to its diameter); approx `3.14159265358979323846`
SQRT1_2	No	No	The value for the square root of ½, which is approx. `0.7071067811865476`
SQRT2	No	No	The number value of the square root of 2, which is approx `1.4142135623730951`

Note that every method of the Math object first carries out a `toNumber()` operation on each of the arguments, then performs a computation on the resulting value(s). For familiar expressions (eg acos, asin etc) the implementor will use available mathematical libraries, such as those available to C programmers. ECMAScript recommends the use of the freely downloadable Maths library `fdlibm`.

Method Name	Arguments	Values	Description
abs()	x	absolute number	Returns the absolute value of x; in general, has the same magnitude as the value but a positive sign
acos()	x	Number in radians	Approximates the inverse cosine of the argument; expressed in radians.
asin()	x	Number in radians	Approximates the inverse sine of the argument; expressed in radians
atan()	x	Number in radians	Approximates the inverse tan of the argument; expressed in radians
atan2()	y, x	Number in radians	Returns the inverse tan of the quotient y/x where the argument signs determine the quadrant of the result.
ceil()	x	Integer number	Returns the smallest mathematical integer larger than x. If x is already an integer, then equal to x.
cos()	x	Number in radians	Gives an implementation-dependent approximation of the cosine of the argument.

Table Continued on Following Page

Method Name	Arguments	Values	Description
exp()	x	Number value	Returns an approximation of e to the power x.
floor()	x	Number value	Returns the greatest mathematical integer smaller than x. If x is already an integer, then return is equal to x.
log()	x	Number value	Approximates the natural logarithm of x.
max()	x, y	x or y	Returns the larger of the two arguments.
min()	x, y	x or y	Returns the smaller of the two arguments.
pow()	x, y	x^y	Returns x to the power y
random()	None	Number value	Returns a randomly generated number greater than or equal to 0, less than 1.
round()	x	Integer	Returns the closest integer to the argument; rounds up if two are equally close. If x is an integer, then return = x
sin()	x	Number in radians	Gives an implementation-dependent approximation of the sine of the argument.
sqrt()	x	Number value	Returns an approximation of the square root of the argument.
tan()	x	Number value	Gives an implementation-dependent approximation of the tan of the argument.

Date

The Date object contains a number that represents a given time in milliseconds, relative to Midnight, January 1st, 1970. Readers are referred to the ECMAScript standard for full details of the operations carried out to convert this number to specific dates and times under implementations of ECMAScript. Note that Months are represented by an integer from 0 to 11, inclusive, with 0 being January and 11 being December. Days of the week are integers from 0 to 6, with 0 being Sunday and 6 being Saturday. Note that UTC is Universal Coordinated Time, or GMT.

Property Name	Read/Write?	Enumerable?	Description
length	No	No	Initial value is 7

Method Name	Arguments	Return	Description
parse(*string*)			
UTC(*year,* [*month,* [*date,* [*hours,* [*minutes,* [*seconds, ms*]]]]])		Number	Creates a date value in UTC, rather than a local time date. Note that arguments can not be 'skipped', and that if date or larger unit is omitted (e.g. month, year) then result is implementation dependent.
toString()		String	Implementation dependent, but intended to return a human readable time value. Not generic
getTime()	Value stored in Date object.	time value	Returns the time value of the object
getYear()	Value stored in Date object.	19xx	Specified only for backward compatibilty; returns two digit year.
getFullYear()	Value stored in Date object.	xxxx	Returns four digit year in human readable form. Based on local time
getUTCFullYear()	Value stored in Date object.	xxxx	As above; based on UTC.
getMonth()	Value stored in Date object.	0-11	Calculates month, based on local time
getUTCMonth()	Value stored in Date object.	0-11	Calculates month, based on UTC.
getDate()	Value stored in Date object.	1-31	Calculates date, based on local time.
getUTCDate()	Value stored in Date object.	1-31	Calculates date, based on UTC.
getDay()	Value stored in Date object.	0-6	Calculates day, based on local time.
getUTCDay()	Value stored in Date object.	0-6	Calculates day, based on UTC.
getHours()	Value stored in Date object.	0-23	Calculates hour, based on local time
getUTCHours()	Value stored in Date object.	0-23	Calculates hour, based on UTC time

Table Continued on Following Page

Method Name	Arguments	Return	Description
getMinutes()	Value stored in Date object.	0-59	Returns number of minutes past the hour according to local time.
getUTCMinutes()	Value stored in Date object.	0-59	Returns number of minutes past the hour according to UTC time.
getSeconds()	Value stored in Date object.	0-59	Returns number of seconds past the minute according to local time.
getUTCSeconds()	Value stored in Date object.	0-59	Returns number of seconds past the minute according to UTC time.
getMilliseconds()	Value stored in Date object.	0-999	Returns number of milliseconds past the minute according to local time.
getUTCMilliseconds ()	Value stored in Date object.	0-999	Returns number of milliseconds past the minute according to UTC time.
getTimezoneOffset( )		Integer	Returns difference between UTC time and local time in minutes.
setTime(*time*)	time	time	sets Date object's value to specified time
setMilliseconds (*ms*)	integer	date value(integer)	Sets Date object's value to specified milliseconds, local time
setUTCMilliseconds (*ms*)	integer	date value(integer)	Sets Date object's value to specified milliseconds, UTC
setSeconds (*sec*[,*ms*])	integer,	date value(integer)	Sets Date object's value to specified seconds and milliseconds, local time.
setUTCSeconds (*sec*[,*ms*])	integer	date value(integer)	Sets Date object's value to specified seconds, UTC.
setMinutes (*min*[,*sec*[,*ms*]])	integer	date value(integer)	Sets Date object's value to specified minutes, local time.
setUTCMinutes (*min*[,*sec*[,*ms*]])	integer	date value(integer)	Sets Date object's value to specified minutes, UTC.

Method Name	Arguments	Return	Description
setHours (*hour*[,*min*[,*sec*[,*ms*]]])	integer	date value(integer)	Sets Date object's value to specified minutes, local time
setUTCHours (*hour* [,*min*[,*sec*[,*ms*]]])	integer	date value(integer)	Sets Date object's value to specified minutes, UTC
setDate (*date*)	integer	date value(integer)	Sets Date object's value to specified date, local time
setUTCDate (*date*)	integer	date value(integer)	Sets Date object's value to specified date, UTC
setMonth (*mon*[, *date*])	integer	date value(integer)	Sets Date object's value to specified month, local time
setUTCMonth (*mon*[,*date*])	integer	date value(integer)	Sets Date object's value to specified month, UTC
setFullYear (*year*[,*mon*[,*date*]])	integer	date value(integer)	Sets Date object's value to specified full year, local time
setUTCFullYear (*year*[,*mon*[,*date*]])	integer	date value(integer)	Sets Date object's value to specified full year, UTC
setYear (*year*)	integer	date value(integer)	Sets Date object's value to specified year, local time, two digits. Deprecated.
toLocaleString ()	value of Date object	string	Returns a human readable string based on local time & representation. Implementation dependent.
toUTCString ()	value of Date object	string	Returns a human readable string based on UTC.
toGMTString ()	value of Date object	string	Returns a human readable string based on GMT (Included for backward compatability)

Note that for set methods, where optional arguments (such as [s]) are omitted, they are retrieved using the appropriate get method.

Core Language Enhancements

The headings in this section match those of Appendix A. JavaScript vendors can't leave the language alone; they have to add features. This section describes those features. Host objects are covered in later sections.

Script Formatting and Comments

Microsoft supports a special formatting comment, @cc, or conditional compilation. This allows the use of new JScript language features without sacrificing compatibility with browsers that don't support them.

Keywords	Description
@cc_on	Activates conditional compilation support.
@if, @elif, @end	Conditionally executes a group of statements.
@set	Allows creation of variables used in conditional compilation statements.

JavaScript Objects

The following predefined variables are available for conditional compilation. If a variable is not true, it is not defined and behaves as NaN when accessed.

Variable	Behavior
@_win32	true if running on a win32 system
@_win16	true if running on a win16 system
@_mac	true if running on an Apple Macintosh system
@_alpha	true if running on a Dec Alpha processor
@_x86	true if running on an Intel processor
@_mc680x0	true if running on a Motorola 680x0 processor
@_PowerPC	true if running on a Motorola PowerPC
@_jscript	Always true
@_jscript_build	Contains the build number of the JScript scripting engine.
@_jscript_version	Contains the JScript version number in major.minor format.

Operators and Expressions

JScript Identity Operators

In addition to the ECMAScript compliant comparison operators, JScript also adds the following comparators:

Operator type	Operators	Evaluation order for like elements
identity operators	===, !==	left to right

These operators behave identically to the equality operators except that no type conversion is done, and the types must be the same to be considered equal.

Support for Regular Expressions

Both JScript and JavaScript provide support for string searches by regarding both regular expressions and strings as objects, providing them with properties and methods as with other objects.

The JScript RegularExpression Object

Regular Expression objects store patterns used when searching strings for character combinations. After the Regular Expression object is created, it is either passed to a string method, or a string is passed to one of the regular expression methods. Information about the most recent search performed is stored in the RegExp object.

Unlike other objects, this can be created in two ways with the following pieces of syntax:

```
var regularexpression = /pattern/
var regularexpression = /pattern/switch
```

or

```
var regularexpression = new RegExp("pattern")
var regularexpression = new RegExp("pattern","switch")
```

"Pattern" denotes the expression string you want to search for, and is obligatory. Switch is optional and denotes the type of search you wish to conduct. Available switches are:

- ❑ **i** (ignore case)
- ❑ **g** (global search for all occurrences of pattern)
- ❑ **gi** (global search, ignore case)

The RegularExpression object has four properties and three methods, as follows:

Property	Description
global	Boolean value denoting whether the global switch (g) has been used.
ignorecase	Boolean value denoting whether the ignore case (i) switch has been used.
lastIndex	Specifies the index point form which to begin the next match.
source	Contains the text of the regular expression pattern.

Method	Description	Return Values	Required Arguments
compile	Compiles a string expression (containing a regular expression pattern) into an internal format.	(internal conversion)	pattern
exec	Searches for a match in the specified string.	null or array	string
test	Tests whether a pattern exists in a string.	boolean	string

The JScript RegExp Object

The RegExp object stores information on regular expression pattern searches. It cannot be created directly—only as a side effect as using the RegularExpression object—but is always available for use. Its properties have undefined as their value until a successful regular expression search has been completed.

The `RegExp` object has nine properties and no methods:

Property	Description
`index`	Returns the beginning position of the first successful match in a searched string.
`input`	Contains the string against which a search was performed. Read-only Also written as `$_` instead of `input`
`lastindex`	Returns where the last successful match begins in a string that was searched.
`lastmatch`	Returns the last matched characters. Read-only. Also written as `$&` instead of `lastmatch`
`lastParen`	Returns the last substring match within parentheses, if any. Read-only. Also written as `$+` instead of `lastParen`
`leftContext`	Returns the input string up to the most recent match. Read-only Also written as ``$` `` instead of `leftContext`
`multiline`	Boolean value specifying whether searching continued across line breaks. Read-only. Also written as `$*` instead of `multiline`
`rightContext`	Returns the input string past the most recent match. Read-only. Also written as `$'` instead of `rightContext`
`$1, $2, ...` `$9`	Returns the nine most-recently memorized strings found during pattern matching. Read-only

The JavaScript RegExp Object

While JavaScript expresses the concept of regular expressions as a single object called `RegExp`, JScript uses two objects, `RegExp` and `RegularExpression` to implement the idea. The JavaScript `RegExp` object uses all the methods and properties that apply to both the JScript objects, and the syntax is also the same.

Regular Expression Syntax

Special characters and sequences are used in writing patterns for regular expressions. The following table details them and includes short examples showing how the characters are used.

Character	Description
`\`	Marks the next character as special. `/n/` matches the character "n". The sequence `/\n/` matches a linefeed or newline character.
`^`	Matches the beginning of the input or line.
`$`	Matches the end of the input or line.

Character	Description
`*`	Matches the preceding character zero or more times. `/zo*/` matches "z" and "zoo."
`+`	Matches the preceding characters one or more times. `/zo+/` matches "zoo" but not "z."
`?`	Matches the preceding character zero or one time. `/a?ve?/` matches the "ve" in "never."
`.`	Matches any single character except a newline character.
`(pattern)`	Matches *pattern* and remembers the match. The matched substring can be retrieved from the resulting Array object elements `[1]...[n]` or the RegExp object's `$1...$9` properties. To match parentheses characters, `()`, use `"\("` or `"\)"`.
`x|y`	Matches either x or y. `/z|food?/` matches "zoo" or "food".
`{n}`	n is a nonnegative integer. Matches exactly n times. `/o{2}/` does not match the "o" in "Bob", but matches the first two o's in "foooood".
`{n,}`	n is a nonnegative integer. Matches at least n times. `/o{2,}/` does not match the "o" in "Bob" and matches all the o's in "fooooood." `/o{1,}/` is equivalent to `/o+/`.
`{n,m}`	m and n are nonnegative integers. Matches at least n and at most m times. `/o{1,3}/` matches the first three o's in "fooooood".
`[xyz]`	A character set. Matches any one of the enclosed characters. `/[abc]/` matches the "a" in "plain".
`[^xyz]`	A negative character set. Matches any character not enclosed. `/[^abc]/` matches the "p" in "plain".
`[\b]`	Matches a backspace (JavaScript only)
`\b`	Matches a word boundary, such as a space. `/ea*r\b/` matches the "er" in "never early".
`\B`	Matches a nonword boundary. `/ea*r\B/` matches the "ear" in "never early".
`\cX`	Where X is a control character. Matches a control character in a string. For example, `/\cM/` matches control-M in a string. (JavaScript only)
`\d`	Matches a digit character. Equivalent to `[0-9]`.
`\D`	Matches a nondigit character. Equivalent to `[^0-9]`.
`\f`	Matches a form-feed character.
`\n`	Matches a linefeed character.
`\r`	Matches a carriage return character.

Table Continued on Following Page

Character	Description
\s	Matches any white space including space, tab, form-feed, and so forth. Equivalent to `[\f\n\r\t\v]`
\S	Matches any nonwhite space character. Equivalent to `[^\f\n\r\t\v]`
\t	Matches a tab character.
\v	Matches a vertical tab character.
\w	Matches any word character including underscore. Equivalent to `[A-Za-z0-9_]`.
\W	Matches any nonword character. Equivalent to `[^A-Za-z0-9_]`.
\num	Matches num, where num is a positive integer. A reference back to remembered matches. `\1` matches what is stored in `RegExp.$1`.
/n/	Matches n, where n is an octal, hexadecimal, or decimal escape value. Allows embedding of ASCII codes into regular expressions. (JScript only)
\o octal \x hex	Where `\o octal` is an octal escape value or `\x hex` is a hexadecimal escape value. Allows you to embed ASCII codes into regular expressions.

Statements and Control Flow

This is a short guide to the non-standard statements used in browser implementations of JavaScript. Except where stated, JavaScript commands are valid for Navigator 2.0 onwards and the most recent implementations of JScript.

break (JavaScript, JScript)

The break statement is available in both JavaScript and JScript. It terminates the current while or for loop and transfers program control to the statement following the terminated loop. If a label is used in conjunction with the break, it will terminate the associated label. The syntax for both JScript and JavaScript is:

```
break [label]
```

The optional label argument specifies the label of the statement you are breaking from.

As an example, this simple function breaks out of the loop when the loop count reaches 3, and returns x times 3:

```
function testBreak(x)
{
var i = 0
   while (i < 6) {
   if (i == 3)
      break
```

```
        i++
      }
    return i*x
  }
```

continue (JavaScript, JScript)

Statement that terminates execution of the block of statements in a `while` or `for` loop, but, unlike `break`, continues execution of the loop with the next iteration. The syntax for both JScript and JavaScript is:

```
continue [label]
```

As with `break`, `label` is an optional argument that transfers the effect of the `continue` statement to the appropriate labeled statement.

do...while (JavaScript, JScript)

Carries out the statement until the test condition evaluates to `false`. The statement is always carried out at least once. Syntax is:

```
do
    statement
while(condition)
```

export (JavaScript)

Allows a signed script to provide properties, functions, and objects to all other signed or unsigned scripts-used for establishing security. The receiving script uses the equivalent, `import`.

```
export name1, name2, ..., nameN
export *
```

The `nameN` parameters supply the names of properties, functions, objects etc to be exported; `*` makes all the script's properties, functions and objects available.

for...in (JavaScript, JScript)

Statement that iterates a specified variable over all the properties of an object (or array, in JScript). For each distinct property, JavaScript executes the specified statements. Note that you cannot control the order in which the statement runs through the properties.

```
for (variable in object | array)
    statement
```

`variable` is the number to be assigned to each element of the object, `object|array` is the object or array to be affected and `statement` (which may be a compound statement).

import (JavaScript)

Allows a script to import properties, functions, and objects from a signed script which has exported the information. Syntax and parameters are similar, but not identical, to those of `export`:

```
import object.name1, object.name2,… object.nameN
import object.*
```

`object` is the object that will hold the names; * will import all the elements of the object.

labeled (JavaScript, Jscript)

Provides an identifier that can be referred to by `break` or `continue` to indicate whether or not the program should continue execution. Syntax is:

```
label :
     statement
```

`statement` can be a block of statements.

switch (JavaScript, JScript)

Allows a program to evaluate an expression and attempt to match the expression's value to one of several case labels. Syntax is:

```
switch (expression)
{
case label :
   statement;
   break;
case label :
   statement;
   break;
   ...
default : statement;
}
```

`expression` is the statement to be evaluated; `label` is the possible result the expression is to be evaluated against. If (and only if) `label` exactly matches the expression result (without a type conversion) then `statement` (which may be a series of statements) will be carried out. `break` is optional, but can be used to jump straight out of the case cycle. `default` is also optional; if it is present, it will be applied if the expression is not matched, but otherwise the program will simply move onto the statements following the `switch`.

while (JavaScript, JScript)

The `while` statement creates a loop that evaluates a boolean expression, and if it is `true`, executes a block of statements. Syntax is:

```
while (expression)
{
   statements
}
```

`expression` is the boolean function to be examined; `statements` are the statements to be carried out until `expression` is false.

Scope, functions and methods

caller (JScript)

The `caller` property of a function contains a reference to the function that invoked the current function. It is described as `functionname.caller`. It is only defined for a function while that function is executing. If the function is called from the top level of a JScript program, caller contains `null`.

Native Objects

JScript Extra Date Methods

Method	Decsription	Required Arguments
getVarDate	Returns the VT_DATE value stored in the Date object.	`date.getVarDate( )`

JScript Array Handling

In addition to the normal array handling methods, there are two additional methods which apply to all arrays. They are as follows:

Method	Description	Required Arguments
concat	Combines two arrays to create a new array.	`array1.concat(array2)`
slice	Returns a section of an array.	`array1.slice(start)`
		`array1.slice(start,end)`

The VBArray Object (JScript)

JScript also provides support for a new kind of object. A **VBArray** provides access to Visual Basic safe arrays. They are read-only, and cannot be created directly. The safeArray argument must have obtained a VBArray value before being passed to the VBArray constructor. This can only be done by retrieving the value from an existing ActiveX or other object.

VBArrays can have multiple dimensions. The indices of each dimension can be different. This object has five methods associated with it.

Method	Description	Required Arguments
dimensions	Returns the number of dimensions in a VBArray	`array.dimensions()`
getItem	Retrieves the item at the specified location	`Array.getItem` `(dimension1,..., dimn)`

Table Continued on Following Page

Method	Description	Required Arguments
`lbound`	Returns the lowest index value used in the specified dimension of a VBArray.	`Array.lbound()` `Array.lbound(dimension)`
`toArray`	Converts a VBArray to a standard JScript array.	`safeArray.toArray( )`
`ubound`	Returns the highest index value used in the specified dimension of the VBArray.	`Array.ubound()` `Array.ubound(dimension)`

JScript and Javascript String Handling

In addition to the ECMA-compliant string object methods in both the major implementations of JavaScript, there are a number of extra methods existing in both JScript and JavaScript which can be divided into the following categories:

String Addition and Subtraction

Identical in name to the array methods, `concat` and `slice` also apply to strings.

Method	Description	Required Arguments
`concat`	Combines two strings to create a new string.	`string1.concat(string2)`
`slice`	Returns a section of a string.	`string1.slice(start)` `string1.slice(start,end)`

String Searches and Regular Expressions

Three methods—`match`, `replace` and `search`—can be used to formulate searches for regular expressions within strings.

Method	Description	Required Arguments
`match`	Executes a search on a string object using the supplied Regular Expression object.	`stringObj.match` `_(RegExp)`

`replace`	Replaces the text found matching a regular expression within a string with some other text.	`stringObj.match`
		`_(RegExp,`
		`_newText)`

`search`	Searches a string for matches to a regular expression.	`stringObj.search` `_(RegExp)`

HTML Creation

The following methods take a text string and then surround it with certain HTML tags.

Method	Description	Required Arguments
anchor	Puts a named HTML anchor around the string text. Returns strVar as `<A NAME="aname">`strVar`</A>`	`Text = Text.anchor(aname)`
big	Puts HTML `<big>` tags around text in the string. Returns Text as `<big>`Text`</big>`	`Text=Text.big( )`
blink	Puts HTML `<blink>` tags around the string text. Returns Text as `<blink>`Text`</blink>`	`Text=Text.blink( )`
bold	Puts HTML `<b>` tags around the string text. Returns Text as `<b>`Text`</b>`	`Text=Text.bold( )`
fixed	Puts HTML `<tt>` tags around the string text. Returns Text as `<tt>`Text`</tt>`	`Text=Text.fixed( )`
fontcolor	Puts colored font tags around the string text. Returns `<font color="fcolor">`Text`</font>`	`Text = Text.fontcolor _("fcolor")`
fontsize	Puts 'sized' font tag around the string text. Returns `<font size='fsize'>`Text`</font>`	`Text.fontsize(fsize)`
italics	Puts HTML `<i>` tags around the string text. Returns Text as `<i>`Text`</i>`	`Text=Text.italics( )`
link	Puts a set of site link tags around the string text. Returns Text as `<A HREF="linkedsite">`Text`</A>`	`Text = Text.link("linke _dsite")`
small	Puts HTML `<SMALL>` tags around the string text. Returns Text as `<SMALL>`Text`</SMALL>`	`Text=Text.small( )`
strike	Puts HTML `<STRIKE>` tags around the string text. Returns Text as `<STRIKE>`Text`</STRIKE>`	`Text=Text.strike( )`
sub	Puts HTML `<SUB>` tags around the string text. Returns Text as `<SUB>`Text`</SUB>`	`Text=Text.sub( )`
sup	Puts HTML `<SUP>` tags around the string text. Returns Text as `<SUP>`Text`</SUP>`	`Text=Text.sup( )`

None of the above methods check to see if the tag has already been applied to the string.

The Enumerator Object (JScript)

Collection members are not immediately accessible. Rather than using array indices, you can only select first or next element of a collection. The JScript Enumerator object provides a way to access any member of a collection.

It has the following four methods:

Method	Description
atEnd()	Returns a Boolean value indicating if the enumerator is at the end of the collection.
item()	Returns the current item in the collection.
moveFirst()	Resets the current item in the collection to the first item.
moveNext()	Moves the current item to the next item in the collection.

JScript ScriptEngine Functions

As a refinement/replacement of the 'language' property which JavaScript uses to return whether a piece of script or applet is written in JavaScript or JScript, Microsoft's scripting language contains four functions which can access a little more detail:

Function	Description	Returns
ScriptEngine	Returns a string representing the scripting language in use.	JScript, VBA or VBScript
ScriptEngineBuild Version	Returns the build version number of the scripting engine in use	For these three functions, the return value corresponds directly to the version information contained in the DLL for the scripting language in use.
ScriptEngineMajor Version	Returns the major version number of the scripting engine in use	
ScriptEngineMinor Version	Returns the minor version number of the scripting engine in use	

The Browser Object Model

The Browser Object Model offers a very useful resource for accessing the properties of the client browser with JavaScript. The diagram below is, strictly, for IE4. However, it shares its basic structure with the Navigator browser object model.

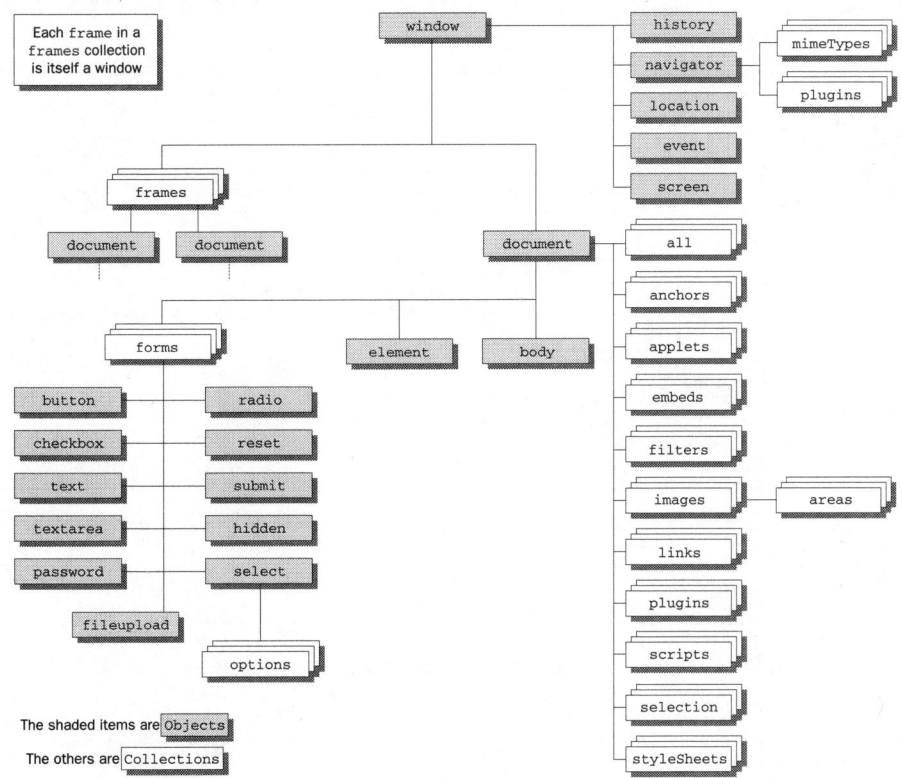

Browser Object Table

This is by no means a complete listing; full details of a browser's Object Models can usually be found in their SDKs. Note that in particular, because of its DOM compliance, IE4 can treat almost all HTML tags as individual objects, and the scriptwriter can access these.

Objects	Browser?	Description
A	IE4	An object that represents an anchor created with `<A NAME="..">` in the document.
area		An area created within a `<MAP>` element by an `<AREA>` tag.
button		An object that represents a control created with an `<INPUT>` tag where `TYPE=BUTTON`.
checkbox	NC	An object that represents a control created with an `<INPUT>` tag where `TYPE=CHECKBOX`.
document		Exposes the contents of the HTML document through a number of arrays and properties.
element	NC4	An object that represents a control in the array of all the controls on a `<FORM>`.
event		The global event object exposed for accessing an event's parameters.
fileUpload	NC	An object that represents a control created with an `<INPUT>` tag where `TYPE=FILE`.
form		An object that represents the section of a page contained within a `<FORM>` tag.
frame		An object that represents a `<FRAME>` within a `<FRAMESET>`.
hidden	NC	An object that represents a control created with an `<INPUT>` tag where `TYPE=HIDDEN`.
history		Contains information on the URLs that the client has visited.
image		An object that represents an element created with an `<IMG>` tag.
layer		An object that represents a `<LAYER>` or `<ILAYER>` in a document.
link		An object that represents a link created in the page with an `<A HREF="..">` tag.
location		Contains information about the current URL being displayed.
mimeType		Contains information about the MIME types supported by the browser.
navigator		An object representing the browser itself, and its properties.
option		An individual `<OPTION>` item in a list created by a `<SELECT>` tag.
password	NC4	An object that represents a control created with an `<INPUT>` tag where `TYPE=PASSWORD`.
plugin	NC4	An object that represents the features of an installed plugin component.

Objects	Browser?	Description
radio	NC4	An object that represents a control created with an `<INPUT>` tag where `TYPE=RADIO`.
reset	NC4	An object that represents a control created with an `<INPUT>` tag where `TYPE=RESET`.
screen		Contains information about the client's screen and rendering abilities.
select	NC4	An object that represents a list control created with a `<SELECT>` tag.
StyleSheet	IE4	Exposes all the styles within a single style sheet in the styleSheets collection.
submit	NC4	An object that represents a control created with an `<INPUT>` tag where `TYPE=SUBMIT`.
text	NC4	An object that represents a control created with an `<INPUT>` tag where `TYPE=TEXT`.
textarea		An object that represents a text area control created with a `<TEXTAREA>` tag.
TextRange	IE4	Represents sections of the text stream making up the HTML document.
window		An object that provides information about the current browser window.

JavaScript Universal Properties and Methods

These properties and methods apply to all objects within the model, since they all apply to the primitive `Object` object.

Property	Description
name	Specifies the name to use to refer to the anchor.

Methods	Description	Required Arguments
eval	Evaluates a string of JavaScript code in the context of the specified object	eval(string)
toString	Returns a string representing the specified object	toString() toString(i) where $2 \leq i \leq 16$
valueOf	Returns the primitive value of the specified object	valueOf()
watch	Watches for a property to be assigned a value and runs a function when that occurs	watch(property)
unwatch	Removes a watchpoint from a property of the object	unwatch(property)

Notes : `eval` *was removed as a method of objects in Navigator 4, but retained as a global function, as specified in ECMAScript*

The ActiveXObject Object (IE)

Enables and returns a reference to an automation object.

No properties or methods.

The Applet Object (Navigator 3+,IE)

Includes a Java applet in a web page.

Has all the properties and methods of a Java applet.

The Area Object (Navigator 3+,IE)

Defines an area of an image as an image map. When the user clicks the area, the area's hypertext reference is loaded into its target window. `Area` objects are a type of `Link` object.

Properties	Description
hash	The string following the **#** symbol, the anchor name, in the URL
host	The **hostname:port** part of the location or URL.
hostname	The **hostname** part of the location or URL.
href	The destination URL or anchor point.
pathname	The file or object path name following the third slash in a URL.
port	The **port** number in a URL.
protocol	Specifies the beginning of the URL, including the colon.
search	Any query string or form data following the **?** in the complete URL.
target	Specifies the window or frame where the new page will be loaded.
text	A string containing the content of the corresponding **<A>** tag

Methods	Description	Required Arguments
handleEvent	Invokes the appropriate event handling code of the object for this event.	handleEvent(eventName)

The Button Object (Navigator 2+)

Represents a control created with an `<INPUT>` tag where `TYPE=BUTTON`.

Properties	Description
form	Specifies the form that contains the button.
name	Specifies the name to use to refer to the button.
type	Must be "**BUTTON**" for a Button element.
value	The caption of the button.

Methods	Description	Required Arguments
blur	Causes the element to lose the focus, and fires its **onBlur** event.	`blur()`
click	Simulates a click on the element, but does not fire its **onClick** event.	`click()`
focus	Causes the element to receive the focus, and fire its **onFocus** event.	`focus()`
handleEvent	Invokes the appropriate event handling code of object for this event.	`handleEvent(eventName)`

The Checkbox Object (Navigator 2+, IE)

Represents a control created with an `<INPUT>` tag where `TYPE=CHECKBOX`.

Properties	Description
checked	Indicates that the checkbox is selected (i.e. 'on' or ticked).
defaultChecked	Denotes if the checkbox is checked by default.
form	Reference to the form object that contains the element.
name	Specifies the name to use to refer to the checkbox.
type	Must be "**CHECKBOX**" for a Checkbox element.
value	The value of the control when checked.

Methods	Description	Required Arguments
blur	Causes the control to lose the focus, and fire its **onBlur** event.	blur()
click	Simulates a click on the control, and fires its **onClick** event.	click()
focus	Causes the control to receive the focus, and fire its **onFocus** event.	focus()
handleEvent	Invokes the appropriate event handling code of the object for this event.	handleEvent(eventname)

The Document Object

Contains information about the current document, and provides methods for displaying HTML output to the user.

Properties	Description
activeElement	Identifies the element that has the focus
alinkColor	The color for active links in the page - i.e. while the mouse button is held down
anchors	An array containing an entry for each anchor in the document
applets	An array containing an entry for each applet in the document
bgColor	Specifies the background color to be used for an element.
body	Read-only reference to the document's implicit body object, as defined by the `<BODY>` tag
cookie	The string value of a cookie stored by the browser.
domain	Sets or returns the domain of the document that served the document for use in cookies and security
embeds	An array containing an entry for each embedded object in the document
fgColor	Sets the color of the document foreground text
formName(NC4)	A separate property for each named form in the document
forms	An array containing an entry for each form in the document
images	An array containing an entry for each image in the document
lastModified	The date that the source file for the page was last modified, as a string, where available
layers	An array containing an entry for each layer in the document
linkColor	The color for unvisited links in the page
links	An array containing an entry for each link in the document
location	The full URL of the document
parentWindow	Returns the parent window that contains the document.
`plugins`(NC4 only)	An array containing an entry for each plugin in the document
readyState	Specifies the current state of an object being downloaded
referrer	The URL of the page that referenced (loaded) the current page
`selection` (NC4 only)	Read-only reference to the document's selection object.
title	Provides advisory information about the element, such as when loading or as a tooltip, contained in the `<TITLE>` tag.

Method	Description	Required Arguments
url	Uniform Resource Locator (address) for the current document or in a `<META>` tag	captureEvents(eventType)
vlinkColor	The color for visited links in the page	
close	Closes a document forcing written data to be displayed, or closes the browser window	close()
createElement(IE4)	Creates an instance of an image or option element object	
createStylesheet (IE4 only)	Creates a Stylesheet	
elementFromPoint(IE4)	Returns the element at the specified x and y coordinates with respect to the window.	
execCommand(IE4)	Executes a command over the document selection or range	
getSelection	Returns a string currently containing the text selected in the document	getSelection()
handleEvent	Invokes the handler for the specified event	handleEvent(eventName)
open(IE4)	Opens a stream to collect output of `write` or `writeln` methods	open() open(mime-type) open(text/html, replace)
queryCommandEnabled (IE4)	Denotes if the specified command is available for a document or TextRange	
queryCommandIndeterm (IE4)	Denotes if the specified command is in the indeterminate state	
queryCommandState (IE4)	Returns the current state of the command for a document or TextRange object.	
queryCommandSupported (IE4)	Denotes if the specified command is supported for a document or TextRange object	

Method	Description	Required Arguments
`queryCommandValue` (IE4)	Returns the value of the command specified for a document or TextRange object	
`releaseEvents`	Releases an event that has been captured back up through the normal event hierarchy	releaseEvents(eventType)
`routeEvent` (NC4 only)	Passes an event that has been captured back up through the normal event hierarchy	
`write` (IE4)	Writes text and HTML to a document in the specified window	write(expr1, ..., expr N)
`writeln` (IE4)	Writes text and HTML to a document in the specified window, followed by a carriage return	writeln(expr1, ..., expr N)

The Element Object (NC4)

Represents a control in the array of all the controls on a `<FORM>`.

Properties	Description
checked	Indicates that a checkbox or radio element is selected (i.e. 'on' or ticked).
defaultChecked	Denotes if a checkbox or radio element is checked by default.
defaultValue	The text displayed as the initial contents of a text-based control.
form	Reference to the form object that contains the element.
length	Returns the number of elements in an element sub-array.
name	Specifies the name to use to refer to the element.
selectedIndex	An integer specifying the index of the selected option in a `<SELECT>` element.
type	The type of the element, such as **TEXT**, **BUTTON** or **RADIO**.
value	The default value of text/numeric controls, or the value when the control is 'on' for Boolean controls.

Methods	Description	Required Arguments
blur	Causes the element to lose the focus, and fire its **onBlur** event.	blur()

Methods	Description	Required Arguments
click	Simulates a click on the element, and fires its **onClick** event.	click()
focus	Causes the element to receive the focus, and fire its **onFocus** event.	focus()
handleEvent	Invokes the appropriate event handling code of object for this event.	handleEvent(eventName)
select	Highlights the input area of a text-based element.	select()

The Event Object (Navigator 4)

The global object provided to allow the scripting language to access an event's parameters.

Properties	Description
altKey (IE4)	Returns the state of the *Alt* key when an event occurs
button (IE only)	The mouse button, if any, that was pressed to fire the event
cancelBubble (IE only)	Set to prevent the current event from bubbling up the hierarchy
clientX (IE only)	Returns the *x* coordinate of the element, excluding borders, margins, padding, scrollbars, etc
clientY (IE only)	Returns the *y* coordinate of the element, excluding borders, margins, padding, scrollbars, etc
ctrlKey (IE only)	Returns the state of the *Ctrl* key when an event occurs
data	The URLs of the objects dropped onto the Navigator window, as an array of strings
fromElement (IE only)	Returns the element being moved from for an **onmouseover** or **onmouseout** event
height	Represents the height of the window or frame
keyCode (IE only)	ASCII code of the key being pressed. Changing it sends a different character to the object.
layerX (NC)	Horizontal position of the mouse pointer in pixels in relation to the containing layer. **layerX** is synonymous with *x*
layerY (NC)	Vertical position of the mouse pointer in pixels in relation to the containing layer. **layerY** is synonymous with *y*
modifiers (NC)	String containing the names of the keys held down for a key-press event. Modifier key values are: ALT_MASK, CONTROL_MASK, SHIFT_MASK, and META_MASK.

Properties	Description
offsetX (IE only)	Returns the *x* coordinate of the mouse pointer when an event occurs, relative to the containing element
offsetY (IE only)	Returns the *y* coordinate position of the mouse pointer when an event occurs, relative to the containing element
pageX (NC)	Horizontal position in pixels of the mouse pointer or a layer in relation to the page
pageY (NC)	Vertical position in pixels of the mouse pointer or a layer in relation to the page
reason (IE)	Indicates whether data transfer to an element was successful, or why it failed
returnValue (IE)	Allows a return value to be specified for the event or a dialog window
screenX (NC)	Returns the *x* coordinate of the mouse pointer when an event occurs, in relation to the screen
screenY (NC)	Returns the *y* coordinate of the mouse pointer when an event occurs, in relation to the screen
shiftKey (IE)	Returns the state of the *Shift* key when an event occurs
srcElement (IE)	Returns the element deepest in the object hierarchy that a specified event occurred over
srcFilter (IE)	Returns the filter that caused the element to produce an onfilterchange event
target	The name of the object where the event was originally sent
toElement (IE)	Returns the element being moved to for an onmouseover or onmouseout event
type (NC)	Returns the name of the event as a string, without the 'on' prefix, such as 'click' instead of 'onclick'
which (IE)	ASCII value of a key that was pressed, or indicates which mouse button was clicked
width (IE)	Represents the width of the window or frame
x (IE)	Returns the *x* coordinate of the mouse pointer relative to a positioned parent, or otherwise to the window
y (IE)	Returns the *y* coordinate of the mouse pointer relative to a positioned parent, or otherwise to the window

The FileUpload Object (Navigator 2+)

Represents a control created with an <INPUT> tag where TYPE=FILE

Properties	Description
form	Reference to the form object that contains the element.

Properties	Description
name	Specifies the name to use to refer to the element.
type	Must be "**FILE**" for a FileUpload element.
value	The text value of the control. i.e. The name of the file to upload.

Methods	Description	Required Arguments
blur	Causes the element to lose the focus, and fire its **onBlur** event.	blur()
focus	Causes the element to receive the focus, and fire its **onFocus** event.	focus()
handleEvent	Invokes the appropriate event handling code of object for this event.	handleEvent(eventName)
select	Selects the input area of the file upload field.	select()

The Form Object (Navigator 2+)

Represents the section of a page contained within a <FORM> tag.

Properties	Description
action	The URL where the form is to be sent.
elements	An array reflecting all the elements in a form.
encoding	Defines the type of mime-encoding to be used when submitting the form.
length	Returns the number of elements in the form.
method	How the form data should be sent to the server; either **GET** or **POST**.
name	Specifies the name to use to refer to the form.
target	Specifies the window or frame where the return page will be loaded.

Methods	Description	Required Arguments
handleEvent	Invokes the appropriate event handling code of object for this event.	handleEvent(eventName)
reset	Simulates a mouse click on a **RESET** button in the form.	reset()
submit	Submits the form, as when the **SUBMIT** button is clicked.	submit()

The Frame Object (Navigator 2+)

Represents a <FRAME> within a <FRAMESET>. Every frame object is also the same as a window object and has the same properties and methods. See 'Window Object' for this list.

The Hidden Object (Navigator 2+)

Represents a control created with an `<INPUT>` tag where `TYPE=HIDDEN`

Properties	Description
form	Specifies the form containing the hidden object
name	Specifies the name to use to refer to the element
type	Must be "`HIDDEN`" for a Hidden element
value	Reflects the current value of the hidden object

The History Object (Navigator 2+)

Contains information about the URLs that the client has visited, as stored in the browser's History list, and allows the script to move through the list.

Properties	Description
current	The current item in the browser's history list
length	Returns the number of elements in the history list
next	Refers to the next item in the browser's history list
previous	Refers to the previous item in the browser's history list

Methods	Description	Required Arguments
back	Loads the previous URL in the browser's History list	back()
forward	Loads the next URL in the browser's History list	forward()
go	Loads a specified URL from the browser's History list	go(part of url in history list) go(number in history list)

The Image Object (Navigator 3+)

Represents an element created with an `<IMG>` tag.

Properties	Description
border	Specifies the border to be drawn around the image.
complete	Indicates if the image has completed loading.
height	Sets the height for the image in pixels.
hspace	The horizontal spacing between the image and its neighbors.
lowsrc	Specifies the URL of a lower resolution image to display.

Properties	Description
name	Specifies the name to use to refer to the image.
prototype	Allows the addition of properties to an image object
src	An external file that contains the source data for the image.
vspace	The vertical spacing between the image and its neighbors.
width	Sets the width for the image in pixels.

Methods	Description	Required Arguments
handleEvent	Invokes the appropriate event handling code of object for this event.	`handleEvent(eventName)`

The Layer Object (Navigator 4)

Corresponds to a layer in an HTML document created by a `<LAYER>` or an `<ILAYER>` tag.

Properties	Description
above	Indicates that the layer should be above another element in the z-order of the page, or returns the element above it.
background	URL of an image to display behind the elements in the layer.
below	Indicates that the layer should be below another element in the z-order of the page, or returns the element below it.
bgColor	Specifies the background color to be used for the layer.
clip.bottom	Y co-ordinate of the bottom of the clipping rectangle for the layer.
clip.height	Height of the clipping rectangle for the layer.
clip.left	X co-ordinate of the left of the clipping rectangle for the layer.
clip.right	X co-ordinate of the right of the clipping rectangle for the layer.
clip.top	Y co-ordinate of the top of the clipping rectangle for the layer.
clip.width	Width of the clipping for the layer.
document	The layer's associated document.
left	Position in pixels of the left-hand side of the layer in relation to its containing layer or the document.
name	Specifies the name to use to refer to the layer.
pageX	Horizontal position of the mouse pointer in pixels with respect to the layer.
pageY	Vertical position of the mouse pointer in pixels with respect to the layer.
parentLayer	Reference to the layer that contains the current layer.

Properties	Description
siblingAbove	Reference to the layer above the current layer if they share the same parent layer.
siblingBelow	Reference to the layer below the current layer if they share the same parent layer.
src	An external file that contains the source data for the layer.
top	Position of the top of the layer.
visibility	Defines whether the layer should be displayed on the page.
zIndex	Position in the z-order or stacking order of the page, i.e. the z co-ordinate.

Methods	Description	Required Arguments
captureEvents	Instructs the layer to capture all events of a particular type.	captureEvents(eventType)
handleEvent	Invokes the appropriate event handling code of the object for this event.	handleEvent(eventName)
load	Loads a file into a layer, and can change the width of the layer it loads the file into.	load(filename, layerWidth)
moveAbove	Changes the z-order so that the layer is rendered above (overlaps) the specified layer.	moveAbove(aLayer)
moveBelow	Changes the z-order so that the layer is rendered below (covered by) the specified layer.	moveBelow(aLayer)
moveBy	Moves the layer horizontally and vertically by a specified number of pixels.	moveBy(horiz, vert)
moveTo	Moves the layer so that the top left is at a position x, y (in pixels) within its container layer.	moveTo(x,y)
moveToAbsolute	Moves the layer to a position specified in x and y with respect to the page and not the container.	moveToAbsolute(x,y)
releaseEvents	Instructs the layer to stop capturing events of a particular type.	releaseEvents(eventType)
resizeBy	Resizes the layer horizontally and vertically by a specified number of pixels.	resizeBy(width, height)
resizeTo	Resizes the layer to a size specified in x and y (in pixels).	resizeTo(width, height)
routeEvent	Passes an event that has been captured back up through the normal event hierarchy.	routeEvent(eventName)

The Link Object (Navigator 2+)

Represents a link created in the page with an <A HREF='...'> tag.
NB. In general, a URL has this form - `protocol://host:port/pathname#hash?search`

Properties	Description
hash	The string following the # symbol, the anchor name, in the **HREF** value.
host	Specifies the host and domain name, or IP address, of a network host.
hostname	Specifies the host:port portion of the URL.
href	The destination URL or anchor point.
pathname	The file or object path name following the third slash in a URL.
port	The port number in a URL.
protocol	The initial sub-string indicating the URL's access method.
search	Any query string or form data following the ? in the complete URL.
target	Specifies the window or frame where the new page will be loaded.
text	A string containing the content of the corresponding **<A>** tag.

Methods	Description	Required Arguments
handleEvent	Invokes the appropriate event handling code of object for this event.	`handleEvent(eventName)`

The Location Object (Navigator 2+)

Contains information on the current URL. It also provides methods that will reload a page
NB In general, a URL has this form - `protocol://host:port/pathname#hash?search`

Properties	Descriptions
hash	The string following the # symbol in the URL
host	Specifies the host and domain name, or IP address, of a network host.
hostname	Specifies the host:port portion of the URL.
href	The entire URL as a string
pathname	The file or object path name following the third slash in a URL
port	The port number in a URL
protocol	The initial substring up to and including the first colon, indicating the URL's access method
search	The contents of the query string or form data following the ? (question mark) in the complete URL

Methods	Descriptions	Required Arguments
assign (IE only)	Loads another page. Equivalent to changing the `window.location.href` property	
reload	(Forces a) reload of the current page in the window	reload() reload(ForceGet)
replace	Loads the specified URL over the current element in the browser's history list	replace('URL')

The Mime-Type Object (Navigator 3+, IE4)

The object representing a Mime-Type supported by the browser

Properties	Description
description	Returns a description of the MimeType
enabledPlugin	Returns the plug-in that can handle the specified MimeType
suffixes	A list of filename extensions used with the specified MimeType
type (NC4)	The name of the mime-type. e.g. video/mpeg.

The Navigator Object (Navigator 2+, IE)

The object representing the browser itself

Properties	Description
appCodeName	The code name of the browser
appName	The product name of the browser
appVersion	The version of the browser
cookieEnabled (IE4 only)	Indicates if client-side cookies are enabled in the browser
language	Returns the language the browser was compiled for
mimeTypes (NC4)	An array of all the mime types supported by the client
platform (NC4)	Returns the name of the operating system the browser was compiled for
plugins (NC4)	An array of all the plugins loaded in by the client.
userAgent (NC4)	The user-agent (browser name) header sent in the HTTP protocol from the client to the server

Method	Description	Return Values	Required arguments
javaEnabled	Returns True or False, depending on whether a Java VM is installed and enabled	true false	javaEnabled()
preference (NC4)	Allows a signed script to get and set certain Navigator preferences.		preference(prefName) preference(prefName, setValue)
taintEnabled	Specifies whether data tainting is enabled (Navigator 3 only, IE)	true false	taintEnabled()

The Option Object (Navigator 2+)

An individual <OPTION> item in a list created by a <SELECT> tag.

Properties	Description
defaultSelected	Specifies the initial selection state of the option.
index (IE only)	Returns the ordinal position of the option in a list.
length (IE only)	Returns the number of elements in an element sub-array.
selected	Specifies the current selection state of the option.
selectedIndex (IE only)	An integer specifying the index of the selected option in a list.
text	The text displayed for the option.
value	The value returned when the option is selected and the form is submitted.

The Password Object (Navigator 2+)

Represents a control created with an <INPUT> tag where TYPE=PASSWORD

Properties	Description
defaultValue	The text displayed as the initial contents of the control.
form	Reference to the form object that contains the control.
name	Specifies the name to use to refer to the control.
type	Must be 'PASSWORD' for a Password control.
value	The text value of the control.

Methods	Description	Required Arguments
blur	Causes the control to lose the focus, and fire its **onBlur** event.	blur()

Methods	Description	Required Arguments
focus	Causes the control to receive the focus, and fire its **onFocus** event.	focus()
handleEvent	Invokes the appropriate event handling code of object for this event.	handleEvent(eventName)
select	Highlights the input area of the control.	select()

The Plugin Object (Navigator 3+)

Represents the features of an installed plugin component.

Properties	Description
description	A description of the plugin
filename	Name of the plugin file on disk
length	Returns the number of mime types the plugin supports
name	Specifies the name to use to refer to the plugin

Methods	Description
refresh	Makes newly installed plug-ins available and optionally reloads open documents that contain plug-ins.

The Radio Object (NC4 only)

Represents a control created with an < INPUT > tag where TYPE=RADIO.

Properties	Description
checked	Lets you set an individual radio object to 'ON'.
defaultChecked	Denotes if the individual radio button is checked.
form	Reference to the form object that contains the element.
name	Specifies the name to use to refer to the group of radio buttons.
type	Must be 'RADIO' for a Radio element.
value	The 'value' attribute given to the radio button when declared.

Methods	Description	Required Arguments
blur	Causes the control to lose the focus, and fire its **onBlur** event.	blur()
click	Simulates a click on the control, and fires its **onClick** event.	click()

Methods	Description	Required Arguments
focus	Causes the control to receive the focus, and fire its **onFocus** event.	focus()
handleEvent	Invokes the appropriate event handling code of the object for this event.	handleEvent(eventName)

The Reset Object (Navigator 2+)

Represents a reset button on an HTML form.

Properties	Description
form	Reference to the form object that contains the element.
name	Specifies the name to use to refer to the element.
type	Must be **'RESET'** for a Reset element.
value	The text used for the reset button's caption.

Methods	Description	Required Arguments
blur	Causes the control to lose the focus, and fire its **onBlur** event.	blur()
click	Simulates a click on the control, and fires its **onClick** event.	click()
focus	Causes the control to receive the focus, and fire its **onFocus** event.	focus()
handleEvent	Invokes the appropriate event handling code of the object for this event.	handleEvent(eventName)

The Screen Object (Navigator 4, IE4)

Contains properties describing the display screen and colors.

Properties	Description
availHeight (NC4)	Height of the available screen space in pixels (excluding screen furniture)
availWidth (NC4)	Width of the available screen space in pixels (excluding screen furniture)
bufferDepth (IE4 only)	Specifies if and how an off-screen bitmap buffer should be used
colorDepth	Returns the number of bits per pixel of the user's display device or screen buffer
height	Returns the height of the user's display screen in pixels
pixelDepth (NC4)	Returns the number of bits used per pixel by the system display hardware

Properties	Description
updateInterval (IE4 only)	Sets or returns the interval between screen updates on the client
width	Returns the width of the user's display screen in pixels

The Select Object (Navigator 2+)

Contains properties describing a selection list in an HTML form.

Properties	Description
form	Reference to the form object that contains the list element.
length	Number of items in the selection list.
name	Specifies the name to use to refer to the list element.
options	Reflects the text associated with the items.
selectedIndex	The numeric position within the list of the (first) selected item.
type	Indicates the type of list, i.e. **SELECT-ONE**, **SELECT-MULTI**.
text (NC4 only)	The text of the currently selected item.

Methods	Description	Required Arguments
blur	Causes the control to lose the focus, and fire its **onBlur** event.	blur()
focus	Causes the control to receive the focus, and fire its **onFocus** event.	focus()
handleEvent	Invokes the appropriate event handling code of the object for this event.	handleEvent(eventName)

The Selection Object (IE4 only)

Returns the active selection on the screen, allowing access to all the selected elements including the plain text in the page.

Properties	Description
type	The type of the selection, i.e. a control, text, a table, or none

Methods	Description
clear	Clears the contents of the selection
createRange	Returns a copy of the currently selected range
empty	Deselects the current selection and sets selection type to none

The Style Object (IE4 only)
(In Netscape as JavaScript Style Properties)

This provides access to the individual style properties for an element. These could have been previously set by a style sheet, or by an inline style tag within the page.

Property Name	Description
background	Specifies a background picture that is tiled behind text and graphics.
backgroundAttachment	Defines if a background image should be fixed on the page or scroll with the content.
backgroundColor	Specifies the background color of the page or element.
backgroundImage	Specifies a URL for the background image for the page or element.
backgroundPosition	The initial position of a background image on the page.
backgroundPositionX	The x coordinate of the background image in relation to the containing window.
backgroundPositionY	The y coordinate of the background image in relation to the containing window.
BackgroundRepeat	Defines if and how a background image is repeated on the page.
border	Specifies the border to be drawn around the element.
borderBottom	Used to specify several attributes of the bottom border of an element.
borderBottomColor	The color of the bottom border for an element.
borderBottomStyle	The style of the bottom border for an element.
borderBottomWidth	The width of the bottom border for an element.
borderColor	The color of all or some of the borders for an element.
borderLeft	Used to specify several attributes of the left border of an element.
borderLeftColor	The color of the left border for an element.
borderLeftStyle	The style of the left border for an element.
borderLeftWidth	The width of the left border for an element.
borderRight	Used to specify several attributes of the right border of an element.
BorderRightColor	The color of the right border for an element.
BorderRightStyle	The style of the right border for an element.
BorderRightWidth	The width of the right border for an element.
borderStyle	Used to specify the style of one or more borders of an element.
borderTop	Used to specify several attributes of the top border of an element.
borderTopColor	The color of the top border for an element.

Property Name	Description
borderTopStyle	The style of the top border for an element.
borderTopWidth	The width of the top border for an element.
borderWidth	Used to specify the width of one or more borders of an element.
clear	Causes the next element or text to be displayed below left-aligned or right-aligned images.
clip	Specifies how an element's contents should be displayed if larger that the available client area.
color	The text or foreground color of an element.
cssText	The text value of the element's entire **STYLE** attribute.
cursor	Specifies the type of cursor to display when the mouse pointer is over the element.
display	Specifies if the element will be visible (displayed) in the page.
filter	Sets or returns an array of all the filters specified in the element's style property.
font	Defines various attributes of the font for an element, or imports a font.
fontFamily	Specifies the name of the typeface, or 'font family'.
fontSize	Specifies the font size.
fontStyle	Specifies the style of the font, i.e. normal or italic.
fontVariant	Specifies the use of small capitals for the text.
fontWeight	Specifies the weight (boldness) of the text.
height	Specifies the height at which the element is to be drawn, and sets the **posHeight** property.
left	Specifies the position of the left of the element, and sets the **posLeft** property.
letterSpacing	Indicates the additional space to be placed between characters in the text.
lineHeight	The distance between the baselines of two adjacent lines of text.
listStyle	Allows several style properties of a list element to be set in one operation.
listStyleImage	Defines the image used as a background for a list element.
listStylePosition	Defines the position of the bullets used in a list element.
listStyleType	Defines the design of the bullets used in a list element.
margin	Allows all four margins to be specified with a single attribute.
marginBottom	Specifies the bottom margin for the page or text block.

Property Name	Description
marginLeft	Specifies the left margin for the page or text block.
marginRight	Specifies the right margin for the page or text block.
marginTop	Specifies the top margin for the page or text block.
overflow	Defines how text that overflows the element is handled.
paddingBottom	Sets the amount of space between the bottom border and content of an element.
paddingLeft	Sets the amount of space between the left border and content of an element.
paddingRight	Sets the amount of space between the right border and content of an element.
paddingTop	Sets the amount of space between the top border and content of an element.
pageBreakAfter	Specifies if a page break should occur after the element.
pageBreakBefore	Specifies if a page break should occur after the element.
pixelHeight	Sets or returns the height style property of the element in pixels, as a pure number, rather than a string.
pixelLeft	Sets or returns the left style property of the element in pixels, as a pure number, rather than a string.
pixelTop	Sets or returns the top style property of the element in pixels, as a pure number, rather than a string.
pixelWidth	Sets or returns the width style property of the element in pixels, as a pure number, rather than a string.
posHeight	Returns the value of the height style property in its last specified units, as a pure number rather than a string.
position	Returns the value of the position style property, defining whether the element can be positioned.
posLeft	Returns the value of the left style property in its last specified units, as a pure number rather than a string.
posTop	Returns the value of the top style property in its last specified units, as a pure number rather than a string.
posWidth	Returns the value of the width style property in its last specified units, as a pure number rather than a string.
styleFloat	Specifies if the element will float above the other elements in the page, or cause them to flow round it.
textAlign	Indicates how text should be aligned within the element.
textDecoration	Specifies several font decorations (underline, overline, strikethrough) added to the text of an element.

Property Name	Description
textDecorationBlink	Specifies if the font should blink or flash. Has no effect in IE4.
textDecorationLineThrough	Specifies if the text is displayed as strikethrough, i.e. with a horizontal line through it.
textDecorationNone	Specifies if the text is displayed with no additional decoration.
textDecorationOverline	Denotes if the text is displayed as overline, i.e. with a horizontal line above it.
textDecorationUnderline	Denotes if the text is displayed as underline, i.e. with a horizontal line below it.
textIndent	Specifies the indent for the first line of text in an element, and may be negative.
textTransform	Specifies how the text for the element should be capitalized.
top	Position of the top of the element, sets the **posTop** property. Also returns topmost window object.
verticalAlign	Sets or returns the vertical alignment style property for an element.
visibility	Indicates if the element or contents are visible on the page.
width	Specifies the width at which the element is to be drawn, and sets the **posWidth** property.
zIndex	Sets or returns the z-index for the element, indicating whether it appears above or below other elements.

MethodName	Description
getAttribute	Returns the value of an attribute defined in an HTML tag.
removeAttribute	Causes the specified attribute to be removed from the HTML element and the current page.
setAttribute	Adds and/or sets the value of an attribute in a HTML tag.

The Stylesheet Object (IE only)

Exposes all the styles within a single style sheet in the styleSheets collection.

Property Name	Description
disabled	Sets or returns whether an element is disabled.
href	The entire URL as a string.
id	Identifier or name for an element in a page or style sheet, or as the target for hypertext links.
owningElement	Returns the style sheet that imported or referenced the current style sheet, usually through a <LINK> tag.

Property Name	Description
parentStyleSheet	Returns the style sheet that imported the current style sheet, or null for a non-imported style sheet.
readOnly	Indicates that an element's contents are read only, or that a rule in a style sheet cannot be changed.
type	Specifies the type of list style, link, selection, control, button, MIME-type, rel, or the CSS language.

Methods	Description
addImport	Adds a style sheet to the imports collection for the given style sheet.
addRule	Creates a new style rule for the **styleSheet** object and returns the index into the Rules collection.

The Submit Object (Navigator 2+)

Represents a Submit button in an HTML form.

Properties	Description
form	Reference to the form object that contains the element.
name	Specifies the name to use to refer to the element.
type	Must be 'SUBMIT' for a Submit element.
value	The text used for the submit button's caption.

Methods	Description	Required Arguments
blur	Causes the control to lose the focus, and fire its **onBlur** event.	blur()
click	Simulates a click on the control, and fires its **onClick** event.	click()
focus	Causes the control to receive the focus, and fire its **onFocus** event.	focus()
handleEvent	Invokes the appropriate event handling code of the object for this event.	handleEvent(eventName)

The Text Object (Navigator 2+)

Represents a single line text input area in an html form

Properties	Description
defaultValue	The text displayed as the initial contents of the control.
form	Reference to the form object that contains the element.

Properties	Description
name	Specifies the name to use to refer to the element.
type	Must be 'TEXT' (or omitted) for a text element.
value	The text currently within the text box.

Methods	Description	Required Arguments
blur	Causes the control to lose the focus, and fire its onBlur event.	blur()
focus	Causes the control to receive the focus, and fire its onFocus event.	focus()
handleEvent	Invokes the appropriate event handling code of the object for this event.	handleEvent(eventName)
select	Highlights the input area of the object.	select()

The Textarea Object (Navigator 4)

Represents a multi line text input area in an html form.

Properties	Description
defaultValue	The text displayed as the initial contents of the control.
form	Reference to the form object that contains the element.
name	Specifies the name to use to refer to the element.
type	Information about the type of the control.
value	The text currently within the text box.

Methods	Description	Required Arguments
blur	Causes the control to lose the focus, and fire its onBlur event.	blur()
focus	Causes the control to receive the focus, and fire its onFocus event.	focus()
handleEvent	Invokes the appropriate event handling code of the object for this event.	handleEvent(eventName)
select	Highlights the input area of a form element.	select()

The TextRange Object (IE only)

This object represents the text stream of the HTML document. It can be used to set and retrieve the text within the page.

Property Name	Description
htmlText	Returns the contents of a **TextRange** as text and HTML source.
text	The plain text contained within a block element, a **TextRange** or an **<OPTION>** tag.

Method Name	Description
collapse	Shrinks a TextRange to either the start or end of the current range.
compareEndPoints	Compares two text ranges and returns a value indicating the result.
duplicate	Returns a duplicate of a TextRange object.
execCommand	Executes a command over the document selection or range.
expand	Expands the range by a character, word, sentence or story so that partial units are completely contained.
findText	Sets the range start and end points to cover the text if found within the current document.
getBookmark	Sets String to a unique bookmark value to identify that position in the document.
inRange	Denotes if the specified range is within or equal to the current range.
isEqual	Denotes if the specified range is equal to the current range.
move	Changes the start and end points of a TextRange to cover different text.
moveEnd	Causes the range to grow or shrink from the end of the range.
moveStart	Causes the range to grow or shrink from the beginning of the range.
moveToBookmark	Moves range to encompass the range with a bookmark value previously defined in String.
moveToElementText	Moves range to encompass the text in the element specified.
moveToPoint	Moves and collapses range to the point specified in x and y relative to the document.
parentElement	Returns the parent element that completely encloses the current range.
pasteHTML	Pastes HTML and/or plain text into the current range.
queryCommandEnabled	Denotes if the specified command is available for a document or TextRange.
queryCommandIndeterm	Denotes if the specified command is in the indeterminate state.
queryCommandState	Returns the current state of the command for a document or TextRange object.
queryCommandSupported	Denotes if the specified command is supported for a document or TextRange object.

Method Name	Description
queryCommandValue	Returns the value of the command specified for a document or TextRange object.
scrollIntoView	Scrolls the element or TextRange into view in the browser, optionally at the top of the window.
select	Makes the active selection equal to the current object, or highlights the input area of a form element.
setEndPoint	Sets the end point of the range based on the end point of another range.

The Window Object (Navigator 2+, IE)

The Window object refers to a window or frame on display by the browser.

Property Name	Description
client (IE only)	Returns the navigator object for the browser.
clientInformation (IE only)	A reference that returns the navigator object for the browser.
closed	Indicates if a window is closed.
defaultStatus	The default message displayed in the status bar at the bottom of the window.
dialogArguments (IE only)	Returns the arguments that were passed into a dialog window, as an array.
dialogHeight (IE only)	Sets or returns the height of a dialog window.
dialogLeft (IE only)	Sets or returns the x coordinate of a dialog window.
dialogTop (IE only)	Sets or returns the y coordinate of a dialog window.
dialogWidth (IE only)	Sets or returns the width of a dialog window.
document	Read-only reference to the window's document object.
frames	An array of objects corresponding to child frames (created with the <FRAME> tag) in source order.
history	Read-only reference to the window's history object.
innerHeight (NC4)	Height of the window excluding the window borders.
innerWidth (NC4)	Width of the window excluding the window borders.
length	Returns the number of child frames in a window.
location (NC4)	The current URL in the window.
locationbar (NC4)	Defines whether the address bar will be displayed in the browser window.
menubar	Represents the browser window's menu bar.
name	A string specifying the window's name.

Property Name	Description
offScreenBuffering (IE4 only)	Specifies whether to use off-screen buffering for the document.
opener	Returns a reference to the window that created the current window.
outerHeight (NC4)	Height of the window including the window borders.
outerWidth (NC4)	Width of the window including the window borders.
pageXOffset (NC4)	Horizontal offset of the top left of the visible part of the page within the windows in pixels.
pageYOffset (NC4)	Vertical offset of the top left of the visible part of the page within the windows in pixels.
parent	Returns the parent window or frame in the window/frame hierarchy.
personalbar (NC4)	Represents the browser window's user's personal bar.
returnValue (IE only)	Allows a return value to be specified for the event or a dialog window.
scrollbars (NC4)	Defines whether the window will provide scrollbars if all the content cannot be displayed.
self	Provides a reference to the current window.
status	Text displayed in the window's status bar, or an alias for the value of an option button.
statusbar (NC4)	Defines whether the status bar will be displayed in the browser window.
toolbar (NC4)	Defines whether the toolbar will be displayed in the browser window.
top	The topmost window object.
window	Read-only reference to the current window object, same as _self.

Method	Description	Required Arguments
Alert	Displays an Alert dialog box with a message and an OK button	alert('message')
back	Loads the previous URL in the browser's history list	back ( )
blur	Causes a control to lose focus and fire its **onblur** event	blur ( )
captureEvents (NC4)	Instructs the window to capture events of a particular type	captureEvents(eventType)
clearInterval	Cancels an interval timer that was set with the **setInterval** method.	clearInterval(intervalID)
clearTimeout	Cancels a timeout that was set with the **setTimeout** method.	clearTimeout(timeoutID)

Method	Description	Required Arguments
close	Closes a document forcing written data to be displayed, or closes the browser window.	close ( )
confirm	Displays a Confirm dialog box with a message and OK and Cancel buttons.	confirm('message')
disableExternalCapture (NC4)	Prevents a window that includes frames from capturing events in documents loaded from different locations	disableExternalCapture ( )
enableExternalCapture (NC4)	Allows a window that includes frames to capture events in documents loaded from different locations	enableExternalCapture ( )
execScript (IE only)	Executes a script. The **alert** default language is JScript	
find (NC4)	Returns true if a specified string is found in the text in the current window	find(string) find(string, casesensitive) find(string, casesensitive, backward)
focus	Causes a control to receive the focus and fires its **onfocus** event	focus ( )
forward (NC4)	Loads the next URL in the browser's history list	forward ( )
handleEvent (NC4)	Invokes the appropriate event handling code of the object for this event	handleEvent(eventName)
home (NC4)	Loads the user's home page into the browser window	home ( )
moveBy (NC4)	Moves the window horizontally and vertically	moveBy(horiz, vert)
moveTo (NC4)	Moves the window so that the top left is at a position (x,y)	moveTo (x,y)
open	Opens the document as a stream to collect output of **write** or **writeln** methods	open(URL, windowName) open(URL, windowName, windowFeatures)
print (NC4)	Prints the contents of the window, equivalent to pressing the Print button.	print ( )
prompt (NC4)	Displays a Prompt dialog box with a message and an input field	prompt(message) prompt(message, inputDefault)

Method	Description	Required Arguments
releaseEvents (NC4)	Instructs the window to stop capturing events of a particular type.	releaseEvents(eventType)
resizeBy (NC4)	Resizes te window horizontally and vertically	resizeBy(horiz,vert)
resizeTo (NC4)	Resizes the window to a size *x, y* specified in pixels	resizeTo(x,y)
routeEvent (NC4)	Passes an event that has been captured up through the normal event hierarchy	routeEvent(event)
scrollBy (NC4)	Scrolls the window horizontally and vertically within the window by a number of pixels	scrollBy(horiz, vert)
scrollTo (NC4)	Scrolls the document within the window so that the point *x,y* is at the top left corner	scrollTo(x,y)
setInterval	Denotes a code routine to execute repeatedly every specified number of milliseconds	setInterval(exp, msec) setInterval(function, msec, arg1, ..., argN)
setTimeout	Denotes a code routine to execute a specified number of milliseconds after loading the page	setTimeout(exp, msec) setTimeout(function, msec, arg1, ..., arg N)
showHelp (IE only)	Opens a window to display a Help file	
showModal Dialog (IE only)	Displays an HTML dialog window, and returns the **returnValue** property of its document when closed	
stop (NC4)	Stops the current download, equivalent to pressing the Stop button	stop()

Special JScript Objects

The following objects are unique to JScript, and extend the functionality of the browser within the host system.

Drive Object

Gives the script access to the properties of the drive tree; allows various aspects of the drive system to be manipulated using JScript. The `Drive` object has no available methods.

Property Name	Description
AvailableSpace	Returns the amount of space available on the drive to the user.
DriveLetter	Returns drive letter.
DriveType	Returns drive type as an integer. **0** is unknown, **1** is removable, **2** is fixed, **3** is Network, **4** is CD-ROM, **5** is RAM disk
FileSystem	Returns file system type, such **FAT**, **NTFS** or **CDFS**
FreeSpace	Read-only value giving amount of freespace available to the user
IsReady	Returns **True** if drive is ready, otherwise **False**
Path	Returns the path for the specified drive
RootFolder	Returns a Folder object representing the root drive; read only
SerialNumber	Returns a unique decimal serial number for the specified drive
ShareName	Returns the shared network name for a network drive
TotalSize	Returns the total bytes available on the specified disk
VolumeName	Sets or returns the name of the drive volume; name is a string, in syntax: VolumeName=string

File Object

Allows the browser to treat a file as if it were an object.

Property Name	Description
Attributes	Sets or returns the attributes of the folder. Can read/write as well read only; syntax is **file.Attributes [= newattributes]**. Values are **0** (normal), **1**(ReadOnly), **2**(Hidden), **4**(System), **8**(Disk drive volume label) **16** (folder/directory), **32**(changed file), **64** (link or shortcut), **128** (compressed file).
DateCreated	Read only property that returns the date that the specified file was created.
DateLastAccessed	Read only property that returns date and time of last access
DateLastModified	Read only property that returns date file was last modified.
Drive	Returns the drive letter of the file's home drive.
Name	Read/write value that sets or returns file/folders name.
ParentFolder	Returns a folder object containing the parent object for the specified file
Path	Returns directory path for specified object.
ShortName	Returns a DOS 8.3 naming convention.
ShortPath	Returns a path using the DOS 8.3 naming convention

Property Name	Description
Size	Returns size of the object in bytes. For folders, this is the total of all files and subfolders.
type	Returns a description of the folders type, based on the three letter extension.

Method	Description	Required Arguments
Copy	Copies a file from one location to another; overwrite is an optional Boolean with a default of `true`.	`object.Copy(destination[, overwrite]);`
Delete	Deletes the specified file or folder object. `force` is an optional Boolean with default of `false` that will not allow deletion of read-only files.	`object.Delete(force);`
Move	Moves specified file or folder to the destination drive.	object.Move(destination);
OpenAsTextStream	Opens file and returns a `textstream` object that can be read, written too or appended. `iomode` (optional) is one of three constants: `ForReading`, `ForWriting`, or `ForAppending`. Default `format` is ACSII	object.OpenAsTextStream([iomode,[format]])

FileSystemObject

Allows the browser to access the host computer's file system as if it were an object.

Property Name	Description
drives	Returns a collection of all the drives available on the machine.

Method	Description	Required Arguments
BuildPath Method	Appends a name to the end of a path. Will insert a separator.	BuildPath(path,name)
CopyFile Method	Copies a file from one location to another; overwrite is an optional Boolean with a default of `true`.	CopyFile(source,destination[,overwrite])
CopyFolder Method	Copies a folder from one location to another; overwrite is an optional Boolean with a default of `true`.	CopyFolder(source,destination[,overwrite])
CreateFolder Method	Creates a folder; gives an error if `foldername` is already in use.	CreateFolder(foldername)

Method	Description	Required Arguments
CreateTextFile	Creates a file with name filename, and returns a **TextStream** object that can be used to read/write the file.	CreateTextFile(filename [,overwrite[,unicode]])
DeleteFile	Deletes the specified file object. **force** is an optional Boolean with default of **false** that will not allow deletion of read-only files.	DeleteFile(filespec [,force])
DeleteFolder	Deletes the specified folder object. **force** is an optional Boolean with default of **false** that will not allow deletion of read-only files.	DeleteFolder(folderspec [,force]);
DriveExists	Boolean return value; **True** if it exists, otherwise **false**.	DriveExists(drivespec)
FileExists	Boolean return value; **True** if it exists, otherwise **false**.	FileExists(filespec)
FolderExists	Boolean return value; **True** if it exists, otherwise **false**.	FolderExists(folderspec)
GetAbsolutePathName	Returns an explicit path.	GetAbsolutePathName (pathspec)
GetBaseName	Returns a **string** value of the last item in the specified path, minus any file extension details.	GetBaseName(path)
GetDrive	Returns a **Drive** object for the specified drive;p drive spec can be a letter, letter with colon or network share spec.	GetDrive(drivespec);
GetDriveName	Returns **Drive** name as a **string** for the specified path.	GetDriveName(path)
GetExtensionName	Returns the file type extension for last item in path as a **string**	GetExtensionName(path)
GetFile	Returns a **file** object corresponding to the last file in the path.	GetFile(filespec)
GetFileName	Returns the last item in the **pathspec string** as a **string**. It will return empty string if the path only has drives. Note that it does NOT check path existence; simply parses string.	GetFileName(pathspec)
GetFolder	Returns a **folder** object corresponding to the last folder in the path.	GetFolder(folderspec)

Method	Description	Required Arguments
GetParentFolderName	Returns the parent folder of the last item in the **pathspec** **string** as a **string**. It will return empty string if the path has no folders. Note that it does NOT check path existence; simply parses string.	GetParentFolderName(path)
GetSpecialFolder	Returns the special folder specified as an object. folderspec can be one of **0** (Windows folder), **1**(System Folder), **2** (Temporary folder)	GetSpecialFolder (folderspec)
GetTempName	Provides a temporary file name, not an actual folder. Used for operations requiring a temporary file/folder.	GetTempName();
MoveFile	Moves one or more **file** objects from one location to another. **source** is the path to the files, and may include wildcards; **destination** may not.	MoveFile (source,destination)
MoveFolder	Moves **folders** from one location to another. **source** is the path to the folder, and may include wildcards; **destination** may not.	MoveFolder (source,destination);
OpenTextFile	Opens specified file and returns a **TextStream** object that can be read/written. **iomode** (optional) is one of three constants: **ForReading**, **ForWriting**, or **ForAppending**. Default **format** is ACSII.	OpenTextFile(filename[,iomode[,c reate[,format]]])

Folder Object

Allows JScript to manipulate the files on the browser's computer under suitably secure situations.

Property Name	Description
Attributes	Sets or returns the attributes of the folder. Can read/write as well read only; syntax is **folder.Attributes [= newattributes]**. Values are **0** (normal), **1** (ReadOnly), **2** (Hidden), **4** (System), **8** (Disk drive volume label) **16** (folder/directory), **32** (changed file), **64** (link or shortcut), **128** (compressed file).
DateCreated	Read only property that returns the date that the specified file or folder was created.

Property Name	Description
DateLastAccessed	Read only property that returns date and time of last access.
DateLastModified	Read only property that returns date file was last modified.
Drive	Returns the drive letter of the file's home drive.
IsRootFolder	Returns Boolean value indicating whether specified folder is a root directory or not.
Name	Read/write value that sets or returns folder's name.
ParentFolder	Returns a folder object containing the parent object for the specified file.
Path	Returns directory path for specified object.
ShortName	Returns a DOS 8.3 naming convention.
ShortPath	Returns a path using the DOS 8.3 naming convention.
Size	Returns size of the object in bytes. For folders, this is the total of all files and subfolders.
SubFolders	Returns a **folders** collection consisting of all sub folders in a folder, including hidden or system folders.
type	Returns a description of the folders type, based on the three letter extension.

Method	Description	Required Arguments
Copy	Copies a folder from one location to another; overwrite is an optional Boolean with a default of **true**.	`object.Copy(destination[,o verwrite]);`
Delete	Deletes the specified folder object. **force** is an optional Boolean with default of **false** that will not allow deletion of read-only files.	`object.Delete(force);`
Move	Moves specified folder to the destination drive.	object.Move(destination);
OpenAsTextStream	Opens file and returns a **textstream** object that can be read, written too or appended. **iomode** (optional) is one of three constants: **ForReading**, **ForWriting**, or **ForAppending**. Default **format** is ACSII.	object.OpenAsTextStream([iomod e, [format]])

TextStream

Properties	Description
AtEndOfLine	Returns a boolean value; **true** if at the end of as line; **false** otherwise.

Properties	Description
AtEndOfStream	Returns a boolean value; **true** if at the end of the TextStream, **false** if otherwise.
Column	Returns the column **number** of the current character in the TextStream.
Line	Read-only **number** value for the current line number in the TextStream.

Method	Description	Required Arguments
Close	Closes the TextStream object.	object.Close ( ) ;
Read	Reads the specified number of characters and returns the result as a **string** value.	object.Read(integer)
ReadAll	Returns the entire TextStream as a **string.**	object.ReadAll ( ) ;
ReadLine	Reads a single line form a TextStream; from line start up to (but not including) a new line character.	object.ReadLine ( )
Skip	Skips the specified number of characters when reading a TextStream object.	object.Skip(integer)
SkipLine	Skips the next line while reading the TextStream.	object.SkipLine ( )
Write	Writes the specified string to the TextStream object.	object.Write(string)
WriteBlankLines	Inserts an **integer** number of newline characters, i.e. blank lines.	object.WriteBlankLines(integer)
WriteLine	Writes the specified string followed by a newline character to the TextStream object.	object.WriteLine ([string])

D

HTML Tags & Colors

This section is intended to provide a quick reference to some of the more useful HTML tags and the attributes they support, together with a listing of color values and names sorted by type. A full listing of all the HTML tags is available from the Wrox web site, in the Wrox Ultimate HTML Reference Database. The URL is: **http://webdev.wrox.co.uk/html4db/**.

The HTML tags we have provided here are those directly relevant to JavaScript, and browser compatibility information is also provided.

<A>

Defines a hypertext link. The HREF or the NAME attribute must be specified. **Supported by ALL.**

Attributes	2.0	3.2	4.0	N2	N3	N4	IE2	IE3	IE4
\<event_name\>= script_code	✗	✗	✓	✗	✗	✓	✗	✓	✓
ACCESSKEY= key_character	✗	✗	✓	✗	✗	✗	✗	✗	✓
CHARSET=string	✗	✗	✓	✗	✗	✗	✗	✗	✗
CLASS=classname	✗	✗	✗	✗	✗	✓	✗	✓	✓
COORDS=string	✗	✗	✓	✗	✗	✓	✗	✗	✗
DATAFLD=column _name	✗	✗	✗	✗	✗	✗	✗	✗	✓
DATASRC=id	✗	✗	✗	✗	✗	✗	✗	✗	✓

Attributes	2.0	3.2	4.0	N2	N3	N4	IE2	IE3	IE4
DIR=LTR|RTL	✗	✗	✓	✗	✗	✗	✗	✗	✗
HREF=url	✓	✓	✓	✓	✓	✓	✓	✓	✓
HREFLANG= langcode	✗	✗	✓	✗	✗	✗	✗	✗	✗
ID=string	✗	✗	✓	✗	✗	✓	✗	✓	✓
LANG=language_ type	✗	✗	✓	✗	✗	✗	✗	✗	✓
LANGUAGE= JAVASCRIPT |JSCRIPT| VBSCRIPT |VBS	✗	✗	✗	✗	✗	✗	✗	✗	✓
METHODS=string	✓	✗	✗	✗	✗	✗	✗	✗	✓
NAME=string	✓	✓	✓	✓	✓	✓	✓	✓	✓
REL=SAME|NEXT| PARENT|PREVIOUS |string	✓	✓	✓	✗	✗	✗	✗	✓	✓
REV=string	✓	✓	✓	✗	✗	✗	✗	✓	✓
SHAPE=CIRC| CIRCLE|POLY |POLYGON|RECT| RECTANGLE	✗	✗	✓	✗	✗	✗	✗	✗	✗
STYLE=string	✗	✗	✓	✗	✗	✓	✗	✓	✓
TABINDEX=number	✗	✗	✓	✗	✗	✗	✗	✗	✓
TARGET=<window_ name> |_parent|_blank |_top |_self	✗	✗	✓	✓	✓	✓	✗	✓	✓
TITLE=string	✓	✓	✓	✗	✗	✗	✗	✓	✓
TYPE=BUTTON| RESET|SUBMIT	✗	✗	✓	✗	✗	✗	✗	✗	✓
URN=string	✓	✗	✗	✗	✗	✗	✗	✗	✓

<ADDRESS>

Specifies information such as address, signature and authorship. **ALL**.

Attributes	2.0	3.2	4.0	N2	N3	N4	IE2	IE3	IE4
<event_name>= script_code	✗	✗	✓	✗	✗	✗	✗	✗	✓

Attributes	2.0	3.2	4.0	N2	N3	N4	IE2	IE3	IE4
CLASS=classname	✗	✗	✓	✗	✗	✓	✗	✗	✓
DIR=LTR|RTL	✗	✗	✓	✗	✗	✗	✗	✗	✗
ID=string	✗	✗	✓	✗	✗	✓	✗	✗	✓
LANG=language_type	✗	✗	✓	✗	✗	✗	✗	✗	✓
LANGUAGE= JAVASCRIPT |JSCRIPT| VBSCRIPT|VBS	✗	✗	✗	✗	✗	✗	✗	✗	✓
STYLE=STRING	✗	✗	✓	✗	✗	✓	✗	✗	✓
TITLE=STRING	✗	✗	✓	✗	✗	✗	✗	✗	✓

\<APPLET>

Places a Java applet or other executable content in the page. **HTML 3.2, N2, N3, N4, IE3, IE4, deprecated in HTML 4.0.**

Attributes	2.0	3.2	4.0	N2	N3	N4	IE2	IE3	IE4
<event_name>= script_code	✗	✗	D	✗	✗	✗	✗	✗	✗
ALIGN=TOP| MIDDLE|BOTTOM |LEFT|RIGHT| ABSMIDDLE |BASELINE| ABSBOTTOM |TEXTTOP	✗	✓	D	✓	✓	✓	✗	✓	✓
ALT=text	✗	✓	D	✓	✓	✓	✗	✓	✓
ARCHIVE=url	✗	✗	D	✗	✓	✓	✗	✗	✗
BORDER=number	✗	✗	D	✗	✗	✗	✗	✗	✗
CLASS=classname	✗	✗	D	✗	✗	✓	✗	✗	✓
CODE=filename	✗	✓	D	✓	✓	✓	✗	✓	✓
CODEBASE= Path|url	✗	✓	D	✓	✓	✓	✗	✓	✓
DATAFLD=column_name	✗	✗	✗	✗	✗	✗	✗	✗	✓
DATASRC=id	✗	✗	✗	✗	✗	✗	✗	✗	✓
DOWNLOAD=number	✗	✗	✗	✗	✗	✗	✗	✓	✗
HEIGHT=number	✗	✓	•	✓	✓	✓	✗	✓	✗

Attributes	2.0	3.2	4.0	N2	N3	N4	IE2	IE3	IE4
HSPACE=number	✗	✓	D	✗	✗	✓	✗	✓	✓
ID=string	✗	✗	D	✗	✗	✓	✗	✗	✓
MAYSCRIPT=YES|NO	✗	✗	✗	✗	✗	✓	✗	✗	✗
NAME=string	✗	✓	D	✗	✗	✗	✗	✓	✓
OBJECT=string	✗	✗	D	✗	✗	✗	✗	✗	✗
SRC=url	✗	✗	✗	✗	✗	✗	✗	✗	✓
STYLE=string	✗	✗	D	✗	✗	✓	✗	✗	✓
TITLE=string	✗	✗	D	✗	✗	✗	✗	✓	✓
VSPACE=number	✗	✓	D	✗	✗	✓	✗	✓	✓
WIDTH=number	✗	✓	D	✓	✓	✓	✗	✓	✓

<BODY>

Defines the beginning and end of the body section of the page. **ALL**.

Attributes	2.0	3.2	4.0	N2	N3	N4	IE2	IE3	IE4
<event_name>=script_code	✗	✗	✓	✗	✗	✓	✗	✗	✓
ALINK=color	✗	✓	D	✓	✓	✓	✗	✓	✓
BACKGROUND=string	✗	✓	D	✓	✓	✓	✓	✓	✓
BGCOLOR=color	✗	✓	D	✓	✓	✓	✓	✓	✓
BGPROPERTIES=FIXED	✗	✗	✗	✗	✗	✗	✓	✓	✓
BOTTOMMARGIN=number	✗	✗	✗	✗	✗	✗	✗	✗	✓
CLASS=classname	✗	✗	✓	✗	✗	✓	✗	✓	✓
DIR=LTR|RTL	✗	✗	✓	✗	✗	✗	✗	✗	✗
ID=string	✗	✗	✓	✗	✗	✓	✗	✓	✓
LANG=language_type	✗	✗	✓	✗	✗	✗	✗	✗	✓
LANGUAGE=JAVASCRIPT|JSCRIPT|VBSCRIPT|VBS	✗	✗	✗	✗	✗	✗	✗	✗	✓

Attributes	2.0	3.2	4.0	N2	N3	N4	IE2	IE3	IE4
LEFTMARGIN= number	✗	✗	✗	✗	✗	✗	✓	✓	✓
LINK=color	✗	✓	D	✓	✓	✓	✓	✓	✓
RIGHTMARGIN= number	✗	✗	✗	✗	✗	✗	✗	✗	✓
SCROLL=YES|NO	✗	✗	✗	✗	✗	✗	✗	✗	✓
STYLE=string	✗	✗	✓	✗	✗	✓	✗	✓	✓
TEXT=color	✗	✓	D	✓	✓	✓	✓	✓	✓
TITLE=string	✗	✗	✓	✗	✗	✗	✗	✗	✓
TOPMARGIN= number	✗	✗	✗	✗	✗	✗	✓	✓	✓
VLINK=color	✗	✓	D	✓	✓	✓	✓	✓	✓

\<BUTTON>

Renders an HTML button, the enclosed text used as the button's caption. **HTML 4.0, IE4**.

Attributes	2.0	3.2	4.0	N2	N3	N4	IE2	IE3	IE4
\<event_name>= script_code	✗	✗	✓	✗	✗	✗	✗	✗	✓
ACCESSKEY=ley_ character	✗	✗	✓	✗	✗	✗	✗	✗	✓
CLASS=classname	✗	✗	✓	✗	✗	✗	✗	✗	✓
DATAFLD=column_ name	✗	✗	✗	✗	✗	✗	✗	✗	✓
DATAFORMATAS= HTML|TEXT	✗	✗	✗	✗	✗	✗	✗	✗	✓
DATASRC=id	✗	✗	✗	✗	✗	✗	✗	✗	✓
DIR=LTR|RTL	✗	✗	✓	✗	✗	✗	✗	✗	✗
DISABLED	✗	✗	✓	✗	✗	✗	✗	✗	✓
ID=string	✗	✗	✓	✗	✗	✗	✗	✗	✓
LANG=language_ type	✗	✗	✓	✗	✗	✗	✗	✗	✓
LANGUAGE= JAVASCRIPT |JSCRIPT| VBSCRIPT|VBS	✗	✗	✗	✗	✗	✗	✗	✗	✓
NAME=string	✗	✗	✓	✗	✗	✗	✗	✗	✗

Attributes	2.0	3.2	4.0	N2	N3	N4	IE2	IE3	IE4
STYLE=string	✗	✗	✓	✗	✗	✗	✗	✗	✓
TABINDEX=number	✗	✗	✓	✗	✗	✗	✗	✗	✗
TITLE=string	✗	✗	✓	✗	✗	✗	✗	✗	✓
TYPE=BUTTON|RESET|SUBMIT	✗	✗	✓	✗	✗	✗	✗	✗	✓
VALUE=string	✗	✗							

<EMBED>

Embeds documents of any type in the page, to be viewed in another suitable application. **N2, N3, N4, IE3, IE4**.

Attributes	2.0	3.2	4.0	N2	N3	N4	IE2	IE3	IE4
ALIGN=ABSBOTTOM |ABSMIDDLE| BASELINE |BOTTOM|LEFT| MIDDLE |RIGHT| TEXTTOP|TOP	✗	✗	✗	✗	✗	✓	✗	✗	✓
ALT=text	✗	✗	✗	✗	✗	✗	✗	✗	✓
BORDER=number	✗	✗	D	✗	✗	✓	✗	✗	✗
CLASS=classname	✗	✗	✗	✗	✗	✓	✗	✗	✓
CODE=filename	✗	✗	✗	✗	✗	✗	✗	✗	✓
CODEBASE=url	✗	✗	✗	✗	✗	✗	✗	✗	✓
HEIGHT=number	✗	✗	✗	✓	✓	✓	✗	✓	✓
HIDDEN=string	✗	✗	✗	✗	✗	✓	✗	✗	✗
HSPACE=number	✗	✗	✗	✗	✗	✓	✗	✗	✓
ID=string	✗	✗	✗	✗	✗	✓	✗	✗	✓
NAME=string	✗	✗	✗	✓	✓	✓	✗	✓	✓
PALETTE= FOREGROUND |BACKGROUND	✗	✗	✗	✗	✗	✓	✗	✓	✗
PLUGINSPAGE= string	✗	✗	✗	✗	✗	✓	✗	✗	✗
SRC=url	✗	✗	✗	✓	✓	✓	✗	✓	✓
STYLE=string	✗	✗	✗	✗	✗	✓	✗	✗	✓
TITLE=string	✗	✗	✗	✗	✗	✗	✗	✗	✓

Attributes	2.0	3.2	4.0	N2	N3	N4	IE2	IE3	IE4
TYPE=mime-type	✗	✗	✗	✗	✗	✓	✗	✗	✗
UNITS=EN|EMS|PIXELS	✗	✗	✗	✗	✗	✓	✗	✓	✓
VSPACE=number	✗	✗	✗	✗	✗	✓	✗	✗	✓
WIDTH=number	✗	✗	✗	✓	✓	✓	✗	✓	✓

<FORM>

Denotes a form containing controls and elements, whose values are sent to a server. **ALL**.

Attributes	2.0	3.2	4.0	N2	N3	N4	IE2	IE3	IE4
<event_name>=script_code	✗	✗	✓	✗	✗	✓	✗	✓	✓
ACCEPT-CHARSET=string	✗	✗	✓	✗	✗	✗	✗	✗	✗
ACTION=string	✓	✓	✓	✓	✓	✓	✓	✓	✓
CLASS=classname	✗	✗	✓	✗	✗	✓	✗	✗	✓
DIR=LTR|RTL	✗	✗	✓	✗	✗	✗	✗	✗	✗
ENCTYPE=string	✓	✓	✓	✓	✓	✓	✗	✗	✓
ID=string	✗	✗	✓	✗	✗	✓	✗	✗	✓
LANG=language_type	✗	✗	✓	✗	✗	✗	✗	✗	✓
LANGUAGE=JAVASCRIPT|JSCRIPT|VBSCRIPT|VBS	✗	✗	✗	✗	✗	✗	✗	✗	✓
METHOD=GET|POST	✓	✓	✓	✓	✓	✓	✓	✓	✓
NAME=string	✗	✗	✗	✗	✗	✓	✗	✗	✓
STYLE=string	✗	✗	✓	✗	✗	✓	✗	✗	✓
TARGET=<window_name>|_parent|_blank|_top|_self	✗	✗	✓	✓	✓	✓	✗	✓	✓
TITLE=string	✗	✗	✓	✗	✗	✗	✗	✗	✓

<FRAME>

Specifies an individual frame within a frameset. **HTML 4.0, N2, N3, N4, IE3, IE4**.

Attributes	2.0	3.2	4.0	N2	N3	N4	IE2	IE3	IE4
`<event_name>=script_code`	✗	✗	✗	✗	✗	✓	✗	✗	✓
`ALIGN=CENTER|LEFT|RIGHT`	✗	✗	✗	✗	✗	✓	✗	✓	✗
`BORDERCOLOR=color`	✗	✗	✗	✗	✓	✓	✗	✗	✓
`CLASS=classname`	✗	✗	✓	✗	✗	✓	✗	✗	✓
`DATAFLD=column_name`	✗	✗	✗	✗	✗	✗	✗	✗	✓
`DATASRC=id`	✗	✗	✗	✗	✗	✗	✗	✗	✓
`FRAMEBORDER=NO|YES|0|1`	✗	✗	✓	✗	✓	✓	✗	✓	✓
`ID=string`	✗	✗	✓	✗	✗	✓	✗	✗	✓
`LANG=language_type`	✗	✗	✗	✗	✗	✗	✗	✗	✓
`LANGUAGE=JAVASCRIPT|JSCRIPT|VBSCRIPT|VBS`	✗	✗	✗	✗	✗	✗	✗	✗	✓
`LONGDESC=url`	✗	✗	✓	✗	✗	✗	✗	✗	✗
`MARGINHEIGHT=number`	✗	✗	✓	✓	✓	✓	✗	✓	✓
`MARGINWIDTH=number`	✗	✗	✓	✓	✓	✓	✗	✓	✓
`NAME=string`	✗	✗	✓	✓	✓	✓	✗	✓	✓
`NORESIZE=NORESIZE|RESIZE`	✗	✗	✓	✓	✓	✓	✗	✓	✓
`SCROLLING=AUTO|YES|NO`	✗	✗	✓	✓	✓	✓	✗	✓	✓
`SRC=url`	✗	✗	✓	✓	✓	✓	✗	✓	✓
`STYLE=string`	✗	✗	✓	✗	✗	✗	✗	✗	✓
`TITLE=string`	✗	✗	✓	✗	✗	✓	✗	✗	✓

<FRAMESET>

Specifies a frameset containing multiple frames and other nested framesets. **HTML 4.0, N2, N3, N4, IE3, IE4.**

Attributes	2.0	3.2	4.0	N2	N3	N4	IE2	IE3	IE4
<event_name>= script_code	✗	✗	✓	✗	✗	✗	✗	✗	✗
BORDER=number	✗	✗	D	✗	✓	✓	✗	✗	✓
BORDERCOLOR= color	✗	✗	✗	✗	✓	✓	✗	✗	✓
CLASS=classname	✗	✗	✓	✗	✗	✓	✗	✗	✓
COLS=number	✗	✗	✓	✓	✓	✓	✗	✓	✓
FRAMEBORDER= NO I YES I 0 I 1	✗	✗	✗	✗	✓	✓	✗	✓	✓
FRAMESPACING= number	✗	✗	✗	✗	✗	✗	✗	✓	✓
ID=string	✗	✗	✓	✗	✗	✓	✗	✗	✓
LANG=language_ type	✗	✗	✗	✗	✗	✗	✗	✗	✓
LANGUAGE= JAVASCRIPT I JSCRIPT I VBSCRIPT I VBS	✗	✗	✗	✗	✗	✗	✗	✗	✓
ROWS=number	✗	✗	✓	✓	✓	✓	✗	✓	✓
STYLE=string	✗	✗	✓	✗	✗	✗	✗	✗	✓
TITLE=string	✗	✗	✓	✗	✗	✗	✗	✗	✓

<HEAD>

Contains tags holding unviewed information about the document. **ALL.**

Attributes	2.0	3.2	4.0	N2	N3	N4	IE2	IE3	IE4
CLASS=classname	✗	✗	✗	✗	✗	✓	✗	✗	✓
DIR=LTR I RTL	✗	✗	✓	✗	✗	✗	✗	✗	✗
ID=string	✗	✗	✗	✗	✗	✓	✗	✗	✓
LANG=language_ type	✗	✗	✓	✗	✗	✗	✗	✗	✗
PROFILE=url	✗	✗	✓	✗	✗	✗	✗	✗	✗
TITLE=string	✗	✗	✗	✗	✗	✗	✗	✗	✓

<HTML>

The outer tag for the page, which identifies the document as containing HTML elements. **ALL**.

Attributes	2.0	3.2	4.0	N2	N3	N4	IE2	IE3	IE4
DIR=LTR|RTL	✗	✗	✓	✗	✗	✗	✗	✗	✗
LANG=language_ type	✗	✗	✓	✗	✗	✗	✗	✗	✗
TITLE=string	✗	✗	✗	✗	✗	✗	✗	✗	✓
VERSION=url	✗	✗	✓	✗	✗	✗	✗	✗	✗

<IFRAME>

Used to create in-line floating frames within the page. **HTML 4.0, IE3, IE4**

Attributes	2.0	3.2	4.0	N2	N3	N4	IE2	IE3	IE4
ALIGN=ABSBOTTOM |ABSMIDDLE| BASELINE |BOTTOM|LEFT| MIDDLE |RIGHT| TEXTTOP|TOP	✗	✗	D	✗	✗	✗	✗	✗	✓
BORDER=number	✗	✗	D	✗	✗	✗	✗	✗	✓
BORDERCOLOR= color	✗	✗	✗	✗	✗	✗	✗	✗	✓
CLASS=classname	✗	✗	✓	✗	✗	✗	✗	✗	✓
DATAFLD= column_name	✗	✗	✗	✗	✗	✗	✗	✗	✓
DATASRC=id	✗	✗	✗	✗	✗	✗	✗	✗	✓
FRAMEBORDER= NO|YES|0|1	✗	✗	✓	✗	✗	✗	✗	✗	✓
FRAMESPACING= number	✗	✗	✗	✗	✗	✗	✗	✗	✓
HEIGHT=number	✗	✗	✓	✗	✗	✗	✗	✗	✓
HSPACE=number	✗	✗	✗	✗	✗	✗	✗	✗	✓
ID=string	✗	✗	✓	✗	✗	✗	✗	✗	✓
LANG=language_ type	✗	✗	✗	✗	✗	✗	✗	✗	✓
LANGUAGE= JAVASCRIPT |JSCRIPT| VBSCRIPT|VBS	✗	✗	✗	✗	✗	✗	✗	✗	✓

Attributes	2.0	3.2	4.0	N2	N3	N4	IE2	IE3	IE4
LONGDESC=url	✗	✗	✓	✗	✗	✗	✗	✗	✗
MARGINHEIGHT= number	✗	✗	✓	✗	✗	✗	✗	✗	✓
MARGINWIDTH= number	✗	✗	✓	✗	✗	✗	✗	✗	✓
NAME=string	✗	✗	✓	✗	✗	✗	✗	✗	✓
NORESIZE= NORESIZE |RESIZE	✗	✗	✗	✗	✗	✗	✗	✗	✓
SCROLLING= AUTO|YES|NO	✗	✗	✓	✗	✗	✗	✗	✗	✓
SRC=url	✗	✗	✓	✗	✗	✗	✗	✗	✓
STYLE=string	✗	✗	✓	✗	✗	✗	✗	✗	✓
TITLE=string	✗	✗	✓	✗	✗	✗	✗	✗	✓
VSPACE=number	✗	✗	✗	✗	✗	✗	✗	✗	✓
WIDTH=number	✗	✗	✓	✗	✗	✗	✗	✗	✓

\<ILAYER>

Defines a separate area of the page as an inline layer that can hold a different page. **N4 only**.

Attributes	2.0	3.2	4.0	N2	N3	N4	IE2	IE3	IE4
\<event_name>= script_code	✗	✗	✗	✗	✗	✓	✗	✗	✗
ABOVE=object_id	✗	✗	✗	✗	✗	✓	✗	✗	✗
BACKGROUND= string	✗	✗	✗	✗	✗	✓	✗	✗	✗
BELOW=object_id	✗	✗	✗	✗	✗	✓	✗	✗	✗
BGCOLOR=color	✗	✗	D	✗	✗	✓	✗	✗	✗
CLASS=classname	✗	✗	✗	✗	✗	✓	✗	✗	✗
CLIP= number[,number, number,number]	✗	✗	✗	✗	✗	✓	✗	✗	✗
ID=string	✗	✗	✗	✗	✗	✓	✗	✗	✗
LEFT=number	✗	✗	✗	✗	✗	✓	✗	✗	✗
NAME=string	✗	✗	✗	✗	✗	✓	✗	✗	✗
PAGEX=number	✗	✗	✗	✗	✗	✓	✗	✗	✗

Attributes	2.0	3.2	4.0	N2	N3	N4	IE2	IE3	IE4
PAGEY=number	✗	✗	✗	✗	✗	✓	✗	✗	✗
SRC=url	✗	✗	✗	✗	✗	✓	✗	✗	✗
STYLE=string	✗	✗	✗	✗	✗	✓	✗	✗	✗
TOP=number	✗	✗	✗	✗	✗	✓	✗	✗	✗
VISIBILITY=SHOW |HIDE |INHERIT	✗	✗	✗	✗	✗	✓	✗	✗	✗
WIDTH=number	✗	✗	✗	✗	✗	✓	✗	✗	✗
Z-INDEX=number	✗	✗	✗	✗	✗	✓	✗	✗	✗

<IMG>

Embeds an image or a video clip in the document. **Supported by ALL**.

Attributes	2.0	3.2	4.0	N2	N3	N4	IE2	IE3	IE4
<event_name>= script_code	✗	✗	✓	✗	✗	✓	✗	✗	✓
ALIGN=BASBOTTOM |ABSMIDDLE| BASELINE |BOTTOM|LEFT| MIDDLE |RIGHT| TEXTTOP|TOP	✓	✓	D	✓	✓	✓	✓	✓	✓
ALT=text	✓	✓	✓	✓	✓	✓	✓	✓	✓
BORDER=number	✗	✓	D	✓	✓	✓	✓	✓	✓
CLASS=classname	✗	✗	✓	✗	✗	✓	✗	✓	✓
CONTROLS	✗	✗	✗	✗	✗	✗	✓	✓	✗
DATAFLD=column_ name	✗	✗	✗	✗	✗	✗	✗	✗	✓
DATASRC=id	✗	✗	✗	✗	✗	✗	✗	✗	✓
DIR=LTR|RTL	✗	✗	✓	✗	✗	✗	✗	✗	✗
DYNSRC=string	✗	✗	✗	✗	✗	✗	✓	✓	✓
HEIGHT=number	✗	✓	✓	✓	✓	✓	✓	✓	✓
HSPACE=number	✗	✓	✓	✓	✓	✓	✓	✓	✓
ID=string	✗	✗	✓	✗	✗	✓	✗	✓	✓
ISMAP	✓	✓	✓	✓	✓	✓	✓	✓	✓
LANG=language_ type	✗	✗	✓	✗	✗	✗	✗	✗	✓

Attributes	2.0	3.2	4.0	N2	N3	N4	IE2	IE3	IE4
LANGUAGE= JAVASCRIPT |JSCRIPT| VBSCRIPT|VBS	✗	✗	✗	✗	✗	✗	✗	✗	✓
LONGDESC=url	✗	✗	✓	✗	✗	✗	✗	✗	✗
LOOP=number	✗	✗	✗	✗	✗	✗	✓	✓	✓
LOWSRC=url	✗	✗	✗	✓	✓	✓	✗	✗	✓
NAME=string	✗	✗	✗	✗	✗	✓	✗	✗	✓
SRC=url	✓	✓	✓	✓	✓	✓	✓	✓	✓
START= number|string	✗	✗	✗	✗	✗	✗	✓	✓	✗
STYLE=string	✗	✗	✓	✗	✗	✓	✗	✓	✓
TITLE=string	✗	✗	✓	✗	✗	✗	✗	✓	✓
USEMAP=url	✗	✓	✓	✓	✓	✓	✓	✓	✓
VSPACE=number	✗	✓	✓	✓	✓	✓	✓	✓	✓
WIDTH=number	✗	✓	✓	✓	✓	✓	✓	✓	✓

<INPUT>

Specifies a form input control, such as a button, text or check box. **Supported by ALL**.

Attributes	2.0	3.2	4.0	N2	N3	N4	IE2	IE3	IE4
<event_name>= script_code	✗	✗	✓	✗	✗	✓	✗	✓	✓
ACCEPT=string	✗	✗	✓	✗	✗	✗	✗	✗	✗
ACCESSKEY=key_ character	✗	✗	✓	✗	✗	✗	✗	✗	✓
ALIGN=CENTER| LEFT|RIGHT	✓	✓	D	✓	✓	✓	✓	✓	✓
ALT=text	✗	✗	✓	✗	✗	✗	✗	✗	✗
CHECKED= FALSE|TRUE	✓	✓	✓	✓	✓	✓	✓	✓	✓
CLASS=classname	✗	✗	✓	✗	✗	✓	✗	✓	✓
DATAFLD=column_ name	✗	✗	✗	✗	✗	✗	✗	✗	✓
DATAFORMATAS= HTML|TEXT	✗	✗	✗	✗	✗	✗	✗	✗	✓
DATASRC=id	✗	✗	✗	✗	✗	✗	✗	✗	✓

Attributes	2.0	3.2	4.0	N2	N3	N4	IE2	IE3	IE4
DIR=LTR|RTL	✗	✗	✓	✗	✗	✗	✗	✗	✗
DISABLED	✗	✗	✓	✗	✗	✗	✗	✗	✓
ID=string	✗	✗	✓	✗	✗	✓	✗	✓	✓
LANG=language_type	✗	✗	✓	✗	✗	✗	✗	✗	✓
LANGUAGE=JAVASCRIPT |JSCRIPT| VBSCRIPT|VBS	✗	✗	✗	✗	✗	✗	✗	✗	✓
MAXLENGTH=number	✓	✓	✓	✓	✓	✓	✓	✓	✓
NAME=string	✓	✓	✓	✓	✓	✓	✓	✓	✓
NOTAB	✗	✗	✗	✗	✗	✗	✗	✓	✗
READONLY	✗	✗	✓	✗	✗	✗	✗	✗	✓
SIZE=number	✓	✓	✓	✓	✓	✓	✓	✓	✓
SRC=url	✓	✓	✓	✓	✓	✗	✓	✓	✓
STYLE=string	✗	✗	✓	✗	✗	✓	✗	✓	✓
TABINDEX=number	✗	✗	✓	✗	✗	✗	✗	✓	✓
TITLE=string	✗	✗	✓	✗	✗	✗	✗	✓	✓
TYPE=BUTTON| CHECKBOX |FILE|HIDDEN| IMAGE |PASSWORD| RADIO|RESET |SUBMIT|TEXT	✓	✓	✓	✓	✓	✓	✓	✓	✓
USEMAP=url	✗	✗	✓	✗	✗	✗	✗	✗	✗
VALUE=string	✓	✓	✓	✓	✓	✓	✓	✓	✓

<LABEL>

Defines the text of a label for a control-like element. **HTML 4.0, IE4**.

Attributes	2.0	3.2	4.0	N2	N3	N4	IE2	IE3	IE4
<event_name>= script_code	✗	✗	✓	✗	✗	✗	✗	✗	✓
ACCESSKEY=key_character	✗	✗	✓	✗	✗	✗	✗	✗	✓
CLASS=classname	✗	✗	✓	✗	✗	✗	✗	✗	✓

Attributes	2.0	3.2	4.0	N2	N3	N4	IE2	IE3	IE4
DATAFLD=column_name	✗	✗	✗	✗	✗	✗	✗	✗	✓
DATAFORMATAS=HTML|TEXT	✗	✗	✗	✗	✗	✗	✗	✗	✓
DATASRC=id	✗	✗	✗	✗	✗	✗	✗	✗	✓
DIR=LTR|RTL	✗	✗	✓	✗	✗	✗	✗	✗	✗
FOR=element_name	✗	✗	✓	✗	✗	✗	✗	✗	✓
ID=string	✗	✗	✓	✗	✗	✗	✗	✗	✓
LANG=language_type	✗	✗	✓	✗	✗	✗	✗	✗	✓
LANGUAGE=JAVASCRIPT|JSCRIPT|VBSCRIPT|VBS	✗	✗	✗	✗	✗	✗	✗	✗	✓
STYLE=string	✗	✗	✓	✗	✗	✗	✗	✗	✓

<LAYER>

Defines a separate area of the page as a layer that can hold a different page. **N4 only**.

Attributes	2.0	3.2	4.0	N2	N3	N4	IE2	IE3	IE4
<event_name>=script_code	✗	✗	✗	✗	✗	✓	✗	✗	✗
ABOVE=object_id	✗	✗	✗	✗	✗	✓	✗	✗	✗
BACKGROUND=string	✗	✗	✗	✗	✗	✓	✗	✗	✗
BELOW=object_id	✗	✗	✗	✗	✗	✓	✗	✗	✗
BGCOLOR=color	✗	✗	D	✗	✗	✓	✗	✗	✗
CLASS=classname	✗	✗	✗	✗	✗	✓	✗	✗	✗
CLIP=number [,number,number,number]	✗	✗	✗	✗	✗	✓	✗	✗	✗
ID=string	✗	✗	✗	✗	✗	✓	✗	✗	✗
LEFT=number	✗	✗	✗	✗	✗	✓	✗	✗	✗
NAME=string	✗	✗	✗	✗	✗	✓	✗	✗	✗
PAGEX=number	✗	✗	✗	✗	✗	✓	✗	✗	✗
PAGEY=number	✗	✗	✗	✗	✗	✓	✗	✗	✗

Attributes	2.0	3.2	4.0	N2	N3	N4	IE2	IE3	IE4
SRC=url	✗	✗	✗	✗	✗	✓	✗	✗	✗
STYLE=string	✗	✗	✗	✗	✗	✓	✗	✗	✗
TOP=number	✗	✗	✗	✗	✗	✓	✗	✗	✗
VISIBILITY=SHOW |HIDE |INHERIT	✗	✗	✗	✗	✗	✓	✗	✗	✗
WIDTH=number	✗	✗	✗	✗	✗	✓	✗	✗	✗
Z-INDEX=number	✗	✗	✗	✗	✗	✓	✗	✗	✗

<LINK>

Defines a hyperlink between the document and some other resource. **HTML 2.0, 3.2 & 4.0, IE3, IE4**.

Attributes	2.0	3.2	4.0	N2	N3	N4	IE2	IE3	IE4
<event_name>= script_code	✗	✗	✓	✗	✗	✗	✗	✗	✗
CHARSET=charset	✗	✗	✓	✗	✗	✗	✗	✗	✗
CLASS=classname	✗	✗	✓	✗	✗	✗	✗	✗	✗
DIR=LTR|RTL	✗	✗	✓	✗	✗	✗	✗	✗	✗
DISABLED	✗	✗	✗	✗	✗	✗	✗	✗	✓
HREF=url	✓	✓	✓	✓	✓	✓	✗	✓	✓
HREFLANG= langcode	✗	✗	✓	✗	✗	✗	✗	✗	✗
ID=string	✗	✗	✓	✗	✗	✓	✗	✗	✓
LANG=language_ type	✗	✗	✓	✗	✗	✗	✗	✗	✓
MEDIA=SCREEN| PRINT| PROJECTION| BRAILLE|SPEECH| ALL	✗	✗	✓	✗	✗	✗	✗	✗	✓
METHODS=string	✓	✗	✗	✗	✗	✗	✗	✗	✗
REL= relationship	✓	✓	✓	✓	✓	✓	✗	✓	✓
REV= relationship	✓	✓	✓	✓	✓	✓	✗	✓	✗
STYLE=string	✗	✗	✓	✗	✗	✓	✗	✗	✗

Attributes	2.0	3.2	4.0	N2	N3	N4	IE2	IE3	IE4
TARGET=<window_name>|_parent|_blank|_tope|_self	✗	✗	✓	✗	✗	✗	✗	✗	✗
TITLE=string	✓	✓	✓	✓	✓	✓	✗	✓	✓
TYPE=MIME-type	✗	✗	✓	✗	✗	✓	✗	✓	✓
URN=string	✓	✗	✗	✗	✗	✗	✗	✗	✗

<OBJECT>

Inserts an object or other non-intrinsic HTML control into the page. **HTML 4.0, IE3, IE4**.

Attributes	2.0	3.2	4.0	N2	N3	N4	IE2	IE3	IE4
<event_name>=script_code	✗	✗	✓	✗	✗	✗	✗	✗	✓
ACCESSKEY=key_character	✗	✗	✗	✗	✗	✗	✗	✗	✓
ALIGN=ABSBOTTOM|ABSMIDDLE|BASELINE|BOTTOM|LEFT|MIDDLE|RIGHT|TEXTTOP|TOP	✓	✓	D	✗	✗	✗	✗	✓	✓
ARCHIVE=urllist	✗	✗	✓	✗	✗	✗	✗	✗	✗
BORDER=number	✗	✗	D	✗	✗	✗	✗	✓	✗
CLASS=classname	✗	✗	✓	✗	✗	✗	✗	✗	✓
CLASSID=string	✗	✗	✓	✗	✗	✗	✗	✓	✓
CODE=filename	✗	✗	✗	✗	✗	✗	✗	✗	✓
CODEBASE=url	✗	✗	✓	✗	✗	✗	✗	✓	✓
CODETYPE=url	✗	✗	✓	✗	✗	✗	✗	✓	✓
DATA=string	✗	✗	✓	✗	✗	✗	✗	✓	✓
DATAFLD=column_name	✗	✗	✗	✗	✗	✗	✗	✗	✓
DATASRC=id	✗	✗	✗	✗	✗	✗	✗	✗	✓
DECLARE	✗	✗	✓	✗	✗	✗	✗	✓	✗
DIR=LTR|RTL	✗	✗	✓	✗	✗	✗	✗	✗	✗
EXPORT	✗	✗	✓	✗	✗	✗	✗	✗	✗

Attributes	2.0	3.2	4.0	N2	N3	N4	IE2	IE3	IE4
HEIGHT=number	✗	✗	✓	✗	✗	✗	✗	✓	✓
HSPACE=number	✗	✗	✓	✗	✗	✗	✗	✓	✗
ID=string	✗	✗	✓	✗	✗	✗	✗	✗	✓
LANG=language_type	✗	✗	✓	✗	✗	✗	✗	✗	✓
LANGUAGE=JAVASCRIPT|JSCRIPT|VBSCRIPT|VBS	✗	✗	✗	✗	✗	✗	✗	✗	✓
NAME=string	✗	✗	✓	✗	✗	✗	✗	✓	✓
NOTAB	✗	✗	✗	✗	✗	✗	✗	✓	✗
SHAPES	✗	✗	✓	✗	✗	✗	✗	✓	✗
STANDBY=string	✗	✗	✓	✗	✗	✗	✗	✓	✗
STYLE=string	✗	✗	✓	✗	✗	✗	✗	✗	✓
TABINDEX=number	✗	✗	✓	✗	✗	✗	✗	✓	✓
TITLE=string	✗	✗	✓	✗	✗	✗	✗	✓	✓
TYPE=MIME-type	✗	✗	✓	✗	✗	✗	✗	✗	✗
USEMAP=url	✗	✗	✓	✗	✗	✗	✗	✓	✗
VSPACE=number	✗	✗	✓	✗	✗	✗	✗	✓	✗
WIDTH=number	✗	✗	✓	✗	✗	✗	✗	✓	✓

<OPTION>

Denotes one choice in a SELECT drop-down or list element. **ALL**.

Attributes	2.0	3.2	4.0	N2	N3	N4	IE2	IE3	IE4
<event_name>=script_code	✗	✗	✓	✗	✗	✗	✗	✗	✓
CLASS=classname	✗	✗	✓	✗	✗	✓	✗	✗	✓
DIR=LTR|RTL	✗	✗	✓	✗	✗	✗	✗	✗	✗
DISABLED	✗	✗	✓	✓	✓	✗	✗	✗	✗
ID=string	✗	✗	✓	✗	✗	✓	✗	✗	✓
LABEL=string	✗	✗	✓	✗	✗	✗	✗	✗	✗
LANG=language_type	✗	✗	✓	✗	✗	✗	✗	✗	✗

Attributes	2.0	3.2	4.0	N2	N3	N4	IE2	IE3	IE4
LANGUAGE= JAVASCRIPT |JSCRIPT| VBSCRIPT|VBS	✗	✗	✗	✗	✗	✗	✗	✗	✓
PLAIN	✗	✗	✗	✓	✓	✓	✗	✗	✗
SELECTED	✓	✓	✓	✓	✓	✓	✓	✓	✓
STYLE=string	✗	✗	✓	✗	✗	✓	✗	✗	✗
TITLE=string	✗	✗	✓	✗	✗	✗	✗	✗	✗
VALUE=string	✓	✓	✓	✓	✓	✓	✓	✓	✓

\<PARAM\>

Used in an \<OBJECT\> or \<APPLET\> tag to set the object's properties. **ALL except HTML 2.0.**

Attributes	2.0	3.2	4.0	N2	N3	N4	IE2	IE3	IE4
DATAFLD=column_ name	✗	✗	✗	✗	✗	✗	✗	✗	✓
DATAFORMATAS= HTML|TEXT	✗	✗	✗	✗	✗	✗	✗	✗	✓
DATASRC=id	✗	✗	✗	✗	✗	✗	✗	✗	✓
ID=string	✗	✗	✓	✗	✗	✗	✗	✗	✗
NAME=string	✗	✓	✓	✓	✓	✓	✗	✓	✓
TYPE=string	✗	✗	✓	✗	✗	✗	✗	✓	✗
VALUE=string	✗	✓	✓	✓	✓	✓	✗	✓	✓
VALUETYPE=DATA| REF|OBJECT	✗	✗	✓	✗	✗	✗	✗	✓	✗

\<SCRIPT\>

Specifies a script for the page that will be interpreted by a script engine. **HTML 3.2, 4.0, N2, N3, N4, IE3, IE4.**

Attributes	2.0	3.2	4.0	N2	N3	N4	IE2	IE3	IE4
ARCHIVE=url	✗	✗	✗	✗	✗	✓	✗	✗	✗
CHARSET=charset	✗	✗	✓	✗	✗	✗	✗	✗	✗
CLASS=classname	✗	✗	✗	✗	✗	✓	✗	✗	✓
DEFER	✗	✗	✓	✗	✗	✗	✗	✗	✗

Attributes	2.0	3.2	4.0	N2	N3	N4	IE2	IE3	IE4
EVENT= <event_name>	✗	✗	✗	✗	✗	✗	✗	✗	✓
FOR= element_name	✗	✗	✗	✗	✗	✗	✗	✗	✓
ID=string	✗	✗	✗	✗	✗	✓	✗	✗	✓
LANGUAGE= JAVASCRIPT |JSCRIPT| VBSCRIPT|VBS	✗	✗	D	✓	✓	✓	✗	✓	✓
SRC=url	✗	✗	✓	✗	✓	✓	✗	✓	✓
STYLE=string	✗	✗	✗	✗	✗	✓	✗	✗	✓
TITLE=string	✗	✗	✗	✗	✗	✗	✗	✗	✓
TYPE=string	✗	✗	✓	✗	✗	✗	✗	✓	✓

<SELECT>

Defines a list box or drop-down list. **ALL.**

Attributes	2.0	3.2	4.0	N2	N3	N4	IE2	IE3	IE4
<event_name>= script_code	✗	✗	✓	✗	✗	✓	✗	✗	✓
ACCESSKEY=key_c haracter	✗	✗	✗	✗	✗	✗	✗	✗	✓
ALIGN=ABSBOTTOM |ABSMIDDLE| BASELINE |BOTTOM|LEFT| MIDDLE |RIGHT| TEXTTOP|TOP	✗	✗	✗	✗	✗	✗	✗	✗	✓
CLASS=classname	✗	✗	✓	✗	✗	✓	✗	✗	✓
DATAFLD=column_ name	✗	✗	✗	✗	✗	✗	✗	✗	✓
DATASRC=id	✗	✗	✗	✗	✗	✗	✗	✗	✓
DIR=LTR|RTL	✗	✗	✓	✗	✗	✗	✗	✗	✗
DISABLED	✗	✗	✓	✗	✗	✗	✗	✗	✓
ID=string	✗	✗	✓	✗	✗	✓	✗	✗	✓
LANG=language_ type	✗	✗	✓	✗	✗	✗	✗	✗	✓

Attributes	2.0	3.2	4.0	N2	N3	N4	IE2	IE3	IE4
LANGUAGE= JAVASCRIPT I JSCRIPT I VBSCRIPT I VBS	✗	✗	✗	✗	✗	✗	✗	✗	✓
MULTIPLE	✓	✓	✓	✓	✓	✓	✓	✓	✓
NAME=string	✓	✓	✓	✓	✓	✓	✓	✓	✓
SIZE=number	✓	✓	✓	✓	✓	✓	✓	✓	✓
STYLE=string	✗	✗	✓	✗	✗	✓	✗	✗	✓
TABINDEX=number	✗	✗	✓	✗	✗	✗	✗	✗	✓
TITLE=string	✗	✗	✓	✗	✗	✗	✗	✗	✓

<STYLE>

Specifies the style properties (i.e. the style sheet) for the page. **HTML 3.2, 4.0, N4, IE3, IE4.**

Attributes	2.0	3.2	4.0	N2	N3	N4	IE2	IE3	IE4
DIR=LTR I RTL	✗	✗	✓	✗	✗	✗	✗	✗	✗
DISABLED	✗	✗	✗	✗	✗	✗	✗	✗	✓
ID=string	✗	✗	✗	✗	✗	✓	✗	✗	✗
LANG=language_ type	✗	✗	✓	✗	✗	✗	✗	✗	✗
MEDIA=SCREEN I PRINT I PROJECTION I BRAILLE I SPEECH I ALL	✗	✗	✓	✗	✗	✗	✗	✗	✓
SRC=url	✗	✗	✗	✗	✗	✓	✗	✗	✗
TITLE=string	✗	✗	✓	✗	✗	✗	✗	✓	✓
TYPE=string	✗	✗	✓	✗	✗	✓	✗	✓	✓

<TITLE>

Denotes the title of the document and used in the browser's window title bar. **ALL.**

Attributes	2.0	3.2	4.0	N2	N3	N4	IE2	IE3	IE4
DIR=LTR I RTL	✗	✗	✓	✗	✗	✗	✗	✗	✗
ID=string	✗	✗	✗	✗	✗	✓	✗	✗	✓

Attributes	2.0	3.2	4.0	N2	N3	N4	IE2	IE3	IE4
LANG=language_ type	✗	✗	✓	✗	✗	✗	✗	✗	✗
TITLE=string	✗	✗	✗	✗	✗	✗	✗	✗	✓

Colors Sorted by Group

Blues

Color Name	Value	IE4 Color Constant
azure	F0FFFF	htmlAzure
aliceblue	F0F8FF	htmlAliceBlue
lavender	E6E6FA	htmlLavender
lightcyan	E0FFFF	htmlLightCyan
powderblue	B0E0E6	htmlPowderBlue
lightsteelblue	B0C4DE	htmlLightSteelBlue
paleturquoise	AFEEEE	htmlPaleTurquoise
lightblue	ADD8E6	htmlLightBlue
blueviolet	8A2BE2	htmlBlueViolet
lightskyblue	87CEFA	htmlLightSkyBlue
skyblue	87CEEB	htmlSkyBlue
mediumslateblue	7B68EE	htmlMediumSlateBlue
slateblue	6A5ACD	htmlSlateBlue
cornflowerblue	6495ED	htmlCornflowerBlue
cadetblue	5F9EA0	htmlCadetBlue
indigo	4B0082	htmlIndigo
mediumturquoise	48D1CC	htmlMediumTurquoise
darkslateblue	483D8B	htmlDarkSlateBlue
steelblue	4682B4	htmlSteelBlue
royalblue	4169E1	htmlRoyalBlue
turquoise	40E0D0	htmlTurquoise
dodgerblue	1E90FF	htmlDodgerBlue

Color Name	Value	IE4 Color Constant
midnightblue	191970	htmlMidnightBlue
aqua	00FFFF	htmlAqua
cyan	00FFFF	htmlCyan
darkturquoise	00CED1	htmlDarkTurquoise
deepskyblue	00BFFF	htmlDeepSkyBlue
darkcyan	008B8B	htmlDarkCyan
blue	0000FF	htmlBlue
mediumblue	0000CD	htmlMediumBlue
darkblue	00008B	htmlDarkBlue
navy	000080	htmlNavy

Greens

Color Name	Value	IE4 Color Constant
mintcream	F5FFFA	htmlMintCream
honeydew	F0FFF0	htmlHoneydew
greenyellow	ADFF2F	htmlGreenYellow
yellowgreen	9ACD32	htmlYellowGreen
palegreen	98FB98	htmlPaleGreen
lightgreen	90EE90	htmlLightGreen
darkseagreen	8FBC8F	htmlDarkSeaGreen
olive	808000	htmlOlive
aquamarine	7FFFD4	htmlAquamarine
chartreuse	7FFF00	htmlChartreuse
lawngreen	7CFC00	htmlLawnGreen
olivedrab	6B8E23	htmlOliveDrab
mediumaquamarine	66CDAA	htmlMediumAquamarine
darkolivegreen	556B2F	htmlDarkOliveGreen
mediumseagreen	3CB371	htmlMediumSeaGreen
limegreen	32CD32	htmlLimeGreen

Color Name	Value	IE4 Color Constant
seagreen	2E8B57	htmlSeaGreen
forestgreen	228B22	htmlForestGreen
lightseagreen	20B2AA	htmlLightSeaGreen
springgreen	00FF7F	htmlSpringGreen
lime	00FF00	htmlLime
mediumspringgreen	00FA9A	htmlMediumSpringGreen
teal	008080	htmlTeal
green	008000	htmlGreen
darkgreen	006400	htmlDarkGreen

Pinks and Reds

Color Name	Value	IE4 Color Constant
lavenderblush	FFF0F5	htmlLavenderBlush
mistyrose	FFE4E1	htmlMistyRose
pink	FFC0CB	htmlPink
lightpink	FFB6C1	htmlLightPink
orange	FFA500	htmlOrange
lightsalmon	FFA07A	htmlLightSalmon
darkorange	FF8C00	htmlDarkOrange
coral	FF7F50	htmlCoral
hotpink	FF69B4	htmlHotPink
tomato	FF6347	htmlTomato
orangered	FF4500	htmlOrangeRed
deeppink	FF1493	htmlDeepPink
fuchsia	FF00FF	htmlFuchsia
magenta	FF00FF	htmlMagenta
red	FF0000	htmlRed
salmon	FA8072	htmlSalmon
lightcoral	F08080	htmlLightCoral

Color Name	Value	IE4 Color Constant
violet	EE82EE	htmlViolet
darksalmon	E9967A	htmlDarkSalmon
plum	DDA0DD	htmlPlum
crimson	DC143C	htmlCrimson
palevioletred	DB7093	htmlPaleVioletRed
orchid	DA70D6	htmlOrchid
thistle	D8BFD8	htmlThistle
indianred	CD5C5C	htmlIndianRed
mediumvioletred	C71585	htmlMediumVioletRed
mediumorchid	BA55D3	htmlMediumOrchid
firebrick	B22222	htmlFirebrick
darkorchid	9932CC	htmlDarkOrchid
darkviolet	9400D3	htmlDarkViolet
mediumpurple	9370DB	htmlMediumPurple
darkmagenta	8B008B	htmlDarkMagenta
darkred	8B0000	htmlDarkRed
purple	800080	htmlPurple
maroon	800000	htmlMaroon

Yellows

Color Name	Value	IE4 Color Constant
ivory	FFFFF0	htmlIvory
lightyellow	FFFFE0	htmlLightYellow
yellow	FFFF00	htmlYellow
floralwhite	FFFAF0	htmlFloralWhite
lemonchiffon	FFFACD	htmlLemonChiffon
cornsilk	FFF8DC	htmlCornsilk
gold	FFD700	htmlGold
khaki	F0E68C	htmlKhaki
darkkhaki	BDB76B	htmlDarkKhaki

Beiges and Browns

Color Name	Value	IE4 Color Constant
snow	FFFAFA	htmlSnow
seashell	FFF5EE	htmlSeashell
papayawhite	FFEFD5	htmlPapayaWhite
blanchedalmond	FFEBCD	htmlBlanchedAlmond
bisque	FFE4C4	htmlBisque
moccasin	FFE4B5	htmlMoccasin
navajowhite	FFDEAD	htmlNavajoWhite
peachpuff	FFDAB9	htmlPeachPuff
oldlace	FDF5E6	htmlOldLace
linen	FAF0E6	htmlLinen
antiquewhite	FAEBD7	htmlAntiqueWhite
beige	F5F5DC	htmlBeige
wheat	F5DEB3	htmlWheat
sandybrown	F4A460	htmlSandyBrown
palegoldenrod	EEE8AA	htmlPaleGoldenRod
burlywood	DEB887	htmlBurlywood
goldenrod	DAA520	htmlGoldenRod
tan	D2B48C	htmlTan
chocolate	D2691E	htmlChocolate
peru	CD853F	htmlPeru
rosybrown	BC8F8F	htmlRosyBrown
darkgoldenrod	B8860B	htmlDarkGoldenRod
brown	A52A2A	htmlBrown
sienna	A0522D	htmlSienna
saddlebrown	8B4513	htmlSaddleBrown

Whites and Grays

Color Name	Value	IE4 Color Constant
white	FFFFFF	htmlWhite
ghostwhite	F8F8FF	htmlGhostWhite
whitesmoke	F5F5F5	htmlWhiteSmoke
gainsboro	DCDCDC	htmlGainsboro
lightgray	D3D3D3	htmlLightGray
silver	C0C0C0	htmlSilver
darkgray	A9A9A9	htmlDarkGray
gray	808080	htmlGray
lightslategray	778899	htmlLightSlateGray
slategray	708090	htmlSlateGray
dimgray	696969	htmlDimGray
darkslategray	2F4F4F	htmlDarkSlateGray
black	000000	htmlBlack

JavaScript Objects

Javascript Reserved Words

There is an extensive range of words that, for a number of reasons, are reserved in JavaScript, and can not or should not be used as identifiers. Some of these are common across all implementations of JavaScript; others are reserved in only some implementations. Others still–particularly in ECMAScript–cover proposed extensions to the language, which have not yet been implemented, and so are called future reserved words. Furthermore, because JavaScript can be combined with a number of other languages, as well as aspects of HTML and CSS, it is advisable to also avoid reserved words for these languages as well.

JavaScript-Specific Keywords

These are organized by implementation; if you've decided to specialize in a single browser implementation, then you may choose not to worry about reserved keywords for other browsers, though we advise against this. Ticks mean the word is reserved (or is a future reserved word), crosses that it is free for use.

	JavaScript	JScript	ECMAScript
abstract	✓	✗	✓
boolean	✓	✗	✓
break	✓	✓	✓
byte	✓	✗	✓
case	✓	✓	✓
catch	✓	✓	✓
char	✓	✗	✓

Table Continued on Following Page

	JavaScript	JScript	ECMAScript
class	✓	✓	✓
const	✓	✓	✓
continue	✓	✓	✓
debugger	✓	✓	✓
default	✓	✓	✓
delete	✓	✓	✓
do	✓	✓	✓
double	✓	✗	✓
else	✓	✓	✓
enum	✗	✓	✓
export	✗	✓	✓
extends	✓	✓	✓
false	✓	✓	✗
final	✓	✗	✓
finally	✓	✓	✓
float	✓	✗	✓
for	✓	✓	✓
function	✓	✓	✓
goto	✓	✗	✓
if	✓	✓	✓
implements	✓	✗	✓
import	✓	✓	✓
in	✓	✓	✓
instanceof	✓	✗	✓
int	✓	✗	✓
interface	✓	✗	✓
long	✓	✗	✓
native	✓	✗	✓
new	✓	✓	✓
null	✓	✓	✗

	JavaScript	JScript	ECMAScript
package	✓	✗	✓
private	✓	✗	✓
protected	✓	✗	✓
public	✓	✗	✓
return	✓	✓	✓
short	✓	✗	✓
static	✓	✗	✓
super	✓	✓	✓
switch	✓	✓	✓
synchronized	✓	✗	✓
this	✓	✓	✓
throw	✓	✓	✓
throws	✓	✗	✓
transient	✓	✗	✓
true	✓	✓	✗
try	✓	✓	✓
typeof	✓	✓	✓
var	✓	✓	✓
void	✓	✓	✓
volatile	✗	✗	✓
while	✓	✓	✓
with	✓	✓	✓

Keywords in Java

The following keywords are reserved in Java so you should avoid using them as names in your programs, regardless of implementation:

abstract	finally	protected
boolean	float	public
break	for	return

Table Continued on Following Page

byte	goto	short
case	if	static
catch	implements	super
char	import	switch
class	instanceof	synchronized
const	int	this
continue	interface	throw
default	long	throws
do	native	transient
double	new	try
else	null	void
extends	package	volatile
final	private	while

You should also not attempt to use the boolean values `true` and `false` as names in your programs.

Reserved Words in C

The words in the following list are **keywords** in C, so you should avoid using them as names in your programs, regardless of implementation:

auto	enum	signed
break	extern	sizeof
case	float	static
char	for	struct
const	goto	switch
continue	if	typedef
default	int	union
defined	long	unsigned
do	register	void
double	return	volatile
else	short	while

StyleSheet/JSS property names

This is a listing of all the properties used in stylesheets as defined in CSS1 and their JavaScript StyleSheet (JSS) equivalents, where appropriate. As with reserved words, they should be avoided in JavaScript programming.

CSS1	JSS
font	
font-family	fontFamily
font-size	fontSize
font-style	fontStyle
font-variant	
font-weight	fontWeight
color	color
background	
background-attachment	
background-color	backgroundColor
background-image	backgroundImage
background-position	
background-repeat	
letter-spacing	
line-height	lineHeight
text-align	textAlign
text-decoration	textDecoration
text-indent	textIndent
text-transform	textTransform
vertical-align	verticalAlign
word-spacing	
border	
border-bottom	
border-bottom-width	borderBottomWidth
border-color	borderColor
border-left	
border-left-width	borderLeftWidth

Table Continued on Following Page

border-right	
border-right-width	borderRightWidth
border-style	borderStyle
border-top	borderTopWidth
border-top-width	
border-width	borderWidths()
clear	clear
display	display
float	align
height	height
left	
list-style	
list-style-image	
list-style-position	
list-style-type	listStyleType
margin	margins
margin-bottom	marginBottom
margin-left	marginLeft()
margin-right	marginRight
margin-top	marginTop
overflow	
padding	paddings()
padding-bottom	paddingBottom
padding-left	paddingLeft
padding-right	paddingRight
padding-top	paddingTop
position	
top	
visibility	
white-space	whiteSpace
width	width
z-index	

HTML Tags

You should, of course avoid using any of the HTML tags, properties or attributes as anything except themselves in JavaScript programming. See Appendix D for a list of HTML tags or for a complete reference, consult the Wrox Press book

Instant HTML Programmer's Reference (ISBN 1-861001-56-8)

To quickly check the availability of any names, use the Wrox Press Ultimate HTML database, available online at `http://webdev.wrox.co.uk/html4db`.

Standards

This table provides a guide to the location of all the standards mentioned in the book. Except where indicated, all of these are free for download, and provide an invaluable selection of resources for the JavaScript programmer determined to get the most out of JavaScript and its related technologies.

Standards	Location
HTML 4.0	http://www.w3.org/TR/PR-html40/
HTML 3.2	http://www.w3.org/TR/REC-html32
ECMAScript	http://www.ecma.ch/stand/ecma-262.htm
JavaScript 1.0, 1.1, 1.2, 1.3	http://developer.netscape.com/docs/manuals/index.html
JSRef JScript 1.0, 2.0, 3.0, 3.1	http://msdn.microsoft.com/scripting/ default.htm
CSS1, CSS1 Positioning.	http://www.w3.org/TR/REC-CSS1
DOM	http://www.w3.org/DOM/
URL Encoding, RFC1738	http://www.scit.wlv.ac.uk/~c9451595/rfc/ rfc17xx/RFC1738.html
Unicode 2.0, 2.1	http://www.unicode.org/unicode/standard/ standard.html
Perl Reg. Exps.	http://reference.perl.com/query.cgi?regexp
CGI Standards	http://hoohoo.ncsa.uiuc.edu/cgi/ interface.html
POSIX	http://www.pasc.org/abstracts/1003p1.htm
C - ANSI X3.159-1989	ftp://ftp.uu.net/doc/standards/ansi/X3.159-1989
floating point ANSI/ IEEE 1754-1985	available to buy from IEEE

Support and Errata

One of the most irritating things about any programming book can be when you find that bit of code you've just spent an hour typing in simply doesn't work. You check it a hundred times to see if you've set it up correctly and then you notice the spelling mistake in the variable name on the book page. Grrr! Of course, you can blame the authors for not taking enough care and testing the code, the editors for not doing their job properly, or the proofreaders for not being eagle-eyed enough, but this doesn't get around the fact that mistakes do happen.

We try hard to ensure no mistakes sneak out into the real world, but we can't promise that this book is 100% error free. What we can do is offer the next best thing by providing you with immediate support and feedback from experts who have worked on the book and try to ensure that future editions eliminate these gremlins. The following section will take you step by step through the process of posting errata to our web site to get that help. The sections that follow, therefore, are:

- ❑ Wrox Developers Membership
- ❑ Finding a list of existing errata on the web site
- ❑ Adding your own errata to the existing list
- ❑ What happens to your errata once you've posted it (why doesn't it appear immediately?)

There is also a section covering how to e-mail a question for technical support. This comprises:

- ❑ What your e-mail should include
- ❑ What happens to your e-mail once it has been received by us

So that you only need view information relevant to yourself, we ask that you register as a Wrox Developer Member. This is a quick and easy process, that will save you time in the long-run. If you are already a member, just update your membership to include this book.

Wrox Developer's Membership

To get your FREE Wrox Developer's Membership click on Membership in the navigation bar of our home site

www.wrox.com.

This is shown in the following screen shot:

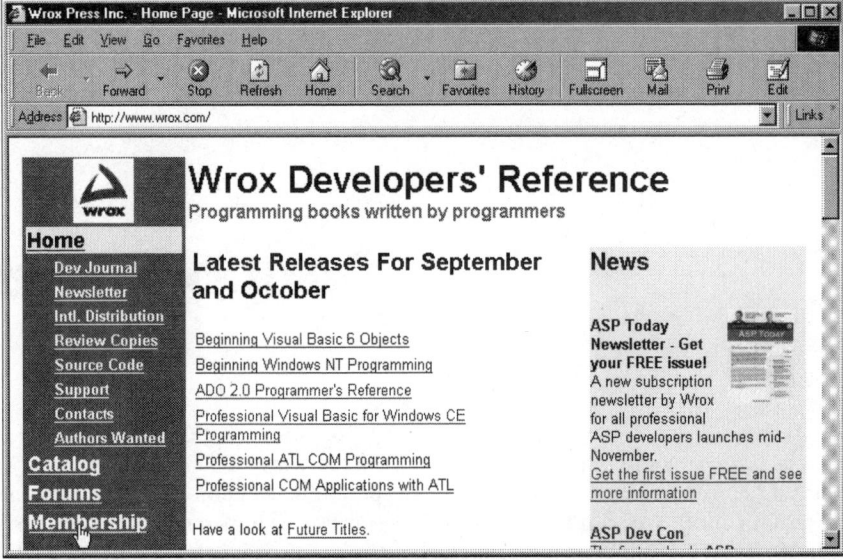

Then, on the next screen (not shown), click on **New User**. This will display a form. Fill in the details on the form and submit the details using the **submit** button at the bottom. Before you can say 'The best read books come in Wrox Red' you will get this screen:

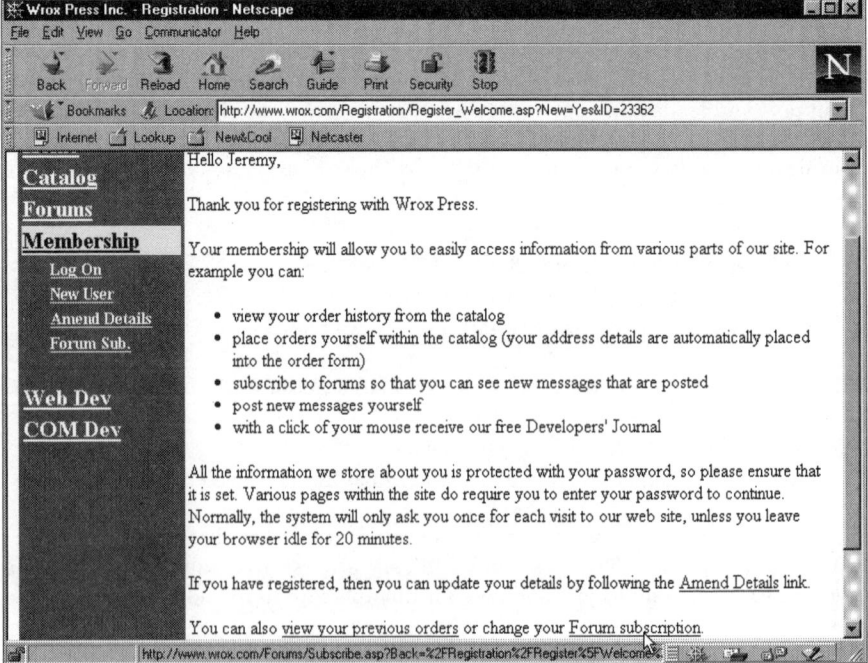

Finding an Errata on the Web Site

Before you send in a query, you might be able to save time by finding the answer to your problem on our web site: http:\\www.wrox.com.

Each book we publish has its own page and its own errata sheet. You can get to any book's page by clicking on support from the left hand side navigation bar.

From this page you can locate any books errata page on our site. Select your book from the pop-up menu and click on it.

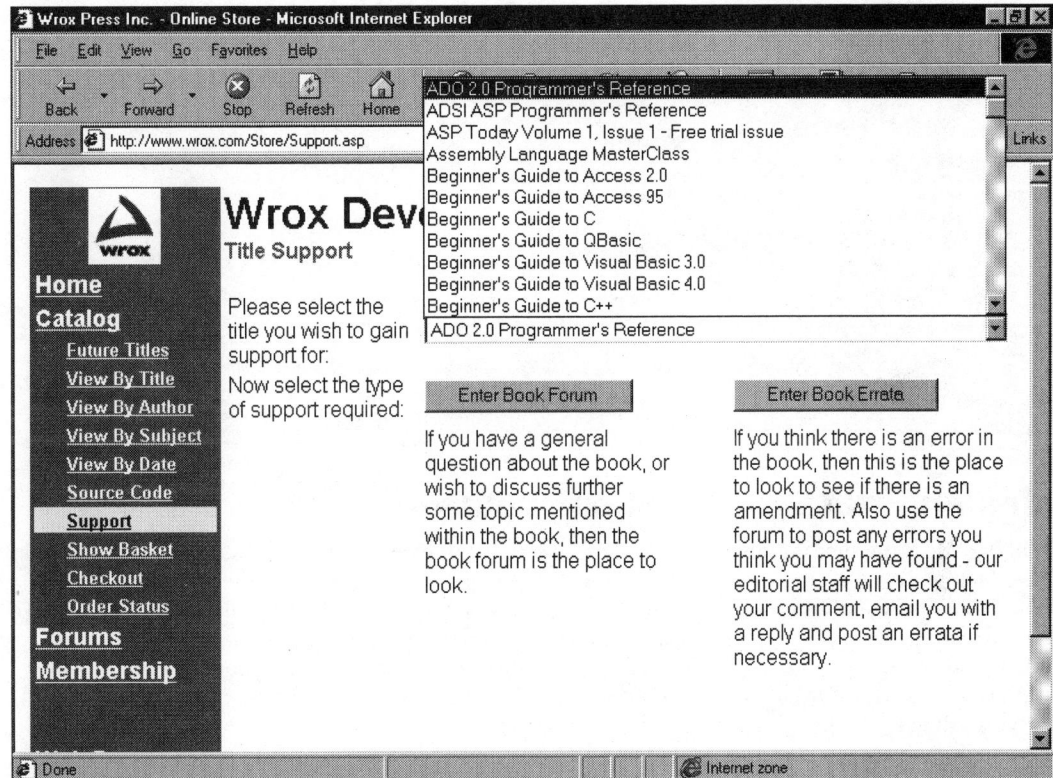

Then click on Enter Book Errata. This will take you to the errata page for the book. Select the criteria by which you want to view the errata, and click the apply criteria button. This will provide you with links to specific errata. For an initial search, you are advised to view the errata by page numbers. If you have looked for an error previously, then you may wish to limit your search using dates. We update these pages daily to ensure that you have the latest information on bugs and errors.

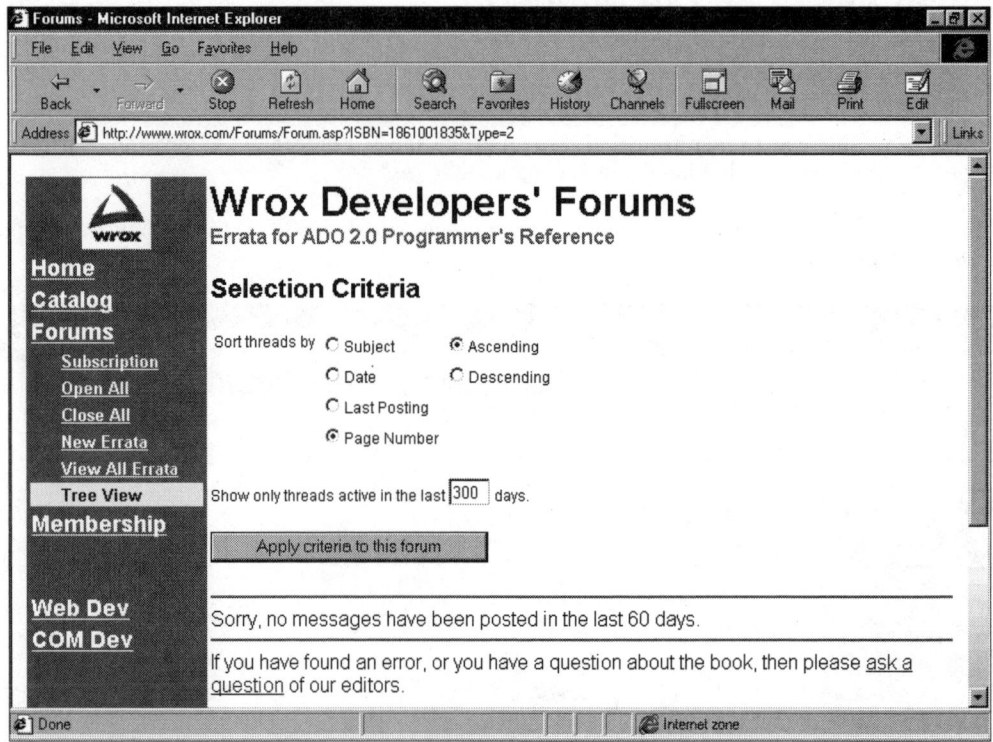

Adding an Errata to the Sheet Yourself

It's always possible that you may find that your error is not listed, in which case you can enter details of the fault yourself. It might be anything from a spelling mistake to a faulty piece of code in the book. Sometimes you'll find useful hints that aren't really errors on the listing. By entering errata you may save another reader hours of frustration, and of course, you will be helping us provide even higher quality information. We're very grateful for this sort of advice and feedback. You can enter errata using the 'ask a question' of our editors link at the bottom of the errata page. Click on this link and you will get a form on which to post your message.

Fill in the subject box, and then type your message in the space provided on the form. Once you have done this, click on the Post Now button at the bottom of the page. The message will be forwarded to our editors. They'll then test your submission and check that the error exists, and that the suggestions you make are valid. Then your submission, together with a solution, is posted on the site for public consumption. Obviously this stage of the process can take a day or two, but we will endeavor to get a fix up sooner than that.

E-mail Support

If you wish to directly query a problem in the book with an expert who knows the book in detail then e-mail support@wrox.com, with the title of the book and the last four numbers of the ISBN in the subject field of the e-mail. Your e-mail MUST include the title of the book the problem relates to, otherwise we won't be able to help you. The diagram below shows what else your e-mail should include:

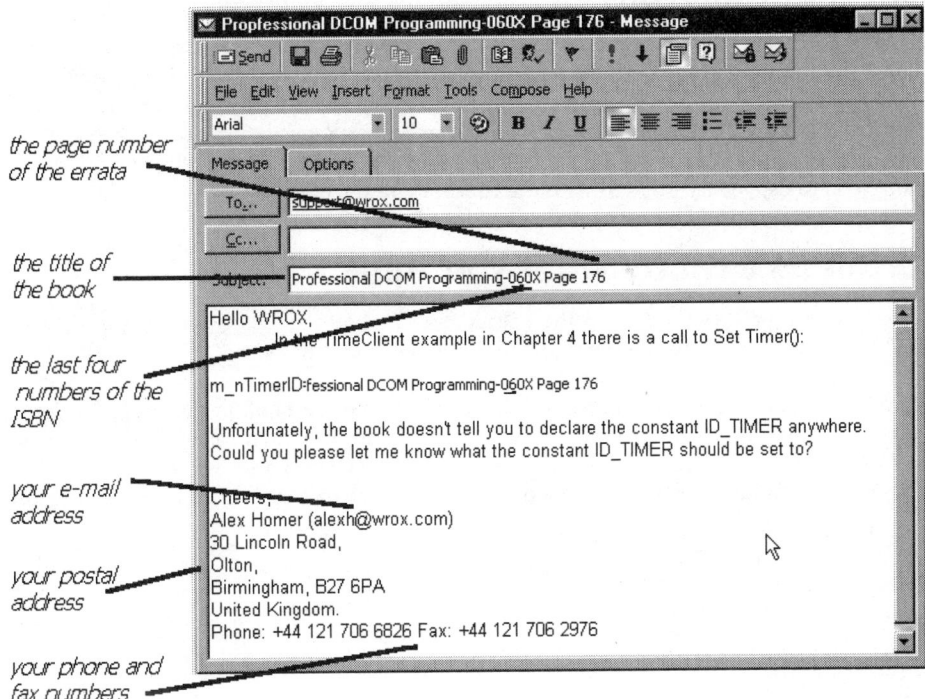

the page number
of the errata

the title of
the book

the last four
numbers of the
ISBN

your e-mail
address

your postal
address

your phone and
fax numbers

We won't send you junk mail. We need the details to save your time and ours. If we need to replace a disk or CD we'll be able to get it to you straight away. When you send an e-mail it will go through the following chain of support:

Customer Support

Your message is delivered to one of our customer support staff who are the first people to read it. They have files on most frequently asked questions and will answer anything general immediately. They answer general questions about the book and the web site.

Editorial

Deeper queries are forwarded to the technical editor responsible for that book. They have experience with the programming language or particular product and are able to answer detailed technical questions on the subject. Once an issue has been resolved, the editor can post the errata to the web site.

The Authors

Finally, in the unlikely event that the editor can't answer your problem, s/he will forward the request to the author. We try to protect the author from any distractions from writing. However, we are quite happy to forward specific requests to them. All Wrox authors help with the support on their books. They'll mail the customer and the editor with their response, and again all readers should benefit.

What we can't answer

Obviously with an ever growing range of books and an ever-changing technology base, there is an increasing volume of data requiring support. While we endeavor to answer all questions about the book, we can't answer bugs in your own programs that you've adapted from our code. So, while you might have loved the help desk systems in our Active Server Pages book, don't expect too much sympathy if you cripple your company with a live adaptation you customized from Chapter 12. But do tell us if you're especially pleased with the routine you developed with our help.

How to tell us exactly what you think

We understand that errors can destroy the enjoyment of a book and can cause many wasted and frustrated hours, so we seek to minimize the distress that they can cause.

You might just wish to tell us how much you liked or loathed the book in question. Or you might have ideas about how this whole process could be improved. In which case you should e-mail `feedback@wrox.com`. You'll always find a sympathetic ear, no matter what the problem is. Above all you should remember that we do care about what you have to say and we will do our utmost to act upon it.

Index

loadRow() method, 215, 217
local files, accessing, 309-313
location object, 109
login state, 268
lookup facility, 210, 238, 250
vs. search facility, 223
with search facility, 239
lookup() method, 210, 222-223, 251
lookupCrit() function, 223
lookupTree() method, 237, 239, 250-251
loops. *see* statements: iterative

M

main() method, 316
makeHeaderTree() function, 164-165
makeRow() function, 226
makeSelect() function, 280
makeTextRange() function, 286, 287
makeTree() method, 235, 242-246, 254
map() function, 55-57, 60-62
match() method, 54
Math Class, 19, 51, 139
memory stack, function calls held in, 130
merging work of multiple users, 273
METHOD attribute, 199
methods
adding to objects, 45-49, 124
definition, 26, 43
dynamic binding to objects, 117
extracting arguments from forms, 235
Java methods called from JavaScript, 303
overloading, 254, 257
overriding, 116, 126
retrieving arguments for, 219, 226, 243, 250-251
static, 296
vs. global functions, 48-49
MFC library. *see* Microsoft Foundation Classes (MFC) library
Microsoft Foundation Classes (MFC) library, 125
modulo operator. *see* % operator
mouseclick event, 141
mouseover event handler, 275
moveEnd() method, 277
moveStart() method, 277

N

NAME attribute, 89, 90, 96
name spaces, 19, 26
NaN, 32, 33

native code
calling from Java, 318-323
native methods, 319
negated classes in regular expressions, 35
NetFileHandler class, 314, 317
NetFileServer application, 318
Netscape Communicator
JavaScript implementation, 6
networking
with TCP/IP protocol, 313-318
new operator, 18, 64, 97, 124
newModeFn() function, 245
NewStringUTF() function, 322
Next() method, 217
nextP() method, 221-222
node determiners, 246
allowing prefixes for, 249
nodes
comparing, 244
constructing, 244, 246
elements of, 244
in tree controller, 151-153
internal
associating data with, 237, 239-242, 250, 254
referring to documents, 180, 182
Tree Class based on, 174
nouns, analyzing as classes, 266-267
null literal, 34
Number Class, 51
number bases, 33
numbers
converting arrays to, 33
converting strings to, 32, 48
hexadecimal, 33
octal, 33

O

Object Class, 69, 74
in Java, 295
<OBJECT> tag, 309
Object-Oriented Analysis and Design, 261
object-oriented programming (OOP), 113-148
advantages in JavaScript, 4
advantages of, 113
principles of, 114-117
objects
adding methods to, 45-49
adding properties to, 45
as associative arrays, 70-71
class types in JavaScript, 51
copying, 223
creating, 18